HARVARD STUDIES
IN INTERNATIONAL AFFAIRS
Number 44

The Diplomacy of Surprise:

Hitler, Nixon, Sadat

Michael I. Handel

Center for International Affairs
Harvard University

Copyright © 1981 by the President and Fellows of Harvard College
Library of Congress Card Number 81-81004
ISBN 0-87674-048-4 (Cloth)
ISBN 0-87674-049-2 (Paper)
Printed in the United States of America

Typeset by Publishers Graphics, Peabody, MA
Printed by Hamilton Printing Company
Rensselaer, N.Y.

The Center is happy to provide a forum for the expression of responsible views. It does not, however, necessarily agree with them.

Created in 1958, the Center for International Affairs fosters advanced study of basic world problems by scholars from various disciplines and senior officials from many countries. The research of the Center focuses on economic, social, and political development; the management of force in the modern world; the problems and relations of advanced industrial societies; transnational processes and international order; and technology and international affairs.

The Harvard Studies in International Affairs, which are listed at the back of this book, may be ordered from Publishers Marketing Group, P.O. Box 350, Momence, Ill. 60954, at the prices indicated. Recent books written under the auspices of the Center, listed on the last pages, may be obtained from bookstores or ordered directly from the publishers.

About the Author

Michael Handel received his Ph.D. from Harvard. Most recently he has been a Research Associate at the M.I.T. Center for International Studies and at the Harvard Center for International Affairs. Among his books and monographs are *The Israeli Political-Military Doctrine* (Harvard Center for International Affairs, 1973); *Perception, Deception and Surprise: The Case of the Yom Kippur War* (1976); *The Study of War Termination* (1979); *Weak States in the International System* (London: Frank Cass, 1981).

CONTENTS

To Jill and Yael

PREFACE

Shortly after President Sadat's startling declaration of his readiness to come to Jerusalem and negotiate directly with Israel (November 9, 1977), it occurred to me that it might be useful to look for similar examples of diplomatic surprise. The number of such surprises in modern history (i.e., in the post-World War I era) was much smaller than I had anticipated. Unlike military men, diplomats and run-of-the-mill political leaders do not like to surprise each other. On the whole, they prefer stability and continuity even in circumstances that might justify a constructive shift in allies, political concepts, or national goals.

I began by looking for any previous research on diplomatic surprise but was unable to find anything that had been written on the subject; hence I decided to examine a few well-known case studies to determine if the beginnings of a general theory could be developed.

My initial focus was on questions similar to those usually asked in the study of military surprise. Is the record of avoiding unpleasant surprises better in diplomacy than in military affairs? What kind of "concepts" do political intelligence analysts develop? What kind of warning signals are available to facilitate the prediction of a radical change in foreign policy? Is deception a commonly used tactic? What circumstances, if any, tend to increase the likelihood of an unexpected diplomatic maneuver? What are the differences and similarities between military and diplomatic surprise?

In answering these questions, my attention centered on four case studies. The first was Hitler's series of *faits accomplis* that began with his *Machtergreifung* and ended with the remilitarization of the Rhineland; the second was the Ribbentrop-Molotov agreement of August 1939; the third, Nixon's China policy from his election in 1968 to the July 15, 1971 announcement of his intended visit to the People's Republic of China; and the last was President Sadat's frequent use of surprise in diplomacy between 1971 and 1977, culminating in his visit to Jerusalem. These were among the most obvious case studies—I have by no means exhausted the menu. Other studies, to mention only a few, might include the Rapallo

Agreement between Germany and the Soviet Union in 1922, or de Gaulle's diplomacy.

It was relatively easy to find the documents relevant to Hitler's surprises, especially the German documents pertaining to the Ribbentrop-Molotov agreement. This also holds for the documents of the Western Allies. It is, of course, impossible to gain access to similar information concerning the evolution of the Soviet Union's foreign policy during that period. This is also true for the foreign policies of China and to a lesser extent, Egypt. Both America's and Israel's foreign policy are discussed in detail in the newspapers of these nations, as well as in the published memoirs of their leaders.

The memoirs of leaders such as Richard Nixon, President Sadat, and Golda Meir are generally very disappointing, though still useful if corroborated by other sources. The recently published memoirs of Henry Kissinger are of exceptional interest in regard to how his mind works, though they reveal little that is new concerning the China policy of the United States. Former Prime Minister Rabin's memoirs, recently published in Israel and also in an abbreviated English translation, are very useful since they include a critical discussion of Israeli foreign policy between 1969 and 1973.

In the reconstruction of each case study, I have focused on the development of the circumstances that eventually gave rise to the unexpected and/or radical shift in policy; on the negotiation and signaling process (if more than one state intitiated the surprise); the role of mediators from other states; on the role of individual leaders, and in particular the creative process which motivates leaders to make changes in their political concepts ahead of, and often against, the advice of their counselors. I have also examined the specific goals the surprise was intended to achieve; the perceptions of the intended victims; and the perceptions of the countries that the initiator of the surprise sought to collaborate with. The results of each diplomatic surprise are also discussed, although I have, for the most part, limited myself to the processes and mechanisms involved *until* the moment of surprise. The immediate goals and effects are easy to summarize, but the long-range effects have become history.

As I continued with my research, it became clear that more attention must be devoted to questions such as the formation of foreign policy in general; and the differences between normal or routine diplomacy and what I have called creative diplomacy. Diplomatic surprise, unlike its military counterpart, does not always lead to conflict or destruction—it can instead reduce tensions, thus improving relations between states. It demonstrates beyond doubt (if any doubts still exist) that secret diplomacy can be constructive—and not necessarily dangerous, as Wilsonians have assumed. It is not secrecy itself that is the potentially destructive element, but rather the goals of the diplomacy.

The pivotal role of the individual leader needs to be emphasized. The use of surprise as a means in diplomacy is often associated with the type of political leader who tends to work alone and is willing to take higher risks. Being politically creative, he can therefore transcend the political concepts of his colleagues. This is only one of the areas touched upon in this book which should be studied in more depth.

I have presented the general observations drawn from the case studies in the first chapter. Many of these ideas are tentative and I am sure some will be modified by further research. The chapter is a theoretical summary and distillation of the empirical evidence presented in this book. The reader who is less interested in theory may benefit by first reading the historical chapters.

I would like to thank my friend Richard K. Betts of the Brookings Institution for his help and comments; Major General Shlomo Gazit, former Director of Israeli Military Intelligence, for his insights and suggestions; my student, Arie Ofri for his creative suggestions and help, Peter Jacobsohn, the Center's Editor of Publications, who encouraged me to publish this book and whose thoughtful criticism and advice helped give it final shape, and finally, my wife—without whose encouragement, editorial help, and imaginative criticism, this book would have remained only an idea.

Parts of this book were written under the auspices of the Leonard Davis Institute for International Relations at the Hebrew University of Jerusalem, the MIT Center for International Studies, and the Center for International Affairs at Harvard University.

Cambridge, Spring 1981
Harvard Center for International Affairs

Michael I. Handel

1
SURPRISE AND CHANGE IN DIPLOMACY*

Surprise is an inherent part of human affairs—it occurs in politics, economics, technology, literature, and music, as well as in war; yet research on the subject has thus far been confined to its military use alone.[1] Problems such as the causes of frequent intelligence failures; the methods used in predicting surprise attacks; the role of deception; and the optimal timing of a surprise attack have all been thoroughly explored.[2]

In at least one respect there is little difference between military and diplomatic surprise—as far as the difficulty in avoiding a surprise is concerned. Although developed in the study of military surprise, the following theories serve as valid explanations in the diplomatic realm: noise to signal ratio;[3] deception; rigid concepts projected upon the enemy; pathologies in communication and organization; uncertainties and contradictions inherent in intelligence work; and alert fatigue or the so-called cry wolf syndrome. (See Bibliography.)

NORMAL AND SURPRISE DIPLOMACY

In *The Structure of Scientific Revolutions*, Thomas S. Kuhn makes a distinction between normal science and revolutionary science.[4] Normal science consists of the routine, day-to-day research with which the majority of scientists are concerned. Revolutionary science, which arises in response to scientific anomalies and crises in research, advances new concepts that involve a shift in paradigms. A similar distinction can also be made in the world of diplomacy. Normal or routine diplomacy characterizes most diplomatic activity—and revolutionary or surprise diplomacy[5] involves radical changes in well-established policies. The following diagram schematically illustrates these poles of diplomatic activity and the gradations of conduct that can occur between them.

---

* A slightly different version of this chapter appeared in *International Security*, Vol. 4, No. 4.

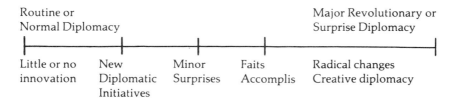

Routine or   Major Revolutionary or
Normal Diplomacy   Surprise Diplomacy

Little or no   New   Minor   Faits   Radical changes
innovation   Diplomatic   Surprises   Accomplis   Creative diplomacy
                    Initiatives

Most foreign policy is based on a high degree of continuity, inertia, and incremental decision-making that is rarely questioned by those who participate in implementing it. Nevertheless, it is often claimed that "the uncertain nature of international affairs creates a demand for flexibility as a safety valve."[6] In reality, the shapers of foreign policy seldom avail themselves of this safety valve. Instead of exploring new, imaginative courses of action in order to cope with uncertainty, political leaders usually cling to the "security" of traditional policies. Such behavior is typical of most bureaucracies, not only those responsible for the implementation of foreign policies. As a result, most of the actions taken by states in foreign affairs are readily predictable. Moreover, the adherence to obsolete policies on major issues often prevents the improvement of relations between states and diverts attention from more basic problems.

The normal solution to a stubborn foreign policy problem is the *new policy initiative*, which is a new but not unexpected move in a familiar direction. A new initiative is usually intended to avoid stagnation or crises rather than to facilitate a change in policy. Slightly more than an incremental change, the policy initiative is a variation on a theme; in this category we can include, for example, the numerous American mediation efforts between Israel and its Arab neighbors prior to the Sadat peace initiative in 1977, and the new American or Soviet proposals in the SALT talks. As will be shown below, in a basic typology of surprise in international politics, we can distinguish between surprises according to the *impact* they have on the international system (either major or minor), and according to the *number* of states participating in launching the surprise (that is, whether the surprise is unilateral, requiring no collaboration, or a bilateral surprise, requiring the collaboration of two or more states).

When a new initiative is not sufficient to bring about the desired change in the international environment, or in the relations between two states, a statesman may resort to the use of a *minor suprise* or even of a *fait accompli*—something approaching a major surprise. A minor surprise can be defined as an unexpected move which is intended to change the trend in relations between two or more states although it *does not* have a radical impact on the balance of power in the international system and may be reversible. Sadat's first peace initiative on February 4, 1971, or his decision to open the Suez Canal in 1975—i.e., earlier than expected—are examples of unilateral minor surprise. However, minor surprise can also be bilateral, as is demonstrated by the joint American-Soviet statement on the Middle East which was issued on October 1, 1977.

Furthermore, there are situations in which old policies can only be changed either through a major diplomatic surprise or a *fait accompli*. A shift in policy that could otherwise take decades to accomplish—if at all—may, as the result of a daring diplomatic maneuver, be compressed into a considerably shorter period of time. Sadat's decision to embark on a peace initiative in 1977 is the most obvious example. By going to Jerusalem, he circumvented the prolonged negotiations, cut short the formalities, and accelerated the chance of achieving peace in the Middle East—goals which would have taken years to accomplish at the scheduled Geneva Peace Conference.

Surprise diplomacy can be used to transcend old policies through two interrelated elements, namely, secrecy and shock. Secrecy provides a safe atmosphere in which the two (or possibly more) sides in a bilateral or multilateral surprise can negotiate and make the necessary preparations for fundamental policy changes. In this kind of situation, surprise is not necessarily a goal in its own right—it is merely the by-product of the secrecy which is needed to protect the embryonic relationship from the interference of other states. Secrecy is always important, but in some cases, the element of shock is the goal of the diplomatic surprise. Shock is intended to throw the adversary off balance and force him to change a policy in a more advantageous direction. The purpose is to facilitate a breakthrough in routine and stagnant situations; and while the adversary is still paralyzed from the effect of the shock, quick action must be taken to prevent a return to the routine. Surprise in this case is almost always unilateral, as in President Sadat's expulsion of the Soviet military experts in 1972, or his peace initiative in 1977. By expelling the Soviet Union's experts, Sadat compelled the USSR to supply his country with massive weapons shipments that it had previously refused to provide.[7] (For a detailed discussion, see Chapter 5.) By coming to Jerusalem to negotiate directly with Israel, Sadat forced Israel to bypass the Geneva conference and make greater concessions.

A *fait accompli* is usually defined as any *unilateral act* (which can involve either a major or minor surprise) committed by one state against the interests of another. In the context of this book, the term *fait accompli* will be more specifically defined in order to distinguish it from a major diplomatic surprise with which it can have elements in common. In the above diagram, a *fait accompli* appears between a major and minor surprise.

Like a major diplomatic surprise, a *fait accompli* can have a decisive effect on the balance of power in the international system (i.e., Hitler's declaration in March 1935 of Germany's intention to rearm, and the remilitarization of the Rhineland in March 1936). The difference between the two, however, is that while having a strong impact, a *fait accompli* is only a surprise in terms of *timing*. Thus, Hitler's decision to remilitarize the Rhineland surprised most observers only by his choice of time, but not by his choice of object. (See Chapter 2.) The Western democracies were fully aware of Hitler's intention to rearm Germany and his long-range plan to remilitarize the Rhineland. Similarly, from Taiwan's point of view, the American decision in January 1979 to establish full diplomatic relations with the People's Republic of China and simultaneously sever relations with Taiwan must have come only as a surprise in timing. By the same token, should the United States decide to negotiate with or recognize the Palestinian Liberation Organization, it could surprise Israel only by its timing. A major diplomatic surprise, on the other hand, is unexpected in terms of timing and object. In addition, a *fait accompli* is a unilateral act, while a major surprise can be a unilateral act or the outcome of collaboration between two or more states. Thus, a *fait accompli* is an important surprise whose impact is tempered by the fact that its object was known in advance.

A major diplomatic surprise is an unexpected move which has considerable impact on the real or expected division of power in the international system or a major subsystem. Such a surprise involves the great powers either directly or indirectly and has implications that transcend the regional system. In contrast, an unanticipated agreement between Libya and Chad, Morocco and Algeria, or Uganda and Tanzania does not seriously affect the global balance of power.

The completely unexpected Treaty of Rapallo concluded in 1922 between the Soviet Union and the German Weimar Republic was—wrongly—perceived by the Western democracies as a major shift in the European balance of power.[8] The rapprochement between the same two countries in August 1939, on the other hand, became, by unleashing World War II, one of the turning points in world history. The American-Chinese rapprochement of 1971 also had global—though not cataclysmic—repercussions: it improved Japanese-Chinese relations and caused tensions in American-Japanese relations. (See Chapter 4.) The Soviet Union may have been induced to seek accommodation with the United States through the SALT talks or with NATO in order to counterbalance the American tilt toward China. Alternatively, the new U.S.-P.R.C. relationship could force the Soviet Union to invest more in its national security. The Russians, as a matter of fact, seemed to do *both* things. Immediately following Nixon's announcement of his planned trip to

Peking, the Russians hastily unfroze negotiations on Berlin and on the problem of guarding against accidental nuclear war which had been deadlocked for months (see Kissinger's *White House Years*, pp. 766-767). At the same time, they continued to increase their nuclear and conventional arsenals. In total, the agreement could gradually transform the loose bipolar international system into a world with three power centers. It is effects such as these that characterize the major diplomatic surprise.

Finally, Sadat's peace initiative transformed the regional balance of power in the Middle East by at least temporarily eliminating Egypt from the military coalition of Arab confrontation states arrayed against Israel; and it also led to the exclusion of the Soviet Union from the Middle East peace process while the United States was able to intensify its involvement. Obviously, it also had implications for the oil export policies of Saudi Arabia and the Persian Gulf states.

It is important to distinguish between major bilateral and unilateral diplomatic surprises. The bilateral surprise requires a coordinated change of policy by two or more states. The often prolonged and public signalling process that takes place between the two states before they arrive at an agreement makes it easier—only in theory, not in practice—for the intelligence organizations of other powers to gain some inkling of an impending rapprochement. A major unilateral surprise as well as a *fait accompli* are initiated by one state, often by the decision of a single leader. When a single leader springs a surprise without even consulting his close advisers, that type of surprise is undoubtedly very difficult to anticipate because of the limited, perhaps nonexistent, warning signals. Table 1 categorizes examples of surprise according to the above analysis.

Commitments to allies and the degree of dependence on other countries play another important role in the initiation of major shifts in foreign policy. If allies agree to modify existing relations, the new foreign policy will be easily implemented. However, a state planning to reorient its policies usually cannot afford to consult its allies for two principal reasons: 1) Its allies would never agree to a move that jeopardizes their own interests; and 2) Secrecy would be compromised. For example, the United States could not consult Taiwan (or even Japan) regarding its decisions to approach the People's Republic of China because Taiwan could never be expected to agree to a move which was diametrically opposed to its interests. And, of course, any state resenting such a move would breach the secrecy in an attempt to foil the rapprochement. In the extreme case of the Middle East, it is obvious that Sadat would never have achieved his aim if he had consulted with his Arab allies on his decision to negotiate directly with Israel. (Sadat shrewdly consulted his Arab allies *after* he had committed himself to go to Jerusalem.)

Table 1

	Minor Surprises	Faits Accomplis — Major Surprises
Bilateral Surprises	—Joint American-Soviet Middle East declaration, October 1977	—Rapallo Agreement, 1922 —Nazi-Soviet Non-Aggression Pact, 1939 —American-Chinese rapprochement, 1971 —Arab oil embargo, 1973
Unilateral Surprises	—Soviet recognition of Israel, 1948 —Sadat's first Peace Initiative, February 1971 —Sadat's declaration of his intention to open the Suez Canal, 1975	—Hitler's *faits accomplis:* German rearmament, 1935 —Remilitarization of the Rhineland, 1936 —Mendès-France's decision to terminate French involvement in Indo-China, 1954 —Sadat's Peace Initiative, November 1977

In the Middle East, certain American commitments to Israel have hampered the ability of the United States to redirect its policy with regard to the Palestinian Liberation Organization. Earlier American promises to Israel not to negotiate with the PLO as long as the PLO refused to amend its national covenant and recognize United Nations Security Council Resolution 242, mean that the slightest deviation from this promise would evoke loud cries of protest from those who had been betrayed. Usually, the government initiating a diplomatic surprise has decided that it will sacrifice the interests of its allies.

THE PATTERN OF BILATERAL DIPLOMATIC SURPRISE

The most interesting cases of a major bilateral diplomatic surprise fit a common pattern which can be divided into three main stages. During the first stage, both sides reevaluate their basic interests and conclude that a reorientation in their foreign policies is necessary. In the second stage, they establish a dialogue to determine whether or not an agreement can be reached. The third stage follows once an agreement has been reached and made public.

Stage 1

Both sides begin to realize, at first independently of each other, that their foreign policies must be revised. Often, these policies are no longer logical in view of changing circumstances and goals. For example, the American embargo on trade with the People's Republic of China as well as the ban on American visits to China had lost much of their original purpose by the 1970's. Likewise, Chinese anti-American policy gradually weakened when faced with the mounting Soviet threat in the 1960's.

It must be emphasized that a bilateral surprise (and sometimes even a unilateral one)[9] cannot occur unless *both sides* have more or less simultaneously concluded that earlier policies should be discontinued. A joint diplomatic move by Israel and the PLO has not been possible because the two sides have been unable even to open a dialogue. In 1968, Israeli Defense Minister Dayan tried to arrange a meeting with the PLO's Yasir Arafat through an Arab intermediary (Fadua Tokan of Nablus), but his overture was ignored; in 1970, Israel again signalled the PLO by actually offering refuge to PLO members who were fleeing from Jordan after King Hussein opened an all-out war against them. Again, the signals were disregarded and constructive change was obstructed.

Often a reorientation of basic policies is facilitated by a change in leadership. A new and uncommitted leader may, at first, appear to support wholeheartedly established policies because of the danger of provoking his domestic opposition during a period of transition. Nevertheless, this same leader will eventually find it easier to change the order of national priorities. In Israel, for example, Begin was not committed to the same goals as the Labor Party which had been in power from 1948 to 1977. He was therefore in a better position to respond to Sadat's signals. For his part, Sadat, unlike Nasser, was committed neither to collaboration with the Soviet Union nor to war against Israel. After unabashedly announcing a military victory in 1973 he could afford to change the policy of confrontation with Israel, thereby assigning his "Egypt first" policy top priority.

It is relatively easy for leaders—especially leaders of authoritarian states—to maintain secrecy during the first stage of bilateral diplomatic surprises since relatively few people participate in the formation of high-level policy. While it is, of course, vital that a similar revision of policies occur on both sides, each step in the reevaluation process need not be synchronized—one side may be in a greater hurry, as in the Ribbentrop-Molotov case. Germany and the Soviet Union began to recognize the need for a policy change at about the same time; yet, Hitler was under pressure to reach an agreement by September 1, 1939, because that was the latest date he had set for his attack on Poland. He was thus forced to make many concessions to the Russians. The Russians, on their part, although not in a hurry, could ill afford to refuse German offers and the corresponding pressure for speed.

During the first stage, both sides frequently make use of foreign mediators who are not necessarily told the exact meaning of the messages they convey. The Israelis and Egyptians used the good offices of Rumania and Morocco; and, in order to signal its policy changes to the People's Republic of China, the United States employed the good offices of the French, Rumanians, and Pakistanis. When the preliminary feelers have proven successful, the parties establish direct contact. Symmetrical interests are not necessary, but the existence of a common, viable interest is essential.

Stage 2

At this juncture, each party must determine to its own satisfaction that the other side is serious in its intentions. Secrecy is crucial so that, should the move fail, each side has the option of withdrawing without losing face or undermining existing relationships with other states. During the negotiations between Nazi Germany and the Soviet Union in 1939 most exchanges were oral, and the few documents which did exist were not written on official letterheads. Kissinger's trip to China prior to the American-Chinese rapprochement was covered by an elaborate veil of secrecy and deception, as was the meeting between Israeli Foreign Minister Dayan and Egyptian Deputy Prime Minister Hassan el-Tohamy in Morocco in 1977. Successful preservation of secrecy allows the two sides to build confidence in each other. Should a leak occur, both parties would be quick to deny any contacts, yet subsequent renewal of such contacts would be difficult.

In the first and second stages, *some* signals are transmitted publicly. In fact, it can be argued that some of the signalling must be carried out *in public* in order to convince the other side of serious intentions. In most cases, however, the open signals are received only by the two sides directly involved. As more and more people take part in the preparations for negotiations and cover-up plans, the likelihood of a breach of secrecy increases. In particular, of course, secret information may be passed to third parties by participants who object to the new policies. In the case of the Ribbentrop-Molotov agreement, for example, Germans who opposed Hitler's plans repeatedly warned Britain's Foreign Office as well as its Intelligence Service that Germany was making offers to the Soviet Union.

Although preconceptions, an excessive number of often conflicting signals, and deliberate deception make a clear analysis difficult, alert observers may detect significant changes at this stage. The intricate process of action and reaction continues until the intentions of each side are unmistakable; then the negotiations are usually accelerated and culminate in the surprise agreement. Nazi Germany and the Soviet Union exchanged signals (Stages 1 and 2) for at least six months before concluding the non-aggression pact in late August 1939. According to some analysts,

President Nixon sent signals to the People's Republic of China in his *Foreign Affairs* article of October 1967—which would mean that the American-Chinese exchange of feelers took place over a period of approximately three years.

After basic decisions have been made at the highest level during the first stage, lower level officials can continue the talks. The negotiations do not always directly concern political issues; sometimes, the two sides begin with the less binding subjects of economic and cultural relations. The preliminary United States-China exchange of signals concerned cultural and economic matters (i.e., the Ping-Pong team invitation). Finally, the parties progress to direct talks on political issues that were only obliquely mentioned in previous meetings.

The reevaluation of fundamental policies continues well into the second stage, since the first two stages are overlapping phases comprising the evaluation of basic interests and policies. No one is certain of the final course of action until the last moment, so both sides keep their options open. The continuation of earlier policies while negotiations are in progress as well as the conflicting trends within the political elite of each state add to the plethora of signals of which only a few are meaningful.

Stage 3

The new course of action is made public soon after an understanding is reached. All that remains is to establish the final details of the agreement and to devise strategies to counter the objections of third parties. In theory, diplomatic surprise is simpler to forecast because of the limited number of options, but in practice the record of timely warnings is no better than that of military surprise. Most often, third parties are totally surprised despite the available indicators. President Nixon's announcement that he was going to visit China evoked utter amazement even from knowledgeable observers. "The moment the president completed his surprise announcement, the cameras switched to the studio commentators for a reaction. They were all flabbergasted, and one anchorman was literally speechless as he looked out into the living rooms of America. The country was stunned and so was the world."[10]

DIPLOMACY OF SURPRISE IN DIFFERENT INTERNATIONAL SYSTEMS

Surprise diplomacy can take place in any type of international system where there is a need to break away from old policies. Empirical evidence suggests a connection between the type of international system and the frequency with which major surprise can be expected to occur. The key factor is the ideological character of the system in question. Diplomatic surprises occur more frequently in the classical balance of power system than in a tight bipolar or a multipolar system; and are more likely in a loose bipolar system than in a tight bipolar one. Naturally, the impact of such a diplomatic maneuver is in inverse relation to the probability of its occurrence.

In the classical balance of power system the actors, who share a common ideology and common values, are allowed (and required) to make rapid shifts in alliances in order to enhance their own power and maintain systemic equilibrium.[11] Surprise diplomacy therefore serves as the regulator of the system;[12] and the fact that such maneuvers occur often does not mean that they are any less surprising. The absence of conflicting political beliefs smooths the way for rapid transitions from one alliance to another because there are no ideological barriers. In this system, the higher the number of principal actors or centers of power, the higher the probability of surprise.

The theory of international systems makes a distinction between a homogeneous and a heterogeneous system, which is often a revolutionary one. The homogeneity of the classical balance of power system means that diplomatic surprises are more frequent, and consequently are of lower intensity and impact than those that occur in a heterogeneous, ideologically split bipolar or multipolar system.

In a heterogeneous international structure, incompatible ideologies exacerbate tensions and impede communication between states. All states, in particular the weaker ones, find it more difficult to maneuver.[13] Major diplomatic surprises are much less likely to take place in this environment—but once they do occur, they have a much stronger effect on the division of power. Ideological competition tends to repress creative diplomacy—and promote a routine and unimaginative diplomacy in which states interpret the behavior of other states according to rigid concepts. While it is more difficult for leaders in such circumstances to embark on new policies, dramatic surprise eventually becomes the only way to shake off the restrictions of old patterns of behavior.

The European multipolar system between the two world wars is a good example of a heterogeneous system:[14] it was divided among democratic, fascist, and communist ideologies, which made it increasingly difficult to maneuver and maintain the European equilibrium. Given the venomous ideological conflict between Nazi Germany and Communist Russia in 1939, a treaty uniting them behind a common interest—to divide Poland—seemed to be an extremely unlikely event. When such a treaty was actually signed, it had an enormous effect on the European balance of power and, in fact, on world history. Prior to the completion of the treaty, the British had been repeatedly warned that the two states might reach an agreement, but they misinterpreted the contradictory signals.

Dismissing warnings with the attitude that a treaty between the two countries was impossible, "the British counted confidently on ideological estrangement between Fascism and Communism. . . ."[15]

At the height of the Cold War in the 1950's, intense ideological competition meant that the great powers made extensive efforts to prevent the defection of small allies. The defection of even a relatively unimportant state (i.e., the one implied in the Russian-Egyptian arms deal of 1955, or the "defection" of Cuba to the Eastern bloc) was perceived as having global repercussions.

A more recent example of unforeseen agreements between the adherents of competing ideologies is the American-Chinese rapprochement of 1970-1971. Experienced observers of the twenty-year-long propaganda war between the capitalist and communist systems assumed that the United States and China would be unable even to hold constructive talks, let alone agree to establish diplomatic relations or collaborate in their mutual interest. Similarly, analysts of Middle Eastern politics felt that after five wars and thirty years of bitter propaganda warfare, Egypt and Israel were unlikely to enter into direct and constructive negotiations. In sum, long-standing ideological rivalries and preconceptions made it difficult for observers to anticipate changes in allegiance.

All of these moves across ideological barriers have one element in common. *In the final analysis, the states involved preferred their national interests to their ideological commitments.* Stalin opted for an agreement with Nazi Germany—anathema to communism—in order to preserve the security and interests of the Soviet Union; Nixon preferred a rapprochement with the People's Republic of China to American commitments to Taiwan; and Sadat chose to focus Egypt's energy inward rather than continue the endless war against Israel. The political intelligence analyst must derive an important lesson from these examples: to concentrate on power calculations rather than ideological rhetoric.

The problem of anticipating a major diplomatic surprise is directly related to the more familiar problem of forecasting in international politics.[16] This problem has received more attention, either directly or implicitly, in the theories of *realpolitik* and "interests" as developed by Thucydides (common interests form the best agreement between states); Machiavelli (the ideas of *necessitas* and *raison d'état*); and more recently, Hans Morgenthau (the concept of interest defined in terms of power). *According to these theories, the most important policies of states can be predicted and identified because they operate on a logic of their own, and do not depend on a particular leader.* Hence, an observer can only make valid predictions of a state's actions once he understands its basic interests. Thus, if China feels threatened by the Soviet Union and is not strong enough to defend itself against the threat it must seek help from another country. The only nation with sufficient strength to counter the Soviet menace is the United States, so it is the United States China must turn to. Likewise, since most German governments (regardless of their form) between the two world wars had wanted to dismember Poland, sooner or later Germany had to seek an agreement, even if a temporary one, with the Soviet Union.

Reality is, however, much more complicated than is implied by the theory of *realpolitik*. Although it helps the analyst to explain the inevitable logic of a major diplomatic surprise or *fait accompli* in retrospect, the theory does not enable him to make forecasts with a high degree of accuracy. Even if *raison d'état* could demonstrate that a particular event would have to take place in the long run, it could never predict *when* the event would occur—because such theories do not adequately consider the *human* or *psychological factors* in foreign policy. Different leaders of the same country *do not* have to behave according to the same logic; and countries with different political systems deal with similar circumstances in various ways.

But above all, it is the human element which makes the anticipation of surprises so difficult in international politics. There are few innovative leaders who will run the risk of replacing ossified political concepts; most tend to follow the foreign policies of their predecessors, usually making nothing more than a few incremental changes.

It is not surprising that all major diplomatic surprises have been initiated at the senior policy-making level—and not by professional diplomats. Professional diplomats rarely approach foreign policy with innovative ideas despite their greater familiarity with many issues. This is explained by the fact that diplomats, as members of a bureaucracy, usually strive to secure and consolidate existing ties rather than explore alternative courses of action.

The frequency with which surprise is used in foreign policy therefore depends on the combination of two variables: leadership style and the type of political system. Diplomatic surprise can be carried out in four different situations.

1. An Authoritarian Leader in a Non-Democratic System

This combination is most conducive to the use of surprise tactics because it offers the leader who is inclined to act independently and can afford to disregard parliamentary opposition to his decision maximum secrecy and control of events. Leaders such as Hitler, Stalin, and Sadat had to be cunning and brutal in the prolonged climb to the top; and since surprise and shock tactics were their most valuable tools in the consolidation of domestic power it was logical that they would continue to employ the same tools in the practice of foreign policy.

2. An Authoritarian-Style Leader in a Democratic System

Because of their commanding style of leadership, statesmen such as de Gaulle, and to a lesser extent President Nixon and Prime Minister Begin, were able to channel the foreign policies of their respective nations in radically new directions. Nevertheless, many features of democratic politics reinforce incrementalism and inhibit the use of surprise strategies; the slower reaction of a democratic system often poses problems in a competition between democratic and non-democratic regimes.[17] Strong leadership is the key element that enables surprise to occur in this system.

3. A Democratic Leader in a Democratic System

In this situation, the leader is usually limited to the implementation of incremental changes in major foreign policy issues since he works by consensus and is open to cross-pressures. A rare example of surprise involving this combination was the decision of French Prime Minister Pierre Mendes-France to withdraw from Indo-China in 1954.

4. Collective Leadership in a Non-Democratic System

Surprise does not often take place in this combination because it also works by consensus-building and compromise. Khrushchev's shock diplomacy resulting in the Cuban missile crisis in 1962 may be regarded as a comparatively rare instance of surprise generated by collective leadership in a non-democratic system.

The most important factor in the launching of a diplomatic surprise is the presence of an authoritarian *style* of leadership; the nature of the political system itself is secondary. Nevertheless, the presence of an authoritarian leader is only a necessary but not a sufficient condition—*he must also be creative and inclined to take high risks.* Despite the fact that *raison d'état* may dictate changes in entrenched policies, such changes do not occur very frequently because the right type of leader is not in charge. A change in American policies toward China may have been justified perhaps as early as 1961 (and certainly from the mid-1960's onward), but without President Nixon's initiative, the normalization of relations with China might still not be accomplished today.

MILITARY AND DIPLOMATIC SURPRISE COMPARED

A military surprise attack is a hostile act that is intended to obtain immediate short-range objectives (such as decisive military victory), and it enables the attacker to dictate the direction and pace of developments.

Table 2
Favorable or Unfavorable Conditions for Radical Foreign Policy Changes

	Favorable Conditions	Unfavorable Conditions
Type of Leadership	—Strong, authoritarian style	—Democratic, consensus-building style
	—Little consulting with aides	—Tends to consult excessively with aides
	—Creative, open-minded, secure	—Uncreative, conservative, insecure
	—Inclined to take risks	—Low tendency to take risks
Type of Political System	—Authoritarian	—Democratic, open society
	—Secretive	—Many conflicting and influential interest groups
	—Government-controlled media	—Diplomacy conducted in a visible and open manner (high degree of mass media involvement)
Expectations From Old Policies	—Old policies conflict with national interests	—Continuation of old policies is not perceived as conflicting with national interests
	—Continuation of old policies will create dangerous situations; the state's position will be weakened	
	—New national goals are identified	—No new national goals are identified—no changes in national priorities
Allies and External Factors	—Weak or few conflicting commitments to allies	—Strong commitments to allies who would object to policy change
	—Little dependence or perception of dependence on other states that would be opposed to a change in policy	—Credibility of commitments to other nations may be weakened
		—Heavy dependence on states that would oppose a change
	—A non-ideological international system— homogeneous	—Highly ideological, heterogeneous global system

A diplomatic surprise, which can be either positive (e.g., improve relations between states) or belligerent, also has an immediate dramatic impact, but its most important results often materialize long after the original effect of the shock has worn off.

Perhaps the most important difference is that in military affairs, surprise is an ever-present factor that must be taken for granted. Military men are educated to consider the use of surprise on every level of action —though this does not necessarily make it easier to predict. In diplomacy, on the other hand, stability and continuity are the accepted norms;[18] since it is not an integral part of the education of diplomats and decision-makers, surprise in foreign policy requires an unconventional approach. While the military analyst is always trying to avoid a possible surprise, the political analyst is less attuned to abrupt change, concentrating instead on existing trends.

Military surprise also differs from diplomatic surprise in its much greater complexity, for it can occur on many levels and involve any combination of the following elements: area or areas chosen for the attack; strategy and tactics employed; use of new military doctrines; technological surprise by the use of new weapons systems; surprise in terms of timing, and so on. *In theory*, the task of predicting a diplomatic surprise should be simpler because the number of possible major shifts in the foreign policy of a given state or states is comparatively limited. But in practice, political intelligence analysts commit the same perceptual errors as their military colleagues. A few examples will clarify this point.

In 1921, both Germany and the Soviet Union faced only two feasible foreign policy choices: they could 1) improve diplomatic relations with the Western democracies, or 2) turn to each other. Choice of the latter option would mean the improvement of relations despite all earlier animosity and conflicting interests. Initially, the two countries preferred the first choice, although they never wholly relinquished the second; and in order to keep both options open, they negotiated simultaneously with the Western democracies and with each other. After encountering rejection, if not ostracism—based on the desire for prolonged revenge in the case of Germany, and in the case of Russia, on the fear of Bolshevism— they had no alternative but to turn to each other and in 1922 they concluded the Treaty of Rapallo. Had the Western powers viewed the situation more dispassionately they would not have been so surprised by the German-Soviet accord.

In 1939, history repeated itself. Once Hitler resolved to dismember Poland, he faced two choices in the accomplishment of his goal. Following his earlier moves in Austria and Czechoslovakia, he had to obtain 1) British and French consent, or 2) Russian consent. When Hitler failed to receive the approval of the West for such a move, he could *only* turn

to the Soviet Union. In this case, diplomatic surprise prepared the way
for a military surprise. As regards the Russians, they desired security
through a reliable defense agreement with Great Britain and France or,
alternatively, through an understanding with Germany. As in 1921, each
side initially attempted to reach an agreement with the reluctant French
and British governments while simultaneously conducting negotiations
with each other. (See Chapter 3.) Eventually the USSR and Germany
developed an interest in preventing each other from reaching a separate
understanding with the Western democracies. As in 1922, Britain and
France should have foreseen the "bombshell" of the Ribbentrop-Molotov
non-aggression pact which was at least as much the outcome of their own
policies as it was the result of German and Soviet duplicity. The British
subsequently tried to counter the Russian-German surprise with a bombshell of their own: the ratification of the Anglo-Polish treaty on August
25 did indeed surprise Hitler, but it came too late to change the course of
events.

After the Chinese Communists gained power in 1949, the American-
Chinese relationship steadily deteriorated into the direct military conflict
of the Korean War, and remained hostile until the late 1960's. Hence the
only form which a major diplomatic surprise could take would be the
normalization of U.S.-Chinese relations.

Sadat's epochal visit to Jerusalem is analogous to the American-Chinese rapprochement in that relations between Egypt and Israel could only
improve. In the process, Sadat—for the second time—wrecked the conceptions of Israeli policy-makers and the intelligence community, catch-
ing all sides unawares. This time, though, he destroyed political instead
of military conceptions. Before Sadat's Peace Initiative in November
1977, the Israelis had continuously tried to bring about a meeting between Israeli and Egyptian leaders through the good offices of Rumanian
President Ceausescu and the Shah of Iran. But despite Foreign Minister
Dayan's secret meeting with Egyptian Vice-President Tohamy in Morocco, the Israelis did not put much hope in this kind of meeting which
had been taking place since 1948. At best, they hoped for a ministerial-
level meeting on neutral ground. In the words of a former Israeli Director
of Military Intelligence, Major General Shlomo Gazit, "We encountered a
methodological problem, but we had no established procedures telling us
how to seek out and examine signals indicating a movement toward
peace. We had had much experience involving war—we knew what signals to search for. But what indicated peace? We had seen a form of Arab

expression that was different in both form and content. But could we ignore the possibility that such talk might be Arab propaganda intended to dull our senses and deceive us?"[19] President Sadat had secretly revolutionized his own concepts of the Arab-Israeli conflict and left the rest of the world behind. A similar change had also to precede the U.S.-Chinese rapprochement. According to Kissinger, this change occurred when "the leaders in the two countries had begun for the first time in a generation to regard each other in geopolitical rather than ideological terms."[20]

Diplomatic surprise may appear to be less complicated than military surprise in terms of possible combinations, but it is in fact no easier to anticipate, especially since, as already pointed out, it does not require many participants. Because the number of people taking part in the preparation and execution can be kept to a minimum, the emission of signals can be tightly controlled. And, as mentioned before, in the analysis of diplomatic surprise, heavy emphasis must be placed on the psychological makeup, motives, and perceptions of one political leader.

Almost all military surprises not only require a large number of participants—but also necessitate the movement of troops and supplies, periods of intensified communications, extensive planning efforts, training, and finally, the concentration of the formations to be used in the attack. The emission of signals is thus practically unavoidable. All of Sadat's political surprises were so successful as surprises because he did not even inform anyone of his decisions until just before they were made public. Paradoxically, the only one of his surprises which was preceded by quite a few signals (which were ignored!) was his decision to launch the 1973 war against Israel. Here, military activities provided many signals that were never available in his diplomatic surprises. Obviously, in a unilateral diplomatic surprise or in a *fait accompli*, the preservation of secrecy is even easier because they do not require collaboration with another state.

Military intentions can almost always be corroborated by examination of material evidence and capabilities. The intelligence analyst can at least compare declared intentions of peaceful coexistence with the development of military hardware. If he observes that a state is creating a substantial offensive military capability, he will begin to doubt that state's peaceful intentions, and continuously reevaluate them in light of these developments. The political intelligence analyst, on the other hand, cannot adjust his conclusions on the basis of any "objective" material evidence, but he *can* carefully watch for changes in his adversary's attitude through media reports and the speeches of various leaders. His analysis nevertheless may lack an important dimension which is available to the military analyst, since changes in attitude of the mass media can be controlled and manipulated by an authoritarian government (unlike material military developments). In addition, it is virtually impossible to maintain complete secrecy in bilateral diplomatic surprises because of the dialogue between the states planning the political maneuver.

Military and diplomatic surprise also differ in the emphasis that is placed on assessing the participants' *intentions* and *capabilities.* In the study of military surprise, analysts must devote equal attention to these two factors and their interaction, whereas the study of diplomatic surprise requires that attention be focused primarily on intentions. Obviously, the launching of a military surprise means that the potential attacker must possess a certain minimum of capabilities; and the greater the capabilities, the more attention military analysts should give to the way in which capabilities influence intentions.

This is not usually a primary consideration for the political analyst because he does not deal with actions that necessitate the immediate use of capabilities. In fact, the opposite is true—he should become more alert when a state's power is deficient relative to its most important goals, since diplomatic activity is often intended to compensate for the lack of capabilities. Though weakness can provide incentive to resort to diplomatic surprise, it is not a sufficient condition. Although Israel is a weak and isolated nation, its leaders (with the possible exception of Foreign Minister Dayan) were not creative enough to come up with the kind of new ideas that Sadat produced. Other examples illustrate the importance of weakness in unexpected political maneuvers. The Rapallo agreement of 1922 allied two exhausted states whose capabilities had been seriously drained during World War I. In the case of the Ribbentrop-Molotov treaty in 1939, the Soviet Union signed a non-aggression pact with Germany because it realized, among other things, that war with Germany would be disastrous as long as the Western democracies remained aloof and impotent. Even if Stalin realized that the Soviet Union would eventually have to fight Germany, this agreement still gave him valuable time to prepare for war. Hitler needed the treaty with the USSR primarily because he had to avoid a two-front war with both Russia and the Western powers while he attacked Poland.

The People's Republic of China desired better relations with the United States in order to counterbalance the powerful Soviet threat; and to a lesser extent, the same was true of the United States. Finally, Sadat did not come to Jerusalem as a result of a lifelong devotion to peace—he came because Egypt had not been able to accomplish its goals (e.g., regaining the Sinai) through the use of military force and because of his fear that Israel might possess a nuclear capability. For its part, Israel was aware that it might not retain its military capabilities indefinitely in a protracted war against all Arab states.

COSTS AND BENEFITS OF MILITARY
AND DIPLOMATIC SURPRISE

The act of surprise offers nothing but advantages to the initiating side in war, while in diplomacy it involves a trade-off. Surprise is the multiplier of any military force. As a fundamental part of military planning, it dictates the course of war on the attacker's terms, reduces his casualties, and improves his chance of achieving victory.* However, diplomatic surprise entails both benefits and costs.

When German Foreign Minister Rathenau decided to sign the treaty with Russia at Rapallo, he knew that it would undermine Germany's relations with the Western democracies. Similarly, Hitler's decision to sign a non-aggression pact with the Soviet Union without consulting his allies, Italy and Japan, may have cost him dearly in the later stages of the war. When Mussolini later took his "revenge" and attacked Greece without consulting Hitler he embroiled the Germans in a Balkan war at a strategically difficult time. (See Chapter 3.) Had Hitler not humiliated the Japanese, they might have turned against the Soviet Union in collaboration with the Germans, instead of south against the United States in the Pacific. As for the Russians, the agreement with Nazi Germany damaged their political standing with the Communist parties of Europe, perhaps convincing the Europeans that Russian interests took precedence over communist ideology.

In his visit to Jerusalem, Sadat also had to pay a substantial price. He alienated almost all of the Arab states, thus losing much of his prestige and considerable economic support in the Arab world. Sadat did gain the Sinai Peninsula and American economic and military support for Egypt, but he sacrificed—at least in the short run—the bid for Arab hegemony.

There is also a price to be paid on the domestic scene. The reversal of a policy to which the state and many interest groups have long been committed engenders sharp criticism. The leaders responsible for the change

---

* A common fallacy concerning military surprise attacks is that a true surprise has only taken place if the whole war (of which the surprise is only one battle) ends in victory. The side that initiates a very successful surprise attack may ultimately lose the war (e.g., the Nazi attack on Russia in 1941, the German offensive in the Ardennes in 1945, the Japanese attack on Pearl Harbor in 1941, the Arab attack on Israel in 1973). The major decision is whether or not to go to war. Once one side decides that it will go to war, it is naturally interested in maximizing its gains in the opening move by destroying the largest possible proportion of the enemy's forces. Whether the initiating side ultimately wins or loses, it still profited from the surprise attack. A surprise attack always strengthens the surprising side. Every state wants to avoid being the object of surprise, because even if it has the strength to recuperate from the initial shock, the price it pays will be high. Generally, the attacking side plans to emerge victorious (the Japanese attack on Pearl Harbor and the Arab attack on Israel in 1973 are unusual in the sense that the attacking sides did not necessarily expect to win—but rather planned on making temporary gains that would improve their political bargaining positions).

in policy must therefore be sure that they have adequate support with which to implement the desired new policy—or in non-democratic systems, they must be sure that they possess sufficient power to crush any resistance by force.

As has been noted, it is easier to undertake a major diplomatic revolution in an authoritarian system than in a democratic one: for one thing, government-controlled media can facilitate the people's acceptance of new ideas. This does not guarantee that internal opposition to such moves is nonexistent. Of course, when Stalin and Hitler were at the peak of their power and in full control of their political systems, they faced no real opposition. But in Egypt, Sadat is in a more precarious position. He must contend with opposition from the army, religious groups, and political parties from the left (those who follow the Soviet line) and the right (nationalistic and Pan-Arab groups).

The leader of a democratic country faces stiffer opposition. President Carter's decision to establish full diplomatic relations with the People's Republic of China and unilaterally sever relations with Taiwan brought him under attack in Congress.

In Israel, Prime Minister Begin encountered strong criticism of the negotiations with Egypt from both his own party and the opposition. Since—by simply announcing them—Sadat could guarantee the delivery of certain benefits to Israel, he found it difficult to understand why Begin in order to reciprocate had to undergo the lengthier, more arduous process of obtaining Knesset approval. Soon, Sadat realized the advantages this system held for him and he learned to manipulate the Israeli opposition forces. The difficulties involved in calculating the costs and benefits of a decision to implement a controversial new policy provide some explanation for the infrequency of major diplomatic surprises.

*   *   *   *   *

There is still much to learn about the positive and negative aspects of surprise and abrupt change in diplomacy. The failure to anticipate a surprise and prepare countermoves can have serious implications, as a look at historical examples demonstrates. Had the British and French been more alert to the signals indicating a possible Soviet-German agreement in the summer of 1939, they could have taken diplomatic or military steps to block such an agreement. They could have: 1) pressured the Polish government to allow the presence of Soviet troops on their soil in the event of a German attack; 2) outbidden the Germans by recognizing the Soviet Union's right to an extended sphere of influence along the Baltic; 3) shown more interest in their military negotiations with Moscow by sending a higher-level delegation to attend the confer-

Table 3 21

Military Surprise	Diplomatic Surprise
—An inherent part of military planning. It does not require a shift in military concepts and thinking.	—Not accepted as part of normal procedures. It requires that a leader make a creative shift in his political concepts.
—Forecasting or warning against military surprise is very difficult because of the large variety of possibilities for surprise in terms of time, place, methods, doctrine, and weapons technology. The emission of signals prior to a large-scale military operation is unavoidable.*	—Forecasting is difficult as a result of the small number of participants and the problem of anticipating the changing concepts and perceptions of a single leader. Secrecy is relatively easy to preserve, especially in unilateral surprise. There are always signals preceding a bilateral surprise. A unilateral surprise or *fait accompli* may sometimes not be preceded by any signals at all.
—Has immediate impact. The price paid by the surprised side is heavy.	—The impact can be immediate or delayed. Surprised parties are seldom subject to immediate danger.
—Offers *only* advantages to the attacking side from the military point of view—but can otherwise increase the desire for revenge on the part of the attacked side or evoke a strong political reaction from non-involved states.	—Always involves a trade-off for the initiating side (a trade-off between conflicting interests, goals, and political allies).
—Is always a hostile, "negative" act.	—Can either be a bilateral, cooperative effort—or a unilateral act or *fait accompli.* Can be positive or negative.
—Equal importance must be attached to the complex interaction between the enemy's *intentions* and *capabilities*.	—Attention must primarily, though not exclusively, be paid to intentions (especially those of individual leaders). Lack of capabilities are not a limiting factor in non-coercive diplomacy. (See Appendix to Chapter 2.)

* Without going into detail, it must be mentioned that the signals inevitably emitted can be shrouded by noise through deliberate deception. In other words, the observer can be deliberately misled as to the true goals of the activities that cannot be hidden from public view (e.g., the Soviet and Warsaw pact exercises prior to the invasion of Czechoslovakia, or the Egyptian and Syrian maneuvers before the 1973 war with Israel). Infrequently, an attack can be launched from an almost static position through the use of forces in being. (This last situation also depends on the risks an attacker is willing to take.)

Table 4

	Type of Surprise	Type of International System	Availability of Warning Signals
Hitler's remilitarization of the Rhineland March 1936	Unilateral *Fait accompli*	Multipolar Heterogeneous Ideological tensions	Many warning signals available Surprise in terms of timing only
The Ribbentrop-Molotov Agreement August 1939	Bilateral Major diplomatic surprise	Multipolar Heterogeneous Powerful ideological competition	Considerable number of signals available Major block to prediction of this surprise was the belief that ideological competition precludes political agreement
American-Chinese Rapprochement 1971	Bilateral Major diplomatic surprise	Loose bipolar Heterogeneous Ideological tensions	Many public signals exchanged Deception on the tactical level to maintain secrecy
Sadat's Expulsion of the Soviet Military Advisers from Egypt July 1972	Unilateral Minor diplomatic surprise	Loose bipolar Heterogeneous Ideological competition	Very few, if any signals Not expected because of the belief that Egypt was too dependent on the Soviet Union
Sadat's Peace Initiative November 1977	Unilateral Major diplomatic surprise	Global Loose bipolar Heterogeneous Ideological tension *Local system:* High tensions; zero-sum-game characteristics	No signals

Major States Surprised	Mediation by Other States	Type of Leader and Domestic Political System	Short and Long Range Impact
France Great Britain France's eastern allies		Authoritarian leader in an authoritarian system Very few German decision makers apprised of the decision in advance	Drastic shift in the European balance of power France's East European system collapsed German power grew
Opponents France Great Britain Poland *Allies* Japan Italy Communist parties	Italy for Germany Bulgaria for the Soviet Union Both played a minor role	Authoritarian leaders in authoritarian systems	Immediate result was the division and partition of Poland, and WWII USSR & German collaboration
Opponents USSR *Allies* Japan S. Vietnam Taiwan	Rumania, Pakistan, and France	China: Authoritarian leadership in authoritarian system USA: Strong leadership in a democratic system	Eased American way out of Vietnam Caused friction in American-Japanese relations PRC joined the UN Counterbalanced power of the USSR Enhanced Nixon's popularity before the US elections
USSR USA Israel		Authoritarian leader in authoritarian system No one knew of Sadat's plan until the last moment	Blackmailed the USSR into supplying Egypt with weapons Enabled Egypt to prepare for the 1973 war Showed possibility of a shift to pro-US policy
Opponents Israel USSR *Allies* Other Arab states PLO USA	Morocco and Rumania	Authoritarian leader in authoritarian system Announcement total surprise to everyone, including Egyptian foreign minister	Bypassed the Geneva Peace Conference; accelerated negotiations; excluded the USSR from talks; drove a wedge between Israel and the US; major change in Middle Eastern balance of power

ence; 4) issued strong statements or taken military moves to convince the Germans of British and French readiness to come to Poland's rescue. When the British government finally made such a statement on August 25, 1939, it was too late: the Ribbentrop-Molotov agreement had been signed.

If it had been fully aware of the contacts between the United States and the People's Republic of China from 1969 to 1971, the Soviet Union might have tried to "blow up" the process of rapprochement by starting an intense propaganda campaign or by reducing troop concentrations and tensions on the Soviet-Chinese border.

The "Arab Oil Embargo" that was imposed during the Yom Kippur War caught Western Europe and the United States by surprise, although there had been ample signals that the Arabs would use the oil weapon as part of their war against Israel.[21] A thoughtful evaluation of these signals might have stimulated the planning of countermeasures (e.g., a new policy for storing oil, earlier attention to the problem of developing alternative energy sources, and better political and economic coordination between the Western nations). Such countermeasures would have at least eased the psychological pressure—that is, the sense of helplessness and frustration.

All available evidence indicates that despite the far fewer possibilities for diplomatic surprise it is nevertheless difficult to avoid. Particular attention must be paid to the role of leaders, who are always instrumental in the initiation of a diplomatic surprise. On the positive side, more must be learned about surprise as a means to introduce constructive changes in foreign policy. Study of this topic may also help us to discover more about the conditions for *change* in foreign policy in general, and the circumstances which are more conducive to the emergence of diplomatic surprises. As recent events have proven, diplomatic surprises can be very unwelcome, but they can also present new, positive opportunities.

NOTES

1. The study of military technological surprise, however, is a much neglected subject that would repay investigation. At present, no theoretical study on technological surprise is available to the public. However, Dr. Zeev Bonen, former head of the Israeli Armament and Development Authority, offers, in *Technological Surprise*, some thought-provoking observations on the subject. He suggests that a technological surprise "out of the blue" is rare, if not impossible. "If the equipment is produced in small quantities, as for example in the case of the U-2 or the A-bomb in World War II, it may be kept secret for a long time." (p. 5) But

even in the cases he cites technological surprise was avoidable. His research points to a dynamic of failure similar to that which exists in diplomatic and military surprise. The weakest link, according to Bonen, is not in the intelligence acquisition or analysis process as much as in the lack of acceptance of intelligence reports by decision-makers. For example, he examines one of the classic case studies of technological surprise—that of the launching of the first Russian Sputnik—and draws the following conclusions: "The launching of the Sputnik came as a major surprise and shock to the American public, abruptly challenging American supremacy. Was the Sputnik a technological intelligence surprise? Definitely not. The information was given directly and clearly by the Russians themselves on various occasions before the actual launching (October 4, 1957) . . . . Obviously there was no intelligence surprise. The information was freely available. It was a problem of acceptance. The Americans did not take the Russian challenge seriously. Their strong belief in American scientific supremacy was a very effective filter that discounted and rejected the possibility of being overtaken by the Russians in the satellite race." (pp. 8-9) See also F. J. Krieger, *Behind the Sputniks* (Washington, D.C.: Public Affairs Press, 1958); and Herbert F. York, *Race to Oblivion* (New York: Simon & Schuster, 1971), pp. 106-125. Other preliminary observations on technological surprise are Arthur Lee Burns, "International Consequences of Expecting Technological Surprise," *World Politics*, Vol. 10, No. 4, July 1958, pp. 512-534; some remarks by Patrick J. McGarvey in *C.I.A.: The Myth and the Madness* (Baltimore: Penguin Books, 1972), pp. 109-110; Stefan T. Possony and J. E. Pournelle, *The Strategy of Technology* (Cambridge, Mass.: Dunellen, 1970), pp. 99-100 in particular; George H. Heilmeir, "How to Avoid Technological Surprises," *Air University Review*, Sept.-Oct., 1976, pp. 2-7.

2. Instead of summarizing the findings of military literature, I am presenting below a selected bibliography for the interest of the reader.

3. In the jargon of intelligence, 'signals' refer to valid information, whereas 'noise' refers to information that is either not validated, deliberately misleading, or found to be incorrect in retrospect. Usually 'signal to noise ratio' means the ratio of correct to incorrect information. Since the existence of noise makes it generally impossible to distinguish between correct and incorrect information, we can distinguish between signals and noise only in retrospect.

4. Thomas S. Kuhn, *The Structure of Scientific Revolutions* (Chicago: University of Chicago Press, 1973), second, enlarged edition. For criticism of his theory, see Imre Lakatos and Alan Musgrave, *Criticism and the Growth of Knowledge* (Cambridge: Cambridge University Press, 1970); for the application of his theory to the social sciences and history, see David A. Hollinger, "T. S. Kuhn's Theory of Science and its Implication for History," *American Historical Review*, Vol. 78, No. 2, April 1973, pp. 370-393.

5. George Liska, *Beyond Kissinger: Ways of Conservative Statecraft* (Baltimore: Johns Hopkins University Press, 1975). The author has described routine diplomacy as follows:

> Routine diplomacy smooths and implements established relations with the aid of only marginal adjustments (i.e., it is the opposite of surprise). Its most constructive performance is in evolving formulas

of mutually acceptable compromise which permit the existing configuration to endure and avoid thus the risks of convulsions of radical change. (p. 25)

Creative diplomacy or diplomacy as the means to reach a higher or new level of normal diplomacy, on the other hand, he describes thus:

> Creative diplomacy rearranges the setting within which negotiations for compromise occur . . . the supreme expression of creative diplomacy is the "diplomatic revolution" [i.e., a major diplomatic surprise]: a fundamental recasting or reversal of existing alignments which automatically marks a major stage (and a rare turning point) in the evolution of the international system. Revolutionizing diplomacy is not, therefore, to be confused with revolutionary diplomacy. . . . Creative diplomacy can be either offensive or defensive in strategic purpose; and the transformation sought may be for repose as well as for major or continuing change. (pp. 25-26)

6. Charles Lockhart, "Flexibility and Commitment in International Conflict," *International Studies Quarterly*, Vol. 22, No. 4, December 1978, p. 550. This article discusses the question of flexibility versus commitment in the specific context of direct conflict and bargaining in crisis situations.

7. See Anwar el Sadat, *In Search of Identity: An Autobiography* (New York: Harper Books, 1978), pp. 228-231; Mohamed Heikal, *The Sphinx and the Commissar* (New York: Harper & Row, 1979), Chapter 15, pp. 242-256; and Alvin Z. Rubinstein, *Red Star on the Nile* (Princeton: Princeton University Press, 1977), pp. 188-212.

8. Walter Laqueur, *Russia and Germany: A Century of Conflict* (London: Weidenfeld and Nicolson, 1960), pp. 128-131.

9. Sadat's peace initiative was a unilateral surprise; but through earlier contacts with Israel, Sadat knew in advance that Israel would respond positively to his move.

10. Marvin Kalb and Bernard Kalb, *Kissinger* (Boston: Little, Brown, 1974), pp. 251-252.

11. For the characteristics of the balance of power system, see Edward Vose Gulick, *Europe's Classical Balance of Power* (New York: W. W. Norton, 1967); Morton A. Kaplan, *System and Process in International Politics* (New York: Wiley and Sons, 1967), Part 1; Butterfield, "The Balance of Power" in Herbert Butterfield and Martin Wight, eds., *Diplomatic Investigations* (Cambridge, Mass.: Harvard University Press, 1968), pp. 132-148, 149-175; Hans J. Morgenthau, *Politics Among Nations*, 5th ed. (New York: Alfred A. Knopf, 1973), pp. 167-224; Ernst B. Haas, "The Balance of Power-Prescription, Concept or Propaganda," *World Politics* Vol. 5, July 1953, pp. 442-477; Stanley Hoffmann, "Balance of Power," *The Encyclopaedia of the Social Sciences* (new) Vol. II, pp. 395-399; Kyung-Won Kim, *Revolution and International Systems* (New York: New York University Press, 1970).

12. For the development of this concept, see Richard N. Rosencrance, *Action and Reaction in International Politics* (Boston: Little, Brown, 1963).

13. For a detailed discussion on the bargaining position of weak states in different international systems, see Michael I. Handel, *Weak States in the International System* (London: Frank Cass, 1981), Chapter 4, pp. 169-216.

14. For the multipolar system, see Raymond Aron, *Peace and War* (Garden City, N.Y.: Doubleday, 1966), pp. 94-149; and Stanley Hoffmann, *Gulliver's Troubles* (New York: McGraw-Hill, 1968), pp. 3-52.

15. A. J. P. Taylor, *The Origins of the Second World War* (New York: Atheneum, 1968), p. 229.

16. See, for example, Saul Friedlaender, "Forecasting in International Relations," *Futuribles* (Geneva: Librairie Droz, 1965); Klaus Knorr and Oskar Morgenstern, *Political Conjecture in Military Planning* (Princeton, N.J.: Princeton Center of International Studies, November 1968), Policy Memorandum No. 35.

17. Yehezkel Dror, "How to Spring Surprises on History" (mimeo), a paper presented at the Leonard Davis Institute for International Relations, Jerusalem— International Conference, "When Patterns Change: Turning Points in International Politics," 1979, p. 3. Even if leaders in democratic societies decide to reverse earlier policies either by their own initiative or by public pressure, the process of change will be slowed down and implemented more gradually.

18. I am grateful to Major General Shlomo Gazit, former head of Israeli Military Intelligence, for suggesting this point to me.

19. Quoted from Major General Shlomo Gazit, *Notes: The Arab-Israeli Conflict After the Camp David Agreements*, 1978 (mimeo), p. 6.

20. Henry Kissinger, *White House Years* (Boston: Little, Brown, 1979), p. 685.

21. See Raymond Vernon, ed., *The Oil Crisis* (New York: W. W. Norton, 1976), pp. 12-13, 61-62, 80-81. Typically—despite the large number of explicit warning signals—both the price hike by OPEC and the OAPEC oil embargo came as a total surprise.

BIBLIOGRAPHY

Adelman, Kenneth L. and Robert Ellsworth, "Foolish Intelligence," *Foreign Policy*, Fall 1979, No. 36, pp. 147-159.

Andrew, Christopher, "Whitehall, Washington and Intelligence Services," *International Affairs*, July 1977, Vol. 53, No. 3, pp. 390-404.

Andrew, Christopher, "Governments and Secret Services, A Historical Perspective," *International Journal*, Spring 1979, pp. 167-186.

Andrews, Captain Frank USN, (Ret.), "The Prevention of Preemptive Attack," *U.S. Naval Institute Proceedings*, Vol. 106, No. 5, May 1980.

Andriole, Stephan J. and Robert A. Young, "Toward the Development of an Integrated Crisis Warning System," *International Studies Quarterly*, Vol. 21, No. 2, March 1977, pp. 107-150.

Ashman, Harold Lowell. *Intelligence and Foreign Policy: A Functional Analysis.* (Unpublished Ph.D. dissertation, University of Utah, 1973.)

Axelrod, Robert, "The Rational Timing of Surprise," *World Politics*, Vol. 31, January 1979, No. 2, pp. 228-247.

Belden, Thomas C., "Indications, Warning and Crisis Operations," *International Studies Quarterly*, Vol. 21, March 1977, pp. 181-199.

Ben-Zvi, Abraham, "Hindsight and Foresight: A Conceptual Framework for the Analysis of Surprise Attacks," *World Politics*, Vol. 28, No. 3, April 1976, pp. 381-395.

Betts, Richard K., "Analysis, War and Decision: Why Intelligence Failures are Inevitable," *World Politics*, Vol. 31, October 1978, No. 1, pp. 61-90.

Betts, Richard K., "American Strategic Intelligence: Politics, Priorities and Direction," prepared for the Conference on Intelligence: Deception and Surprise, at the Fletcher School of Law and Diplomacy, April 24-26, 1979.

Betts, Richard K., *Surprise and Defense: The Lessons of Sudden Attacks for U.S. Military Planning*. Washington: Brookings Institution, 1981.

Bingham, Woodbridge, "Historical Training and Military Intelligence," *The Pacific Historical Review*, Vol. 15, No. 2, June 1946, pp. 201-206.

Blackman, Morris, "The Stupidity of Intelligence," in Charles Peters and Timothy Adams, eds., *Inside the System*. New York: Praeger, 1970.

Borodin, Katerina, "Surprise Attack—Problems and Issues." Sweden: Ministry of Defense, 1975. See also "Surprise Attack: The Case of Sweden" in *The Journal of Strategic Studies*, Vol. 1, No. 1, May 1978, pp. 98-110.

Chan, Steven, "The Intelligence of Stupidity: Understanding Failures in Strategic Warning," *American Political Science Review*, Vol. 73, No. 1, March 1979, pp. 171-180.

Corson, William R. *The Armies of Ignorance*. New York: The Dial Press, 1977.

Critchley, Julian, *Warning and Response: A Study of Surprise Attack in the 20th Century and and Analysis of Its Lessons for the Future*. New York: Crane, Russak, 1978.

Cruickshank, Charles. *Deception in World War II*. New York: Oxford University Press, 1980.

de Weerd, H. A., "Strategic Surprise in the Korean War," *Orbis*, Vol. 6, Fall 1962, pp. 435-452.

Dvornik, Francis. *The Origins of Intelligence Services*. New Brunswick: Rutgers University Press, 1974.

Erfurth, General Waldemar. *Surprise*. Translated by Stefan Possony and Daniel Vilfroy. Harrisburg, Pa.: Military Service Publishing, 1943.

Freedman, Lawrence. *US Intelligence and the Soviet Strategic Threat*. Boulder, Colorado: Westview Press, 1977.

George, Alexander L., "The Case for Multiple Advocacy in Making Foreign Policy: Theory and Practice," *American Political Science Review*, Vol. 66, No. 3, September 1973, pp. 751-795.

George, Alexander L. *Presidential Decisionmaking in Foreign Policy: The Effective Use of Information and Advice*. Boulder: Westview Press, 1980.

George, Alexander and Richard Smoke. *Deterrence in American Foreign Policy: Theory and Practice*. New York: Columbia University Press, 1974.

Handel, Michael I. *Perception, Deception and Surprise: The Case of the Yom Kippur War*. Jerusalem: The Leonard Davis Institute, 1976. See also "The Yom

Kippur War and the Inevitability of Surprise," *International Studies Quarterly,* Vol. 21, No. 3, September 1977, pp. 461-501 (an abbreviated version).

Hareven, Aluph, "Disturbed Hierarchy: Israeli Intelligence in 1954 and 1973," *Jerusalem Quarterly,* No. 9, Fall 1978, pp. 5-19.

Hilsman, Roger C., "Intelligence and Policy-Making in Foreign Affairs," *World Politics,* Vol. 5, 1952, pp. 1-45.

Hilsman, Roger C. *Strategic Intelligence and National Decisions.* Glencoe: The Free Press, 1956.

Holst, Johann Jurgen, "Surprise Signals and Reaction," *Cooperation and Conflict,* Vol. 1, No. 2, pp. 31-45.

Hughes, Thomas L. *The Fate of Facts in a World of Men—Foreign Policy and Intelligence Making.* Headline Series No. 233. New York: Foreign Policy Association, Decmeber 1976.

Janis, Irving L. *Victims of Groupthink: A Psychological Study of Foreign-Policy Decisions and Fiascoes,* Boston: Houghton Mifflin, 1972.

Jervis, Robert. *The Logic of Images in International Relations.* Princeton: Princeton University Press, 1970.

Jervis, Robert, "Hypothesis on Misperception," *World Politics,* Vol. 20, No. 3, April 1968, pp. 454-479.

Jervis, Robert, *Perception and Misperception in International Politics.* Princeton, N.J.: Princeton University Press, 1976.

Kent, Sherman, *Strategic Intelligence for American World Policy.* Princeton: Princeton University Press, 1949.

Knorr, Klaus, *Foreign Intelligence and the Social Sciences,* Research Monograph No. 17. Princeton: Center for International Studies, 1964.

Knorr, Klaus, "Failures in National Intelligence Estimates: The Case of the Cuban Missiles," *World Politics,* Vol. 16, April 1964, pp. 455-467.

Knorr, Klaus, "Strategic Intelligence: Problems and Remedies," in Laurence Martin, Ed. *Strategic Thought in the Nuclear Age.* London: Heineman, 1979.

Kurzel, Joseph J., "Military Alerts and Diplomatic Signals," in Ellen P. Stern, ed., *The Limits of Military Intervention.* Beverly Hills: Sage, 1977.

Martin, Wayne R., "The Measurement of International Military Commitments for Crisis Early Warning," *International Studies Quarterly,* Vol. 21, No. 1, 1977, pp. 151-180.

Platt, Washington. *Strategic Intelligence Production: Basic Principles.* New York: Praeger, 1957.

Poteat, George H., "The Intelligence Gap: Hypotheses on the Process of Surprise," *International Studies Notes III,* Fall 1976.

Ransom, Harry Howe, "Strategic Intelligence and Foreign Policy," *World Politics,* Vol. 27, October 1974, pp. 131-146.

Schelling, Thomas C., *The Strategy of Conflict.* New York: Oxford University Press, 1966.

Schelling, Thomas C., *Arms and Influence.* New Haven: Yale University Press, 1966.

Sherman, Kent, "Estimates and Influence," *Foreign Service Journal* 56, April 1969.

Starr, Chester G. *Political Intelligence in Classical Greece.* Leiden (Netherlands): E. J. Brill, 1974.

Stech, Frank J., *Political and Military Intention Estimation: A Taxonomic Analysis*. Bethesda, Maryland: Mathtech, 1980.

Stech, Frank J., "Self-Deception: The Other Side of the Coin," *The Washington Quarterly*, Vol. 3, No. 3, 1980, pp. 130-141.

Trumpener, Ulrich, "War Premeditated? German Intelligence Operations in July 1914," *Central European History*, Vol. 9, No. 1, March 1976, pp. 58-85.

U.S. Congress, House Select Committee on Intelligence Hearing, *U.S. Intelligence Agencies and Activities: The Performance of the Intelligence Community*, 94th Congress, 1st Session, 1975. (See also "Draft Report of the House Select Committee on Intelligence," *Village Voice*, February 16, 1976, pp. 76-81.)

Wasserman, Benno, "The Failure of Intelligence Prediction," *Political Studies*, Vol. 8, No. 2, June 1960, pp. 156-169.

Whaley, Barton. *Codeword Barbarossa*. Cambridge: MIT Press, 1973.

Whaley, Barton, *Stratagem: Deception and Surprise in War*. Cambridge, Mass.: MIT Center For International Studies, 1969.

Wohlstetter, Roberta. *Pearl Harbor: Warning and Decision*. Stanford: Stanford University Press, 1962.

Wohlstetter, Roberta, "Cuba and Pearl Harbor: Hindsight and Foresight," *Foreign Affairs*, July 1965, pp. 691-707.

Wohlstetter, Roberta, "The Pleasures of Self-Deception," *The Washington Quarterly*, Vol. 2, No. 4, Autumn 1979, pp. 54-64.

Woods, Charles E., Captain USN (Ret.), "Surprise in Naval Warfare," U.S. *Naval Institute Proceedings*, Vol. 104, No. 5, May 1978.

2

HITLER'S DIPLOMACY OF FAITS ACCOMPLIS, 1933-1936

Whatever we have signed, we will fulfill to the best of our ability.
Hitler in "devout earnestness" to G. Ward Price[1]

I could not tell a lie to benefit myself, but for Germany there is no lie I would not utter.
Hitler to General Erhard Milch[2]

There is often an inverse relationship between the military strength of a state and its reliance on diplomacy to achieve national goals. The stronger a state, the more it can rely on the threat to use force and disregard the fine points of diplomacy. Conversely, the weaker a state is relative to its goals, the more it tends to substitute diplomatic stratagems for lack of military power. In such cases, the relatively weaker state usually develops better political bargaining skills, augmenting its power through a complex alliance system or a powerful patron.[3] Less frequently, it tries to compensate for weakness by employing a more risky foreign policy—one that involves a diplomatic surprise or *fait accompli*.

One classic case is Hitler's diplomacy of *faits accomplis* between 1933 and 1936, a time when Germany was weak in relation to its neighbors. Through a series of carefully timed *faits accomplis*, Hitler carried Germany to a position of strength while avoiding retaliation from potential adversaries during the crucial transition period. As soon as he had built up Germany's military power, Hitler gradually shifted from the use of diplomatic *faits accomplis* to military ultimatums, and finally to naked force.

Once he had made his domestic position relatively secure after the *Machtergreifung* in 1933, Hitler devoted more attention to foreign policy. From 1934 to 1936, one *fait accompli* followed another in a series of systematic, interrelated coups that repudiated the treaties of Versailles and Locarno. These feats further enhanced Hitler's domestic popularity, for they reflected the wishes of most respectable German citizens—and

also those of all earlier German governments since the end of World War
I, including those in which Gustav Stresemann, the architect of Locarno,
had been either Chancellor or Foreign Minister.[4]

Hitler happened to be the one who attained power at a more opportune time for successful action against the Versailles treaty. His continuous use of deception and bluff, in addition to his willingness to resort
to blackmail and crude threats, brought about the desired result. Only a
man such as Hitler—a parvenu with no respect for bourgeois values or
education—could have pursued this course of action. Other German
politicians such as Stresemann had too much in common with their
British and French counterparts; all of them were Europeans as much as
they were French, British, or German. This difference in background prevented most European leaders—at least initially—from correctly evaluating Hitler's intentions. By the time their eyes had been opened to his
radically different methods, Hitler had already achieved his basic policy
goals: he had renounced the Treaty of Versailles and the Locarno Pact
without incurring retaliation, legitimized his revisionist policies, and
increased Germany's military power. Any attempt to thwart his demands
would by then have meant a general European war, and the West European states wanted to avoid war at any reasonable—or unreasonable—
cost.

Each *fait accompli* was preceded (and followed) by Hitler's declarations of Germany's love of peace, Germany's desire for friendly collaboration with others, and Germany's proposals for disarmament and non-
aggression treaties. At a time when Germany was still vulnerable to
effective sanctions, Hitler followed each *fait accompli* with the solemn
promise that this was the last such action and that Germany would
henceforth stand behind each of its treaty obligations (especially the one
that he intended to repudiate next). But he always added one condition:
Germany would unequivocally abide by its treaty obligations and remain peaceful as long as all other states followed suit. In each "post-
crisis" speech, Hitler then loaded the dice in his favor by setting forth
conditions he knew the other countries could not possibly meet. Each
speech thus contained the justification for the next *fait accompli*.

Hitler's first important act of deception was a peace offensive. On May
17, 1933, he "pleasantly surprised" the world with the famous *Friedensrede*, a masterly speech of deception he delivered before the Reichstag.

On behalf of the German people and the German government, I
have to make the following statement: Germany has disarmed. She
has complied with all obligations imposed upon her in the Peace
Treaty to an extent far *beyond the limits of equity and reason . . .*
Nevertheless, Germany is at any time willing to undertake fur-

ther obligations in regard to international security, *if all the other nations are ready on their side to do the same, and if this security is also to benefit Germany.* Germany would also be perfectly ready to disband her entire military establishment and destroy the small amount of arms remaining to her, *if the neighbouring countries will do the same thing with equal thoroughness.* But if these countries are not willing to carry out the disarmament measures to which they are also bound by the Treaty of Versailles, *Germany must at least maintain her demand for equality* . . .

[Germany] is also entirely ready to renounce all offensive weapons of every sort *if the armed nations, on their side, will destroy their offensive weapons within a specified period,* and if their use is forbidden by an international convention. Germany has only one desire, to be able to preserve her independence and defend her frontiers . . .

The German Government will not reject *any* prohibition of arms as being too drastic *if it is applied in the same manner to all other States. As long as armaments are allowed to other Powers, Germany cannot be permanently deprived of all weapons of defence.* We are fully prepared only to make use of an equal status to an extent to be settled *by negotiation.*

These demands do not imply rearmament but only a desire for the disarmament of other States . . .

Germany is at all times prepared to renounce offensive weapons *if the rest of the world does the same.* Germany is prepared to agree to any solemn pact of non-aggression because she does not think of attacking but only of acquiring security . . .

May the other nations realize the resolute will of Germany to put an end to a period of blundering and to find the way to a final understanding between all, *on the basis of equal rights.*[5] (Emphasis added.)

Hitler reassured his audience of Germany's sincere desire for peace, but he made all of his offers conditional upon their acceptance by *all* other states. Each promise was followed by a demand for reciprocity; yet the conditions he set forth were simply too exorbitant to be accepted in their entirety by the other European states.

That became obvious once Hitler's proposals were brought before the League of Nations disarmament conference in Geneva in 1933. The British were sympathetic and seemed willing to compromise, but they insisted on England's need to retain an air bombardment capacity for police purposes in the Empire. The Japanese raised questions over naval limitations, and the French demanded provisions for inspection and investigation.[6]

Meanwhile, the German delegation waged a "war of nerves." On May

11, a few days before Hitler's speech, Konstantin von Neurath, Germany's Foreign Minister, published an article that cast doubt on the good will of the "armed states," and declared that if the conference failed to produce satisfactory results, Germany would be forced to provide itself with the arms that these states possessed.[7]

Hitler had shrewdly created an excuse to legitimize Germany's rearmament program. When a few months later he decided to leave the League of Nations, he worried over the possibility—as he was later to worry during the Munich Crisis or on the eve of the German attack on Poland—that someone would make a compromise suggestion which would be difficult to reject.[8] In fact, when the German government cabled its decision to withdraw to the Secretary of the League of Nations on October 14, 1933, it stated:

> In light of the course which recent discussions of the powers concerned have taken in the matter of disarmament, it is now clear that the Disarmament Conference will not fulfill what is its sole object, namely, general disarmament. It is also clear that this failure of the conference is due solely to the unwillingness on the part of the highly armed states to carry out their contractual obligation to disarm [i.e., under the Covenant of the League of Nations]. This renders impossible the satisfaction of Germany's recognized claim to equality of rights, and the condition on which the German government agreed at the beginning of this year again to take part in the work of the conference thus no longer exists. The German government is accordingly compelled to leave the Disarmament Conference.[9]

But Hitler's foreign audience had been temporarily intoxicated by his promises of peace in the *Friedensrede* of May. They heard what they wanted to hear and ignored the ominous warning signs. Toward the end of the speech, Hitler had issued a warning:

> It would be difficult for us as a constantly defamed nation to continue to belong to the League of Nations.[10]

Since this was Hitler's first major foreign policy speech, perhaps the European nations cannot be blamed for ignoring his caveat, but they can certainly be blamed for their refusal, in later years, to recognize his true intentions.

And indeed, when the disarmament conference did not—as Hitler had hoped and foreseen—accept his radical proposals, he presented the world with the first in a series of *faits accomplis*. He abruptly announced—in the October 14 telegram—that Germany was immediately withdrawing from the League of Nations and the disarmament conference. ". . . The news struck the public in Berlin like a bomb, as the French chargé d'affaires put it. It shocked Geneva . . . without Germany the disarmament conference was virtually meaningless. Foreign capitals were amazed—and then indignant."[11]

At first, Hitler was apprehensive that the French would demand action against Germany in the League of Nations and complain about secret German rearmament. But three days later, Hitler was able to "assure his cabinet that the 'critical moment' was past and that Germany had nothing to fear."[12] He then called for a plebiscite to show that German public opinion approved his withdrawal from the League of Nations. The plebiscite, which took place on November 12, 1933, resulted in 95.4% approval of Hitler's move. The withdrawal was, however, more than just a popular move—it was also a brilliant tactical maneuver.[13]

"Hitler had found his adversaries' weaknesses . . . Turning his chosen isolation to advantage, Hitler now courted their interest. Ten days after he had shocked them with his abrupt withdrawal from the conference, he outlined to the British Ambassador his idea of a progressive disarmament convention."[14] He also continued to play on British interest in bringing Germany back into the League of Nations. In March 1935 he told Anthony Eden that every German sincerely desired membership in the League of Nations, but that it was impossible unless Germany obtained equal rights.[15] His shrewd maneuvering had created a situation in which Germany had the moral excuse to rearm while her opponents, who did not realize that Hitler would have left the League anyway, were divided and placed in a morally inferior position.

> As long as Germany was a member, she was bound in a web of relationships that obliged her to accommodate her national interests to those of her fellow members and to maneuver among a multitude of pressures. As long as she participated in the disarmament conference, she was engaged in an enterprise incompatible with the vast rearmament program Hitler's purposes required.[16]

Hitler had established the pattern for his later *faits accomplis*. The preparatory stage of deception was intended to divert attention from his actual goal and reassure potential opponents that he did not intend to do what they feared he might. The *fait accompli* was then followed by a flood of new assurances that since Germany desired peace, this was the last such act of its kind; in this manner, he allayed fears and set the stage for the next move.

*   *   *   *   *

Hitler had established Germany's moral right to continue its rearmament, which by then was well under way. But he had to safeguard this still risky enterprise and avoid a preemptive attack or any other military sanctions against Germany. The only real threat to Germany's rearmament was posed by a possible French-Polish attack—a threat which became more serious after Germany's withdrawal from the League of Nations.[17] The Germans were well aware of the rumors that Marshal Pilsudski had considered the possibility of waging a preventive, limited war against Germany during March-April 1933. At the same time, the Polish government had supposedly approached the French government regarding a joint preemptive war against Germany. While nothing concrete ever came of these consultations (assuming that they took place) the danger to Germany was a real one.[18]

Hitler's best possible strategy was to improve relations with Poland. This was not an easy course to take, for the Germans generally disliked, even despised, the Poles even more than they disliked the French, and no German leader since 1918 had seriously considered such a strategy. Being no more favorably disposed toward Poland than his predecessors, Hitler did not include its continued existence in his long-range plans; but in the short run his order of priorities required an understanding with that country. Such opportunistic moves had been difficult for his predecessors—Stresemann had consistently refused to consider an Eastern Locarno agreement with Poland as a complementary treaty to the Locarno Pact.[19] Traditional German dislike of Poland did not make rapprochement a popular undertaking, but Hitler had the advantage of operating within an authoritarian system.[20]

It so happened that the Poles were also interested in developing better relations with Germany. Worried about the policies of the four powers since the French had let them down at Locarno by not guaranteeing Poland's frontiers, the Poles were searching for a foreign policy which would enable them to be less dependent on France. [21] Both Colonel Józef Beck, the Polish Foreign Minister, and Marshal Pilsudski wanted to follow an even-handed policy between France, Russia, and Germany. They had signed a non-aggression agreement with the Soviet Union in January 1932, were allied with the French since 1921, and were now seeking to improve relations with Nazi Germany.

Soon after Germany's withdrawal from the League of Nations on October 14, 1933, Hitler strongly urged Hermann Rauschning, the *Gauleiter* of Danzig, to arrive at an understanding with Poland. On the same day, Józef Lipski, the new Polish Ambassador in Berlin, had a "most friendly talk with von Neurath who explained at length the need to settle all outstanding problems."[22] Early in November 1933, Pilsudski suggested the possibility of a German-Polish agreement, which was discussed on November 15 between Lipski, Hitler, and Neurath. Welcoming Pilsudski's initiative, Hitler lectured Lipski on the "futility of war" and "the need for a bilateral peaceful settlement of all differences" between the two states.[23] A press communiqué released after the meeting referred to the intention of the two states to continue direct negotiations and to renounce the use of force in their relations.[24] At this point, the Germans and Poles opened secret negotiations and on November 28, 1933, Hans von Moltke, the German Ambassador in Warsaw, handed Pilsudski the German draft of the treaty. The German version did not contain the words "non-aggression pact" because this phrase would have implied that Germany was relinquishing its claims on Polish territory; instead, the phrase "no force agreement" was preferred.*[25]

The Declaration of Non-Aggression and Understanding between Germany and Poland, signed on January 26, 1934, declared that mutual relations would be based on "the principles contained in the Kellogg-Briand Pact" (which was universally acknowledged to be totally ineffective). Both parties promised to settle all problems through direct negotiations and without recourse to force. The agreement, which was to remain in effect for 10 years, obliquely mentioned Poland's continued commitment to its League membership and its treaties with other states.[26]

Hitler's first non-aggression pact, concluded with "the very country it was generally expected to be the most likely to attack," caused a political sensation.[27] It cannot be compared to any of his later agreements—not even to the German-Soviet agreement, which was supported by many Germans. It can, however, be compared to Sadat's Peace Initiative of 1977 which was not only a surprise, but was also highly unwelcome in most of the Arab world. Only history will tell whether Sadat's peace agreement with Israel will be a short-range diplomatic stratagem, such as Hitler's pact with Poland, or a basic shift in policy. The new treaty was a diplomatic triumph for Hitler because it considerably increased Germany's freedom to maneuver without renouncing Germany's unalterable claims to Polish territory. By driving a wedge between Poland and France, Hitler had taken the first step since the Locarno Pact to weaken the French alliance system that encircled Germany. Moreover, the treaty served Hitler as an excellent propaganda tool by demonstrating to the world the sincerity of his "peace speeches." The German-Polish non-aggression agreement did not need to be followed by further assurances of Germany's peaceful intentions—it had already, after all, reduced tensions in Europe by reconciling two hostile states.

---

* A similar non-aggression pact suggested by Hitler to the Czechs at the same time was rejected by them out of hand. It is interesting to note that the German-Polish Non-Aggression Pact was modeled on the Soviet-Polish Non-Aggression Pact signed two years earlier, which was part of Col. Beck's attempt to ensure Poland's security by following a balanced policy with regard to both its powerful neighbors. (See Grigore Gafencu, *Last Days of Europe*, New Haven: Yale University Press, 1948, p. 29.)

The Treaty of Versailles stipulated that Germany was permitted to have an army solely for the maintenance of internal order and frontier control. The army was to consist of no more than seven infantry and three cavalry divisions not exceeding 100,000 soldiers including officers. (The number of officers was limited to 4000.) The General Staff had been dissolved and the personnel of the German War Ministry limited to 300. Conscription was abolished and limits were set on the number and type of weapons Germany was permitted to manufacture: Germany's navy was allowed to maintain six warships with a maximum displacement of 10,000 tons; twelve destroyers of up to 3000 tons; and twelve torpedo boats of up to 200 tons. It was forbidden to build or operate submarines or military aircraft of any type. For a nation like Germany which identified so strongly with military power, the limitations imposed by the Treaty of Versailles were, of course, deeply humiliating.

To be sure, no German government ever observed either the spirit or the letter of Versailles. Although Germany initially attempted to maintain a facade of legality, circumvention of the military clauses of the treaty became a national conspiracy. Kept at about 100,000 soldiers, the size of the Reichswehr was small. Its size was, however, deceptive since it was designed to serve as the nucleus of a much larger army—each soldier was trained to be an officer or at least an NCO. The Reichswehr continued to develop and test offensive weapons in collaboration with the Soviet Union in the late 1920's and early 1930's.[28] By the time Hitler came to power, most of the military clauses of the Treaty of Versailles had already been violated, and the German armed forces were preparing for considerable expansion.

While Hitler made one peace speech after another, he was steadily enlarging the Reichswehr.[29] He disclosed his plan to expand German military power during his first meeting with the commanding generals of the army on February 3, 1933. Revealing his intention to introduce conscription, he emphasized that the main problem was "how to rearm without provoking a preventive attack Germany could not resist."[30] He went on:

> This path I have set out to you will take many years to tread. If France has real statesmen, she will set about us during the preparatory period—not herself, but probably using her vassals in the east. So it will be wrong to commit ourselves too much to the idea of equal armaments. We must make all our economic and military preparations in secret, and only come out into the open when they are 100 per cent complete. Then we will have regained the freedom of decision . . .[31]

This first major speech to the generals was cautious, but when Hitler started probing the Western allies and discovered the extent of their lack of unity and resolve, he accelerated the pace of rearmament. Although

Hitler had always intended to expand Germany's military strength, his initial underestimation of Germany's ability to continue undisturbed in its rearmament program lends weight to A.J.P. Taylor's claim that much of Hitler's later aggression stemmed from the absence of a powerful reaction on the part of the Allies.[32]

Hitler now secretly pressed forward with the expansion of Germany's armed forces and the Army was ordered to increase its strength from 100,000 to 300,000 by October 1, 1934. In April 1934, Hitler told the Chief of the General Staff, General Ludwig Beck, of his intention to openly decree conscription by April 1, 1935. Until that time, the utmost secrecy had to be observed.[33]

In November 1932, the German Navy presented the Defense Minister, General Kurt von Schleicher, with plans to expand battleship and submarine construction. When Hitler gave the go-ahead to Admiral Erich Raeder, the Navy's Commander-in-Chief, in February 1933, he specified that the German Navy should be geared toward combatting the French and Soviet Navies, not the British Navy. At an early stage (February 3, 1933), Hitler also told Raeder that he intended to conclude a German-British Naval Agreement that would fix the British and German naval ratios in Britain's favor.[34] On May 1, 1933, the German Navy was allotted eighty million marks for two battle cruisers of supposedly 26,000 tons each. Actually, each was 35,000 tons, which was 25,000 tons in excess of the maximum 10,000 tonnage allowed under the Versailles treaty. In June 1934, Hitler ordered Raeder not to mention the actual displacement of the battle cruisers; Raeder was only to speak of improved 10,000 ton ships and maintain complete secrecy regarding the construction of U-boats. Submarines (whose construction was prohibited by the Versailles treaty) were secretly built in Holland, Finland, and Spain during the Weimar Republic and the components shipped to Kiel, where they were not assembled until 1935.[35]

The German Air Force was also continuously expanding. Until 1931, flight training had been carried out by Lufthansa, the German airline, as well as in the Soviet Union and by a variety of cover organizations such as the "German Flying Sport Association." Hitler's government simply accelerated the clandestine flight training that had begun during the Weimar Republic; Hermann Goering was appointed Reich Commissioner for Aviation and Erhard Milch, the Director of Lufthansa, supervised the rapid expansion of the secret air force.[36] Many officers and NCOs were transferred from the Army and Navy to the Air Force. In May 1933, Milch "commissioned studies for a thousand-aircraft programme, a significant number of which was to be bombers."[37] The target for late 1935 was a force of 600 front-line aircraft, including nine bomber wings.[38]

From 1933 to 1939 Germany annually spent an average of three billion reichsmarks on its Air Force. All of this hectic activity remained clandestine—at least officially—between 1933 and early 1935. As a cover, the *Reichsbahn* (Germany's state-owned railroad) was made responsible for the training of bomber pilots in night flights between Berlin and Koenigsberg. The head office of this clandestine organization, located in Berlin, hid behind the innocent title of "Traffic Inspectorate" and was staffed by "civilian-clothed Reichswehr officers."[39] Above all, the aircraft industry, which had employed no more than 4000 workers at the time of Hitler's rise to power, employed 230,000 workers by 1937.[40] Beginning in 1933, some two million workers were spared the miseries of unemployment—they were put to work building new airfields, emergency landing fields, control towers, and flying schools. In January 1934, the Air Ministry funded research on synthetic fuels and rubber in anticipation of wartime shortages.[41]

Secrecy was imperative for the embryonic Air Force; a preemptive French attack on Germany and its air bases had to be avoided at all costs.[42] Until the Luftwaffe had grown to the point where it was capable of inflicting sufficient damage on a potential enemy to render an attack too costly, secrecy (and, later, bluff—by pretending that their Air Force was larger than it really was) was its only protection.

Obviously, the massive German rearmament effort could not remain hidden from the British and French for long. While in the autumn of 1933 the British Air Ministry estimated that the Germans would have no military aircraft within the next two years, by March 1934 the British realized that Germany possessed some 350 military aircraft and was producing them at the rate of 60 per month. [43] The British were shocked to learn that German plans called for the production of 1,300 first-line military aircraft by October 1936. (Instead of an earlier British forecast of 1,000 aircraft by April 1939, the actual German output was as high as 140 a month.)[44]

In the later part of 1934, British Intelligence realized that German rearmament was progressing faster than had been estimated. A special Cabinet Committee was therefore established to gather and analyze all available information on German rearmament. In its report of November 26, 1934, the committee made a fairly realistic evaluation of the German effort: it believed that the German Army consisted of 21 infantry divisions, 3 cavalry divisions (or a total of approximately 300,000 soldiers) and one or two mechanized divisions which were still being assembled. It was estimated that this army would be fully equipped by April 1935. The committee also made a reasonably accurate assessment of the strength of the German Navy, though it neglected to mention preparations for the construction of the two battle cruisers and the submarines.

The British calculated that the German Air Force would have over 500 battle-ready aircraft by October 1935—rising to 1400 by the following year.[45] There is no doubt, then, that British Intelligence had obtained largely accurate information regarding the German rearmament plan. The vast increase in German military *capabilities* should already at this early stage have told the British (and the French) politicians something about Germany's *future intentions*. Yet, apparently all the intelligence collected failed to influence British and French policies. Until the Munich Agreement of September 1938 the British government seems to have operated as if sealed off from reality regarding its most important foreign policy problem—Nazi Germany—by resolutely closing its eyes to the overriding threat of continually growing German rearmament. This raises serious questions concerning the extent, and indeed the ultimate purpose, of cooperation between the British government and its Intelligence Services.

Winston Churchill dramatically exposed German rearmament efforts in a speech before Parliament on November 29, 1934. On behalf of the government, Prime Minister Baldwin admitted that there was "some place for anxiety," but he hastened to add that "the real German strength is not 50 per cent of our strength in Europe today."[46] The British government simply preferred to evade the issue. Although Baldwin was technically correct when he said that there was no "immediate menace," he failed to realize that the real issue was not the European military balance in 1934 or even 1935, but the danger of a military imbalance in the years to come. Yet even the military balance—clearly in favor of the Western powers—was not as important as the psychological balance. The Western powers were not even prepared to *threaten* Germany with the use of force, let alone use it. Feeling guilty about Germany's prolonged inequality, the British government believed that Hitler's claims were morally justified.[47] It faced a dilemma: since it did not wish to disarm, it was in a difficult position to demand that others disarm or remain disarmed.

The British government therefore decided at an early stage not to take reprisals against Germany's "illegal rearmament" program. The announcement of the German rearmament program in the House of Commons was made—in contrast to Churchill—in a friendly tone, and the ensuing discussion concluded with no recommendation for action against Germany. The only step the British cabinet took was to "politely inform" the German government that it "did not recognize the right of any signatory to the treaty of [Versailles] to free itself from obligations imposed upon it without negotiations and agreement with the other signatories."[48] The note implied that *if* negotiated with, the British government might in fact formally recognize Germany's right to rearm. The Germans understood that they could now proceed without any danger of British—and, almost certainly, French—intervention; without having been formally admitted or made public by the Germans, their rearmament was recognized as a *fait accompli*.

The French government, too, was not prepared to take military action against the German rearmament program. In 1934, however, the French had stubbornly resisted British pressure to acknowledge the German *fait accompli*. At the League of Nations Disarmament Conference in April 1934 the French government rejected a plan proposed by Arthur Henderson, the British Labor leader and president of the conference. The plan called for France to acknowledge the principle of military equality with regard to Germany and to agree that both countries limit their armies to 300,000 men.[49] In May 1934, the French again rejected a British plan— put forward this time by the British Foreign Secretary, Sir John Simon. Simon proposed that England and France recognize Germany's right to rearm in exchange for a comprehensive European settlement including a revision of the Versailles Treaty. The British hoped to contain Germany's military expansion by trading their formal recognition for an upper limit on Germany's rearmament.

After the plebiscite of January 13, 1935, returned the Saar to the German Reich, Hitler redoubled his efforts to convince the world of his peaceful intentions; he courted the French in particular by announcing that Germany had no more claims on French territory. Immediately after hearing the outcome of the Saar plebiscite, Hitler declared in a broadcast address: "Your decision, German fellow countrymen of the Saar, gives me today the opportunity of stating that after the completion of your return, the German Reich will make no further territorial claims on France. That statement is our historical contribution, entailing as it does, heavy sacrifices, toward that pacification of Europe which is so sorely needed."[50] On January 16 and 17, Hitler reiterated these comforting words in the "name of the whole German people."[51]

Hitler's verbal mastery of the politics of peace—of which any "progressive and peace-loving leader" would have been proud—eventually softened France's attitude.[52] By February 1935, the French were ready to join the British in presenting the German government with offers similar to those they had rejected in 1934. While Hitler welcomed such an offer as recognition of Germany's rearmament, he realized that a comprehensive treaty would also curb his ambitions in the east; therefore his response was evasive and noncommittal. By now, Hitler was ready, well in advance of his original intuitive timetable, to proclaim Germany's rearmament.

The British and French furnished him with the pretext to publicly announce rearmament. On the basis of a paper reporting the progress of German rearmament, the British government decided, on March 4, to modestly expand British arms production.[53] At the same time, the French introduced a bill extending compulsory military service from 18 to 24 months.[54]

On Saturday*, March 9, 1935, Hitler made his first open move to repudiate the Treaty of Versailles when the German government officially notified foreign governments that a German Air Force had already been secretly established.[55] Using threshold tactics, Hitler first wanted to test the reaction of the Western powers to this announcement before making the next and more risky move of openly introducing general conscription in Germany. Since the British and French governments already knew that a clandestine German Air Force existed, they did not react in a threatening way. The British government's reaction was simply to confirm in the House of Commons the scheduled visit to Berlin of Foreign Secretary Simon and Anthony Eden, then Lord Privy Seal with special responsibilities for League of Nations affairs.

On Saturday, March 16, Germany promulgated a law establishing universal military service. It provided for a peacetime army of 12 army corps, or 36 divisions—approximately half a million men. The timing and scope of Hitler's decision surprised Germany's military leaders because Germany could not possibly within the next few years supply the number of divisions to be created. (According to General Fritz Erich von Manstein, the Reichswehr's General Staff would have preferred a target of 21, rather than 36 divisions, but Hitler had more ambitious plans.)[57] The projected strength of the new German Army was twice that of the French Army stationed in Europe.[58]

"The British government after making a solemn protest proceeded to ask whether the Fuehrer was still ready to receive Sir John Simon."[59] Britain's willingness to send its Foreign Secretary to Berlin immediately after the announcement of German conscription was an indisputable victory for Hitler's diplomacy of *faits accomplis*. The French addressed an urgent but mildly worded appeal to the League of Nations. The League convened an emergency session at which the French presented a note calling for a "search for conciliation" and discussing the need to dispel the new tension created by the German conscription law.[60] The League's Council condemned Germany's action and appointed a committee to suggest

* All is well known, most of Hitler's surprises occurred on Saturdays. Roehm was murdered on Saturday, June 30, 1934; the formal establishment of the Luftwaffe was disclosed on March 9, 1935 — a Saturday — and the announcement of conscription came a week later on March 16, 1935. The remilitarization of the Rhineland occurred on Saturday, March 7, 1936. "It was quite seriously believed in Berlin that Hitler timed his gambles in foreign policy for Saturdays, when he knew that the British Cabinet members and other high officials were away from London observing their weekend in the country." Others of Hitler's "weekend surprises" were the Austrian *Anschluss* (March 12, 1938), his attack on Scandinavia (April 17, 1940), and his attack on Russia (June 22, 1941).[56]

steps which might thwart Hitler the next time he attempted such a move. Meanwhile, the Germans continued their rearmament program undisturbed.[61] At the Stresa Conference (April 11-14, 1935), the three participants—Great Britain, France, and Italy—condemned Germany's action and reaffirmed their commitment to Austria's independence (at Mussolini's request) and to the Locarno Pact, and agreed to follow a common policy toward Germany. This was the last time the three powers tried to coordinate their policies—but even this last attempt resulted only in empty gestures.

To allay the growing apprehensions of the Western powers Hitler once more embarked on a peace offensive. On May 21 he delivered another of his peace speeches—a speech so full of exaggerated pacifism that had it been delivered by the leader of a Western nation, it would have been considered in bad taste. But from Hitler's mouth it sounded like the confession of a tired warrior who had reached the sincere conclusion that there is no substitute for peace.

> [War] merely means burdens and misfortune. The blood shed on the European continent in the course of the last 300 years bears no proportion to the national result of the events . . . The principal effect of every war is to destroy the flower of the nation . . . National Socialist Germany wants peace because of its fundamental convictions. And it wants peace also owing to the realization of the simple, primitive fact that no war would be likely essentially to alter distress in Europe. It would probably increase it . . . What then could I wish more than peace and tranquility? But if it is said that this is merely the desire of the leaders, I can reply that if only the leaders and rulers desire peace, the nations themselves will never wish for war. . . . Germany needs peace and desires peace . . .[62]

Hitler assured the world that Germany had no further claims on French territory (i.e., Alsace-Lorraine) and did not plan to annex Austria, although his forbearance contravened the principle of self-determination. (This assurance was mainly directed at Italy.) Germany was also ready to negotiate arms control and limitation agreements on a *mutual basis* and had no intention of starting a naval race with Britain similar to the one that had preceded the Great War. Hitler then went on to hold out a bait for the British government; he expressed his willingness to limit the strength of the German Navy to 35% of the Royal Navy (and to 15% below that of the French Navy). He concluded on a less positive note: "History has certainly often shown us Germans that we understand less the art of living reasonably than that of dying nobly. I know that if ever this nation should be attacked, the Germans will do more than their duty, remembering from the experiences of one and a half decades what is the fate of a conquered people."[63] There were other ominous portents. Hitler declared that Germany did not recognize Lithuania's sovereignty over the port city of Memel, but he added that the Memel problem could be peacefully negotiated with the Great Powers who had been responsible for Lithuania's annexation of Memel. Lithuania did not rank very high on Hitler's list of priorities—yet apparently he could not resist making a point in principle about Germany's refusal to accept the territorial clauses of Versailles. But Lithuania was weak and remote, so no one paid much attention to these remarks. Another bad omen was his attack on the "military alliance between France and Russia" which introduced "an element of legal insecurity . . . into the Locarno Pact . . ."[64] Yet the speech had something for everyone—the British, the French, the Italians, Poles, and Austrians—everyone except the poor Lithuanians. But no one asked why Lithuania's control of ethnic Germans should be different from those controlled by Poland or Czechoslovakia.

The British government actually absolved Nazi Germany of its repudiation of the Treaty of Versailles by concluding a naval treaty with it in London in June 1935. The treaty allowed Germany to build a navy one third the size of the British Navy, including 5 battleships, 21 cruisers, and 64 destroyers. This was more than Germany was even capable of producing for almost a decade. The treaty also permitted Germany to build a submarine force with a tonnage equal to 60% of Britain's—and perhaps 100% in exceptional circumstances.[65]

The treaty was negotiated and signed by the British government in complete disregard of its allies' interests.

> The affront to Britain's partners, France and Italy, both of whom were also naval powers, but neither of whom had been consulted, was open and much resented. The solidarity of the Stresa Front, the unanimity of the Powers' condemnation of Germany's rearmament, was destroyed. The British Government, in its eagerness to secure a private advantage, had given a disastrous impression of bad faith. Like Poland, but without the excuse of Poland's difficult position between Germany and Russia, Great Britain had accepted Hitler's carefully calculated offer without a thought of its ultimate consequences.[66]

Britain went so far as to refuse to give France, its closest ally, information about what types of ships, and how many of each, Germany was now allowed to build. The combination of the Anglo-German naval agreement, which had offended the French, and Mussolini's attack on Ethiopia, which was opposed by the British, seriously undermined the possibility of collaboration between Great Britain and France.

*   *   *   *   *

The last of Hitler's unilateral *faits accomplis*** took place exactly a year after the public announcement of German conscription. On March 7, 1936, Hitler announced the remilitarization of the Rhineland. In view of the move's critical implications for the Western powers as well as Germany's relative military weakness, this was one of the boldest maneuvers of Hitler's entire career.

The Rhineland case raises many interesting questions concerning the use of surprise as a political instrument. In the first place, were the Western powers completely surprised by Hitler's move? Can there be a partial surprise? Additional questions include: finding the ideal timing of a surprise; the problem of noise, signals, and warning; and the role played by *a priori* conceptions in the analysis of signals and noise.

Historians have conflicting opinions as to whether the Western powers were surprised by Hitler's remilitarization of the Rhineland. In *The Origins of the Second World War*, A.J.P. Taylor claims that Hitler's reoccupation of the Rhineland did not surprise the French.[68] In *The Rise and Fall of the Third Reich*, William Shirer states, ". . . Germany's action apparently came as a complete surprise to the French and British governments and their general staffs."[69] Nevertheless, this disagreement is not as perplexing as it seems because, as will be shown, the answer to the question is both yes and no.

What is, however, certain is that Hitler considered the element of surprise essential for the success of his *faits accomplis*. In a directive to the German High Command issued on May 2, 1935—three weeks before the peace speech in the Reichstag in which he reassured the Western powers of his intention to respect the Locarno Pact and the territorial clauses of the Treaty of Versailles—Hitler ordered that operation *Schulung* ("Training") was to be "executed by a surprise blow at lightning speed."[70]

The Germans made every effort to ensure the success of the surprise. Only a small number of officers was informed of the plan—in fact, General Werner von Blomberg, the Minister of War as well as Com-

---

* The major crises that Hitler unloosed two years later differ from the *faits accomplis* described in this chapter. The later crises (the *Anschluss* of Austria and the Czech crisis) involved disputes over foreign territory; they were no longer internal "German affairs." In addition, each *fait accompli* was, as the name indicates, a final, completed event as soon as it was publicly announced, whereas the later crises only created new demands and were not terminated by a German decision and a supine Western attitude. The later crises were initiated by Hitler but could only be resolved by concessions of the other side and therefore cannot be considered *faits accomplis*. While the earlier series of *faits accomplis* was accomplished during a period of German military vulnerability and weakness, the second phase of international crises took place when Germany was perceived to have attained military equality. Having experienced Germany's unilateral rejection of its international obligations and the worthlessness of Hitler's promises, politicians should not have been surprised by the second phase of crises. What was amazing during the second phase was, in Eden's words, the fact "that this man could repeat the exercise so often in later years and still find many to excuse him."[67]

mander-in-Chief of the Armed Forces, took the precaution of issuing the order in handwriting.[71] When further discussion of the plan took place on June 16, 1935, Lieutenant Colonel Alfred Jodl, then head of the Home Defense Department, emphasized that only when absolutely necessary should anything be committed to writing and "without exception such material must be kept in safes."[72]

> Throughout the entire period of decisions and preparations, the Chancellor and his consultants managed to preserve the element of *surprise*. This was a vital factor and perhaps even the key to success. If Paris or London had discovered what was pending, they could easily have ruined everything for Hitler, either by publicly warning Germany of the consequences of her action or even by threatening to reply in kind as soon as the violation took place. If either had occurred, it would be difficult to imagine that Hitler would have risked the confrontation which would then have been inevitable.[73] (Emphasis added.)

From what is known of discussions within the British government on March 5, 1936, it is clear that although such a move was considered possible, no one expected it to happen quite so soon.[74] Therefore, the surprise did not concern the nature of Hitler's move, but rather *the timing*.

As is usually the case, there was no lack of repeated warnings. "For more than a year the French government had been receiving warnings that Adolf Hitler was preparing to move German troops into the demilitarized Rhineland."[75] It is important to examine some of the warnings in detail and discover why the timing of Hitler's move came as a surprise.

One warning was a matter of what was *not* said. On October 16, 1935, "the tenth anniversary of the initialing of the Locarno Pact, the German Press remained *unanimously and significantly silent*."[76] The major element of the Locarno agreement was the maintenance of the status quo along Germany's western frontier and the demilitarization of the Rhineland.

The reoccupation of the Rhineland, like many other major surprises, was preceded by a prolonged series of confusing signals and noises, some of which are briefly summarized here.

As early as October 1934, Jean Dobler, the French Consul General in Cologne, took note of German moves which could be construed as preparations for the reoccupation of the Rhineland. On October 17, he reported that the Inspector General of the German Cavalry, General Knochenhauer, was overheard to remark that very soon German troops would resume once again the Watch on the Rhine. In two long reports to the French Foreign Office dated March 23 and April 12, 1935, he described local preparations for receiving troops and aircraft as well as for the construction of barracks, airfields, munitions depots, roads and the like.

On April 26, Dobler reported that in a speech at Koblenz, Goering confirmed that no German fortifications were being constructed in the Rhineland. He noted, however, that no German newspaper reported this part of Goering's speech, and that despite his repeated requests the Germans refused to give him the official text of the speech as they had promised.

Even more interesting was an incident reported by Dobler in April and May 1935. After the middle of March a German brigade marched into the Rhineland. When Dobler was informed of this he immediately protested to Diels, the head of the Cologne government. Within a day the Germans withdrew their troops and Dobler reported the incident to the Quai d'Orsay.

Germany's real intentions became progressively clearer. On May 30, Dobler reported a conversation with Diels, according to which Hitler intended to respect the Demilitarized Zone for the moment, but that in the spring of 1936 he would ask for modifications in the Locarno and Versailles Treaties with regard to the Rhineland. Dobler, obviously a diplomat of unusual acumen and energy, insisted on discussing the situation in person with Foreign Minister Laval. Laval, however, showed little interest in Dobler's presentation, which took place late in May. After being told that the German brigade had been withdrawn from the DMZ, the following conversation ensued:

"Laval merely said,
            'They have left?'
Dobler: 'Yes'
Laval: 'Well then. . .'
Dobler: 'Well then, they will return. . .'
Laval: 'What should be done?'
Dobler: 'We must declare officially in Berlin that as soon as Germany
            introduces troops into the Rhineland, we will also do so.'
Laval: 'That's your opinion?'
Dobler: 'Yes'
Laval: 'Well, it is not mine.'

Here the conversation stopped and I had the feeling that it would not continue so I decided to reanimate the discussion.

Dobler: 'Sir, mine is the advice of a man who did part of his studies
            in Germany before the war, of a man who lived on the eastern
            frontier of Germany for six years, of a man who has been your
            Consul-General in western Germany for four years, and so I
            beg to reiterate: if we do not take such a step, the Rhineland
            will be reoccupied next year.'

This declaration provoked no answer, so I tried for the last time.

Dobler:	'Do you think it's normal that in the DMZ there are 17 secret aviation landing-strips, not counting those of which I may not know?'
Laval:	'Ah! But that's exaggerated. . . (Turning to Léger) Well Léger, what do you think?'
Léger:	(Looking out the window and tapping on the pane) 'Aviation? . . . ah! yes . . . aviation . . . heu! of course aviation . . . aviation! . . .'

Here the interview finally came to an end. It is absolutely clear that Léger and Rochat did not want the Minister to talk about the Rhineland to the French Consul-General in the Rhineland . . . I took the same train to Berlin where I presented myself to Ambassador François-Poncet who told me immediately, 'You should not send telegrams the way you do. They cause people to worry.'

I responded, 'I hope so . . .'[77]

Dobler continued his warnings during the summer of 1935. Despite all his efforts, his reports were ignored and he was not encouraged to continue his intelligence work. Had these early warnings been heeded, France might have prevented Hitler's remilitarization of the Rhineland.

During the fall of 1935, higher French diplomatic and intelligence authorities in Germany reported additional preparations for the possible remilitarization of the Rhineland. This led the Chief of the General Staff, General Maurice Gamelin, to warn the French Foreign Office on October 21, 1935, that "the hypothesis of a German repudiation of the Rhineland statutes must be envisaged before the autumn of 1936."[78]

Following an interview with Hitler on November 21, 1935, André François-Poncet, the French Ambassador in Berlin, reported to the Quai d'Orsay that Hitler's sharp attack on the Franco-Soviet treaty led him to believe that Hitler was just waiting for an excuse to move into the Rhineland. In François-Poncet's opinion, "Hitler's sole hesitancy now concerned the appropriate moment to act."[79]

On December 13, 1935, Sir Eric Phipps, the British Ambassador in Berlin, had the following reaction to an interview with Hitler:

Herr Hitler's attitude and manner . . . was patronising in regard to Locarno, and struck a cynical note of regret at having failed to occupy the zone on the 16th March last. It seems probable that he will proceed to that reoccupation whenever a favourable opportunity presents itself. *This will hardly be, however, before he has made a final effort to "square" Great Britain.*[80] (Emphasis added.)

This report and other evidence accumulated that month prompted Foreign Secretary Eden to request that the Committee of Imperial Defence (C.I.D.) report to him on the defensive value of the Rhineland to

Britain, France, Belgium and, most important of all—Germany.[81] One day after Christmas, Gamelin again wrote to the Quai d'Orsay reporting accelerated German military construction in the area. On the last day of 1935, François-Poncet repeated his warning.[82] On January 11, 1936, Prime Minister Pierre Laval wired Charles Corbin, the French Ambassador in London, and asked him to inform the British government that the Germans had assigned two army corps (clearly an exaggerated number in light of later events) to the Rhineland area and that "total occupation" might take place on January 30, the anniversary of Hitler's rise to power.[83] However, it turned out to be just another false alarm.

In early January 1936, the French Military Attaché in Berne had expressed apprehension over the redistribution of German military forces near Coblenz and over construction work near Donaueschingen, a few miles north of Schaffhausen on the Swiss border. The problems associated with sustaining burdensome military budgets over a long period of time and the current troubled international situation caused the Swiss authorities to anticipate a sudden German decision. The Swiss General Staff forecast as the date January 30, 1936, the anniversary of Hitler's accession to power.[84] Additional warnings were given in January by the Polish Intelligence to the French Ambassador in Warsaw, who transmitted them to Paris.[85]

There is no evidence that this report caused any alarm in France or that precautionary military steps were taken. The fact that January 30 came and went without any German action may in fact have reduced French vigilance. The French Military Attaché certainly did not add to his reputation by his report. (The same Attaché must have further damaged his credibility when he reported on February 25 that autumn was the probable time for the Germans to act.)[86]

During January 1936, the warnings increased in both frequency and urgency. "On January 15, General Renondeau, French Military Attaché in Berlin, warned of an imminent German move into the Rhineland. The same day Military Intelligence, in a 'Very Secret' communication for the eyes of Gamelin only, gave a similar warning. Apparently jogged out of his nonchalance . . . General Gamelin, on behalf of the General Staff, got up a note which he sent three days later . . . to the Supreme Military Committee: 'Recent information permits us to suppose that Germany envisages in the near future the reoccupation of the demilitarized Rhineland, or at least of the right bank of the river.' "[87]

In spite of the increased number of warnings of the possibility of a German march into the Rhineland at the end of January, neither the French nor the British considered any form of mobilization or issuing a formal warning to the German Government. Had they taken firm action in January 1936—regardless of whether the warning signals received were genuine or not—Hitler might have been deterred from taking action later in March. As noted above, the fact that the warnings in January 1936 turned out to be false alarms may have dulled the attention of the British and French intelligence services to the signals received later in February and March.

On January 17, Dobler reported that Diels had approached him concerning the possibility of reaching a negotiated agreement between Germany and France concerning a change in the demilitarized status of the Rhineland. In his cable to Laval, Dobler also mentioned his telegram of May 30, 1935, in which he quoted Diels as saying that the Rhineland issue would be reopened in the spring of 1936.[88] In yet another report on January 22, Dobler reported that the population and administration in the Rhineland were expecting a reoccupation in the spring.[89]

This emphasis in Dobler's reports on the possibility of the remilitarization of the Rhineland in the spring may have been a major factor in the relaxation of attention to incoming signals during February and early March of 1936 that were conveying an imminent threat in the Rhineland.

Other, perhaps less reliable indications of German intentions reached the French Foreign Ministry. Jacques Bardoux, a noted French journalist, was approached on or about February 10 by the chief of the German section of the British Secret Service. The English officer informed Bardoux that he had just spoken with General Keitel, who had let slip that Hitler would reoccupy the Rhineland in March. Bardoux at once informed Flandin, who a few days later told him that his information was totally false.[90]

Dobler, the alert French Consul General in Cologne, sent still another warning note to the Quai d'Orsay describing German activity in the demilitarized zone. He reported that the German Army would soon place a motorized corps of three divisions on the Rhineland border. In early February he received permission (after several refusals) to report in person to the Quai d'Orsay where he warned that the German preparations were nearly complete.'[91] On February 12, General Joseph Maurin, the Minister of War, sent a note to Foreign Minister Flandin (who had replaced Laval in January) telling him of "further German measures that seemed to indicate an early reoccupation of the Rhineland.[92] The next day, Henry Noel, the French Consul in Duesseldorf, wired Flandin that German officers in mufti had arrived to prepare for reoccupation of the demilitarized zone.[93]

Ambassador François-Poncet met with Hitler once more on March 2, 1936. This time, Hitler, who was in an unfriendly mood, sharply denounced the Franco-Soviet treaty that had been ratified by the French Chamber of Deputies only two days earlier and still had to be approved by the Senate. In his report, the Ambassador concluded that Hitler definitely planned to move into the Rhineland—it was only a question of time.[94] He guessed that Hitler would at least wait until the French had ratified and implemented the treaty in order to use it as an excuse for his move.

On the very day François-Poncet spoke with Hitler, the Germans made the final decision to enter the demilitarized zone. The necessary military preparations were delayed as long as possible to ensure maximum secrecy. All of the orders were given on short notice under a tight planning schedule. With only five days to spare, the formal orders for the planning of the operation were issued on March 2. The operations divisions of the three armed services had less than a day to produce the plans and issue the orders which were sent to the relevant departments on March 3, though the actual date for the operation was given only as late as March 5.[95] Thinking that they were involved in regular maneuvers, most of the soldiers participating in the operation did not realize their true objective until they crossed into the demilitarized zone. Most of Hitler's Cabinet members learned about the operation late at night on March 6. They, too, were presented with a *fait accompli*. ". . . Secrecy was maintained by involving a minimum of persons in planning the operation. Although the records are by no means complete, it is probable that Hitler confided in only nine persons during February and the first few days of March. They were Goering, Goebbels, Ribbentrop, Neurath, Buelow, Fritsch, Blomberg, Hassell and Forster."[96] The choice of Saturday, March 7, for the operation was meant to delay the reaction of the Western powers and, in the worst case, prevent intervention for at least a few days.

All the last-minute warning signals were conveniently ignored. "Geneviève Tabouis, the foreign editor of the French newspaper *L'Oeuvre*, received a telephone call from near the Swiss border on the night of March 5. The caller, an anti-Nazi German diplomat, told her that the *coup* would be carried out on Saturday morning, March 7. He spoke of the dissension between the generals and Hitler and of the retreat orders that would be given at the first sign of French resistance. The diplomat begged her to print the story; when she did so the next day the stock market went down, and a high official on the newspaper warned her to watch out or *L'Oeuvre* would be accused of war-mongering. [97] On the same day (March 5), François-Poncet also reported that the German press was falsely accusing the French of placing elite troops on the border for more than defensive purposes. He also noted that the German *Reichstag* had been convened for March 7 and that on the 6th the cabinet was to meet. "Important events are in the offing."

On Friday, March 6, Eden met with the German Ambassador in London, von Hoesch, to discuss the possibility of reopening the air pact negotiations with Germany. During the conversation, the Ambassador said that he would have an important message from Hitler to deliver the next day. The arrival of a special message from Hitler on a Saturday was unusual and should have alerted Eden. Ambassador von Hoesch had received a most secret message on March 3 informing him that Hitler would reply to the recently ratified Franco-Soviet pact of mutual assistance by re-establishing German sovereignty in the Rhineland.[98] Later that day, the British Ambassador in Berlin sent an urgent message to the Foreign Office; he, the French Ambassador, and the Belgian Chargé d'Affaires (all signatories of the Locarno Pact) had been asked to meet with Baron von Neurath on Saturday morning. His diagnosis of the situation was that Germany might be preparing to take some action with regard to the Locarno Pact.[99] What better warning could Eden have asked for?

The explanation for the surprise of the British and French governments lies in the concepts accepted by senior decision-makers, the conflicting evidence, and the secrecy and deception involved in Hitler's last-minute decision. The inability of intelligence organizations and decision-makers to differentiate effectively between signals and noise is, as has been noted, a well-known problem in intelligence work.[100] In this situation, rigid, *a priori* concepts blinded them to certain facts.

It may be unfair to suggest that it was possible to predict the timing of the German move. Signals relating to physical preparations for the reoccupation of the Rhineland (e.g., building barracks, roads, ammunition depots, the visits of German army officers) were abundant, but the final decision to proceed was taken by Hitler as late as March 2. Considering the small number of people in Germany that were apprised of the target date as well as the extraordinary degree of secrecy, it is doubtful that an authoritative warning concerning the date and the time could have been received by the Allies within three or four days.

The set of concepts commonly accepted by major decision-makers in Great Britain and France rendered them less receptive to the idea that Hitler's move was imminent. The following are the most important of these concepts.

There was no doubt of Hitler's ultimate *intention* to remilitarize the Rhineland, but many experts doubted that Germany possessed the military *capability* to undertake the move.[101] If opposed by the French, British, and Belgians the move would jeopardize Hitler's newly established army. Fearful of retaliation, the German generals recommended a quick withdrawal if the French should respond with force, for as far as sheer military capabilities were concerned, Hitler was embarking on a very risky course. But Hitler wagered, against the best judgment of his generals, that the French had no intention of making a military countermove, and he decreased the risk by timing the move so that the French would be less likely to consider the use of force. (See Appendix to this chapter.)

As military men, the German generals based their calculations almost solely on British and French military capabilities and were therefore extremely reluctant to occupy the demilitarized zone.

> It was inconceivable to them that Britain and France would not resist such a violation of their foreign policy . . . There had been warnings that, if such a reoccupation were attempted, both France and Britain would act; Germany would be hopelessly outnumbered and ill-prepared for war, and would have to concede to the Allies' demand. Her emerging political strength would then be halted and her rearmament policy shattered.[102]

Much of the information relating to the impending move was contradictory. The leaders of Britain and France seemed to select the more reassuring signals which supported their wishful thinking. Moreover, they reinforced each other's views that no imminent move was to be expected from Germany concerning the Rhineland and the Locarno Pact. The funeral of George V of England provided them with a good opportunity to exchange views. On January 27, 1936, when Eden spoke with French Foreign Minister Flandin, both agreed that although Hitler certainly had designs on the Rhineland, he would not take action in the near future.

On the next day, Eden met with Belgian Prime Minister Paul Van Zeeland who also expressed the opinion that Hitler would not commit a sudden and flagrant violation of the demilitarized zone.[103] The German Foreign Minister, Baron von Neurath, who also attended the funeral of King George V, reassured Eden that Germany intended to respect the Locarno Treaty.

During February and March 1936, a number of reports indicating that the German Army was *against* military intervention reached both France and Great Britain. Such reassuring and contradictory signals only strengthened the belief that there was no cause for alarm. Reports of this kind were received, for example, from Dobler, the tireless French Consul General in Cologne, who informed his superiors on February 14, 1936, that a German general in Westphalia had been overheard saying the "German army was not urging a military reoccupation of the Rhineland at the time.[104] Sir Eric Phipps, the British Ambassador in Berlin, reported on March 6 (the night before the reoccupation of the Rhineland) that he had learned from private conversations that the army leaders had advised against any immediate military action.[105]

This is a typical case of how correct information can add to the confusion of intelligence analysts. As we have seen, the German military were indeed opposed to the reoccupation of the Rhineland by force. What the analysts did not know was that Hitler completely disregarded the advice of his generals.

Intelligence analysts in England and France could not understand the subtle change that had taken place in the relations between the German

General Staff and its new Commander-in-Chief. For that matter, this change was not even comprehended at that time by the German generals themselves. Traditionally, the generals had wielded an almost always decisive veto power over political decisions involving military moves—but this was no longer true.

As a politician, Hitler focused on the evaluation of French and British intentions and reached the conclusion, partly through evidence and partly through political intuition, that the Western powers were not going to make use of their superior capabilities.

> Hitler took no heed of his generals' warnings and pressed ahead with his plans, basing all hopes of success on a gigantic bluff which would test the willingness of the signatories of the Locarno Pact to act. He believed they would not move. His generals thought differently; Jodl described the atmosphere in the General Staff at that time as "like that of a roulette table when a player stakes his fortune on a single number."[106]

Hitler later acknowledged the enormous disparity in capabilities.

> If the French had marched into the Rhineland, we would have had to withdraw with our tails between our legs, for the military resources at our disposal would have been wholly inadequate for even moderate resistance.[107]

At the height of the Rhineland crisis on March 9, General von Blomberg, having received warning of an impending French military countermove, asked Hitler to withdraw the troops from Aachen, Trier, and Saarbruecken. Hitler's nerves held fast; and he refused to withdraw his men, rejecting the possibility of French intervention.[108] It is not surprising that Hitler considered the Rhineland operation the most nerve-racking forty-eight hours of his life.[109]

The tension between Hitler and his generals was the natural result of different perceptions which to a large extent reflected their different occupations. While the military tend to emphasize military capabilities, Hitler as a politician focused on the political intentions of his adversaries. Hence in intelligence work more importance should be attached to the proper integration of military and political intelligence—the integration of intentions and capabilities.[110] (See Appendix to this chapter.) Strategic intelligence must always be prepared by both political and military analysts, perhaps even with a slight bias in favor of the political analyst.

Yet another weakness of the intelligence evaluation process emerges from this case study. Intelligence estimates do not necessarily improve by the consensus-building or "majority" process. Had the Fuehrer followed his generals' advice he might have chosen the wrong path; the fact that he could not be bothered with the logical analysis of expert

opinion meant that Hitler made his choice against their best judgement.*
He was in a situation similar to that of President Lincoln who, when all
his Cabinet members voted against him in an important meeting, said,
"The vote is nine to one against—but the ayes have it." Similarly, the
consensus in the American intelligence community until a few days
before the Yom Kippur War in October 1973 was that the Arabs would
not attack—there was only one dissenting view. Nevertheless, making
estimates by consensus is still the most rational way to proceed in the
absence of any other fail-safe method. Yet it is useful to note here the
weaknesses in a rational decision-making process that has to deal with
many non-rational elements and in which intuition can be as good as
rational calculations, although this is difficult to prove to the satisfaction
of those who must make the decision.[111]

Because of the disparity in military strength between Germany and
France, many observers expected that Germany would, before actually
moving troops, first test the European reaction by declaring that it intended to remilitarize the Rhineland. But Hitler decided otherwise.

> In examining ways of resisting a coup, almost no thought was given
> to the possibility that Hitler might commit the sort of *massive viola-
> tion* which would justify immediate military retaliation. Germany
> was not regarded as powerful enough or foolish enough to commit
> such a blatant act when less dangerous methods were available.
> Although some consideration was given to piecemeal remilitariza-
> tion, the main thrust of Flandin's efforts was towards determining
> French reaction to a clear-cut, but non-aggressive reoccupation such
> as did occur.[112] (Emphasis added.)

The important point here, however, does not concern the aggressive-
ness of Hitler's move; it concerns the erosion of the Western powers'
credibility. Francois-Poncet, for example, believed that Germany would
be deterred by his strong statements to State Secretary Buelow concerning French reprisals. But he did not realize that although his statements
might deter the impressionable bureaucrats of the German Foreign

* Yet Hitler's intuition may not have been so intuitive after all. He may have received reports from German Military Intelligence ("Abwehr") from Paris, which
suggested that British cooperation with any French move was considered a necessary
condition for any French military action against Germany. At the same time, the German Ambassador in London, von Hoesch, reported unequivocally that the British
would not support the French in any military move. (See Ladislas Farago, *The Game
of the Foxes*, New York: David McKay, 1971, pp. 102-103.) According to David
Irving in *The War Path*, pp. 25-26, and *Breach of Security*, Hitler's decision to remilitarize the Rhineland against the better judgment of the German generals was
based not so much on his famed intuition but rather on intelligence work that had
been brought to his attention by Goering's *Forschungsamt*, which concluded that both
Britain and France would not resist by force the remilitarization of the Rhineland.
While Irving's claim may be correct, there is no conclusive evidence available to sub-
stantiate his claim.

Ministry, they did not have any effect on Hitler.[113] Paradoxically, the French government evaluated German capabilities as too low to risk an early move into the Rhineland, even as the French General Staff persistently overrated German capabilities in order to discourage a French countermove. Once the crisis began, French Military Intelligence also tended to exaggerate German capabilities for the same reason.

A crucial British misconception involving no little self-deception was that the Germans were interested in British friendship—so interested that Hitler would not violate the demilitarized zone until he had made a final effort to "square Britain."[114]

> Not only did this seem plausible in view of Hitler's many pro-British utterances, but it also proved to be a highly seductive thesis and one which appeared in Foreign Office minutes as late as 4 March 1936, when the Southern Department dismissed as 'inconceivable' the suggestion that Berlin would 'throw away' any chance of alliance with Britain by making a fresh *fait accompli*.[115]

In assessing German intentions, the British watched for an early warning which they expected to see in the form of a break in their own conversations with the Germans. Yet, if anything, British desire for improved relations made Hitler, who feared that a conciliatory British attitude would obstruct his plans, accelerate his decision to remilitarize the Rhineland. The British also hoped that they might be able to negotiate the inevitable German move as part of a general package deal, which was the last thing Hitler wanted.[116] Western approval on the Rhineland issue as part of a comprehensive deal would tie his hands elsewhere (such as along Germany's eastern borders).

There were numerous other theories as to what Hitler might do. The French Military Attaché in Berlin speculated that Germany would not act in the Rhineland without first testing French reaction.[117] As has been mentioned, Ambassador François-Poncet maintained that Hitler would not move before the French Senate had ratified the Franco-Soviet treaty. More imaginative observers suggested that Germany would not risk the success of the Olympic games which were scheduled to open in Berlin during August 1936.[118] This theory dovetailed nicely with the speculation that Hitler would not take action until the autumn of 1936 when the new conscripts increased the army's need for more territory.[119]

An additional cause for the lack of alarm was the strong consensus among diplomats and foreign journalists in Berlin that Hitler would not strike as early as March.

> The Berlin diplomatic corps and the great majority of foreign correspondents were taken by surprise, if not by the fact of the zone's disappearance, at least by the *timing* and *method* . . . One reason

for this was undoubtedly the fact that the abolition of articles 42-43 [of the Treaty of Versailles] had been so frequently predicted that journalists and diplomats had come to treat such reports almost as part of their daily routine. Moreover, in the diplomatic world, ambassadors and ministers tended to trust one another. Hitler and his entourage were suspected, but the assurances of Germany's fidelity to Locarno had emanated from Neurath and the *Auswaertige Amt* right up to the end.[120] (Emphasis added.)

Another reason was the fact that a good deal of diplomatic activity and political attention in March 1936 was devoted to the Italian campaign in Ethiopia and to the possibility of including oil in the list of sanctions against Italy.[121]

The ethics of the "old school" diplomats contributed much to the general inability to anticipate Hitler's actions.* In spite of the bad name that diplomats may have acquired over the years ("A diplomat is an honest man sent abroad to lie for his country"), they have traditionally tended to keep their word as much as possible. Lies and deceit were the exception. Faced with Hitler's revolutionary diplomacy, which accepted no conventional obligations, European diplomats found it difficult to accept the fact that someone would consistently use the diplomatic instruments and jargon solely for the purpose of deception. In the

---

* An additional clue to some of the reasons behind the French failure to anticipate the German reoccupation of the Rhineland can be found in an interesting article written by Contre-Amiral (Ret.) Lapotier, "L'Attaque Nous Surprendra" in *Revue de Defense Nationale*, Vol. 17, August-September 1961, pp. 1386-1404.

According to Contre-Amiral Lapotier, Hitler, the amateur, did not abide by the accepted rules of the game. Until Hitler's rise to power, he suggests, war or an aggressive move (such as the remilitarization of the Rhineland) was always expected to follow a prolonged diplomatic crisis, in turn followed by a stage of "general mobilization" of the nation's armed forces and finally preceded by a formal declaration of war, including the exact date and time for the opening of hostilities. In fact, he implies that by the beginning of World War I, international law and the rules of chivalry excluded the possibility of a surprise attack *on the strategic level*. (This certainly was not true of Napoleon's style in warfare, nor does it fit the Japanese attack on Port Arthur in 1905.)

Moreover, wars in Europe usually broke out in the summer after the induction of a new class of recruits, following the harvest. Hitler now wrecked those long-held European traditions. The reoccupation of the Rhineland broke many accepted rules and norms taken for granted by French diplomats. (1) The remilitarization of the Rhineland took place in the winter, not in the summer, during which military activities were supposed to take place. (2) It was a violation of a diplomatic pact (i.e., the Locarno Pact), *not* preceded by any period of unusual diplomatic rise in tensions. (3) Germany did not undertake any general mobilizations while its military strength was considered too weak for a general war. (4) France was not presented with any formal ultimatum or demands before Hitler made his move. Quite to the contrary, Hitler did his best to imply that everything was normal in German-French relations. (5) The action took place on a Saturday, a weekend. (6) The seventh of March was only a few days before Easter and, (7) It took place only a few days before the French general elections and hence no French leader was ready to take decisive action to anticipate or react to the German move.

ten weeks preceding the operation, the German Foreign Ministry issued no less than nine assurances denying Germany's intention to repudiate the Locarno Pact.[122]

Normally, the more frequent the warnings, the higher the probability that they are correct. If, however, such signals extend over a long period of time, they gradually become "routinized" and are therefore discounted. In the jargon of the literature of surprise, this is called the "cry wolf syndrome" or "alert fatigue." This may explain why the French and British did not even issue any warnings to the Germans upon hearing that Hitler might make a move on January 30, the anniversary of his accession to power.

> As for the reports of illicit activity in the Rhineland, they had been coming into the Quai d'Orsay for years and turned out to be largely unprovable, inconclusive or insufficiently important to justify filing a complaint at Geneva. Nor did anyone take the prognosticators too seriously—an attitude whose wisdom was amply proved by the peaceful passing of 30 January.[123]

In a sense, the Western powers' predictions were based on negative reasoning. Without considering the possibility of a bold *fait accompli*, they set forth all possible reasons why Hitler would *not* make a move in early 1936. Political analysts should have also developed positive theories to explain why Hitler might be motivated to take action at any given time.

British Intelligence, however, did not learn the lessons it should have from its failure to give a specific warning of Hitler's planning and timing to reoccupy the Rhineland. As far as we know, there was no attempt to reform the process of intelligence collection and analysis. Apparently, the gentlemen heading the government did not take the possibility of a European war seriously. Hence, even after this fiasco, the British Secret Intelligence Service (SIS) was unsuccessful in obtaining additional funds from the Cabinet. The official history of British Intelligence during World War II notes in particular the lack of coordination between Military and Political Intelligence. As we shall see, the British (and French) intelligence services made an even worse blunder by not anticipating the German-Soviet non-aggression pact during the summer of 1939.[124] British Intelligence (M.I.5 and M.I.6) was described by a historian as lacking professionalism and being overconfident as a result of its reputation as the most efficient in the world. This overconfidence and lack of professionalism, combined with the tendency of British statesmen "to accept what suited their hopes," contributed to the British inability to correctly forecast Hitler's crisis diplomacy.[125]

Hitler originally planned to reoccupy the Rhineland sometime before the spring of 1937, but ideal international conditions during the winter of 1936 seemed to make an earlier move more feasible.[126] The Western powers' internal weaknesses and dissension, Italy's involvement in Ethiopia, and Russia's preoccupation with internal affairs convinced Hitler that this was the opportune moment.

Planning the timing of his move very precisely, Hitler decided that he would act on a Saturday morning when many members of the British Cabinet were relaxing at their country estates.[127] This was calculated to delay any possible reaction on the part of the Western powers by many critical hours. The timing was also advantageous from at least two other angles.

> With a general election approaching in France, none of the ministers could contemplate general mobilization; only a minority supported the recall of reservists. All thought of action disappeared: diplomacy took its place.[128]

Hitler's move occurred at a time when French public opinion firmly opposed military action beyond France's borders; therefore, the French government was very unlikely to retaliate by military action.[129]

Hitler's timing also coincided with a low point in British-Italian relations caused by Italy's war in Ethiopia. Italy's position as one of the guarantors of the Locarno Pact was particularly important. On February 14, 1936, Hitler met in Munich with Ulrich von Hassell, his Ambassador to Italy, to inquire about Mussolini's reaction to a possible German repudiation of the Locarno Pact. Hassell replied that to the best of his understanding, Mussolini, who was deeply involved in the war in Ethiopia and in conflict with the British and French, would not join any sanctions against Germany. On February 22, Hassell had an interview with Mussolini in which it was established that Mussolini would not attempt to block any German initiative. Italy's position had a crucial impact on Hitler's decision to go ahead with his plan.[130]

The timing of Hitler's move was successful from yet another viewpoint. If, as Hitler suspected, the French were not ready to employ military force to preempt the German reoccupation of the Rhineland unilaterally and risk being branded the aggressors, the only other way for them to take action would be through a decision of the League's Council, which was not in session in early March. To convene a special session of the Council would take at least five to seven days. By the time the members had assembled and listened to various arguments, passions would have cooled and Germany would be firmly established in the region.[131] Even Eden was impressed by Hitler's timing.

The appeal was nicely judged. Most members of the British public would certainly see very little harm in Hitler's action. It would merely appear that he was taking full possession of territory which was his by right. The timing was perfect, including the usual choice of a weekend. France had a new Foreign Minister and a government more than usually provisional, for a general election was due to be held. Mussolini had estranged himself from his former allies, and was certainly cool to his Locarno engagements.[132]

Hitler also tried to guarantee the success of operation *Schulung* by presenting it in a comparatively unprovocative light. He could simply have renounced the Locarno Pact and the remaining security clauses of the Treaty of Versailles. But although this was the least provocative strategy, it was only a half-hearted measure that might have induced the French to make a preemptive move into the Rhineland. Instead, he chose the more dangerous option of moving German troops into the demilitarized zone. He was walking a thin line. On the one hand, he wanted to assert Germany's right to remilitarize the Rhineland, a move that was a precondition for the fulfillment of his grand design; on the other hand, he wanted to avoid a French countermove. According to the Locarno Pact, the entry of German troops into the demilitarized zone without demonstrating offensive intentions constituted a non-flagrant or "qualified" breach of the treaty (i.e., one that did not require a military response). Since Hitler wanted to present his move as a symbolic action (and thus as a non-flagrant violation of the Locarno Pact), he decided to send "only" 19 battalions and 13 artillery units, 22,000 soldiers in all, into the demilitarized zone. With the addition of the local *Landespolizei*, which was supposed to be immediately incorporated into the German armed forces, a total of 36,500 soldiers, supported by 156 artillery pieces and 54 fighter aircraft, would be available in the area. To make the force less conspicuous, only a small portion of it was sent to the French border region. Only three infantry battalions (or less than 3000 soldiers) were sent to Aachen, Trier, and Saarbruecken. The majority of the troops were left east of the Rhine with a few on the western bank, and special care was taken to ensure that no offensive weapons such as tanks or bombers were used.[133] Historians have generally assumed that the Germans would have withdrawn in the event of a French counterattack,[134] but there is, as already noted, some disagreement on this subject.

When the German Foreign Minister informed the French, British, and Italian Ambassadors and the Belgian Chargé d'Affaires of Germany's final renunciation of the Locarno Pact, he called it a symbolic move.[135] Hitler justified this renunciation on the pretext that the French had already violated the treaty by concluding the Franco-Soviet pact. This excuse was intended to put the French on the defensive and undermine their moral position, thus making it more difficult for them to resort to unilateral action.

In order to weaken British support for a possible French action and erode French determination, Hitler took two more diversionary measures. On the same day that German troops reoccupied the Rhineland, he addressed the Reichstag and appealed to the German public for approval by announcing new elections. In his speech he rehashed all of the old themes: he spoke of the need to maintain good relations in the European family of nations; elaborated at length on his sincere efforts to improve German-French relations; and accused France of violating the Locarno Pact through its military alliance with Russia, an act which destroyed the European equilibrium by bringing the massive Soviet armed forces into the balance of power. Using a favorite Teutonic phrase, he said, "The Locarno Rhine Pact has lost its inner meaning . . ." After sarcastically criticizing "international pactomania," he proposed a new, supposedly more practicable version of the Locarno Pact. The obviously infeasible proposals were, briefly, as follows:

(1) Germany would be willing to reestablish a demilitarized zone if France and Belgium were ready to demilitarize their border areas as well.

(2) Germany, France, and Belgium should enter into a twenty-five-year non-aggression treaty to ensure "the sanctity and inviolability of the boundaries of the West."

(3) Britain and Italy could, à la Locarno, be the guarantors of the treaty.

(4) Holland could be included in the treaty system.

(5) Germany was willing to enter into an air pact with the Western powers.

(6) Germany was even willing to extend the idea of a non-aggression treaty to the states on Germany's eastern borders. Lithuania could be included if it agreed to grant autonomy to Memel.

(7) Having attained sovereignty over its original territory, Germany was willing to consider re-entering the League of Nations as soon as a few problems were resolved through negotiation.

Then Hitler melodramatically declared:

Gentlemen, Members of the German Reichstag. In this historic hour, as German troops are moving into their future peace garrisons in the western provinces of the Reich let us all unite in two sacred vows.

First, we swear an oath that we will yield before no power and before no coercion in our determination to restore the honour of our nation . . .

And, secondly, we proclaim now more than ever before our wish to further the cause of mutual understanding between the nations of Europe and particularly an understanding among our western nations [sic] and neighbours.[136]

Above all, he promised that Germany had no further claims to put forward in *Europe*—a promise which was repeated in a March 10 interview with his favorite British journalist, G. Ward Price. But in the interview he was not as magnanimous: "Germany has no more claims to make from [sic] *France*, nor will she make any.[137] (Emphasis added.)

The Western powers were surprised by the timing of Hitler's move, but it is safe to assume that their behavior would not have been very different if they had received advance warning. Hitler's political intuition was correct—perhaps even more so than he originally realized.

The French government reacted like a second-rate power. From the beginning, it was disinclined to make any military countermove for two major reasons: the negative attitude of the British government, and the lack of fighting spirit of its own generals. So far as the French military were concerned, they took the necessary steps to ensure that the government would not opt for offensive action. The French High Command had not prepared contingency plans for military intervention in the demilitarized zone. Thus, even had the French government decided to undertake a military move against the judgement of the military experts there would have been no plans available with which to implement its orders.

In 1936, Britain's refusal to commit itself to any military move necessary for the defense of the European status quo further weakened the already flagging French resolve to undertake unilateral action. Perhaps the most important principle underlying French diplomacy between the two world wars was the cultivation of the good will of the British government.[138] Britain, however, chose to act as an arbiter, not as an ally.[139] With the exception of a few ministers, the French government wanted to save the British commitment for a major war—a threat to their basic security interests—and not waste it on relatively minor threats.[140] Hence, the French were interested in coordinating all of their diplomatic and military moves with those of the British government. By thus surrendering their freedom of action to the British, the French mortgaged their immediate security for potential British assistance and gradually became psychologically dependent as well. Reluctant to take military action for fear of losing British sympathy and support (the bitter memory of their embarrassing intervention in the Ruhr in 1925 was still fresh), the French turned to diplomacy for the solution. All they could do after Hitler's *fait accompli* was to consult the other Locarno signatory states and register a protest at the League's Council.[141]

The negative British attitude reinforced internal developments in

France. As mentioned above, the public opposed moves involving the use of force. Ironically, this was also true of the French Army. Since 1930, the French Army, after withdrawing from the Rhineland, had completely discounted this strategically important region as an area for military operation. The French High Command had only prepared *defensive* contingency plans for a full-fledged war—even though France was committed to the assistance of its eastern allies. French military thinking was dominated by the so-called Maginot mentality; military plans called for a general mobilization and the manning of the Maginot line should a threat arise.

In fact, the French High Command had no plans for less than an all-out mobilization.

> The French army of 1936 had no strike force capable of marching as far as Mainz, to say nothing of occupying the whole of the demilitarized zone. Nor did it possess a single unit which could be made instantly combat-ready. Gamelin could not act at all on German soil without *couverture,* which required eight days and involved the call-up of enough reservists to put 1.2 million men *sur pied.*[142]

France's problem was not lack of military capabilities but lack of planning and preparations for a strike-force action; in brief, it had no plans for what is now called gradual deterrence or limited war.[143]

Some of the ministers in the French government displayed a more offensive spirit than the generals. At first ready to expel the Germans from the Rhineland by force, they were, however, quickly discouraged by the Army's advice. On the day of the German march into the demilitarized zone, Gamelin only recommended that precautionary measures be taken, while Joseph Paul-Boncour, Minister of State for League of Nations Affairs, said that he would like to see the French Army in Mainz as soon as possible. General Gamelin replied, "Ah, that's another affair. I would like nothing better. But you must give me the means.[144] He meant that a general mobilization was the precondition for any move into the Rhineland.

The role played by the French High Command was certainly atypical for an army so superior in capabilities to its enemy. Normally, under a favorable ratio of power and facing such a clear threat to the basic security interests of the state, the civilian government would have to restrain the military leaders; in this case, the army leaders restrained the government.[145] The major role of an army in times of crisis is to provide the government with options for military action; yet instead of expanding the options, the French Army narrowed them by stressing the dangers of escalation as a result of even limited action. The army misled the government concerning the real power ratios involved (i.e., they underestimated French and overestimated German strength), thereby influencing the government against choosing the option of military action.[146]

What could the French government have done, had it been warned of the timing of the German move and had the military demonstrated greater readiness to employ force?

To begin with, as has been noted, it might have tried to deter Hitler by disclosing his plans and issuing strongly-worded warnings. A bluff might have been sufficient, especially if accompanied by some tangible measures such as an open partial mobilization, the movement of troops closer to the border, and a few reconnaissance flights. In addition, the French government might have insisted on reviewing the army's offensive plans in advance instead of finding itself without any when the crisis occurred.[147]

A more sophisticated response would have been to put French armed forces on secret alert, partially mobilize, and then wait for the Germans to make the first move. As soon as the Germans took the initial action, the French could have launched an interceptive strike.[148]

The difference between a preemptive strike and an interceptive strike is important. A preemptive strike is made before the enemy makes his first move, which therefore makes it difficult to prove who is morally responsible for starting the conflict. An interceptive attack lets the enemy make the first move while the interceptive force takes action the moment the enemy has begun the attack. Naturally, the advantage of an interceptive attack is that it leaves no doubt as to which side is the aggressor.[149] An interceptive strike would have enabled the French to take military action without appearing as the aggressors. Obviously, such a bold move would have required information on German plans as well as the determination to act, neither of which was available to the French in March 1936.

Hitler's move into the Rhineland was a unique combination of diplomatic and military surprise. It was military in the sense that troops and materiel were involved—physical, observable evidence was available to corroborate German intentions. Nevertheless, the political and diplomatic elements were dominant in this *fait accompli*, for an attempt to predict this surprise involved, most of all, the proper consideration and evaluation of intentions. The object of the next German move was never in doubt.

> But the full sovereignty of Germany could not be restored while one stone of the structure of the Versailles treaty remained upon another. Reparations had gone; disarmament was ended; the relations with the League of Nations had been ruptured; there remained only that zone of the Rhineland whose demilitarization had been accepted by Germany under Articles 42-44 of the Peace Treaty and volun-

tarily confirmed by the Pact of Locarno. Once this last link of 'the shackles of Versailles' had been shattered, the Fuehrer could turn his attention to the planning of his next moves in the south and east.[150]

Logic indicated *where* Hitler's next move would take place, but it could not have indicated the timing.

From a theoretical point of view, Hitler's *fait accompli* in the Rhineland can be classified as a major unilateral diplomatic surprise since it was the turning point in his expansionist policies. The Germans could now fortify the Rhineland and then turn south and east. France had lost its credibility as an ally; if it was not ready to defend its own vital interests, why should its allies such as Poland* and the Little Entente (Czechoslovakia, Yugoslavia, and Rumania) rely on its promises of aid? France's allies in East and Central Europe had to find alternative ways to insure their security.

The impact of the reoccupation of the Rhineland on the European balance of power following France's paralysis in the face of Hitler's aggression has been succinctly summarized by Ronald Goodman:

> The German move into the Rhineland was an abrupt and destabilizing event which was profoundly to the disadvantage of France; the resolution of the situation was to alter significantly the orientation of the [European] system, in that the Central European countries almost immediately began to effect a rapprochement with Germany, the path was cleared for an Italo-German alliance, Great Britain began to rearm in earnest, the leaders of the Reich felt free to pursue an aggressive policy in Central and Eastern Europe that was to culminate in a general war.[152]

From now on Hitler knew as well as foreign observers that for some time at least Germany could only grow stronger and less vulnerable as it continued to rearm and fortify its western border. Its position, it seemed, could only get better, its risks decrease, as the war France and Britain had been unwilling to chance when they were in a strong position would become more and more dangerous for them.[153]

Almost a year later, in his January 30, 1937, Reichstag speech, Hitler said that the restoration of German honor, equality, and military power would have been impossible to carry out through negotiation.

---

* Determined to resist Germany by force if necessary, the Polish government offered on March 9 to make their military alliance with France operational. They later found themselves in an unpleasant position when the Germans learned of their gesture.[151] In fact, the Polish government was not alone in offering its aid to the French. The governments of the Soviet Union, Czechoslovakia, and Yugoslavia hastened to assure the French of their unqualified support.

That I carried out the measures which were necessary for this pur-pose without consulting our former enemies in each case, and even without informing them, was due to my conviction that the way in which I chose to act would make it easier for the other side to accept our decisions, for they would have had to accept them in any case. I should like to add here that, as all this has now been accomplished, the so-called period of surprises has come to an end.[154]

The reoccupation of the Rhineland is a curious case of a surprise of the first order against two first-rank powers who were not ready to take any action—whether they were surprised or not—at a critical point at which counter-measures whose effectiveness could not be doubted were easy to take. For Hitler a failure in the Rhineland would most likely have been fatal at a time when his control over Germany was not yet fully consoli-dated and the German Army Command was not yet emasculated and completely under his control. Having laid the foundation for Germany's military power, undermined the Western powers' determination to resist, and weakened their alliance system, Hitler no longer needed diplomatic surprises; from now until the summer of 1939 direct ultimatums and the use of force took over.[155]

THE CYCLE OF HITLER'S FAITS ACCOMPLIS

Declarations, Speeches, or Agreements Made for Deceptive or Diversionary Purposes	Faits Accomplis

May 17, 1933
"Friedensrede"—Hitler expresses Germany's desire for peace but emphasizes the need for German equality. (Followed by many similar speeches.)

October 14, 1933
Hitler withdraws from the League of Nations ostensibly to protest Germany's lack of equality with other nations. Germany claims that other nations are rearming while it remains disarmed.

January 26, 1934
Non-aggression pact with Poland is ratified.

January 1935
A series of peace speeches by Hitler.

March 9, 1935 (Saturday)
Formal announcement of the formation of the Luftwaffe.

March 16, 1935 (Saturday)
The German conscription law and plans for rearmament are announced. The pretext is that the French Chamber of Deputies has expanded the French conscription law, and the British have announced a limited expansion of arms production.

March 17, 1935
Hitler gives reassurances of his peaceful intentions in an interview with British journalist G. Ward Price. He confirms Germany's intention to honor all of its treaties (i.e., what is left of the Treaty of Versailles and the Locarno Pact).

May 1, 1935
Hitler declares in his May Day speech that Germany is willing to sign a Western air convention and implies

THE CYCLE OF HITLER'S FAITS ACCOMPLIS

Declarations, Speeches, or Agreements Made for Deceptive or Diversionary Purposes	Faits Accomplis

that Germany might consider returning to the League of Nations.

May 21, 1935
Another of Hitler's grandiose peace
speeches. He says that war does
not improve any state's position and
that Germany needs and desires peace.
He proposes a new German disarmament program, indicates readiness to sign non-aggression
treaties with all neighboring states
(except Lithuania), guarantees French
borders, and warns that French
negotiations with the Soviet Union
undermine the Locarno Pact. He
promises not to intervene in Austrian
affairs and proposes a naval agreement
between Germany and Britain.

June 1935
Germany and Great Britain sign
a naval agreement to "limit the naval
arms race" and set the ratio of
German to British sea power.
This is followed by numerous
assurances that Germany will
peacefully adhere to its treaty
obligations.

March 7, 1936 (Saturday)
Germany reoccupies the Rhineland.
The pretext for this move is that
the French-Soviet military
agreement is contradictory to both
the spirit and the letter of the
Locarno Pact.

*Following the reoccupation of
the Rhineland*
Hitler declares that Germany may
consider resuming its membership
in the League of Nations, that it has
no more claims on the Western
Powers, and that it is willing to
conclude an air agreement with the
Western Powers and renegotiate a
Locarno-type agreement in the West.

CHRONOLOGY

January 30, 1933	Hitler becomes German Chancellor.
February 3	In a meeting with top military commanders, Hitler discloses his intention to introduce conscription and expand the armed forces.
May 17	Hitler's *Friedensrede* (Peace Speech).
October 17	Germany leaves the League of Nations.
November 12	In a plebiscite 95.4% of the voters approve Hitler's decision to leave the League of Nations.
January 26, 1934	Signing of the Declaration of Non-Aggression and Understanding between Poland and Germany.
June 30	"The Night of the Long Knives"— S. A. Leader Roehm is murdered on Hitler's orders and the power of the S. A. broken.
October	Jean Dobler, the French Consul General in Cologne, warns his government of German preparations to remilitarize the Rhineland.
November 26	A British Cabinet committee publishes its findings on the German rearmament program.
November 29	Churchill exposes German rearmament efforts in a speech in the House of Commons.
January 13, 1935	The Saar is returned to Germany following a plebiscite.
January 16 and 17	In two speeches Hitler reiterates Germany's desire for peace.
March 9	The German government officially announces the existence of a German air force.

March 16	Germany announces the introduction of conscription.
Late March	A German brigade enters the Demilitarized Zone and is withdrawn following a French protest.
April 11	At the Stresa Conference, Great Britain, France, and Italy agree to follow a common policy with regard to Germany.
April 12	Consul General Jean Dobler again warns the French Foreign Office of Germany's military preparations for remilitarization of the Rhineland.
May 21	Another of Hitler's "sincere" peace speeches, but he declares that Germany does not recognize Lithuania's right to control Memel.
May 29	Diels, head of the Cologne government, tells Dobler that in spring 1936 Hitler intends to renegotiate the Versailles and Locarno Treaty clauses concerning the Rhineland.
June	Germany and Great Britain conclude a naval treaty allowing the Germans to construct a navy one-third, and a submarine force three-fifths the size of the British. The French government is *not* consulted and only informed after the conclusion of the treaty.
June-July	Dobler sends several reports warning of remilitarization of the Rhineland.
October 16	The German press completely ignores the tenth anniversary of the Locarno Treaty.
October 21	Chief of the General Staff General Gamelin warns the French Foreign

Office of the possibility of a German repudiation of the Versailles clauses relating to the Rhineland.

November 21, 1935

André François-Poncet, the French Ambassador in Berlin, concludes in a report that Hitler is waiting for an excuse to remilitarize the Rhineland.

December 13

Sir Eric Phipps, the British Ambassador in Berlin, reports that Hitler will remilitarize the Rhineland at the first possible opportunity, though not before trying to improve Germany's relations with Great Britain.

December 26

Gamelin reports to the Quai d'Orsay on accelerated German military construction in the Rhineland.

December 31

François-Poncet repeats his warning concerning Hitler's designs on the Rhineland.

Early January 1936

The French Military Attaché in Berne reports unusual German military activity and a Swiss Intelligence forecast that Germany will remilitarize the Rhineland on January 30—the anniversary of Hitler's accession to power.

January 7

François-Poncet sends a memorandum to the Political Section of the Quai d'Orsay that the German generals oppose any high-risk policy in the Rhineland but would not oppose such an action if Hitler decided on it. He sends a similar report on the 15th.

January 10

The French Ambassador to Switzerland, Clauzel, passes a warning from Col. Dubois, head of the Information Section of the Swiss Army, regarding an imminent

	German move in the Rhineland to the Quai d'Orsay.
January 11	Premier Pierre Laval instructs the French Ambassador in London to warn the British Government of the possibility of a large-scale German military reoccupation of the Rhineland on January 30.
January 15	The French Military Attaché in Berlin warns of an imminent German move into the Rhineland. A similar warning is forwarded by the Polish Intelligence through the French Military Attaché in Warsaw.
	French Military Intelligence transmits a similar warning to General Gamelin.
January 17	Diels discusses with Dobler the possibility of reaching a Franco-German accord regarding the Rhineland.
January 18	General Gamelin issues a warning to the Supreme Military Committee concerning the possibility of Germany's intention to remilitarize the Rhineland.
January 27	During the funeral of King George V of England the Foreign Ministers of England, France, and Belgium agree that a German move into the Rhineland is not likely to occur soon. Germany's Foreign Minister, Baron von Neurath, reassures Eden that Germany intends to respect the Locarno Treaty.
Early February	Dobler, the French Consul General in Cologne, personally informs the Quai d'Orsay about German military preparations to remilitarize the Rhineland.

February 10, 1936

François-Poncet reports a conversation between Goering and British Ambassador Sir Eric Phipps in which Goering states that a Franco-Soviet Pact would contravene the Locarno Pact. François-Poncet believes that a denunciation of Locarno is likely.

February 12

General Maurin, the Minister of War, notifies Foreign Minister Flandin (who replaced Laval) that there is evidence of preparations for an early German military reoccupation of the Rhineland.

February 13

Henry Noel, the French Consul in Duesseldorf, reports the arrival of German officers in mufti to prepare the remilitarization of the Rhineland.

February 14

Dobler informs Paris that he has learned that the German Army was not urging the military reoccupation of the Rhineland.

February 27

French Chamber overwhelmingly ratifies Franco-Soviet Pact.

March 2

François-Poncet meets with Hitler who is in an irritable mood and denounces the Franco-Soviet treaty ratified two days before by the French Senate. François-Poncet reports that the remilitarization of the Rhineland by the Germans is just a question of time.

Hitler makes the final decision to reoccupy the Rhineland on March 7.

March 3

All pertinent orders for carrying out the military invasion of the Rhineland are issued. The actual date for the beginning of the remilitarization is given only to a few commanding generals. The troops are given the impression that they are preparing for military exercises and are notified of the real purpose of the operation only on March 5.

March 5

Genevieve Tabouis, the foreign editor of the French newspaper *L'Oeuvre*, receives a telephone call from Switzerland informing her that the German Army will move into the Rhineland on the morning of March 7.

March 6

The British Ambassador in Berlin, Sir Eric Phipps, reports that he has learned from private conversations that the German Army leaders have advised against any immediate military action in the Rhineland.

Eden meets with von Hoesch, the German Ambassador to Great Britain, who informs him that he will have an important message from Hitler to deliver the next day. Later the same day the British Ambassador in Berlin sends an urgent message to the Foreign Office informing it that the representatives of Great Britain, France, and Belgium have been asked to meet with Baron von Neurath on Saturday morning.

Saturday, March 7

At dawn, German troops march across the bridges of the Rhine.

NOTES

1. Norman Baynes, *The Speeches of Adolf Hitler: April 1922-August 1939*, Vol. 2 (New York: Howard Fertig, 1969), p. 1108. (Hereafter cited as Baynes, *Hitler's Speeches*.)

2. David Irving, *The Rise and Fall of the Luftwaffe* (London: Futura Publications, 1976), p. 39.

3. See, for example, Annette Baker Fox, *The Power of Small States: Diplomacy in World War II* (Chicago: University of Chicago Press, 1959); Michael Handel, *Weak States in the International System* (London: Frank Cass, 1981).

4. Henry L. Bretton, *Stresemann and the Revision of Versailles* (Stanford: Stanford University Press, 1953); Hans W. Gatzke, *Stresemann and the Rearmament of Germany* (Baltimore: The Johns Hopkins University Press, 1954).

5. Baynes, *Hitler's Speeches*, pp. 1052-1058.

6. F.P. Walters, *A History of the League of Nations* (London: Oxford University Press, 1965), p. 548.

7. Christoph M. Kimmich, *Germany and the League of Nations* (Chicago: University of Chicago Press, 1976), p. 178.

8. *Ibid.*, p. 187.

9. *Ibid.*, p. 189; Walters, *A History of the League of Nations*, p. 550. To be exact, three different announcements followed Hitler's decision to withdraw from the League of Nations on October 14, 1933. The first was a proclamation by Hitler (see Baynes, *Hitler's Speeches*, pp. 1088-1090). The second, given on the same day, was a proclamation by the government to the German people (see Baynes, pp. 1090-1092), and the third was a broadcast by Hitler (see Baynes, pp. 1092-1104). In this proclamation, Hitler said, ". . . While the German Government asserts afresh its unalterable will for peace, in the face of these humiliating and dishonouring suggestions, to its profound regret it declares that it is forced to leave the Disarmament Conference. And in consequence it must also give notice of its retirement from the League of Nations. The Government places this, its decision, together with a new profession of loyalty to a policy of sincere love for peace and readiness to reach an understanding, before the German people for its judgement, and expects from the German people that it will make known that while it has the same love for peace, the same readiness for peace, it also holds the same view of national honour and is as resolute as is the Government." Baynes, pp. 1089-1090.

An earlier warning signal that may well have indicated Nazi Germany's attitude toward the League of Nations and international organizations in general was its withdrawal from the International Labor Organization in June 1933. Walters, *A History of the League of Nations*, p. 565.

10. Baynes, *Hitler's Speeches*, p. 1057.

11. Kimmich, *Germany and the League of Nations*, p. 188, p. 190.

12. *Ibid.*, p. 191.

13. David Irving, *The War Path* (New York: The Viking Press, 1978), p. 32; Baynes, *Hitler's Speeches*, p. 1143.

14. Kimmich, *Germany and the League of Nations*, p. 191.

15. *Ibid.*, p. 193.

16. *Ibid.*, p. 173; also E. M. Robertson, *Hitler's Pre-War Policy and Military Plans 1933-1939* (New York: Citadel Press, 1967), p. 24.

17. Gerald L. Weinberg, *The Foreign Policy of Hitler's Germany* (Chicago: Chicago University Press, 1970), p. 69. (Hereafter cited as Weinberg, *Hitler's Foreign Policy*).

18. *Ibid.*, pp. 60-62.

19. See Christian Hoeltje, *Die Weimarer Republik und das Ostlocarno-Problem, 1919-1934* (Wuerzburg: Holzner, 1955).

20. William L. Shirer, *The Rise and Fall of the Third Reich* (New York: Simon and Schuster, 1960), p. 213. (Hereafter cited as Shirer, *The Rise and Fall*).

21. Joseph Korbel, *Poland Between East and West* (Princeton: Princeton University Press, 1963). Polish foreign policy was shortsighted. Poland was searching for more freedom of action not only because it distrusted French policy after Locarno but also because it had ambitions to play the role of a middle, or great, power. But Poland's position in relation to Germany and the Soviet Union, both of which had powerful claims to territory that they considered to be occupied by Poland, was, in fact, one of weakness. The only issue on which the Germans and Russians could agree after Hitler's accession to power was their common dislike of Poland. Instead of trying to strengthen their alliance with France, the only great power with which they had common interests, the Poles proceeded to weaken France and strengthen their real enemies. The Poles' mistaken perception of their strength and of the salience of their geographic position may have been temporarily justified in the 1920's when Germany and the Soviet Union were exhausted, but it was an anachronism by 1934 and certainly by 1939. For Polish foreign policy in this period, see also: Bodhan B. Budurowycz, *Polish-Soviet Relations 1932-1939* (New York: Columbia University Press, 1963); Roman Debicki, *The Foreign Policy of Poland 1919-1939* (London: Pall Mall Press, 1963); Harold von Riekhoff, *German-Polish Relations 1918-1933* (Baltimore: The Johns Hopkins University Press, 1971); Henry L. Roberts, "The Diplomacy of Colonel Beck" in Gordon A. Craig and Felix Gilbert, *The Diplomats 1919-1939* (Princeton: Princeton University Press, 1953), Chapter 15, pp. 579-614; Hans Roos, *Polen und Europa, Studien zur polnischen Aussenpolitik 1931-1939* (Tuebingen: Mohr, 1957). For Poland's attitude toward the League of Nations, see Walters, *A History of the League of Nations*, Chapter 52, Poland and the League: Danzig, pp. 615-623; George Sakwa, "The Franco-Polish Alliance and the Remilitarization of the Rhineland," *The Historical Journal*, Vol. 16, No. 1, 1973, pp. 125-146.

22. Weinberg, *Hitler's Foreign Policy*, p. 70.

23. *Ibid.*, p. 70.

24. *Ibid.*, p. 70.

25. Korbel, *Poland Between East and West*, p. 285.

26. *Ibid.*, p. 286.

27. Weinberg, *Hitler's Foreign Policy*, p. 73; Alan Bullock, *Hitler: A Study in Tyranny*, revised edition (New York: Harper & Row, 1962), p. 325. (Hereafter cited as Bullock, *Hitler*).

28. Hans W. Gatzke, "Russo-German Military Collaboration during the Weimar Republic," *American Historical Review*, Vol. 43, No. 3 (April 1958), pp.

565-597; Lionel Kochan, *Russia and the Weimar Republic* (Cambridge: Bowes & Bowes, 1954); Harvey Leonard Dyck, *The Weimar Republic and Soviet Russia 1926-1933* (New York: Columbia University Press, 1966); Francis L. Carsten, "The Reichswehr and the Red Army," *Survey*, No. 44-45 (October 1962), pp. 114-132.

29. Edward W. Bennett, *German Rearmament and the West 1932-1933* (Princeton: Princeton University Press, 1979); Gerhard Meinck, *Hitler und die deutsche Aufruestung 1933-1937* (Wiesbaden: Steiner, 1959); Georges Castellan, *Le rearmament clandestin du Reich 1930-1935* (Paris: Plon, 1954); Donald Cameron Watt, *Too Serious a Business* (Berkeley: University of California Press, 1975).

30. Weinberg, *Hitler's Foreign Policy*, p. 36. (Quoting General Wilhelm Adam.)

31. Irving, *The War Path*, p. 29. (From notes of the speech taken by Major Horst von Mellenthin, adjutant of General Kurt von Hammerstein-Equord, the Commander-in-Chief of the Army.)

32. John Wheeler-Bennett expresses a similar opinion. "It must not be thought that Adolf Hitler operated to a carefully prepared timetable. Only the general scheme of things to come was clear in his mind. Neither the time, nor even the sequence of events was defined long beforehand." John W. Wheeler-Bennett, *The Nemesis of Power*, 2nd ed. (London: Macmillan, 1964), p. 345. (Hereafter cited as *Nemesis of Power*.)

33. Shirer, *The Rise and Fall*, p. 281.

34. Irving, *The War Path*, pp. 30-31.

35. Shirer, *The Rise and Fall*, p. 281.

36. Irving, *The War Path*, p. 29. See also Karl-Heinz Voelker, "Die Geheime Luftruestung der Reichswehr und ihre Auswirkung auf den Flugzeugsbestand der Luftwaffe bis zum Beginn des Zweiten Weltkrieges," *Wehrwissenschaftliche Rundschau*, Vol. 12 (1962), pp. 540-549; Karl-Heinz Voelker, *Die Deutsche Luftwaffe 1933-1939* (Stuttgart: Deutsche Verlags-Anstalt, 1967).

37. Irving, *The Rise and Fall of the Luftwaffe*, p. 31.

38. *Ibid.*, pp. 31, 33. See also Weinberg, *Hitler's Foreign Policy*, p. 176.

39. Irving, *The Rise and Fall of the Luftwaffe*, p. 34.

40. *Ibid.*, p. 35.

41. *Ibid.*, pp. 38-39; Shirer, *The Rise and Fall*, p. 282.

42. Irving, *The Rise and Fall of the Luftwaffe*, p. 38.

43. N. H. Gibbs, *Grand Strategy, Vol. 1, Rearmament Policy* (London: Her Majesty's Stationery Office, 1976), p. 135.

44. *Ibid.*, p. 135. See also F. H. Hinsley, *British Intelligence in the Second World War*, Vol. 1 (New York: Cambridge University Press, 1979), p. 61. As early as the summer of 1934, Goering openly violated the Versailles Treaty by allowing squadrons of what was to become the Luftwaffe to fly in parades. Robertson, *Hitler's Pre-War Policy*, p. 51.

45. Gibbs, *Rearmament Policy*, p. 137.

46. *Ibid.*, p. 139. See also Correlli Barnett, *The Collapse of British Power* (London: Eyre Methuen, 1972), pp. 396-398.

47. Barnett, *Collapse of British Power*, pp. 388-395.

48. Gibbs, *Rearmament Policy*, p. 141.

49. William L. Shirer, *The Collapse of the Third Republic* (New York: Simon and Schuster, 1969), pp. 241-242. (Hereafter cited as Shirer, *Collapse of the Third Republic*.)

50. Baynes, *Hitler's Speeches*, p. 1195.

51. *Ibid.*, pp. 1197-1198.

52. "It was an essential factor in the Hitlerian technique that each step on the road to aggression must be carefully camouflaged as a defensive measure. The object of this procedure was to convince the German people that their peace-loving Fuehrer was being deflected from his avowed aims of pacific settlement by the intransigence and the intrigue of the Western Powers, against whose constant machinations he was ever defending the interests of the Reich." Wheeler-Bennett, *The Nemesis of Power*, p. 346.

53. Gibbs, *Rearmament Policy*, p. 151; Shirer, *Rise and Fall*, p. 283.

54. Shirer, *Rise and Fall*, p. 283.

55. Irving, *The Rise and Fall of the Luftwaffe*, p. 44. There seems to be some confusion concerning the date of the announcement and who made it. In *The Rise and Fall of the Luftwaffe*, David Irving states that the announcement was made on March 10 at the attaché level only. In his more recent book, *The War Path: Hitler's Germany 1933-1939*, Irving gives the date as March 9 (p. 45). In *The Rise and Fall of the Third Reich*, Shirer gives the date as March 10, and claims that the news was first announced by Goering in an interview with Ward Price of the London "Daily Mail" (p. 283). in *The Rise and Fall of the Luftwaffe*, Irving says that Hitler signed a decree during February 1935 that on March 1 the 'Reich Luftwaffe' would be founded as a third service (alongside the Reich Army and Navy) and that Goering would be its first commander-in-chief (p. 44).

56. Shirer, *Collapse of the Third Republic*, p. 263n.

57. Shirer, *Rise and Fall*, p. 284; Bullock, *Hitler*, pp. 332-333; Wheeler-Bennett, *Nemesis of Power*, p. 339n; Robertson, *Hitler's Pre-War Policy*, p. 56. Wheeler-Bennett has this to say on Hitler's decision:

> The thirty-six divisions which the Fuehrer had somewhat embarrassingly presented the Army on March 16, 1935, would have kept them [the German Generals] 'fully' satisfied and occupied for a considerable period of time. As the result of the *embarras de richesse*, the military position of Germany was at its weakest from 1935-7 and the *Generalitaet* were profoundly desirous of a period of peace and quiet to enable them to absorb this boa-constrictor meal of man-power and organization which they had been forced to consume. They were extremely grateful for what they had received and when they had completed the process of digestion, they would be ready to fight, but until that time, they were weak and torpid, unwilling to engage in active or aggressive exercise. [Wheeler-Bennett, pp. 344-345.]

58. Shirer, *Collapse of the Third Republic*, p. 244.

59. Bullock, *Hitler*, p. 333.

60. *Ibid.*, p. 334.

61. Shirer, *Rise and Fall*, p. 285.

62. Baynes, *Hitler's Speeches*, pp. 1218-1247. Incredible as it may appear in

light of later events, Hitler was able to make war more and more certain, and yet, by the art of his speeches, to renew again and again the hope, that, in the end, he would show himself a man of peace. See also Walters, *A History of the League of Nations*, p. 547.

63. *Ibid.*, p. 1247.

64. *Ibid.*, p. 1237.

65. Shirer, *Rise and Fall*, p. 289. For an analysis of the Anglo-German Naval Treaty as an art of self-deception see Roberta Wohlstetter, "The Pleasures of Self-Deception," *The Washington Quarterly*, Vol. 2, No. 4, Autumn 1979, pp. 56-57.

66. Bullock, *Hitler*, pp. 338-339. See also E. M. Robertson, *Hitler's Pre-War Policy and Military Plans 1933-1939*, pp. 63-64.

67. Anthony Eden, *Facing the Dictators* (Boston: Houghton Mifflin), p. 382.

68. A. J. P. Taylor, *The Origins of the Second World War* (New York: Atheneum, 1968) p. 970.

69. Shirer, *Rise and Fall*, p. 292n.

70. Shirer, *Rise and Fall*, p. 290; Shirer, *The Collapse of the Third Republic*, pp. 251-252. *Nazi Conspiracy and Aggression*. Part of the Nuremberg documents, *(NCA)* VI, pp. 951-952, No. C-139; *Trial of the Major War Criminals*. Nuremberg documents and testimony *(TMWC)*, XV, pp. 445-448. Western intelligence services somehow became aware of these preliminary orders for the remilitarization of the Rhineland fairly early despite the secrecy involved. This is the viewpoint of John C. Cairns in "March, 1936, Again: The View from Paris" in Hans Gatzke, *European Diplomacy Between the Wars 1919-1939* (Chicago: Quadrangle Books, 1974) p. 174.

71. *TMWC*, p. 446.

72. *Ibid.*, p. 449.

73. John Thomas Emmerson, *The Rhineland Crisis* (Ames: Iowa State University Press, 1977). This is one of the best monographs on the Hitler crises in the 1930's, and the most detailed study of the Rhineland Crisis, p. 100. To be cited hereafter as Emmerson, *Rhineland Crisis*. There are also three interesting unpublished Ph.D. dissertations on the subject: Aaron Leon Goldman, *Crisis in the Rhineland: Britain, France and the Rhineland Crisis of 1936*, Indiana University, 1967 (to be cited hereafter as Goldman, *Crisis in the Rhineland*), Lawrence Warner Hill, *British Official Reaction to the Rhineland Crisis, November, 1935 - May 1936*, Texan Christian University, 1972 (to be cited as *Reaction to the Rhineland Crisis*), and Ronald E. M. Goodman, *The Rhineland Crisis and The Politics of Dependence: A Case Study in Bureaucratic Government and Irresponsible Leadership*. Unpublished Ph.D. Dissertation, Princeton University 1978. To be cited as Goodman, *The Politics of Dependence.*

74. Gibbs, *Rearmament Policy*, p. 234. "Although Whitehall had been more than half expecting the German occupation of the Rhineland in 1936 . . . the SIS [Special or Secret Intelligence Service], like the embassies and the other overt sources gave no advance warning of these moves." F. H. Hinsley, *British Intelligence in the Second World War* Vol. 1 (New York: Cambridge University Press, 1979), p. 58.

75. Shirer, *The Collapse of the Third Republic*, p. 251.

76. Wheeler-Bennett, *Nemesis of Power*, p. 348. (Emphasis added.)

77. The conversation between Dobler and Laval is quoted from Goodman, *The Politics of Dependence*, pp. 52-54.

78. Shirer, *Collapse of the Third Republic*, p. 252.

79. *Ibid.*, p. 252.

80. Quoted in Gibbs, *Rearmament Policy*, p. 230. See also Emmerson, *Rhineland Crisis*, p. 63.

81. For these reports see Gibbs, *Rearmament Policy*, pp. 230-233.

82. Shirer, *Collapse of the Third Republic*, p. 252. It should be noted that Goering's *Forschungsamt* (literally "research office," but actually an electronic listening post) intercepted and deciphered the diplomatic communications of François-Poncet and probably those of the British Ambassador as well. See Ladislas Farago, *The Game of the Foxes*, New York: David McKay, 1971, p. 102. See also D. C. Watts, Introduction to David Irving's (Ed.) *Breach of Security: The German Secret Intelligence File on Events Leading to the Second World War*, London: William Kimber, 1968.

83. *Ibid.*, p. 253.

84. Hill, *Reaction to the Rhineland Crisis*, p. 52.

85. Goodman, *The Politics of Dependence*, p. 69.

86. Goldman, *Crisis in the Rhineland*, p. 63.

87. Shirer, *Collapse of the Third Republic*, p. 257.

88. Goodman, *The Politics of Dependence*, pp. 80-81.

89. *Ibid.*, p. 85.

90. *Ibid.*, p. 122.

91. Shirer, *Collapse of the Third Republic*, p. 259.

92. *Ibid.*, p. 259.

93. *Ibid.*, p. 259. Also in Goldman, *The Rhineland Crisis*, p. 63.

94. See John C. Cairns, "March 7, 1936, Again: The View from Paris" in Gatzke, *European Diplomacy Between the Wars 1919-1939*, p. 175.

95. Emmerson, *Rhineland Crisis*, p. 101.

96. *Ibid.*, pp. 101-102; also p. 291n.

97. Goldman, *Crisis in the Rhineland*, pp. 109-111, quoting Genevieve Tabouis, *They Called Me Cassandra* (New York: Charles Scribner, 1942), pp. 273-274; Goodman, *The Politics of Dependence*, pp. 80-81.

98. Ian Colvin, *Vansittart in Office* (London: Victor Gollancz, 1965) p. 96.

99. Hill, *Reaction to the Rhineland Crisis*, p. 95.

100. On the difficulty of separating signals and noise, see, for example, Roberta Wohlstetter, *Pearl Harbor: Warning and Decision* (Stanford: Stanford University Press, 1962); Robert Jervis, "Hypothesis on Misperception", *World Politics*, Vol. 20, No. 3, (April 1968), pp. 454-479; and Robert Jervis, *The Logic Of Images in International Relations* (Princeton: Princeton University Press, 1970); Michael I. Handel, *Perception, Deception and Surprise: The Case of the Yom Kippur War* (Jerusalem: The Leonard Davis Institute for International Relations, Jerusalem Papers on Peace Problems, No. 19, 1976), especially pp. 14-15.

101. Emmerson, *Rhineland Crisis*, pp. 40-41. François-Poncet, for example.

102. Matthew Cooper, *The German Army 1933-1945* (London: Macdonald and Jane's, 1978), p. 53. See also Goldman, *Crisis in the Rhineland*, pp. 112-123.

103. Hill, *Reaction to the Rhineland Crisis*, pp. 55-56.

104. Goldman, *Crisis in the Rhineland*, p. 64. A similar analysis concerning the positions of the German military leadership was sent to the Quai d'Orsay by François-Poncet on January 11 and 15, 1936. He concluded that even though the German Generals would be reluctant to take any risks in the Rhineland region, they would be unable to resist a demand by Hitler to take such action. Goodman, *The Politics of Dependence*, p. 75.

105. Hill, *Reaction to the Rhineland Crisis*, p. 96.

106. Cooper, *The German Army 1933-1945*, pp. 53-54.

107. Quoted in Shirer, *The Collapse of the Third Republic*, p. 281. New evidence suggests, however, that the Germans had made plans to fight back if necessary. See D. C. Watts, "German Plans for the Reoccupation of the Rhineland: A Note", *Journal of Contemporary History*, October 1966, pp. 193-199; Emmerson, *Rhineland Crisis*, pp. 98-99.

108. Cooper, *The German Army*, p. 54; Shirer, *The Rise and Fall*, p. 294. On March 13 Blomberg received a most urgent telegram from the three German Service Attachés in London who were convinced that the British were alerting their fleet and sending an expeditionary force to France. The cable read "Situation grave, 50-50 peace/war." Blomberg was alarmed and approached Hitler again. Hitler remained calm and brushed his warning aside. See Heinz Hoehne, *Canaris*, (Garden City, N.Y.: Doubleday, 1979), p. 203. The alarming reports of the German Military Attaché in London, Col. Baron Geyr von Schweppenburg, came after he had been invited to the War Office and had been left in a room of the German Section showing a map with both British and French troop dispositions. (See Major-General Sir Kenneth Strong, *Intelligence at the Top*, London: Cassell, 1968, p. 19, also Ladislas Farago, *The Game of the Foxes*, New York, David McKay, 1971, pp. 98-112.) As soon as the crisis was over, Hitler ordered Blomberg to recall both the Military and Naval Attaché in London.

109. Shirer, *The Rise and Fall*, p. 293; Shirer, *The Collapse of the Third Republic*, p. 281.

110. For a detailed discussion, see Michael I. Handel, *Perception, Deception and Surprise: The Case of the Yom Kippur War*, p. 62. "More attention must be paid to *intentions*, as the enemy almost always has the capabilities to initiate some sort of attack, surprise further strengthening these capabilities. Above all, where political gains are more important than military victory, the decision to initiate a war is not always directly related to one's relative capabilities. It must also be borne in mind that, in the context of deterrence, one can influence the enemy's mind, i.e., his intentions to go to war, but one cannot have any impact on his capabilities." In deciding to move into the Rhineland, Hitler correctly concluded that while the British and French had more than enough military capabilities to counter the German move, they did not have the intention or will to do so.

The coordination of British military and political intelligence was weak and little definite information was available concerning Hitler's intentions. The problem was summarized in *British Intelligence in the Second World War* in the following way. "On Hitler's intentions there was no lack of intelligence, even if it was not all reliable. As to what Hitler would do if other governments moved to check or deflect his expansionistic plans, no agent, however well placed, could provide the answer, or could be believed if he professed to do so, for not even Hitler and his immediate entourage knew what the answer would be." p. 59.

111. See Handel, *Perception, Deception and Surprise: The Case of the Yom Kippur War*. For dangers involved in consensus building in social groups and intelligence work, see also Irving L. Janis, *Victims of Groupthink*, (Boston: Houghton Mifflin, 1972).

112. Emmerson, *Rhineland Crisis*, pp. 47-48. Whether or not Hitler's move was aggressive is a matter of judgment. Emmerson feels that it was a non-aggressive move. Since it involved the movement of a large number of German troops into the area—troops that were ready to fight back, as the latest evidence as cited by Emmerson suggests—it seems that the move must be interpreted as aggressive.

113. Under the Nazi regime, the German Foreign Ministry was not a major policy-making organization. It had almost nothing to do with the decision concerning the Non-Aggression Treaty with Poland in 1934, the Anglo-German Naval Pact (1935), the decision to reoccupy the Rhineland, and Hitler's later coups. "These major policy departures were the work of Hitler and a close coterie of 'amateur advisers.' " Paul Seabury, *The Wilhelmstrasse* (Berkeley: University of California Press, 1954), p. 91. The Wilhelmstrasse passively followed Hitler's foreign policy and "swung into line" after the launching of each new fait accompli. *Ibid.*, p. 91.

114. This was Ambassador Phipps' position. See Emmerson, *Rhineland Crisis*, pp. 64-65.

115. Emmerson, *Rhineland Crisis*, pp. 64-65.

116. *Ibid.*, p. 66.

117. Weinberg, *Hitler's Foreign Policy*, p. 243.

118. Emmerson, *Rhineland Crisis*, p. 41.

119. *Ibid.*, p. 41.

120. *Ibid.*, p. 101.

121. Esmonde Robertson, "Hitler and Sanctions: Mussolini and the Rhineland". *European Studies Review*, Vol. 7, 1977, pp. 409-435.

122. Emmerson, *Rhineland Crisis*, p. 291n.

123. *Ibid.*, p. 40.

124. Hinsley, *The History of British Intelligence*, pp. 58-59.

125. Keith Middlemas, *Diplomacy of Illusion: The British Government and Germany, 1937-1939*, (London: Weidenfeld & Nicolson, 1972), pp. 93-95. See also F. W. Winterbotham, *The Nazi Connection* (New York: Dell, 1979), pp. 10-11.

126. William Carr, *Arms, Autarky and Aggression* (London: Edward Arnold, 1972), p. 66. Hitler told Hassell (the German Ambassador in Rome) in February 1936 that he had previously considered the spring of 1937 as the most favorable date for the remilitarization of the Rhineland. See Robertson, *Hitler's Pre-War Policy*, pp. 58; 71.

127. Barnett, *The Collapse of British Power*, p. 382.

128. Taylor, *The Origins of the Second World War*, p. 99. See also R. A. C. Parker, "The First Capitulation: France and the Rhineland Crisis of 1936," *World Politics*, Vol. 8, No. 3, April 1956, p. 362.

129. Emmerson, *Rhineland Crisis*, p. 78.

130. For Hitler's timing of the remilitization of the Rhineland, see also Barnett, *The Collapse of British Power*, pp. 382-383. For a very different, theoretical approach to the question of the best timing of a surprise attack in war, see Robert Axelrod, "The Rational Timing of Surprise" in *World Politics*, January 1979, No. 2, pp. 228-247. Hitler sensed that the war in Ethiopia was nearing its end and that the conflict between Italy, Britain, and France over the Ethiopian war might be forgotten once the Italians brought the war to its conclusion. Watt, *Too Serious a Business*, pp. 105-106.

131. Emmerson, *Rhineland Crisis*, p. 97.

132. Eden, *Facing the Dictators*, p. 382.

133. Emmerson, *Rhineland Crisis*, p. 97; Watt, *Too Serious a Business*, p. 105.

134. By Shirer, for example, in both of his books cited.

135. Shirer, *The Collapse of the Third Republic*, p. 261.

136. Baynes, *Hitler's Speeches*, pp. 1299-1300.

137. *Ibid.*, p. 1304.

138. For a detailed analysis of the French dependence on British military, economic, and technological support, see Robert J. Young, *In Command of France* (Cambridge, Mass.: Harvard University Press, 1978), pp. 20-22. What Young misses in his revisionist approach to the study of French military strategy in the 1930's is in my opinion the fact that the French could have lessened their dependence on the British if they had had the will to do so. The French conveniently ignored the fact that the Polish and Czech armies, individually, let alone combined, outnumbered the German military establishment. See Telford Taylor, *Munich: The Price of Power* (New York: Doubleday, 1979) p. 141. Their dependence on Great Britain was not an inescapable fact to which there was no alternative. The French consciously tried to shackle the British to themselves (as they did on the eve of World War I) by increasing rather than decreasing their dependence on them. The author's assertion that France's military inferiority forced her to choose a defensive and passive strategy towards Germany is not very convincing either. Indeed, the best time for the French to make a successful military move against the Germans was during the Rhineland Crisis, a period in which their military superiority could not be in doubt, or even later when the Germans attacked Poland in the autumn of 1939. Even by 1940 the numerical strength (in manpower, tanks, aircraft, artillery, etc.) of the French Army was equal to that of the Germans. French passivity was the result of a psychological attitude—not a military necessity.

139. Robertson, *Hitler's Pre-War Plans*, p. 53.

140. France's decision not to undertake any unilateral military action for fear of losing British support resembles Israel's behavior on the eve of the 1973 war. The Israeli government decided not to preempt the Syrian and Egyptian attacks for fear of alienating the United States and losing its support. See the memoirs of Golda Meir, *My Life* (New York: G. P. Putnam's Sons, 1975), pp. 426-431. In either case, it is impossible to judge whether this attitude of dependence on another country and the enormous investment in the future good will of other states was justified. The short-run price was very heavy on both occasions, but *may* have been justified in the long run when in 1940 the British fulfilled their treaty obligations to fight with the French or when the United States started the

airlift to Israel during the Yom Kippur War. It is difficult to determine whether the help received later in both cases would have been offered anyway.

141. Emmerson, *Rhineland Crisis*, pp. 42-43.

142. *Ibid.*, p. 105. See Parker, "The First Capitulation," *World Politics*, Vol. 8, No. 3, 1956, pp. 362-364. It is interesting to note that following the failure of the French military to prevent the German reoccupation of the Rhineland, no French policy to reform or improve their decision-making process was initiated; nor did the French armed forces formulate any plans to meet a future crisis. Goodman, *The Politics of Dependence*, p. 184.

143. Watt, *Too Serious a Business*, pp. 94-95. See also, Young, *In Command of France*, Chapter 5. Henry Owen, "Nato Strategy: What is Past is Prologue," *Foreign Affairs*, Vol. 43, No. 4, 1965, pp. 685-688.

144. Shirer, *The Collapse of the French Republic*, p. 262. For a detailed discussion of the difference in attitude between the civilian ministers in the French government (who favored a countermove) and the ministers of the armed forces who objected to any military move, see Goldman, *Crisis in the Rhineland*, Chapter 6, pp. 134-169.

145. Shirer, *The Collapse of the French Republic*, pp. 262-263.

146. *Ibid.*, p. 263; Weinberg, *Hitler's Foreign Policy*, pp. 243-244; Wheeler-Bennett, *The Nemesis of Power*, p. 349. Gamelin produced inflated figures of the German forces in the Rhineland. He declared them to be no less than the equivalent of 21 or 22 divisions. This formidable total was reached in this way:

Army troops

30,000 *Wehrmacht* (Army)	forming 6 or
30,000 *Landespolizei* (Police)	7 divisions
30,000 *Arbeitsdienst* (Labor Corps)	

Auxiliary troops

30,000 N.S.K.K. (Nazi Party Motorized Corps)	forming the base of 15 divisions of
25,000 S.S.	*Grenzsicherung*
150,000 S.A.	(Border Police) assembled on the Franco-Belgian Front.

Source, Parker, "The First Capitulation," *World Politics*, Vol. 8, No. 3, 1956, pp. 364-366. As we have seen, the real strength of the German troops participating directly in the reoccupation of the Rhineland was in no way near the French estimate. The actual number of German soldiers (including the para-military *Landespolizei*) was 36,500. The inflated numbers produced by the French High Command served as an excellent excuse for nonaction. See also Telford Taylor, *Munich*, pp. 141-142. For a detailed comparison of the German, French, Polish, and Czech armed forces, see Walter Bernhardt, *Die deutsche Aufruestung 1934-1939*, Frankfurt: Bernard & Graefe, 1969.

By comparison, the French had 30 first-rate divisions available that could be emplaced within 6 hours, and an additional 450,000 second-echelon B troops that could be mobilized within 48 hours. Under a full mobilization within 6 days, the French could expand their armed forces to 1.1 million soldiers. The British, by comparison, had only two divisions available for deployment in Europe. This makes nonsense, of course, of the "dependence" of the French on the British, which was obviously self-inflicted.

147. Shirer, *The Collapse of the French Republic*, pp. 262-263; Weinberg, *Hitler's Foreign Policy*, p. 243.

148. An excellent alternative for an all-or-nothing mobilization could have been the establishment of an ". . . assault force *(force de choc)* of a hundred thousand or so men, ready to march at the first signal." See Parker, "The First Capitulation," *World Politics*, Vol. 3, No. 3, 1956, p. 364.

149. Michael I. Handel, *Israel's Political-Military Doctrine* (Cambridge: Harvard Center for International Affairs, 1973), p. 4.

150. Wheeler-Bennett, *The Nemesis of Power*, p. 345.

151. Bullock, *Hitler*, p. 345. George Sakwa, "The Franco-Polish Alliance and the Remilitarization of the Rhineland," *The Historical Journal*, Vol. 16, No. 1, 1973, pp. 125-146.

152. Goodman, *The Politics of Dependence*, p. 316.

153. Weinberg, *Hitler's Foreign Policy*, p. 263.

154. Baynes, *Hitler's Speeches*, p. 1336.

155. Carr, *Arms, Autarky and Aggression*, p. 66. "After the reoccupation of the Rhineland . . . he relied increasingly on violence, or threat of violence, to attain his objects."

BIBLIOGRAPHY

Adamthwaite, Anthony, *France and the Coming of the Second World War 1936-1939*. London, Cass, 1977.

Baumont, M. "The Rhineland Crisis" in Neville Waites (ed.), *Troubled Neighbours: Franco-British Relations in the Twentieth Century*. London: Weidenfeld & Nicolson, 1941.

Baynes, Norman. *The Speeches of Adolf Hitler*, Vol. II. New York: Howard Fertig, 1969.

Bennett, Edward W. *German Rearmament and the West 1932-1933*. Princeton: Princeton University Press, 1979.

Bernhardt, Walter. *Die deutsche Aufruestung 1934-1939*. Frankfurt: Bernard & Graefe, 1969.

Braubach, Max. *Der Einmarsch deutscher Truppen in die entmilitarisierte Zone am Rhein im März 1936*. Mainz: Westdeutscher Verlag, 1956.

Bretton, Henry L. *Stresemann and the Revision of Versailles*. Stanford: Stanford University Press, 1953.

Bullock, Alan. *Hitler: A Study in Tyranny*. Revised edition. New York: Harper and Row, 1962.

Carr, William. *Arms, Autarky and Aggression: A Study of German Foreign Policy 1933-1939*. London: Edward Arnold, 1972.

Cooper, Matthew, *The German Army 1933-1945*. London: Macdonald and Jane's, 1978.

Debicki, Roman, "The Remilitarization of the Rhineland and its Impact on the French-Polish Alliance," *Polish Review*, 14:4. Autumn 1969, pp. 45-55.

Eden, Anthony, *Facing the Dictators*. Boston: Houghton Mifflin, 1962.

Emmerson, John Thomas. *The Rhineland Crisis*. Ames: Iowa State University Press, 1977.

François-Poncet, André. *The Fateful Years: Memoirs of a French Ambassador in Berlin, 1931-1938*. New York: Harcourt, Brace & Co., 1949.

Gatzke, Hans W., (ed.). *European Diplomacy Between the Wars, 1919-1939*. Chicago: Quadrangle Books, 1972.

———. *Stresemann and the Rearmament of Germany*. Baltimore: Johns Hopkins University Press, 1954.

Gibbs, N. H., *Grand Strategy*. Vol. 1, *Rearmament Policy*. London: Her Majesty's Stationery Office, 1976.

Goldman, Aaron L., *Crisis in the Rhineland: Britain, France and the Rhineland Crisis of 1936*. Unpublished Ph.D. dissertation: University of Indiana, June 1967.

Goodman, Ronald E. M., *The Rhineland Crisis and the Politics of Dependence: A Case Study in Bureaucratic Government and Irresponsible Leadership*. Unpublished Ph.D. dissertation, Princeton, N.J., June 1978.

Hall, Hines H., "The Foreign Policy-Making Process in Britain, 1934-1935 and the Origins of the Anglo-German Naval Agreement." *The Historical Journal*, Vol. 19, No. 2, pp. 477-499.

Hill, Lawrence, W., *British Official Reaction to the Rhineland Crisis November 1935-May 1936*. Unpublished Ph.D. dissertation: Lamar State College of Technology, Beaumont, Texas, May 1972.

Hinsley, F. H., et al., *British Intelligence in the Second World War: Its Influence on Strategy and Operations*, Vol. 1. New York: Cambridge University Press, 1979.

Hoehne, Heinz, *Canaris*. Garden City, N.Y.: Doubleday, 1979.

Irving, David, *The Rise and Fall of the Luftwaffe*. London: Futura Publications, 1976.

———. *The War Path*. New York: Viking Press, 1978.

———. (Ed.) *A Breach of Security: The German Secret Intelligence File on Events Leading to the Second World War*. London: William Kimber, 1968.

Jacobson, Jon. *Locarno Diplomacy*. Princeton: Princeton University Press, 1972.

Kimmich, Christoph M. *Germany and the League of Nations*. Chicago: Chicago University Press, 1976.

Kirkpatrick, Lyman B., Jr. *Captains Without Eyes: Intelligence Failures in World War II*. London: Macmillan, 1969.

Korbel, Joseph. *Poland Between East and West*. Princeton: Princeton University Press, 1963.

Lepotier, Contre-Amiral (Ret.), "L'Attaque Nous Surprendra," *Revue de Defense Nationale*, August-September 1961, Vol. 17, pp. 1386-1404.

Mason, Herbert Molloy. *The Rise of the Luftwaffe*. New York: Dial Press, 1973.

Meinck, Gerhard. *Hitler und die deutsche Aufruestung 1933-1937*. Wiesbaden: Franz Steiner, 1959.

Mueller, Klaus-Juergen. *Das Heer und Hitler*. Stuttgart: Deutsche Verlags-Anstalt, 1969.

Owen, Henry, "NATO Strategy: What is Past is Prologue." *Foreign Affairs*, July 1965, Vol. 43, No. 4, p. 682-690.

Parker, R. A. C., "The First Capitulation: France and the Rhineland Crisis of 1936," *World Politics*, Vol. 8, No. 3, April 1956, pp. 355-373.

Robertson, E. M., *Hitler's Pre-War Policy and Military Plans 1933-1939*. New York: Citadel Press, 1967.

Robertson, Esmonde, *Hitler and Sanctions: Mussolini and the Rhineland*. European Studies Review, Vol. 7, 1977, pp. 409-435.

Sakwa, George, "The Franco-Polish Alliance and the Remilitarization of the Rhineland," pp. 125-146. *The Historical Journal*, Vol. 16, No. 1.

Seabury, Paul. *The Wilhelmstrasse*. Berkeley: University of California Press, 1954.

Shirer, William L. *The Collapse of the Third Republic*. New York: Simon and Schuster, 1960.

Strong, Major General Sir Kenneth. *Intelligence at the Top*. London: Cassell, 1968.

Tabouis, Genevieve. *They Called Me Cassandra*. New York: Charles Scribner, 1942.

Thompson, Neville. *The Anti-Appeasers: Conservative Opposition to Appeasement in the 1930's*. London: Oxford University Press, 1971.

Voelker, Karl-Heinz. *Die deutsche Luftwaffe 1933-1939*. Stuttgart: Deutsche Verlags-Anstalt, 1967.

Walters, F. P. *A History of the League of Nations*. London: Oxford University Press, 1952.

Watt, Donald Cameron. *Too Serious a Business*. Berkeley: University of California Press, 1975.

Watt, Donald C., "German Plans for the Reoccupation of the Rhineland: A Note," *Journal of Contemporary History*, Vol. 1, No. 4, 1966, pp. 193-199.

Weinberg, Gerhard L. *The Foreign Policy of Hitler's Germany: 1933-1936*. Chicago: Chicago University Press, 1971.

——————. *The Foreign Policy of Hitler's Germany: Starting World War II, 1937-1939*. Chicago: Chicago University Press, 1980.

Wheeler-Bennett, John. *The Nemesis of Power*, 2nd ed. London: Macmillan, 1964.

Wohlstetter, Roberta. "The Pleasures of Self-Deception," *The Washington Quarterly*, Vol. 2, No. 2, Autumn 1979, pp. 54-64.

Yeuell, Col. Donovan P., "The German Occupation of the Rhineland." *U.S. Naval Institute Proceedings*, Nov. 1955, pp. 1105-1215.

Young, Robert J. *In Command of France: French Foreign Policy and Military Planning, 1933-1940*. Cambridge, Mass.: Harvard University Press, 1978.

APPENDIX

THE INTELLIGENCE EVALUATION PROCESS OF INTENTIONS AND CAPABILITIES

One's Own Intentions

Time and again the victim of a surprise attack has enjoyed the *status quo* and derived satisfaction from it—or at least has not entertained offensive designs himself. Often he presumes that what is good for him must also be good for the enemy; therefore the enemy must not be planning an offensive either. Even if offensive designs are attributed to an enemy, one's own desire for peace and for the maintenance of the *status quo* makes the enemy's aggressive intentions appear somewhat abstract and remote, so that a threat is rarely perceived as immediate. There is a strong element of wishful thinking, escapism, and even resignation in such attitudes. Related to this is the fear that if the threat of war is taken seriously and adequate preparations to meet it are made, such preparations would antagonize, provoke, or frighten the enemy, strengthen the more aggressive interest groups in his society, and supply them with an excuse to take pre-emptive action. Preparations for war are thus perceived as a form of self-fulfilling prophecy, while ignoring threatening signals seems to contribute to peace. Such a policy of self-defeat and resignation was undoubtedly Stalin's policy towards Germany in 1940-41,[1] and, to a certain extent, Israel's as well on the eve of the Yom Kippur War. Conversely, if one's own goals are offensive, the tendency to project such intentions onto the enemy and to be more suspicious result in one's being more alert and attentive to incoming signals indicating the possibility of approaching danger. Examples of such situations are German and British behavior before their invasion of Norway, the British anticipatory invasion of Iceland, and Russia's occupation of the Baltic states in 1940; all actions were taken in anticipation of German occupation of these states.[2] Another possibility is that one side is so pre-occupied with planning its own attack that it plans in a vacuum, paying no attention to its adversary, who might be simultaneously involved in similar designs. The case of the Americans, surprised by the Germans during their Ardennes offensive, comes to mind here. [3]

One's Own Capabilities

The development of capabilities is meant to facilitate the implementation of one's intentions and goals as well as to match the opponent's capabilities and his present and possible future intentions. In the short range, intentions are limited by one's own capabilities, which can be expanded only in the medium or long range. In order to deceive an enemy one often attempts to create an impression of inaction by indicating that one's capabilities do not yet match one's intentions. This was one of the deception strategies pursued by the Arab states on the eve of the Yom Kippur War.

Measuring One's Own Capabilities against the Opponent's

Two basic errors in evaluation can occur at this stage. The first, and possibly more common, is the overestimation of one's own capabilities, on which

Program No. 2   The Mutual Balance of Capabilities and Intentions: The Basis of
                 Evaluation of the Probability of the Outbreak of War by Each
                 Side.

— Material Data   — Political Military
— Military Doctrine   Goals
— Balance of Deterrence   — Readiness to Undertake
— Credibility/   Risks
  Non-Credibility   — Image of the Other
                                                     Side

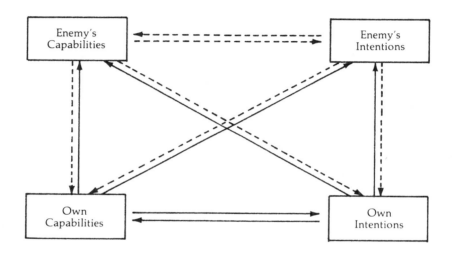

— Material Data   — Political-Military
— Military Doctrine   Goals
— Balance of Deterrence   — Readiness to Undertake
— Credibility/   Risks
  Non-Credibility   — Image of the Other
                                                     Side

1. One's intentions are constrained in the short range by available capabilities.
2. Capabilities are developed according to intentions, and can be expanded in
   the longer run.
3. One's capabilities are also built and designed to match or surpass the enemy's
   capabilities and are continuously evaluated against the enemy's capabilities:
   balance of deterrence.
4. The enemy's intentions and willingness to undertake risks are evaluated. The
   enemy's intentions also influence one's own.
5. One's own capabilities are adapted to enemy's intentions.
6. One's intentions are constrained by enemy's capabilities. Enemy's capabilities
   must be taken into account before his intentions.

complete information is available, and the underestimation of the opponent's material, technical and doctrinal capabilities, which are often discovered only after surprise has been achieved. This can be the natural result of inadequate information on the enemy's capabilities, combined with over-confidence in one's own. The Germans had very little information on Soviet capabilities on the eve of "Barbarossa." In February 1941 they estimated that the Russians had 155 divisions; by April this estimate had been upgraded to a total of 247 divisions. Soon after the invasion took place, the Germans had identified 360 Soviet divisions. "Probably no major campaign has ever been launched upon less intelligence . . . This lack of intelligence was the root cause of the ultimate disaster."[4] In 1941, the United States underestimated Japanese capabilities, and Russia underestimated Germany's capability to fight a two-front war[5] (although this does not contradict Stalin's overestimation of Germany's power in other respects, and his consequent underestimation of his own power to wage war). The Egyptians, for example, helped Israeli intelligence reach such conclusions by, on the one hand, spreading rumors of the inadequate maintenance of and lack of spare parts for their anti-aircraft missiles (deception) and, on the other hand, successfully concealing from the Israelis the addition of new weapons and their improved performance (secrecy).

The second error which intelligence services and military establishments can make is overestimation of their opponent's capabilities. The cause of such misassessments can be: (a) Possession of the wrong information or absence of adequate information regarding the enemy's real strength; this can be compounded by the enemy's deception and his dissemination of misinformation. A good example is the American intelligence community's short-lived overestimation of Russian strategic missile power in 1958, during the 'missile gap' period; the Russians, including Khrushchev himself, happily contributed false information. (b) Lack of self-assurance as a result of an earlier defeat and/or the enemy's performance elsewhere. Israel's previous victories clearly led the Egyptians and Syrians to overestimate Israel's capabilities in certain respects. Similarly, Germany's earlier victories over Russian forces in World War I, combined with Hitler's impressive performance in Poland and the West, led Stalin to overestimate German power in many ways. (c) A deliberate attempt to overestimate the enemy's capabilities in order to 'play it safe.' This is often combined with deliberate manipulation of intelligence data. (d) The desire to obtain larger budgets for military expenditures.[6]

Underestimating or overestimating the enemy's capabilities can lead to different types of mistakes in policy decisions. Underrating the enemy's capabilities is usually translated into exaggeratedly favorable estimates of one's own deterrent posture, and hence into unjustified over-confidence. One incorrectly concludes that the enemy is effectively deterred by one's assumed superiority, while in reality one's forces, rather than serving as a deterrent, are actually viewed by the enemy as a target: a deterrent can make a superb target.[7] Such overestimation is a dangerous mistake since "so long as deterrence is not openly challenged, the defender is inclined to assume that deterrence is working. But the impression that deterrence is successful may be illusory."[8]

The converse mistake—overestimating the enemy's capabilities—can result in a timid policy which can lead one to lose important opportunities for action or, even worse, can lead the enemy to underestimate one's own deterrence posture in light of hesitant and weak policies, and hence can lead to war.

Capabilities are put into action by means of a military doctrine, and the same capabilities can yield radically different results according to the choice of military doctrine. Therefore the enemy's doctrine must be taken into account when gauging his capabilities. This can prove rather difficult, for many doctrines have never been tested in battle, and they are often changed, updated and/or reversed or determined just before action.

An error common to intelligence services and military decision-makers is the projection of the assumptions of their own military doctrine onto the enemy, thereby categorizing the opposing doctrine as a variant of their own. Military doctrines, as abstract sets of principles and creative innovations, are much more difficult for an opponent to reconstruct than are material capabilities. On the eve of World War II, the English and the French, whose military capabilities were either equal or superior to those of the Germans, projected their military doctrine onto the enemy, and were thus quite unprepared to counter the German *Blitzkrieg* strategy and tactics. Similarly, in 1973 the Israelis projected their own preoccupation with air superiority onto the Egyptians and the Syrians, and were surprised to discover that the Arabs were content to merely neutralize Israel's control of the skies rather than dominate the skies themselves.

Evaluating the Enemy's Intentions

One's own intentions are to a certain extent influenced by perceptions of enemy intentions. While one's intentions are determined by autonomous goals (but also by external constraints), an opponent's continued hostility can lead to more aggressive intentions on one's part.

The most critical problem in this context lies in evaluating the enemy's intentions, forming a proper image of his character and his willingness to undertake risks. It is impossible to perceive exactly how the mental processes of an adversary in a different culture operate.

> Intelligence prediction is the estimation of the likely actions or intentions of foreign nations, and its failure can be reduced in the last analysis to a misunderstanding of foreigners' conceptual frameworks, i.e., a failure to understand properly the assumptions or interpretations of the situation upon which foreigners base their decisions. Such misunderstanding is due to . . . the uncritical interpretations of the actions and intentions of foreign states in terms of an inapplicable conceptual framework that makes these irrational and senseless.[9]

This is what Klaus Knorr has termed "apparently irrational behavior": "The behavior of people with a culture different from one's own often *appears* irrational when in fact they act rationally, but evaluate the outcomes of alternative courses of action in terms of values that differ sharply from ours. Thus, different societies differ in the value they place on individual life or on the political integrity of the individual."[10]

This cultural noise barrier is accentuated when Western culture collides with other types of culture in their approaches to war. The Western approach is best summarized by Clausewitz's observations; central to his theory is the notion that war is a tool meant to serve political ends which, according to Western (i.e., European and American) experience, can be served only through victory. Thus in Western experience and rationality, a state never resorts to war if it has little or no chance to win militarily; political goals cannot be achieved by defeat. Many non-Western cultures have departed from Western logic. They agree with Clausewitz on the primacy of politics and the subordinate role of military action to politics. But war is considered a worthwhile undertaking even if military success is *not* guaranteed, so long as political goals can be attained, including, often, the preservation of one's honor and pride. Paradoxically—in terms of Western experience—political aims are frequently obtained even through defeat.

This has created a serious perceptual gap in Western observers' understanding of non-Western states' behavior. In Western eyes, non-Western societies have often tended to assume much greater risks in war than those considered rational or profitable by Western standards. The Arabs were willing to risk military defeat (which is what happened) in order to improve thereby their political position (which, again, is exactly what happened). The Israelis could not anticipate such behavior. For a society in which there is no substitute for victory (as most Israelis perceive their situation), there could be little understanding of a military action which *a priori* could not lead to military victory. The Israelis projected their own experience and rationality onto the Arabs—and paid a high price for it. Similarly, the Americans could not perceive Japanese and North Vietnamese readiness to accept risks which were highly unacceptable by U.S. standards. This was one of the major reasons why the Americans could not envision a direct Japanese attack on the United States in 1941. They could not believe "that a power as small as Japan would make the first strike against a power as big as the United States. Even in retrospect, it is difficult to understand the magnitude and the particular characteristics of Japanese rashness."[11]

> What [they] miscalculated was the ability and willingness of the Japanese to accept such high risks . . . [national] sanity would dictate against such an event, but Japanese sanity cannot be measured by our own standards of [logic] . . . Our own standards . . . reckoned the risks to the Japanese as too large and therefore not likely to be taken.[12]

Such misunderstanding of the risks which leaders of different cultures (or different mentalities, such as Hitler's) are willing to accept can work in favor of those willing to take such inordinately high risks; the risks can actually be reduced and the surprise effected can act to multiply lesser military capabilities.

Evaluation of the Enemy's Intentions According to One's Own Capabilities

The enemy's intentions are to a large extent influenced by his knowledge of our own capabilities. The greater and more impressive our capabilities are, and the more he knows about them, the less aggressive his intentions are likely to be: i.e., he is deterred. If, however, the enemy's knowledge of our true capabilities is deficient or only partial, it also becomes more difficult for us to evaluate his intentions (or in other words, the effectiveness of our deterrence is lessened). If the enemy underrates our capabilities, his intentions might become more aggressive as a result. If he overrates our capabilities (because of past experience, miscalculation, or simply faulty information) and thus entertains less aggressive intentions, he is effectively deterred. One way or another, in order to evaluate the enemy's intentions we have to know what *he* does or does not know about us. Often, however, it is easier to learn about the enemy's capabilities than it is to acquire information about his knowledge of our capabilities and how he views them. This complicates our attempts to evaluate the enemy's intentions and can create serious gaps in our knowledge about the possibility of an enemy's surprise attack. Thus, both the Russians and the Americans on the eve of the German and Japanese attacks were not fully aware of the fact that their own power was considerably underrated by their enemies.

Comparing One's Own Intentions with the Enemy's Capabilities

The last element in the complex process of intelligence assessment is obvious, and need not be discussed at length. Suffice it to say that the greater the enemy's capabilities, the less one's readiness to undertake high risks, and the more restrained (deterred) one is in the choice of options. In the final analysis, it is always safer to gear one's decisions and plans less to the enemy's *intentions* than to his *capabilities*. It is also important for us to know how the enemy evaluates our intentions in light of our estimation of his capabilities. For example, if the enemy thinks we underrate his capabilities and thus develop aggressive intentions towards him, he might choose to take pre-emptive action and thus surprise us before we surprise him.

While it is possible to break down such an analysis into several parts, in reality all steps are closely interrelated and cannot be treated separately. Interweaving all steps is an intricate and delicate process in which a mistake at any point affects the rest and distorts the final intelligence estimates.

The difficulties involved in making intelligence predictions are endless. In this context, only two more will be mentioned, the first of which is known as the 'cry wolf' syndrome. Intelligence services frequently pass information to their armies and governments indicating a possible enemy attack. They must try to minimize the number of warnings, for every false alert is very costly.[13] But as long as no fail-safe criteria are developed to differentiate between, on the one hand, real offensive intentions of the enemy and, on the other hand, mere mobilizations for maneuvers, for tests of our preparedness, or for conditioning us to false alerts, then all precautionary measures must be taken, especially if one's own defenses are highly vulnerable to surprise attack. Another danger in issuing false alarms is that mobilizing one's armed forces, even as a precautionary move, can also lead to the outbreak of undesired and unplanned war by triggering an automatic mobilization/counter-mobilization process on the part of the antagonists—which is what happened on the eves of World War I and the Six-Day War of 1967.[14] The side enjoying the *status quo* should therefore be very careful not to mobilize, for fear of self-fulfilling prophecy, unless it is very sure that the outbreak of war is inevitable. Almost every strategic surprise is preceded by false alerts, which in the course of time tend to reduce attention to them so that they become a routine, almost symbolic ritual, and are not taken as seriously as they should be. Barton Whaley has found that

> instances of surprise are indeed somewhat more commonly preceded by false alerts than those instances *not* involving surprise. Moreover, the trend is that the greater the number of false alerts, the greater the chance of their being associated with surprise . . . the false alarms serve mainly to undermine the credibility of the source and dull the effect of subsequent warnings. Thus, we see that the "cry wolf" syndrome constitutes an important perturbation in intelligence estimates of future enemy action.[15]

The choice intelligence services have to make between "being popular (i.e., cheap) and alert"[16] is not an easy one.

NOTES TO APPENDIX

1. See John Erickson, *The Soviet High Command: A Military-Political History 1918-1941* (London: Macmillan, 1962), chap. 17.

2. For the mutual suspicions and calculations of the British and the Germans on the eve of the Norwegian campaign, see T. K. Derry, *The Norwegian Campaign* (London: HMSO, 1952); George Burns Williams, "Blitzkrieg and Conquest: Policy Analysis of Military and Political Decisions Preparatory to the German Attack upon Norway, April 9, 1940" (Ph.D. dissertation, Yale University, 1966). For the British invasion of Iceland, see Donald E. Neuchterlein, *Iceland: Reluctant Ally* (Ithaca, New York: Cornell University Press, 1961). For Russia's anticipatory invasion of the Baltic states, see Albert N. Tarulis, *Soviet Policy Toward the Baltic States 1918-1949* (South Bend, Indiana: Notre Dame University Press, 1959).

3. See H. Baldwin, *Battles Lost and Won*: "The American front, though frustrated and weary, was 'offensive minded.' The mental approach from the lowliest man in the front line to the highest brass on the staffs was one of attack." (pp. 403-404).

4. David Irving, *Hitler's War* (New York: Viking 1977), pp. 204-206. Hitler candidly told Italian Foreign Minister Galeazzo Ciano several months after the invasion of Russia that had he known Russia's real strength he would not have opened a Second Front. See also Lyman B. Kirkpatrick, *Captains Without Eyes: Intelligence Failures in World War II* (London: Macmillan, 1969) pp. 15, 51, 268, and Barry A. Leach, *German Strategy Against Russia 1939-1941* (Oxford: Oxford University Press, 1973), pp. 91-94 and Appendix IV, p. 270. Albert Seaton, *The Russo-German War 1941-45.* (New York: Praeger, 1972) Chapter 3. 'A Little Knowledge', pp. 43-50. Seweryn Bialer, ed., *Stalin and his Generals* (New York: Pegasus, 1969).

5. Roberta Wohlstetter, *Pearl Harbor: Warning and Decision*, (Stanford:

Stanford University Press, 1962), pp. 337-338; 369-370. See also Klaus Knorr, "Failures in National Intelligence Estimates: The Case of the Cuban Missiles." *World Politics* Vol. 16, April 1964, pp. 455-467. p. 462.

6. Examples of the last two causes can be quoted from Samuel Huntington's "Arms Races: Prerequisites and Results," in *Public Policy* (Cambridge, Massachusetts: Harvard University Graduate School of Public Administration, 1958): "The armed services inevitably overstate the military capabilities of the opponent; in 1914, for instance, the Germans estimated the French army to have 121,000 more men than the German army; the French estimated the German army to have 134,000 more men than the French army, but both countries agreed in their estimates of the military forces of third powers" (p. 54, quoting Bernadotte E. Schmitt's *The Coming of the War: 1914*). On the last possibility, Huntington cites the following example: "In 1956 reports of Soviet aircraft production, later asserted to be considerably exaggerated, influenced Congress to appropriate an extra $900 million for the Air Force." (p. 54). It is a recurring phenomenon that before the defense budget is decided, news about new Soviet naval or other capabilities are made public by Pentagon officials.

7. Thomas C. Schelling, Introduction to *Pearl Harbor*, by R. Wohlstetter, p. viii. Americans viewed their navy as a deterrent rather than as a target on the eve of the Pearl Harbor attack. See *ibid.*, pp. 56, 118, 231, 278, 398.

8. A. George and R. Smoke, *Deterrence in American Foreign Policy* (New York: Columbia University Press, 1974), p. 567.

9. Benno Wasserman, "The Failure of Intelligence Prediction," *Political Studies*, Vol. 8, No. 2, June 1960, pp. 156-169; pp. 166-167.

10. Klaus Knorr, "Failures in National Intelligence Estimates," p. 459. See also G. B. Williams, *Blitzkrieg and Conquest*, p. 52.

11. R. Wohlstetter, *Pearl Harbor*, p. 349.

12. *Ibid.*, p. 354.

13. Herman Kahn says of false alarms: "First a nation may react to a false alarm and thus be subject to some needless cost or risk which might dangerously increase the probability of war; if one reacts whenever there is ambiguous evidence, the number of false alarms increases the likelihood of being taken by surprise if the event proves genuine." (Herman Kahn, *On Thermonuclear War* (Princeton: Princeton University Press, 1958), p. 257, quoted in G. B. Williams, *Blitzkrieg and Conquest*, p. 51). "It is a very delicate balance. The exact point of balance in Kahn's diagnosis depends on the rate of false alarms and the 'cost' of reaction." (G. B. Williams, *ibid.*, p. 51n).

14. For the 'point of no return' in this mobilization and counter-mobilization process, see L. L. Farrar, "The Limits of Choice: July 1914 Reconsidered," *Journal of Conflict Resolution*, 16, 4, No. 1, March 1972, pp. 1-24.

15. Barton Whaley, *Codeword Barbarossa*. Cambridge, Mass: MIT Press, 1973.

16. R. Wohlstetter, *Pearl Harbor*, p. 302.

3
THE RIBBENTROP-MOLOTOV AGREEMENT

"I content myself with saying . . . that what the English do not know is far less prodigious than what they do not want to know."

Lord Vansittart, quoted in Ernst von Weizsaecker, *Memoirs*

"A statesman must know how to jump over his shadow. Let's rather agree on a common policy instead of advancing the interests of third parties and tearing each other to pieces."

Georgi Astakhov to Peter Kleist, quoted in Peter Kleist, *Zwischen Hitler und Stalin*

"I do not attempt to conceal from the House that the announcement [of the Russo-German Pact] came to the Government as a surprise, and as a surprise of very unpleasant character . . . "

Prime Minister Chamberlain in Parliament on the 24th of August, 1939.

"The news has acted like a bombshell all over the world. The decision represents a sensational turning point in the relations between the two countries, and it reaches back to the traditional community of German-Russian interests. The historical premises for such a formulation of policy have to be gone into deeply . . . It can certainly be stressed that the announcement found a deep response in the nation. While the democracies talked, we and the Russians have acted."

Germany's Ministry of Propaganda instructions for newspaper editors on coverage of the Ribbentrop-Molotov Agreement.

STAGE 1. October 1938 to the End of April: The Reevaluation of Basic Interests Begins

The Munich Agreement of September 1938, by which Britain and France permitted Germany to annex Czechoslovakia's Sudetenland, clearly demonstrated the Western democracies' weakness and lack of resolve. By failing to honor their obligations they demonstrated their impotence, thus undermining their basic interests. For one thing, the appearance of avoiding war at any cost naturally diminished their credibility among potential allies. And the lessons of Munich could, of course, not be ignored by the Soviet Union in its search for security.

The next target for German aggression was Poland. The Poles were not likely to give in to German demands; unlike the Czechs, they gave the impression that they would meet force with force.

> In viewing this situation, the Soviet leaders may well have reasoned approximately as follows. If Germany attacks Poland, Britain will either back out and leave Poland to her fate or declare war on Germany. If Britain failed to keep her promise, and Munich led the Russians to suspect that she probably would, then Soviet Russia might easily find herself fighting Germany alone. If Britain did fight, then why not let the Germans and the Western Powers fight it out? In either case, if agreement with Germany were possible, such an agreement would enable Russia to profit substantially from the overthrow of what was left of the European order.[1]

Thus, the demonstration of British and French weakness persuaded the Russians that there was little logic in trying to form an alliance in which they would not only supply most of the military muscle, but would also be the first to get embroiled in hostilities. They would carry the burden of the alliance and "pull the chestnuts out of the fire" for the Western democracies.

With the Germans, at least, the Russians shared the same opinion of Poland. They both detested it and hoped to add to their territory by the dismemberment of Poland, to which, in any case, they thought they had historical claims. Since the Western democracies were committed to the defense of Poland, they were obviously the wrong party to which to address any plans for that country's dismemberment. The Germans, however, as already noted, had by their 1934 non-aggression pact with the Poles weakened French-Polish ties and were possibly ready to divide Poland with the Soviet Union.

Thus, after Munich, the Soviet Union began to turn toward Germany. In order to attract German interest, Stalin had to improve his bargaining position vis-à-vis that country. For this purpose, it was best to pretend that he was negotiating a treaty with the Western democracies. But in order to whet their appetite, Stalin had to pretend that negotiations with Nazi Germany were already in progress. Paradoxically, in order to start negotiations with Germany, Stalin had to pretend that they had already begun. Adam Ulam describes the intricate diplomatic maneuvers as follows:

> In fact, rumors of a German-Soviet "deal" that circulated in the fall of 1938 were largely inspired by Soviet sources and for obvious reasons. Munich undoubtedly lowered the Kremlin's opinion of the

British and French regimes. It must have strengthened the suspicion, never absent, that at least some official persons in London and Paris would not be unhappy to see Hitler's further aggression directed eastward. But, unlike Hitler, Stalin did not shape his foreign policies according to whether he got mad at this or that country or regime. A resumption of at least the appearance of collaboration with the West was a vital necessity for the Soviet Union *even and especially if she sought* an agreement with Germany. Hitler was not going to bargain with Stalin out of ideological sympathy, but only if the latter had some cards in his hands. And the strongest card of all would be the possibility of a binding military alliance between the U.S.S.R. and the Western Powers.[2] (Emphasis in the original.)

In his memoirs, Baron Ernst von Weizsaecker, State Secretary in the Foreign Ministry, suggests that Stalin made the first move in the German-Soviet rapprochement. He claims that Stalin's isolation after Munich in the *salon des refusés* led him to initiate the contacts with Germany.[3]

The Soviets' problem, however, was that given Hitler's traditional animosity toward communism in general and Russia in particular, they were not sure that a bargain could be struck. They needed time to carefully evaluate Germany's intentions—time to find out whether the interests of both countries overlapped. There was a need to determine the value of earlier policies and assess ideological animosities. For these reasons, the Soviet Union *continued* to pursue earlier anti-Nazi policies while examining the alternatives.

As has been noted in the preceding chapter, the desire to eliminate Poland had been a major objective of all German governments since Versailles. In the 1920's, the Germans lacked the power to accomplish this goal. By 1939, it was merely a question of timing. The German attitude was aptly expressed by General von Seeckt in 1922.

Poland's existence is intolerable and incompatible with the essential conditions of Germany's life. Poland must go and will go—as a result of her own internal weaknesses and of action by Russia—with our aid. The obliteration of Poland must be one of the fundamental drives of German policy . . . [and] is attainable by means of, and with the help of, Russia.[4]

On November 29, 1938, Hitler issued a directive to the Commanders-in-Chief of the Armed Forces in which he stated that if favorable political conditions should develop they must be exploited to occupy Danzig by means which fell short of full-scale war. Hitler wanted to occupy Danzig and Poland, but he was not yet ready to risk a general European war. As reported by General Walter von Brauchitsch, the Army Commander-in-Chief, this was still Hitler's opinion in March 1939.

For the time being, the Fuehrer does not intend to solve the Polish question. However, it should be worked on. A solution in the near future would have to be based on especially favorable political conditions. In that case, Poland should be knocked down so completely that it need not be taken into account as a political factor for the next few decades. The Fuehrer has in mind as such a solution a borderline advanced from the eastern border of East Prussia to the eastern tip of Upper Silesia.[5]

In a speech to the House of Commons on March 31, sixteen days after Hitler had entered Prague, Prime Minister Chamberlain declared:

In the event of any action which clearly threatened Polish independence and which the Polish Government accordingly considered it vital to resist with their national forces, His Majesty's Government would feel themselves bound at once to lend the Polish Government an assurance to this effect. I may add that the French Government have authorized me to make it plain that they stand in the same position in this matter.[6]

The risk of a general European war over Poland had substantially increased as a result of the loss of credibility of the British and French governments. Hitler was, nevertheless, determined to "solve the Polish problem" and issued his directive for the planning of "Case White"—the attack on Poland—on April 3, 1939.

TOP SECRET

Case White

The present attitude of Poland requires . . . the initiation of military preparations to remove, if necessary, any threat from this direction for ever.

1. *Political Requirements and Aims.* The aim will be to destroy Polish military strength and create in the East a situation which satisfies the requirements of national defense. The Free State of Danzig will be proclaimed a part of the Reich territory at the outbreak of hostilities, at the latest.

The political leaders consider it their task in this case to isolate Poland if possible, that is to say, to limit the war to Poland only.

The development of increasing internal crises in France and the resulting British cautiousness might produce such a situation in the not too distant future.

Intervention by Russia, if she were in the position to intervene, cannot be expected to be of any use to Poland because this would mean Poland's destruction by Bolshevism. Italy's attitude is determined by the Rome-Berlin Axis.

2. *Military Conclusions.* The great objectives in the building up of the German armed forces will continue to be determined by the antagonism of the Western democracies. "Case White" constitutes only a precautionary complement to these preparations . . .

The isolation of Poland will be all the more easily maintained, even after the outbreak of hostilities, if we succeed in starting the war with sudden, heavy blows and in gaining rapid successes . . .

3. *Tasks of the Armed Forces.* The task of the Wehrmacht is to destroy the Polish armed forces. To this end a surprise attack is to be aimed at and prepared. Camouflaged or open general mobilization will not be ordered earlier than the day before the attack and at the latest possible moment.

Preparations must be made in such a way that the operation can be carried out at any time from September 1, 1939, onward.[7]

Hitler's decision to attack Poland if she did not yield peacefully to his demands by September 1939 made it necessary to approach the Soviet Union. As he stated in his "Case White" directive, it was necessary to isolate Poland before such an attack could take place. Thus, in the event of war Hitler had to prevent unilateral intervention by the Soviet Union on Poland's side, and in order to prevent a two-front war he had to block a possible agreement or alliance between the Soviet Union and the British and French governments to help Poland, and finally, of course, it was necessary to keep the British and French out of a German-Polish conflict.

The first two conditions required close collaboration with the Soviet Union and hence a realignment of Germany's policy toward Russia. This was all the more urgent in view of Chamberlain's recent declaration in the House of Commons. Because of his timetable for the Polish campaign, Hitler was under great pressure to approach the Soviet Union and reach an agreement concerning the future of Poland. Yet he took his time in reaching it. A possible explanation is that he was psychologically reluctant to start such a move. (Hitler never visited the U.S.S.R., nor did he participate directly in the conversations at any stage. He may already have made up his mind that Russia, not Poland, was his ultimate goal.)[8] In addition, he may have been certain that he could always make the Soviet Union an offer she could not refuse. The long delays in his decision to approach the Soviet Union certainly contributed to the secrecy of the process.

On May 3, 1939, the Soviet press announced that Maxim Litvinov, the Commissar for Foreign Affairs, had resigned. Like Hitler, the Soviet Union had also perceived the need to shift its policy toward its ideological adversary in order to secure its vital interests. By the end of April both states had completed the process of reevaluating their basic interests. The second stage of probing each others' intentions and exchanging signals had already begun in March 1939, if not earlier.

STAGE 2.   *March 1939 to August 1939:*
            The exchange of Signals and the
            Reciprocal Process of Evaluating
            Intentions between Germany and
            the Soviet Union

By November 1938, as we have seen, Hitler had already decided to in-
corporate Danzig into the German Reich if this would not lead to a
general European war. By mid-April 1939, however, he had made up his
mind to occupy not only Danzig, but also the rest of Poland, regardless
of the consequences.

German pressures on Poland developed gradually. Seeking a revision
of the status of Danzig in accordance with German interests, Joachim
von Ribbentrop, the Reich Foreign Minister, began applying pressure as
early as the end of October 1939, less than a month after Munich. While
Ribbentrop made demands *in secret*, Hitler reassured the Polish Ambassador of Germany's peaceful intentions, stating (January 5, 1939) that
while "Danzig is German . . . will always remain German, and will
sooner or later become part of Germany", nevertheless "no *fait accompli*" would be engineered in Danzig.[9] For the Polish government
these were ominous signs; threats, not words of reassurance. But such
statements kept the new German pressures secret until April 1939.[10]

Hitler was not ready to turn his full attention to the "Polish problem"
as long as the occupation of Czechoslovakia was not completed. While
the support of either the Western democracies and/or the Soviet Union
concerning his next move in Poland's direction was not yet secured, his
specific intentions remained unclear. Why should he prematurely disclose his intentions? Why make public demands on the Polish
government and provoke the Poles and their allies to form a common
anti-German front *before* Germany's preparations for action had been
completed?

Hitler's anniversary speech to the Reichstag on January 30, 1939, must
be considered a masterpiece of deception, as well as one of the first signals to the Russians. The very fact that he did not attack the Soviet
Union in this speech should have been an early warning signal to astute
political observers. Hitler's praise of the "friendship" between Germany
and Poland was also extraordinary. Certainly, a positive attitude toward
both Poland and the Soviet Union contradicted earlier German patterns
of behavior and policy. At about the same time, the Germans also suggested to their allies to convert the Anti-Comintern Pact into a general,
not a specifically anti-Soviet military alliance.

As we shall see, both the German and Soviet governments found it
convenient to start signaling and evaluating each other's intentions on
the relatively noncommittal economic level. Using economic dialogue to

begin the process of mutual probing offered some advantages. The use of "non-political" officials in the probing process was also helpful because it drew much less attention than the participation of high-level politicians; trade talks are often held routinely on a yearly basis. Also, trade talks could always be extended, if desired, to political issues. If a digression to political issues in the course of economic talks proved successful, they could either be discussed by the economic conference, or trigger the formation of a special political conference. Touching upon political issues in this type of situation is always informal and does not obligate the sides involved. If the political probings fail, both sides can claim a misunderstanding by non-political officials, continue the economic discussion as if nothing of a political nature had ever been mentioned, and thus avoid loss of prestige. The negotiations are always *under the control* of the governments involved. This is, in part, also due to the fact that trade talks are usually held by relatively low-level officials who cannot enter into definite commitments on behalf of their governments. If political issues are raised "indirectly" or "unexpectedly" by the economic experts, the "politically inexperienced" delegates, who have no authority to deal with political issues, must refer back to their governments for advice. The pace of negotiations is slowed down, and this slow-motion dialogue helps both sides gain time to carefully weigh their next steps.[11]

One of the first books on the development of German-Soviet relations to appear after World War II describes the careful way in which both sides approached each other.

[The Soviet Government's orders to Alexi Merekalov, the Ambassador, and Georgi Astakhov, the Chargé d'Affaires in Berlin] . . . were oral and were performed with discretion, since they were groping about in the dark and were very much on their guard. If they succeeded, they were replaced by the official negotiators; if they failed, they could be repudiated . . .

Since the two suspicious partners—Hitler's Germany and Stalin's Russia—wished to avoid showing their cards and giving away the lead, they often made use of friendly or neutral diplomats through whom they could throw out feelers. Moscow made one of the first attempts to sound Germany's intentions towards Russia, as well as the first offer of a non-aggression pact, through M. Draganov, the Bulgarian Minister in Berlin. And in June, 1939, Ciano, then Italian Foreign Minister, passed on to the Soviet representative in Rome—by the method which might be called that of the "inspired leakage"—certain German proposals for a pact of non-aggression.

To all this were added the numerous contacts which industrial circles and the chiefs of the Wehrmacht kept up with the Soviet agents. These contacts were sometimes allowed to drop, but were never completely broken off. There was nothing official about them; they were a survival between the two regimes of a system of collaboration which had become precarious in the course of recent years, but which could at any moment be fished out again to act as bait.[12]

That this was the case is also corroborated by the Weizsaecker memoirs. He claims that Hitler ". . . deliberately refrained from showing any undue eagerness; for he was afraid of a setback and that he would get a refusal from Moscow accompanied by mocking Tartar laughter. He therefore still kept economic matters in the foreground."[13]

The first German-Soviet trade talks, held in both Berlin and Moscow, started at the end of December 1938 and lasted until March 1939. At this stage the discussions were exclusively devoted to economic issues. In March, the Russians insisted that they be moved to Moscow in an attempt to determine the degree of German interest in improving "economic" relations with the Soviet Union. The Germans, who were in need of Russian raw materials, agreed to send a delegate to Moscow, though they insisted that the agreements would be signed, as previously decided, in Berlin. The negotiations opened in Moscow on February 10, 1939. However, when by early March the Germans had not met the Russian demands, the negotiations were broken off. The failure of these talks clearly reflected the fact that the first phase in the basic reevaluation and reexamination of Germany's interests and policies concerning Poland and the Soviet Union had not yet been completed.* The failure of these economic talks made the Russians feel that the Germans had not treated them fairly during the negotiations and were not really serious about the talks.[14] Had Hitler been more sure of his future plans and interests at that stage and had he been able to conclude a trade agreement, it might have simplified the process of reaching a political agreement with the Soviet Union later on. As it was, the economic talks were deferred until June 1939, and their resumption at that time proved, as we shall see, to be much more complicated.

In his speech before the Eighteenth Congress of the Communist Party on March 10, however, Stalin did not exclude the possibility of a future Soviet-German rapprochement. He made it clear that the Soviet Union would not let itself be drawn into a war against Germany on behalf of the "weak Western democracies," which he also accused of trying to instigate a senseless conflict between the Soviet Union and Germany. He said that the Soviet Union will ". . . not . . . let our country be drawn into conflict by warmongers, whose custom it is to let others pull their chestnuts out of the fire."[15] The German Ambassador in Moscow, Count Friedrich

* Once Hitler finally decided to attack Poland and realized the need to obtain Soviet support, the Germans were suddenly ready to make all necessary economic concessions to the Soviet Union.

Werner von der Schulenburg, took note of the fact that Stalin had criticized the Western democracies more severely than Germany.[16] While this signaling does not prove that Stalin had already made up his mind to collaborate with Germany and coordinate Soviet and German policies, he certainly indicated that the Soviet Union had no desire to become involved in a war against Germany. These signals did not go unnoticed by the Germans.[17] On April 16, Goering met with Mussolini in Rome and said he had been impressed with Stalin's speech. He drew Mussolini's attention to the fact that Hitler had deliberately not mentioned Russia in his latest speeches, and said he would recommend that Hitler make cautious overtures to the Soviet Union.[18]

Stalin's signals to Germany did not mean that he had discarded all other options (i.e., an agreement with the Western democracies), *but rather that he was exploring alternative policies.* Following Stalin's speech and the German occupation of Czechoslovakia, Commissar of Foreign Relations Litvinov suggested, on behalf of the Soviet government, a European Six Power Conference to discuss ways to stop any further aggression by Hitler (March 18, 1939). Since the Soviet Union was exchanging signals with both Germany and the Western democracies, it was, in effect, emitting contradictory signals.

Stalin's contradictory signaling served two purposes: (a) it kept the Soviet Union's options open, and (b) if Stalin decided to collaborate with Germany, negotiations with the Western democracies could force the Germans to bid higher than they would otherwise have done.

On April 3, as mentioned above, Hitler issued the orders for the O.K.W. (High Command of the Armed Forces) and O.K.H. (High Command of the Army) to prepare plans for the attack on Poland. This decision meant that Hitler would have to find ways to harmonize German and Soviet interests in Poland and Eastern Europe in order to prevent a clash between the two countries.

The last specifically anti-Soviet act of the German government was the push for publication of Spain's adherence to the Anti-Comintern Pact on April 6, 1939. That was also the last time that an anti-Soviet cartoon appeared in the *Schwarze Korps,* the official S.S. newspaper. General orders for the German press to exercise restraint toward Russia were only issued at the beginning of May.[19] Ribbentrop's special expert on Soviet affairs, Peter Kleist, was instructed on April 7 to improve his personal relations with members of the Soviet Embassy in Berlin.

The probing between the two sides was kept at a low level until the end of April. The Germans, for their part, began to worry about the possibility of the creation of an anti-German Triple Entente between the British, the French, and the Russians. They had, therefore, to move adroitly, try to lessen tensions, and clear the air before they could approach the

Soviet Union. Most of the contacts made during April were between German officials of the Foreign Ministry and members of the Soviet Embassy in Berlin. Of these meetings, the most important was between German State Secretary Weizsaecker and Soviet Ambassador Merekalov on April 17, 1939. The excuse for the meeting was German-Soviet economic relations, but they soon moved on to discuss political matters of common interest. The two major themes discussed were Russia's desire to isolate herself from any possible European war and Germany's fear of a possible Triple Entente. Toward the end of their discussion the Russian Ambassador hinted at the possibility of an improvement of Soviet-German relations. He said, according to Weizsaecker's summary of the discussion, that

> Russian policy had always followed a straight course. *Ideological differences had very little adverse effect on relations between Russia and Italy and need not disturb those with Germany either.* Russia had not exploited the present friction between Germany and the Western democracies against us, neither did she wish to do that. As far as Russia was concerned, there was no reason why she should not live on a normal footing with us, and out of normal relations could grow increasingly improved relations.
>
> With this remark, toward which he had been steering the conversation, M. Merekalov ended the talk. He intends to visit Moscow in a day or two.[20]

Merekalov implied that the contents of the discussion would soon be personally reported by him to Moscow. An additional positive signal from the German side was the German agreement to fulfill certain armament contracts that had been signed earlier between the Soviet government and the Czech Skoda Company prior to the complete German occupation of Czechoslovakia in March.

On April 15, President Roosevelt made an appeal to Hitler in which he asked, "Are you willing to give assurances that your armed forces will not attack or invade the territory of the following independent states?" (A list of 31 states was included.) Hitler answered Roosevelt's question in a long speech to the Reichstag on April 28, 1939. He gave the question a sarcastic but positive answer, and mentioned the names of all the states referred to by Roosevelt with one exception—Poland—an omission which went unnoticed by all observers at the time. The sheer length of the speech combined with the number of issues touched upon (including the denunciation of the Anglo-German Naval Treaty of 1935 and the German-Polish Non-Aggression Pact of 1934) could have been the reason that observers did not notice the omission of Poland's name. In any case, the denunciation of Germany's Non-Aggression Pact with Poland indicated the possibility of a German attack on Poland. Hitler, himself, however, continued his deception tactics in the same speech by denying the rumors of a possible German attack on Poland as "mere inventions of the international press."[21] None of his listeners could, of course, know that only three weeks earlier he had ordered his armed forces to prepare for the destruction of Poland by September 1. (Though Hitler had originally specified September 1 as the earliest date for the attack on Poland, he later advanced his timetable to make September 1 the last possible date.)

During the speech, Hitler signaled to the Soviet Union by not only omitting his usual tirade against the U.S.S.R., but by failing even to mention her.

The next important signal came from the Soviet Union. Litvinov was dismissed by Stalin, and Molotov was appointed to take his place on May 3.[22] In the absence of Ambassador Schulenburg, Werner von Tippelskirch, the German Charge d'Affaires, wrote the following report of the incident.

> The appointment of Molotov as Foreign Commissar, while retaining his office of Chairman of the Council of People's Commissars, is published by the Soviet press in large headlines as an Ukase of the Presidium of the Supreme Soviet of May 3. The dismissal of Litvinov appears on the last page in the 'News in Brief' column. The sudden change has caused the greatest surprise here, as Litvinov was in the midst of negotiations with the British Delegation, had appeared in close proximity to Stalin on the saluting-base at the Parade on May 1, and as there had been no recent indications that his position was weakening.[23]

Litvinov's dismissal was a symbolic gesture, indicating a major shift in Soviet foreign policy. "Litvinov's resignation as Foreign Minister struck Hitler like a cannonball," Grossadmiral Raeder later recalled.[24] Its meaning was not lost for a moment on Hitler, who later described the replacement of Litvinov as "decisive."[25] Litvinov was well-known as a major proponent of collaboration between the Soviet Union and the Western democracies, and he advocated the idea of pursuing a policy of collective security through the League of Nations. Litvinov's policies failed miserably primarily because of the short-sighted diplomacy of the Western democracies. Litvinov, who was a Jew, was replaced by a non-Jew, making direct negotiations between the two countries much easier. The appointment of Molotov, who was, in Tippelskirch's words, Stalin's "most intimate friend and closest collaborator," also indicated Stalin's growing personal involvement in foreign affairs. Churchill immediately perceived a Soviet turn toward Germany in Litvinov's dismissal.[26] After this event, an intensified level of probing commenced on May 5, with a discussion between Georgi Astakhov, the Soviet Chargé d'Affaires in

Berlin, and Julius Schnurre, the German Foreign Office expert on East European economic affairs. After the meeting, Schnurre reported that:

> . . . Astakhov touched upon the dismissal of Litvinov and tried, without asking direct questions, to learn whether this event would cause a change in our attitude toward the Soviet Union. He stressed very much the great importance of the personality of Molotov, who was by no means a specialist in foreign policy, but who would have all the greater importance for future Soviet foreign policy.[27]

At the same meeting, Astakhov also suggested that their two countries continue the trade negotiations which had been broken off in early March.

"In Germany, the reaction to Litvinov's dismissal was immediate. A change in the tone of the German press was ordered, and this was quickly noted by the Russians."[28] On May 6, Hitler was briefed on Germany's political, military, and economic relations with the Soviet Union. The same day, Ribbentrop spoke with the Italian Foreign Minister Count Ciano on the need for, and the possibility of, a rapprochement with the Soviet Union. On the seventh of May, Goering's liaison officer to Hitler, General Karl Bodenschatz, leaked, on Goering's orders, information to the French Embassy on the possibility of a German-Soviet rapprochement. (He leaked the same information to the Polish Embassy on May 29.) The reasons for the leaks on Goering's initiative are not clear, but they were either the result of his rivalry with Ribbentrop, or a German attempt to blackmail the Poles into accepting the German demands peacefully.[29] The French Ambassador did, indeed, report to his government that Germany was trying to reach an agreement with the Soviet Union which might lead, among other things, to the fourth partition of Poland. The existence of these leaks is important because it shows that the Western democracies had enough signals, at this early stage, to be aware of a possible German-Soviet agreement. The fact that nothing materialized as a result of these warnings may have contributed to the development of the so-called "cry wolf" syndrome among Western intelligence analysts and dulled their interest in subsequent warnings.

Though Stalin had dismissed Litvinov, he still pursued a cautious policy of maintaining only low-level contacts between the Soviet Union and Germany.

> Having made the first move (i.e., Litvinov's dismissal), Stalin expected Hitler to make the next. But Hitler, too, would not yet commit himself. Stalin now allowed only an obscure official, the Counsellor of the Russian Embassy in Berlin, Georgi Astakhov, to sound more freely the German Foreign Office and to drop meaningful remarks. In case of failure, Stalin could easily disavow Astakhov and make him a scapegoat. In his caution Stalin went so far as

to recall Merekalov, the Ambassador, from Berlin and to keep him away from his post throughout the spring and the summer. The Ambassador's prolonged absence was doubly useful: it burdened Moscow with less formal responsibility for Astakhov's contacts, and it served to camouflage their actual importance.[30]

On May 17, Astakhov met with Schnurre at the Foreign Office, on the pretext of discussing mutual trade problems, but again the conversation drifted quickly to political matters. According to Schnurre, Astakhov stated that

> there were no conflicts in foreign policy between Germany and the Soviet Union and that therefore there was no reason for any enmity between the two countries. It was true that in the Soviet Union there was a distinct feeling of being menaced by Germany. It would undoubtedly be possible to eliminate this feeling of being menaced and the distrust in Moscow. During this conversation he again mentioned the Treaty of Rapallo. In reply to my incidental question he commented on the Anglo-Soviet negotiations to the effect that, as they stood at the moment, the result desired by Britain would hardly materialize.
>
> To substantiate his opinion concerning the possibility of a change in German-Soviet relations, Astakhov repeatedly referred to Italy and stressed that the Duce had let it be known, even after the creation of the Axis, that there were no obstacles to a normal development of the political and economic relations between the Soviet Union and Italy.[31]

At this stage, the signals exchanged between the two governments became somewhat clouded. On May 20, 1939, Schulenburg met with Molotov. Molotov was friendly, but he firmly stated that economic negotiations could only be resumed after the necessary political bases had been established. He did not explain, even when Schulenburg insisted, what he meant by "political bases."[32] This was a new Russian approach in which the order of progress in the relations between the two states was the opposite of that which the Germans had in mind. The immediate German reaction was negative, and, on May 21, the German Foreign Office instructed Schulenburg to adopt a passive attitude and leave the initiative to the Russians.[33] This was the last time the German government would hesitate in its approach to the Soviet Union.

On May 23, Hitler met in secret with his military chiefs, and told them that any further success in Europe could only be achieved by the use of force. He had finally made up his mind to "attack Poland on the first suitable opportunity." He then spoke of the crucial need to isolate Poland, which raised the question of Russia's attitude. Hitler said that, "It is not ruled out that Russia might disinterest herself in the destruction of

Poland."[34] In fact, Hitler reached similar conclusions to those which had been expressed by Molotov in his May 20 meeting with Schulenburg. "Economic relations (Hitler said) are possible only if the political relations have improved."[35] Having reached the decision to attack Poland, Hitler's desire for an understanding with the Soviet Union now became urgent.

In the meantime, the Germans became worried about a potential agreement between Great Britain, France and the U.S.S.R. after Chamberlain announced in the House of Commons on May 24, 1939, that "an understanding with Russia had been reached on most important points and that an agreement would probably be signed soon."[36] While this statement was premature, and contradicted his earlier statement of May 17, it still had an important impact upon the Germans.[37] They had to find a way to simultaneously thwart a possible Anglo-Russian agreement and ease tensions with the Soviet Union; they had to further probe Russian intentions before beginning any serious negotiations. Approaching the Russians was a delicate matter. On May 25, State Secretary Weizsaecker made the following suggestions to Ribbentrop on this matter.

A German move in Moscow at the present moment is only of value if it is taken seriously by the Russians; otherwise it would be worthless or even dangerous: that is, Moscow would, inter alia, forthwith play it off against us in Tokyo.

The following might therefore be contemplated:

a) A conversation by Herr Hilger in the Russian Foreign Ministry in continuation of his normal conversations there. Herr Hilger could here refer to the preparatory economic work, at which he had been present in Berlin during recent weeks, and which was concerned with intensifying Russo-German trade. There would also be no objection to Herr Hilger mentioning quite casually of his own accord that he did not wish to touch on politics but that, nevertheless, he thought all possibilities remained open between Germany and Russia.

b) A request to the Italian Ambassador in Moscow, Signor Rosso, to make clear in a suitable manner German readiness for Russo-German contacts. Here Signor Rosso could refer to recent information about Ciano's visit to Berlin.

A request to this effect to Rosso by Count Schulenburg would naturally need to be supported by instructions from Rome to Rosso.

c) A conversation between the Foreign Minister and the Russian Ambassador, Merekalov, concerning the date of whose return enquiries have been made in Moscow. A reply to these is still outstanding.[38]

It is important to note that Weizsaecker emphasized the need to make all such approaches appear serious and credible to the Soviet government.

On May 26, Ribbentrop handed Hitler a copy of his new instructions to the German Ambassador in Moscow (telling him that under no circumstances should he leave *any* written documents with the Russians).[39] Schulenburg was instructed to tell Molotov that:

> . . . A real opposition of interests in foreign affairs does not exist between Germany and Soviet Russia . . . The time has come to consider a pacification and normalizing of German-Soviet Russian foreign relations . . . The chief factor in German foreign policy is the close relationship with Italy, now sealed by the Pact of Alliance. This Alliance, as is evident from the very nature of things, is not directed against Soviet Russia and . . . it is exclusively directed against the Anglo-French combination.
>
> If, however, against our wishes, it should come to hostilities with Poland, we are firmly convinced that even this need not in any way lead to a clash of interests with Soviet Russia. We can, even today, go so far as to say that when settling the German-Polish question— in whatever way this is done—we would take Russian interests into account as far as possible.[40]

Ribbentrop then added what he thought was an offer the Russians could not refuse:

> When the real balance of forces and interests are soberly weighed up, we are unable to see what could really induce Soviet Russia to play an active part in the game of the British policy of encirclement. From the reports available it seems to us that Moscow also realises that this would mean Soviet Russia undertaking a onesided liability without any really valuable British *quid pro quo* . . . Britain is by no means in a position to offer Soviet Russia a really valuable *quid pro quo*, no matter how the treaties may be formulated . . . We are therefore convinced that Britain will once more remain faithful to her traditional policy of letting other Powers pull her chestnuts out of the fire.[41]

Hitler, still under the impression made by Chamberlain's misleading statement, thought that Ribbentrop's instructions to the German Ambassador went too far and ordered them held up. Since he was afraid of a humiliating rejection of German offers, he advocated a more cautious approach.[42] (It should also be noted that another reason for Germany's hesitation during the end of May was the cool response of Germany's closest allies —Italy and Japan—to the proposed move in Moscow.[43])

The fear that one's approach to a former enemy will be rebuffed is a typical problem in surprise diplomacy. Finding a safe way to approach the prospective political partner is one of the most crucial steps in this lengthy process.

This was the problem that the Germans faced toward the end of May. But, fearing the possibility of an Anglo-Russian agreement, the Germans had to act quickly. They finally decided to approach the Russians at a lower level in Berlin, thus leaving themselves more leeway, rather than through a direct meeting with Molotov in Moscow. It was decided that Weizsaecker would meet Astakhov, the Soviet Chargé d'Affaires in Berlin, once again under the pretext of trade talks. "Weizsaecker would allude to Astakhov's past reference to the possibility of 'normalizing' Russo-German relations . . . and . . . develop the theme that although Germany saw no insurmountable obstacle to such a possibility, the *real intentions* of the Soviet government would have to be clarified in view of the negotiations which the Soviets were conducting with Great Britain."[44] Hitler approved this milder approach on May 29.[45] The carefully planned meeting took place on the next morning. Astakhov responded to the German "feelers" in a noncommittal but positive way by saying that Molotov had no "intention of barring the door against further Russo-German discussions."[46]

This meeting was the turning point in the series of moves that finally led to the Ribbentrop-Molotov agreement. The Soviet government remained very suspicious of German intentions, but they were not making any progress in their simultaneous conversations with the French and British, so they were certainly receptive to German proposals. On May 29, "Tass, the official Soviet news agency, published a communiqué denying a story which had appeared in an English publication that a German commercial delegation had been obliged to return to Germany because the Soviet government had rejected its proposals for Russo-German trade."[47] The emphatic Russian denial stressed the fact that no German trade delegation had ever reached Moscow. In *Germany and the Soviet Union 1939-1941*, Weinberg suggests that the Russians were signaling the Germans that a German trade delegation would be welcome in Moscow. On May 30, the German Economic Counselor in Moscow received instructions from Berlin to resume negotiations on economic matters.

On the following day, apparently in response to Weizsaecker's pressure, Molotov declared in the Supreme Soviet that:

> While conducting negotiations with Great Britain and France we by no means consider it necessary to renounce business relations with countries like Germany and Italy . . . At the beginning of 1939 the People's Commissariat of Foreign Trade was informed that a special German representative . . . was leaving for Moscow for the purpose of these negotiations. Subsequently, the negotiations were . . . discontinued on account of disagreement. To judge by certain signs, it is not precluded that the negotiations may be resumed.[48]

The favorable Soviet response meant that the two sides could begin negotiations. From June to mid-July 1939, the negotiations were conducted erratically, and little progress was made. On June 29, as a matter of fact, Hitler, for reasons which have never been fully explained, ordered a freeze of the economic conversations in Moscow. The contacts were nevertheless not entirely broken off. Most of the discussions took place in Moscow between low-level German officials and Anastas Mikoyan, the Soviet Foreign Trade Commissar. The main stumbling blocks were political, not economic. The Russians were afraid that the Germans simply wanted to put a "spoke in the wheel" of the Anglo-French-Russian negotiations, while the Germans were afraid that the Russians were only using them to obtain a better deal from the Western democracies. Both sides continued to scrutinize each other's intentions, using the progress (or lack of it) in their economic discussions as an indicator. This was the stage at which both sides experimented with the use of intermediaries. Astakhov hinted through Draganov, the Bulgarian Minister in Berlin (June 14), that the Soviet Union had three basic options available: (1) to reach an agreement with the British and French; (2) to delay the present negotiations; or, (3) to come to an agreement with Germany. He stated that Russia would prefer the third option; readiness on Germany's part to sign a non-aggression treaty would induce Russia to abandon her treaty negotiations with England.[49] Draganov indicated that the Soviet Union would prefer to reach an agreement with Germany because it refused to recognize Rumania's occupation of Bessarabia (which the British and French did). If the Germans were to recognize the Soviet Union's revisionistic goals a German-Soviet agreement would become possible. This Soviet trial balloon indicated for the first time what Molotov had in mind when he talked about the need to build a "political base." Astakhov added that, "If Germany would declare that she would not attack the Soviet Union or that she would conclude a non-aggression pact with her . . ."[50] Still apprehensive about the status of Anglo-Russian negotiations, Germany continued to hesitate.

At about the same time, the Germans approached the Soviet Union through Count Galeazzo Ciano, the Italian Foreign Minister. Ciano transmitted three main proposals to the Soviet Chargé d'Affaires in Rome.

(1) Germany would help to improve relations between Russia and Japan.

(2) Germany would sign a non-aggression pact with Russia, which would include a guarantee for the Baltic states.

(3) There would be a large-scale commercial agreement.

There is proof that these proposals did in fact reach Moscow, since

Molotov mentioned them in his talk with von der Schulenburg on 15th August.[51]

On the instructions of Ribbentrop, Schulenburg, while in Berlin, met with Astakhov on June 26 and assured him that Germany had no intention of attacking the U.S.S.R. He expressed Germany's wish to cooperate with the Soviet Union as long as the Soviets did not participate in any anti-German acts such as the resurrection of the Triple Entente. If political understanding between the two states was desired, he suggested that the Soviet government adopt a more definitive stance.[52] The Ambassador made similar overtures to Molotov in Moscow on June 28, but Molotov's reaction was cold and reserved. Stating that he disapproved of the Russian attitude, Hitler decided on June 29 to break off the talks. A complete breakdown in the economic and, by implication, the political negotiations appeared imminent. "By the end of June—beginning of July the game was interrupted. The first round has shown that the different interests of both great powers could not as yet be brought together under one roof. Both still believed that other alternatives were available."[53]

In the meantime, the Anglo-French-Soviet negotiations reached an impasse over the question of guarantees to Poland, Rumania, and the Baltic States. These countries had agreed to accept the Anglo-French guarantees but adamantly refused to consider the possibility of a Soviet guarantee. Molotov requested that the British government send Foreign Secretary Halifax to Moscow in order to break the deadlock, but the British only wanted to send a relatively low-level official from the Foreign Office. The appointment of such a low-ranking official was viewed negatively by the Soviet Union and taken as an indication of a half-hearted British attitude toward the formation of an anti-Hitler alliance.[54] Talks with the British official lasted from June 14 to June 29, and yielded no positive results. Instead of working on a final agreement, the British and French were only interested in having preliminary discussions on the possibility of reaching such an agreement in the future. The British and French attitudes only intensified Stalin's lack of faith in their intention to use force against Hitler, and thus created the conditions which finally pushed the Russians and Germans into each other's arms.

Regardless of the negotiations, Hitler continued making plans to attack Poland "on schedule." On June 15, he received General von Brauchitsch's plan for the army operations against Poland, and a week later General Keitel presented the preliminary timetable for "Case White." The German mobilization was scheduled to start on August 20.

The Germans decided to make what they presented as one last attempt to reach agreement with the Russians. On July 4, the Italian Ambassador in Moscow had a discussion with Vladimir Potemkin, the Soviet Deputy Commissar for Foreign Affairs, and told him (as instructed by Rome and

Berlin) of the German government's sincere desire to improve relations with the Soviet Union. Potemkin replied that good relations between the two states would have a stabilizing effect and help to safeguard peace. Four days later, new instructions were on their way to the German economic representative outlining more German concessions. The information was transmitted to Mikoyan on July 10, and the Russians spent more than a week deliberating over the next step.[55]

The next initiative came from the Russians, when Babarin, the Soviet trade representative in Berlin, met with Dr. Schnurre, the German Foreign Office expert on East European economic matters, on July 18 (July 22 is the date suggested by Weinberg). Babarin began with the general statement that the Soviet Union was interested in enlarging the scope of Soviet-German economic relations, and then presented a detailed memorandum setting forth the Soviet perception of the German concessions received on July 10, and called for a new trade agreement. He declared that if matters were clarified in a satisfactory way, he was empowered to sign such a trade agreement in Berlin.[56]

On the night of July 21, an announcement was made on Radio Moscow declaring the resumption of negotiations between Germany and the Soviet Union "with regard to trade and credit." A similar announcement was made in the Soviet press on the following day. The renewed economic talks lasted from July 22 until August 13.

On July 22, Weizsaecker wired Schulenburg in Moscow cancelling the freeze orders of June 29. The cable said that:

> . . . We will here [in Berlin] act in a markedly forthcoming manner, since a conclusion, and this at the earliest possible date, is desired for general reasons.
> As far as the purely political aspect of our conversations with the Russians is concerned, we regard the period of waiting stipulated for you in our telegram No. 134 as having expired. You are therefore empowered to pick up the threads again there, without in any way pressing the matter . . .[57]

In early June, the French government had received information on a conversation between Hitler and Generals Brauchitsch and Keitel, in which the two generals emphasized the need to secure Soviet neutrality before any war was begun. Daladier, the French Prime Minister, passed these reports on to the British in order to warn them against any further delays in their negotiations with the Soviet Union. The British viewed the reports with great suspicion. They felt that the French had a vested interest in the reports and they also feared that the reports had been disseminated by the Soviet Union in order to improve its own bargaining position. The British distrusted *all* information which they could not verify themselves—but no such reliable information was available. There was always the possibility that such information had been doctored by the French, the Germans, or the Russians.[58]

Yet intelligence information showing German-Soviet political collusion kept coming in. On June 2, agents of the Director of Naval Intelligence reported that Ribbentrop had sent "three of his best assistants to Moscow to help in the negotiations." In mid-June, Field Marshal Goering told the British Ambassador in Berlin, Sir Nevile Henderson, that "Germany and Russia will not always be enemies."[59]

In a frank reply to a British question, Astakhov himself said that economic talks between the Soviet Union and Germany were proceeding. He added that "they were of an informatory character only" and that no concrete proposals had yet been accepted.[60] But how could any intelligence analyst expect the Soviet Chargé d'Affaires in Berlin to be telling the truth? As often happens, the truth was the best lie.

On June 16, Sir Robert Vansittart, the Diplomatic Adviser to the Government, sent a report to Lord Halifax, the Foreign Secretary, stating that "the [German] military are delighted to have got Hitler on the path to an agreement with Soviet Russia and assure him that this prospect has frightened the British statesmen and made them uncertain again."[61] In the same report, he added that Hitler, in collusion with Russia, planned to surround Germany with "friendly or vassal states."

On June 15, Dr. Erich Kordt, Senior Counsellor in the Foreign Ministry, was sent to London by Weizsaecker—a lukewarm opponent of the Nazis—to warn the British of the possibility of a German-Soviet rapprochement. The next day, he passed the warning on to the British Foreign Office through a French journalist friend, who said that, "the Germans are seeking to reach an agreement with the Soviet and that only an Anglo-Russian agreement would be a strong deterrent to war."[62] But the British did not feel that they could trust the words of a German official. Throughout the month of June, rumors of an impending Russo-German alliance proliferated. Hence a special report was prepared by the Intelligence Department of the War Office, but there was no secret intelligence to corroborate these rumors.[63]

There was, however, contradictory evidence which indicated certain problems that the Germans and Russians were having in their relationship. The British Foreign Office possessed

> . . . at least one most secret report indicating that the Germans held the view that the elimination of Stalin was essential for their plans. Another most secret report from a reliable source on the Russian side stated that Stalin was very bitter on account of German intrigues in the Ukraine and that, so long as he remained, no question of a rapprochement was possible. A further report early in June

stated that although certain sections of influential Soviet opinion might be against active co-operation with the Western Powers, yet the feeling against Germany was still very bitter.[64]

Of course, there was a factual basis for the contradictory reports. While most of the German military and Foreign Ministry officials felt the urgent need for a treaty with the Soviet Union, Hitler continued to delay. When the "economic conversations which were supposed to be held in Moscow between Schnurre and Mikoyan were delayed by the Russians' insistence on ironing out existing differences, Hitler, as has been noted, lost his patience and ordered the discussions halted 29 June, 1939.[65] Faced with contradictory signals, the War Office chose to advocate a middle-of-the-road attitude.

> [There exists] . . . an atmosphere which, in spite of the personal antagonisms of Stalin and Hitler, may be conducive to the possibility of a future rapprochement, for there is much economic logic to recommend it and there are leading personages in both countries, but particularly in Germany, who desire to bring it about. Although there seem immense ideological difficulties, no opportunist change of policy is impossible to Stalin, and Hitler might well excuse himself by coming to an agreement with Soviet Russia while maintaining his antagonism to the world-revolution policy of the Comintern. The danger of such a rapprochement cannot therefore be discounted, and it is still wise to watch the situation very carefully.[66]

What the report ignored was the speed with which an economic agreement could be reached. The War Office experts did not consider that an economic agreement could serve as a pretext for the creation of the appropriate environment in which to rapidly conclude a political agreement. These rumors and signals, which began before the German-Soviet negotiations took a positive turn, should have been corroborated with signals related to Germany's preparations for war on Poland. It is not known whether such an analysis was ever made or whether adequate information on Germany's war preparations was available.

The Western democracies also assumed that if *they* were having difficult, painstakingly slow negotiations with the Russians, then the Germans must be having the same problems. However, British and French moral and treaty obligations to Eastern European states inhibited their political conversations with the Russians and precluded speedy decisions or meaningful concessions on their part. The Germans were not bound by such constraints. Their position was much less complex, because once they decided to act, they could instantly make the concessions necessary for reaching an agreement with the U.S.S.R.

On July 26, Schnurre, on the instructions of Ribbentrop, dined with Astakhov, the Soviet Chargé d'Affaires, and Babarin, the Soviet trade delegate. In the course of a comprehensive discussion of political and economic problems, both Astakhov and Babarin declared that a Soviet-German political rapprochement corresponded with the vital interests of both countries. In Moscow, Astakhov said, they had thus far felt very threatened by Germany's foreign policy and were naturally suspicious of German intentions. Therefore, the process of rapprochement would have to take place gradually in order to establish mutual trust. Schnurre replied by saying that

> . . . German policy in the East had taken an entirely different course in the meantime. On our part there could be no question of menacing the Soviet Union . . . German policy was aimed against Britain. That was the decisive factor. I could imagine a far-reaching arrangement of mutual interests with due consideration for vital Russian problems. However, this possibility would be barred the moment the Soviet Union, by signing a treaty, aligned itself with Britain against Germany . . . The time was opportune now but would no longer be so after the conclusion of a pact with London . . .What could Britain offer Russia? At best participation in a European war and the hostility of Germany . . . What could we offer as against this? Neutrality and keeping out of a possible European conflict and, if Moscow wished, a German-Russian understanding on mutual interests which, just as in former times, would work out to the advantage of both countries . . . Controversial problems of foreign policy . . . did not in my opinion exist anywhere along the line from the Baltic Sea to the Black Sea and to the Far East. In addition, despite all the divergencies in philosophies of life (*Weltanschauung*) there was *one* thing common to the ideology of Germany, Italy and the Soviet Union: opposition to the capitalist democracies.[67]

Astakhov promised to immediately report the contents of the conversation to Moscow and asked whether similar views were held by higher German representatives. Schnurre replied in the affirmative. The Germans were eager to know the Soviet reaction to these feelers. Weizsaecker sent Ambassador Schulenburg in Moscow a copy of Schnurre's report and a special dispatch that included a clear reference to the possibility of a German-Soviet partition of Poland.

> It would be important for us to know whether the remarks made to Astakhov and Babarin have met with any response in Moscow. If you see an opportunity of arranging a further conversation with Molotov, please sound him out on the same lines. If this results in Molotov abandoning the reserve he has so far maintained you could go a step further in your exposition and put into a little more

concrete form what is expressed in general terms in the [Schnurre] memorandum. This applies in particular to the Polish question. We would be prepared, however the Polish question may develop, whether peacefully as we desire, or in some other way that is forced upon us, to safeguard all Soviet interests. . . . In the Baltic question too, if the talks took a positive course, the idea could be advanced of so adjusting our attitude to the Baltic states as to respect vital Soviet interests in the Baltic sea.[68]

The Germans were impatient (though they tried unsuccessfully to hide their haste from the Russians) not only because they feared that some progress was being made in the Anglo-French-Russian talks, but because Hitler had set September 1 as the last date for his planned invasion of Poland. On July 23, the British and French finally acquiesced to the Russian demands to start their military talks in Moscow the following month.

On August 2, Ribbentrop held a conversation with Astakhov on the trade talks—the same topic that Schnurre and Astakhov had discussed over dinner on July 26. Confirming Schnurre's offers, Ribbentrop presented the German view that political agreements could also be reached if certain conditions were fulfilled. He promised to present more concrete terms for a political agreement upon receiving an official, positive indication of commitment from the Soviet Union. On August 3, Ribbentrop cabled a summary of his discussion with Astakhov to Schulenburg in Moscow who was supposed to meet Molotov later the same day.

Yesterday I had a lengthy conversation with Astakhov, on which a telegram follows.

I expressed the *German* wish for remolding German-Russian relations and stated that from the Baltic to the Black Sea there was no problem which could not be solved to our mutual satisfaction. In response to Astakhov's desire for more concrete conversations on topical questions . . . I declared myself ready for such conversations if the Soviet Government would inform me through Astakhov that they also desired to place German-Russian relations on a new and definite basis.[69]

An hour later Weizsaecker sent an additional cable to Schulenburg:

In view of the political situation and in the interests of speed, we are anxious, without prejudice to your conversation with Molotov today, to continue in more concrete terms in Berlin the conversations on harmonizing German-Soviet intentions. To this end Schnurre will receive Astakhov today and will tell him that we would be ready for a continuation on more concrete lines . . . We would propose . . . that Astakhov obtain instructions from Moscow. We should then be prepared to speak quite concretely concerning problems of possible interest to the Soviet Union.[70]

That same day, even before Schulenburg's meeting with Molotov, Schnurre met once again with Astakhov in Berlin and urged speed in the economic negotiations so that a political agreement could quickly follow. Astakhov stated that he had received a rather unfavorable answer from Molotov in response to the German proposals. While Moscow wanted to improve its relationship with Germany "so far nothing concrete was known of Germany's attitude." A few hours later, Molotov reiterated this answer to Schulenburg. He implied that Russia was interested in coming to an understanding with Germany, but that Germany's actions (i.e., Germany's adherence to the Anti-Comintern Pact, which also implied Japan's support of Germany against Russia, and the exclusion of Russia from the Munich agreements) could only cause the Soviet Union to be suspicious. The Russians, Molotov said, would not commit themselves until they had evidence that the German attitude had indeed changed.[71] The Russians were perhaps stalling until they could determine the results of the military staff conversations to be held with the French and British later that month. Or, having noted Germany's ill-disguised desire to reach a speedy agreement, they may have hoped to extract a few more concessions from the Germans. Astakhov met with Schnurre on August 10, and by way of answering Ribbentrop's proposals of August 2, he used the occasion to define the major problems between the U.S.S.R. and Germany which required clarification. On August 12, Astakhov again met with Schnurre and suggested that the questions which were raised on the tenth could be the subject of formal political discussion in Moscow.[72] He did add, however, that Molotov had emphasized the fact that the discussions must be "undertaken *only* by degrees." The Germans were quick to agree, thus clearing the way for the commencement of political negotiations.

September 1 had been set as the date for the attack on Poland.[73] Time was running out for the Germans. They had to make swift, radical changes in their relationship with the U.S.S.R.—not changes "by degrees." Meanwhile, the Soviet government did its best to intensify German fears.

> . . . By inviting the British and French Governments to send military missions to Moscow, Stalin secured another advantage. It allowed him to exert stronger pressure on the German leaders, or, to put it bluntly, to "blackmail" them the more effectively. Stalin could thus raise the price of his co-operation even higher.[74]

On August 14, the German Foreign Office, on the instructions of Ribbentrop, sent two important telegrams to Ambassador von der Schulenburg in Moscow. The first, and less important one, urged him to do his best to counter any arguments in favor of a Russian-English agreement. He was to argue that the British were militarily too weak to wage land warfare on any meaningful scale against Germany, and that therefore the Russians would ultimately bear the burden of such an alliance.[75] These arguments did not fall on deaf ears, as the Russians (especially Stalin) had reached similar conclusions. In August 1942 Stalin told Churchill that

> We formed the impression that the British and French Governments were not resolved to go to war if Poland were attacked, but that they hoped the diplomatic line-up of Britain, France and Russia would deter Hitler. We were sure it would not. "How many divisions," Stalin had asked, "will France send against Germany on mobilization?" The answer was: "About a hundred." He then asked: "How many will England send?" The answer was: "Two, and two more later." "Ah, two, and two more later," Stalin had repeated. "Do you know," he asked, "how many divisions we shall have to put on the Russian front if we go to war with Germany?" There was a pause. "More than three hundred."[76]

The second, more important telegram sent on the 14th included a German counteroffer which the Russians could not resist. Apparently written by Hitler and Ribbentrop the day before, the detailed telegram explicitly instructed Schulenburg to read the telegram *verbatim* to Molotov, and not, under any circumstances, to give it to anyone in writing:

> There exist no real conflicts of interests between Germany and Russia . . . There is no doubt that German-Russian policy today has come to an *historic turning point*. The decisions with respect to policy to be made in the immediate future in Berlin and Moscow will be of decisive importance for the development of relations between the German and Russian peoples for generations . . . The crisis which has been produced in German-Polish relations by English policy, as well as English agitation for war and the attempts at an alliance which are bound up with that policy, *make a speedy clarification of German-Russian relations* necessary. Otherwise matters might . . . take a turn which would deprive both Governments of the possibility of *restoring German-Russian friendship and in due course clarifying jointly territorial questions in Eastern Europe.* The leadership of both countries, therefore, should not allow the situation to drift, but should take action at the proper time. It would be fatal if, through mutual ignorance of views and intentions, the two peoples should finally drift apart.
>
> As we have been informed, the Soviet Government also feel the desire for a clarification of German-Russian relations. Since, however, according to previous experience this clarification can be

achieved only slowly through the usual diplomatic channels, I am prepared to make a short visit to Moscow in order, in the name of the Fuehrer, to set forth the Fuehrer's views to M. Stalin. In my view, only through such a direct discussion can a change be brought about, and it should not be impossible thereby to lay the foundations for a final settlement of German-Russian relations.[77] (Emphasis added.)

Ribbentrop, unlike the British Foreign Secretary, was more than willing to go to Moscow on the condition that he could have "a detailed discussion" with Stalin. By August 15, German preparations for war were advancing rapidly. The "Party Rally of Peace" to be held in Nuremberg in September was secretly cancelled; soldiers and railroads were mobilized; and the Navy reported that in addition to 21 submarines its pocket battleships *Graf Spee* and *Deutschland* were prepared to move to their stations in the Atlantic.[78] On the same day, Weizsaecker dropped hints to both the British and French Ambassadors in Berlin about the possible development of a German-Russian coordinated policy concerning Poland.

At 8 that evening Schulenburg, as ordered, delivered to Molotov the German message of August 14th. This time Molotov was more responsive. He inquired as to the degree of German interest in a mutual non-aggression pact, emphasizing that such an agreement was possible only upon the fulfillment of certain conditions. These conditions included: (1) German willingness to pressure Japan to improve its relations with Russia and (2) the possibility of what Molotov euphemistically referred to as a "joint guarantee of the Baltic States" by the U.S.S.R. and Germany. Molotov was, as usual, in no particular hurry, and indicated that the negotiating process must be gradual if it was to yield tangible results. From the German point of view, the Russian response was favorable, but the pace was frustratingly slow. Schulenburg's report on his discussion with Molotov reached Ribbentrop (and Hitler) early on August 16.[79]

The U.S. State Department was well informed on the German-Soviet negotiations, and received immediate reports on events taking place in both Moscow and Berlin. The information was said to come from "certain members" of the German Embassy in Moscow. On August 16, only a day after the talks took place, Ambassador Laurence Steinhardt sent a report to Washington on the Schulenburg-Molotov discussions, including information on Russia's offer to sign a non-aggression pact. The Americans promptly forwarded this piece of information to the British. This was intelligence that proved to be more accurate than anything made available to the British government during that period.

Upon receiving the information, Sir Ronald Lindsay, the British Ambassador in Washington, sent it in an enciphered telegram to London's Foreign Office Communications Department at 9 p.m. on August 17. It was received in London the following morning at 9:30, but was not immediately deciphered. In fact, the telegram reached the Central Department only five days later, on August 22, and was mentioned for the first time at the Cabinet meeting at 3 p.m. the same day. How can this delay be explained? Among the explanations offered is that the month of August 1939 was a time of acute crisis in Europe. "The volume of telegraphic traffic through the Foreign Office was increasing to the extent of causing 'serious delays' to occur. Telegrams from Washington would not have had the highest priority."[80] According to Shirer's version of the incident in *The Collapse of the Third Republic* (p. 462), Ambassador Lindsay, instead of urgently cabling London, sent the information by air mail which was much slower. The dispatch was therefore only received in London on August 22. In *1939: The Making of the Second World War*, Aster states that Lindsay did cable this information while a letter was also sent by air mail. The letter sent by air (due to arrive on August 20) only contained information on the source of the news in the telegram. For reasons of secrecy, Undersecretary Sumner Welles had asked the British Ambassador not to include the source (Steinhardt) in the cable. It was therefore included in the letter. This sequence of events was typical of crisis situations—the overflow of coded messages during crises creates bottlenecks which delay the deciphering process. In this case, the telegram was deciphered too late to have a serious impact on the government's decisions. (A similar well-known case occurred in the last days before the Japanese attack on Pearl Harbor when information of the greatest national importance was not deciphered in time because of "bottlenecks" and low priority.)[81]

A second, though less convincing, explanation for the four-day delay in the deciphering of this important message is that one of the most important cipher clerks at the Communications Department of the Foreign Office was a Soviet spy who purposely delayed passing on the contents of the cable. This interpretation is based on the fact that a cipher clerk by the name of Captain John Herbert King was arrested on September 27, 1939, and sentenced to 10 years imprisonment on October 18.[82] This explanation is speculative at best. The "bottleneck" explanation seems more credible since it is based on similar occurrences during other crises.

The Germans accepted all of Molotov's suggestions without reservation, but pressed for an immediate acceleration of the negotiations. By mid-day of August 16, the German Foreign Office had sent an urgent message to Schulenburg in Moscow instructing him to request another interview with Molotov, and then wait for further orders. Ribbentrop's instructions arrived a few hours later—Schulenburg was to inform

Molotov that the German government had, in essence, accepted all of his suggestions.

> . . . Germany is prepared to conclude a non-aggression pact with the Soviet Union and, if the Soviet Government so desire, one which would be undenounceable for a term of twenty-five years. Further, Germany is ready to guarantee the Baltic States jointly with the Soviet Union. Finally, it is thoroughly in accord with the German position, and Germany is prepared, to exercise influence for an improvement and consolidation of Russian-Japanese relations.
>
> The Fuehrer is of the opinion that, in view of the present situation, and of the possibility of the occurrence, any day, of serious events (please at this point explain to M. Molotov that Germany is determined not to endure Polish provocation indefinitely), a basic and rapid clarification of German-Russian relations and of each country's attitude to the questions of the moment is desirable. For these reasons I am prepared to come by aeroplane to Moscow at any time after Friday, August 18, to deal, on the basis of full powers from the Fuehrer, with the entire complex of German-Russian questions, and, if the occasion arises, to sign the appropriate treaties.
>
> Annex: I request that you again read these instructions word for word to M[olotov] and ask for the views of the Russian Government and of M. Stalin immediately. Entirely confidentially, it is added for your guidance that it would be of very special interest to us if my Moscow trip could take place at the end of this week or the beginning of next week.[83]

The telegram arrived at the German embassy at 1:00 a.m. on the 17th, and early that day, Schulenburg requested an interview with Molotov. The interview took place on the same day at 8 p.m. In terms of bargaining, the German need for speedy negotiations made them vulnerable to the Russians. Molotov opened the interview with the presentation of a written reply to the previous German suggestions. Beginning on the now familiar note of suspicion, it stated that "the Soviet Government, up till very recently, have proceeded on the assumption that the German Government are seeking an occasion for clashes with the Soviet Union, are preparing themselves for such clashes . . . Not to mention the fact that the German Government, by means of the so-called Anti-Comintern Pact, were endeavouring to create, and have created, the united front of a number of States against the Soviet Union. . . ."[84] The note continued that the U.S.S.R. welcomed a serious change in the political attitude of Germany. It repeated that Russo-German relations must be improved by careful steps, of which the first was to be the completion of a trade and credit agreement. Only then could the two parties implement the second step and conclude a non-aggression or neutrality pact. The second step would include "a special protocol defining the interests of the contracting parties in this or that question of foreign policy"—a hint at the possible division of Eastern Europe. As far as Ribbentrop's desire to come immediately to Moscow was concerned, Molotov said that this proved the seriousness of German intent, and was in marked contrast to the British refusal to send a high-level official to Moscow. He then added that such an important journey could not take place immediately because it required thorough preparation.[85]

Late on the 18th, Ribbentrop sent another most urgent telegram to Schulenburg, who received it early the next morning. It instructed him to relay the following message to Molotov as soon as possible.

> We, too, under normal circumstances, would naturally be ready to pursue a realignment of German-Russian relations further through diplomatic channels, and to carry it out in the customary way. But the present unusual situation makes it necessary, in the opinion of the Fuehrer, to employ a different method which would lead to quick results. German-Polish relations are becoming more acute from day to day. . . . The Fuehrer considers it necessary that we be not taken by surprise by the outbreak of a German-Polish conflict while we are striving for a clarification of German-Russian relations. He therefore considers a previous clarification necessary, if only to be able to take into account Russian interests in case of such a conflict. . . .
>
> We have in mind here the following . . . points, which I would ask you to read to M. M[olotov], but not to hand to him.
>
> Article 1. The German Reich and the U.S.S.R. will in no event resort to war, or to any other use of force, with respect to each other.
>
> Article 2. This treaty shall enter into force immediately upon signature, and shall be valid and not liable to denunciation thereafter for a term of twenty-five years.[86]

Schulenburg was to tell Molotov that the trade and credit talks had been successfully concluded the same day (August 18) in Berlin, and the time had arrived to move on to the second step. He added that negotiations in Moscow would enable him to more fully "take Russian wishes into account."

> Please state . . . that I should also be in a position to sign a special protocol regulating the interests of both parties in questions of foreign policy of one kind or another; for instance, the settlement of spheres of interest in the Baltic area. . . . Such a settlement . . . will only be possible . . . at an oral discussion.
>
> Please emphasize, in this connection, that German foreign policy has today reached an historic turning-point. This time, please

conduct the conversation, except for the above treaty articles, not in the form of reading out these instructions, but by pressing emphatically, in the sense of the foregoing statements, for a rapid realization of my journey, and by opposing appropriately any fresh Russian objections. . . . You must keep in mind the decisive fact that an early outbreak of open German-Polish conflict is probable, and that we, therefore, have the greatest interest in having my visit to Moscow take place immediately.[87]

August 19 was the day on which all German warships and submarines had to sail if they were to be at their battle stations by late August, the target date for the attack on Poland. The army would have to make immediate preparations for the invasion.[88] The ceremony for signing the trade agreement was planned for mid-day on August 19, but the Russian delegates asked for a delay, telling the Germans they had to get further instructions from Moscow. The Germans were naturally worried about the reasons for the delay. Ribbentrop wired Schulenburg to report any information he could get concerning Russian intentions. The only positive signal was an announcement by Tass concerning the differences of opinion between the Russian and the Anglo-French military delegations. There was, therefore, still a chance for a Soviet-German pact.[89]

At 7:10 p.m. on August 19 the Germans received their answer.

SECRET
MOST URGENT

The Soviet Government agree to the Reich Foreign Minister's coming to Moscow one week after the announcement of the signature of the economic agreement. Molotov stated that, if the conclusion of the economic agreement is made public tomorrow, the Reich Foreign Minister could arrive in Moscow on August 26 or 27.

Molotov handed to me a draft of a non-aggression pact.

A detailed account of the two conversations I had with Molotov today, as well as the text of the Soviet draft, follows by telegram at once.

SCHULENBURG[90]

On the 19th, Schulenburg had met with Molotov twice. The first meeting, which took place at 2 p.m., was brief and not particularly successful. Molotov insisted that Ribbentrop's offer to visit Moscow was premature—such an important trip required preparation. The issues to be covered in the protocol had to be precisely stated by Germany and finally, the trade and credit agreement had to be signed, published, and achieve its effect abroad before Ribbentrop's visit could be considered. The German Ambassador's protests were ignored.

At 4:30 p.m. Schulenburg was suddenly asked to meet with Molotov again. The Soviet government had reconsidered the German suggestions and was now ready to invite Ribbentrop to Moscow on either August 26 or 27, if the trade agreement was signed and published the next day (August 20). Molotov still would not agree to set an earlier date for Ribbentrop's visit to Moscow. He did, however, hand Schulenburg the Soviet government's draft of the proposed non-aggression treaty.[91]

The sudden change in the Russian position must have reflected Stalin's change of attitude. Stalin must have decided to sign a non-aggression treaty with Germany sometime during the afternoon of August 19, for he reported his decision to the Politburo later the same day.

The Germans now had no choice but to speed up the pace of negotiations—the timetable for the attack on Poland would have to be scrapped if Ribbentrop could not visit Moscow well before August 26. (At that time, August 26 was the scheduled date for the attack on Poland.) On August 19, in the meantime, German pocket battleships and submarines actually sailed to their battle stations in the Atlantic. Clearing the way for a political agreement, the German-Soviet trade agreement was hastily signed early on the 20th (2 a.m.), although it was dated the 19th. Many of the details were not fully settled, but its immediate importance, in any case, was political—not commercial.

At this stage, Hitler decided to intervene personally. He sent a message to Stalin asking to receive his Foreign Minister in Moscow at once. His telegram was sent on Sunday, August 20, at 6:45 p.m., only 12 hours after Schulenburg's report of his second meeting with Molotov had been received in Berlin.

> *M. Stalin, Moscow.*   1) I sincerely welcome the signing of the new German-Soviet Commercial Agreement as the first step in the reshaping of German-Soviet relations.
>
> 2) The conclusion of a non-aggression pact with the Soviet Union means to me the establishment of German policy for a long time. Germany thereby resumes a political course that was beneficial to both States during bygone centuries. The Government of the Reich are therefore resolved in such a case to accept all the consequences of such a far-reaching change.
>
> 3) I accept the draft of the non-aggression pact that your Foreign Minister, M. Molotov, handed over, but consider it urgently necessary to clarify the questions connected with it as soon as possible.
>
> 4) The substance of the supplementary protocol desired by the Government of the Soviet Union can, I am convinced, be clarified in the shortest possible time if a responsible German statesman can come to Moscow himself to negotiate . . .
>
> 5) The tension between Germany and Poland has become intolerable. Polish demeanour toward a great Power is such that a crisis may arise any day. Germany is at any rate determined . . . to look after the interests of the Reich with all the means at her disposal.

6) In my opinion, it is desirable . . . not to lose any time. I therefore again propose that you receive my Foreign Minister on Tuesday, August 22, but at the latest on Wednesday, August 23. The Reich Foreign Minister has the fullest powers to draw up and sign the non-aggression pact as well as the protocol. A longer stay by the Reich Foreign Minister in Moscow than one to two days at most is impossible in view of the international situation. I should be glad to receive your early answer. *Adolf Hitler.*[92]

While trying to reach an agreement with the Soviet Union, Germany was simultaneously pressuring the Polish government for concessions regarding Danzig. The mounting pressures should have alerted the Western democracies to the events of the following day.

With great apprehension, the Germans waited 24 hours for Stalin's answer. Stalin's positive answer was received with considerable relief in Berlin on August 21, at 9:35 p.m.

August 21, 1939.   To the Chancellor of the German Reich, Herr A. Hitler. I thank you for the letter. I hope that the German-Soviet non-aggression pact will bring about a decided turn for the better in the political relations between our countries.

The peoples of our countries need peaceful relations with each other. The assent of the German Government to the conclusion of a non-aggression pact provides the foundation for eliminating the political tension and for the establishment of peace and collaboration between our countries.

The Soviet Government have instructed me to inform you that they agree to Herr von Ribbentrop's arriving in Moscow on August 23.   *J. Stalin.*[93]

Thus, Stalin's favorable response secured Russian neutrality and removed the last obstacle to Germany's attack on Poland.

Hitler received Stalin's answer at 10:30 p.m. and at 11 p.m. German radio stations interrupted their regular programming to announce that "The Reich government and the Soviet Union have agreed to conclude a pact of non-aggression with each other. The Reich Minister for Foreign Affairs will arrive in Moscow on Wednesday, August 23, for the conclusion of the negotiations." The Russians announced Ribbentrop's visit and their intention to sign a treaty with Germany in the morning newspapers on August 22.[94]

On the same day, Hitler gathered his military commanders at Obersalzberg and told them that the war against Poland would start on the 26th. He then analyzed the Russian change of attitude toward Germany and the major characteristics of the negotiations conducted with Russia.

The enemy had another hope, that Russia would become our enemy after the conquest of Poland. The enemy did not reckon with my great strength of purpose. Our enemies are small fry. I saw them in Munich.

I was convinced that Stalin would never accept the English offer. Russia has no interest in preserving Poland, and Stalin knows that it would mean the end of his regime, no matter whether his soldiers emerged from a war victorious or vanquished. *Litvinov's replacement was decisive. I brought about the change toward Russia gradually. In connection with the commercial treaty we got into political conversations.* Proposal for a non-aggression pact. Then came a comprehensive proposal from Russia. Four days ago I took a special step, which led to Russia replying yesterday that she is prepared to sign. Personal contact with Stalin is established. The day after tomorrow von Ribbentrop will conclude the treaty. Now Poland is in the position in which I wanted her.

We need not be afraid of a blockade. The East will supply us with grain, cattle, coal, lead and zinc.

Today's announcement of the non-aggression pact with Russia came as a bombshell. The consequences cannot be foreseen . . . The effect on Poland will be tremendous.[95] (Emphasis added.)

The second stage in the process of "surprise diplomacy" between Germany and Russia was thus concluded with the announcement of their intention to sign a non-aggression pact.

The process is best summarized in the words of Weizsaecker's August 22 telegram to all the important German missions abroad.

For some months the normalization and improvement of relations between Germany and the Soviet Union have been prepared by slow and steady development. The starting-point was the resumption of the economic and credit negotiations, leading to an agreement on August 19, which placed German-Soviet trade on a broader and deeper foundation. Concurrently with these negotiations, political soundings were taken which led in recent weeks to an intensive exchange of views between Berlin and Moscow. For some months this trend was expressed in the moderate tone of the German press. Outward signs of it were, in particular, the presence of the Soviet Chargé d'Affaires at the "Day of German Art" in Munich, the sending of an official German delegation to the Agricultural Exhibition in Moscow, and the official attendance of members of the Soviet Embassy and Trade Delegation here at the Eastern Fair in Koenigsberg.[96]

STAGE 3. *August 22-23: Third Parties Are Surprised.*
The Signing of the German-Soviet
Non-Aggression Pact in Moscow

The third stage follows in the wake of the "diplomatic surprise." This is the stage of implementation for the initiating sides—and the stage of confusion and shock for the surprised parties. The unexpected shift in policy by the parties involved is, at this point, translated into some form of action. It can be a symbolic action, such as an exchange of state visits, or a more concrete move such as a specific agreement concerning the political, economic, or military interests of both states; a joint declaration; mutual diplomatic recognition and the establishment of normal diplomatic connections, and so on. The impact of the results of surprise can be of immediate practical consequences or it can be deferred until further progress is made.

In Churchill's words, "The sinister news broke upon the world like an explosion."[97] The British and French were completely caught by surprise despite the signals and information they had received.[98] On the evening of August 22 Ribbentrop left for Moscow via Koenigsberg. The same evening the British had a minor surprise of their own for Hitler. The British Ambassador in Berlin informed State Secretary Weizsaecker by telephone of the contents of a message sent by Chamberlain to Hitler. Chamberlain clearly stated that England would fulfill her obligations to Poland (i.e., go to war if necessary), regardless of what agreements the Germans might sign with the Soviet Union. The British government irrevocably committed itself to the Poles. The Ambassador delivered the message in person to Hitler on the following day.

> . . . Apparently the announcement of a German-Soviet Agreement is taken in some quarters in Berlin to indicate that intervention by Great Britain on behalf of Poland is no longer a contingency that need be reckoned with. No greater mistake could be made. Whatever may prove to be the nature of the German-Soviet Agreement, it cannot alter Great Britain's obligation to Poland . . .
>
> It has been alleged that, if His Majesty's Government had made their position more clear in 1914, the great catastrophe would have been avoided. Whether or not there is any force in that allegation, His Majesty's Government are resolved that on this occasion there shall be no such tragic misunderstanding.
>
> If the case should arise, they are resolved, and prepared, to employ without delay all the forces at their command, and it is impossible to foresee the end of hostilities once engaged . . .[99]

Chamberlain's message came as a complete surprise to Hitler. Britain's firm commitment stood in contrast to the entire history of its appeasement of Hitler. Hitler was convinced that the British and French would not fight. A few days earlier (August 14) during a military conference at Obersalzberg, he had decided that "England, unlike 1914, will not allow herself to blunder into a war lasting for years . . . What should England fight for? You don't get yourself killed for an ally . . . The men of Munich will not take the risk . . . while England may talk big, even recall her Ambassador, perhaps put a complete embargo on trade, she is sure not to resort to armed intervention in the conflict."[100] In his speech to his military commanders at Obersalzberg on August 22 he proved to his satisfaction that England was too weak to fight, and too vulnerable to air attacks. "England does not want the conflict to break out for two or three years . . . England does not really want to support Poland . . . she will not take any risks."[101] Chamberlain had now upset Hitler's calculations and perceptions. He was shaken, but after delaying his decision to go to war by a few days, he decided to go ahead as planned anyway. For the second time in the 20th century, the British had committed themselves too late to prevent war.

It is interesting to note that Goering's *Forschungsamt*, intercepting British diplomatic communications, warned Hitler that the British would honor their obligations to Poland and would declare war on Germany. D. C. Watt, in his Introduction to David Irving's book, *Breach of Security*, explains why Hitler disregarded these warnings, and comments on Hitler's reluctance to listen to and consider intelligence reports that contradicted his own plans.

> Hitler completely rejected the 'pessimistic material of the *Forschungsamt*,' showing the probability of British and French intervention in a German-Polish conflict as it 'disturbed the formation of his intuition.' He certainly took little or no interest in their activities or in following up any of the information that reached him from them. The truth is probably that in this period he was so set on war with Poland that he was not prepared to listen to anything that might controvert his decision. His distrust of professional expertise, so apparent in his general attitude to his professional military and diplomatic advisers, would have reinforced him in this rejection, which was supported by von Ribbentrop's continual insistence that Britain and France were bluffing. Thus signs of a weakening in French morale which the *Forschungsamt* claimed to have detected in conversations between the French Embassy and Paris, and of Polish dilatoriness detected in similar telephone communications between Warsaw and the Polish Embassy in Berlin probably were used to confirm his prejudices, while the other evidence was dismissed. He was amply confirmed in his prejudices by von Ribbentrop, whose antipathy to Goering and to the office whose output infringed his monopoly as Foreign Minister has already been mentioned.

When Hitler received the British ultimatum on September 3, his surprise was not the result of any failure on the part of professional German intelligence, just as it was not for lack of any official warning from the British government, or his own Foreign Ministry officials or his Italian allies. He did not believe because his intuition was otherwise, and Ribbentrop, his jackal, feared to lose position if he gave the lie to his master. (pp. 39-40.) See also David Irving, *The War Path*, pp. 243-244.*

In the meantime the German delegation headed by Ribbentrop arrived in Moscow at noon on August 23 and was received in the Kremlin at 3:30 p.m. To their surprise, the Germans found that Stalin himself, in addition to Molotov, was present at the discussions. Stalin's presence at such an early stage of the meetings was not expected, but it helped the talks to proceed more rapidly. The non-aggression pact itself posed only minor problems since Hitler had already accepted the greater part of the preliminary draft submitted by the Russians. Stalin agreed to shorten the proposed duration of the treaty from 25 to 10 years. He also agreed to have the pact come into force, with no further ratification necessary, as soon as it had been signed by both parties. All major issues were settled within three hours. At a second meeting later the same day, they agreed on a secret protocol which divided Eastern Europe and the Baltic States into "two spheres of interests." The treaty itself was signed in the early hours of August 24, but was dated the previous day.[102] It is interesting to note that even with such a radical and surprising shift in Soviet foreign policy, Ribbentrop could not convince Stalin to sign a communiqué or a preamble to the treaty warmly praising the new German-Soviet friendship. Even Machiavellian cynical realpolitik has its limits. Stalin said that "The Soviet Government could not suddenly present to the public assurances of friendship after they had been covered with pails of manure by the Nazi Government for six years."[103]

ANALYSIS

As we have seen, from March 1939 onwards the Western democracies received a large number of warnings concerning the ongoing negotiations. The following is a partial list of those signals and warnings.

General Ludwig Beck and Colonel Hans Oster of the German Army conveyed warnings to the London *News Chronicle*'s Berlin correspondent. The correspondent met with Foreign Office officials in London on March 29. Later, he also met with Sir Alexander Cadogan, the Permanent Undersecretary for Foreign Affairs, Lord Halifax, and Neville Chamberlain and reported Germany's intention to attack Poland.[104]

---

* Weizsaecker, in his memoirs, refers to the work of the *Forschungsamt* as follows: "The art of decoding enciphered text had been brought to a high degree of perfection in the Third Reich. Under the supreme direction of Goering this had been brought to such a pitch that we could read half the telegrams sent to foreign diplomats in Berlin." *Memoirs of Ernst von Weizsaecker*, p. 165.

On April 28, when Hitler delivered his major speech to the Reichstag, he omitted his usual abuse of Bolshevik Russia. A State Department official, in a conversation with a member of the British Embassy in Washington, made a point of drawing attention to this omission.

During April and May the American press was full of sensational disclosures by W. G. Krivitsky, a former Chief of Soviet Military Intelligence in Western Europe, who had defected in October 1937. Krivitsky gave details, later proved to be accurate, of Stalin's attempts since 1934 to make a deal with Hitler. Despite continued rebuffs and in order to keep the U.S.S.R. out of a war, Krivitsky claimed, Stalin was still searching for terms which were acceptable to Hitler. (The British, who had treated these revelations with skepticism, had no idea of the real earlier identity of "Krivitsky," though they received, on July 14, a hint from a State Department official.)[105]

In early May the Polish Ambassador in Budapest was warned by the Hungarian Intelligence (which had tenuous connections with the *Abwehr*) of Soviet-German contacts concerning a new partition of Poland.[106]

On May 7, General Karl Bodenschatz, Goering's liaison officer with Hitler, on Goering's orders, leaked the possibility of a Russo-German rapprochement to the French Embassy in Berlin (and to the Polish Embassy on May 27).

Also on May 7, the French Ambassador in Berlin, Robert Coulondre, reported at length to the French government on Hitler's determination to secure Danzig and reunite East Prussia with the Reich. Until the right moment arrived, he said, Hitler would seek an agreement with the Soviet Union in order to prevent intervention by the Western Powers and perhaps effect a fourth partition of Poland.[107]

On May 29, General Bodenschatz invited the Polish Military Attaché Szymanski and told him that Hitler was seeking an alliance with the Soviet Union.[108]

On June 1, Ambassador Coulondre warned his government of a possible German-Soviet rapprochement. Reporting information obtained from a "reliable intermediary," he said that the German Army High Command was of the opinion that a war against Poland could *only* be won if Russia's neutrality had been secured.[109]

In early June the Japanese Military Attaché in Warsaw asked Colonel Josef Smolenski, the Chief of Polish Intelligence, to act as an intermediary between the German military and Japan because Japan did not look with favor on the growing German-Soviet contacts. This request on the part of the Japanese—certainly coordinated with Tokyo—appears to be extremely naive given the fact that Poland was the major target of the German-Soviet contacts!

During the first week of June, Daladier, the French Prime Minister, transmitted Coulondre's warning to Sir Eric Phipps, the British Ambassador in Paris.[110]

Coulondre sent an additional report on June 13, apparently based on information from someone in Ribbentrop's "immediate entourage." Ribbentrop was convinced that the Polish question could only be solved through German-Soviet collaboration.[111] He also reported about Hitler's speech during a review of the Condor Legion which fought for Franco, in which Hitler never referred to the fact that it was sent to Spain to fight "Bolshevism" and "Communism." Instead the speech was directed against the "Democracies," the warmongers and war profiteers, "the promoters of 'encirclement.' "[112]

While on a visit in London on June 15, Erich Kordt of Ribbentrop's secretariat, warned officials of the British Foreign Office (through a French journalist) that Berlin and Moscow were definitely considering political collaboration.

Toward the end of June, the Kordt brothers, in a discussion with Sir Robert Vansittart, Chief Diplomatic Adviser to the Foreign Secretary, warned that despite the personal insults exchanged between Soviet Russia and Nazi Germany, Hitler would not hesitate to sit down at the same table with the Russians or to make major concessions to Stalin. He had, in fact, already taken steps to open talks with Moscow and the approaches had not been rejected. If Hitler teamed up with Stalin it would mean war. Erich Kordt based his claims on a personal discussion with Hitler. Hitler had recently said, "Should Chamberlain close with Stalin, I will undertake nothing but rather summon a party congress of peace in the fall. If not, I can smash Poland since the Western Powers will not stir and I will have my back free."[113]

Throughout June and July, Laurence Steinhardt, the American Ambassador in Moscow, sent Washington warnings of an impending Soviet-German deal, which President Roosevelt passed on to the British, French, and Polish Embassies.

On July 14, the French Consul in Hamburg reported that there were rumors in commercial circles of the possibility of a German-Soviet non-aggression pact should Britain and France fail to secure such an agreement themselves.

On July 16, Georgi Astakhov, the Soviet Chargé d'Affaires, attended Hitler's "Day of German Art" in Munich.[114]

On August 1, an official German delegation attended the opening of the Agricultural Exhibition in Moscow. This was the first such visit in three or four years.[115]

Weizsaecker met with the British and French Ambassadors in Berlin on August 15. Both reported that Weizsaecker was convinced that a German-Soviet political agreement would be reached. At the time, Weizsaecker hinted to the British Ambassador that the Germans had requested that Ribbentrop make a visit to Moscow.[116]

On August 16, Laurence Steinhardt, the American Ambassador in Moscow, warned Washington that the Russians had offered to sign a non-aggression pact with the Germans.

On August 17, Sumner Welles, the U.S. Undersecretary of State, informed the British Ambassador in Washington of Steinhardt's warning of a possible Soviet-German non-aggression pact.

Members of the Soviet Embassy and trade delegation attended the Eastern Fair in Koenigsberg on August 20.[117]

On August 20, Daladier received a Havas Press Agency dispatch from Moscow which purported to give the minutes of the Politburo meeting of August 19. At that meeting, Stalin spoke of his decision to sign a non-aggression treaty with Germany. Stalin's arguments, as contained in the Havas dispatch, were as follows:

1) If the U.S.S.R. signed a military pact with the Western democracies, Germany might seek another *modus vivendi* with the West which would be dangerous to the U.S.S.R.

2) If the U.S.S.R. signed a non-aggression pact with Germany she would be able to stay out of the war for perhaps a decade while the Western democracies and Germany exhausted themselves in an extended conflict. In the meantime, as a result of such an agreement, the U.S.S.R. would be able to obtain parts of Poland, the Baltic States, and Bessarabia.

After reading the dispatch, Daladier believed that it was authentic, although he had no way of verifying it.[118]

Many of these warnings were premature. As we have seen, neither the Germans nor the Russians were sure of each other's intentions until the middle of August. Nevertheless, these signals, warnings, and rumors should at least have alerted the Western democracies to the *growing probability* of a German-Russian political agreement.

In addition to the unpublished warnings, there were also public statements and certain actions and decisions of both Germany and the Soviet Union that indicated possible German-Russian collusion. Among these are the following:

Germany's initially secret *demands and pressures on Poland* began soon after the Munich crisis with the cancellation of the Polish-German non-aggression pact of 1934 by Hitler on April 28, 1939. These pressures culminated in open threats and intensified propaganda warfare during August. This should have alerted observers to the possibility of a German attack on Poland and hence to the pressing German need to reach an agreement with Russia. The possibility of such an agreement over Poland should have been further enhanced by the following factors: the traditional Polish-Russian animosity and distrust, Soviet territorial claims on Poland, and the Poles' stubborn refusal to allow Russian troops to enter Poland in the event of a German attack which could also endanger the Soviet Union.

The gradual change in public attitudes adopted by both Germany and the Soviet Union since the winter of 1939 was reflected in both Hitler's and Stalin's speeches, as well as in their respective newspapers and publications. In his speech on January 30, Hitler omitted his usual diatribe on communism and the Soviet Union. Stalin "responded" in his speech on March 10 by *not* attacking Germany, while at the same time accusing the Western democracies of trying to provoke a German-Russian conflict. Hitler again avoided any attacks on the Soviet Union in his Reichstag speech on April 28. He used the same occasion to terminate the German-Polish non-aggression pact of 1934 and the Anglo-German naval agreement of 1935. Five days later, Litvinov, the Soviet Commissar for Foreign Affairs, and the symbol of Soviet pro-Western policy, was dismissed. In addition, any content analysis of German newspapers beginning in April 1939, but especially from May on, would have indicated a positive change in their attitude toward the Soviet Union.

The lack of progress during the Anglo-French-Soviet talks in the spring and summer of 1939 should have led the allies to consider the possibility that the Soviet Union was seeking an alternative approach to enhance its security. The Western democracies did not seriously consider the fact that their appeasement policy toward Nazi Germany undermined their deterrent posture and value as potential military and political allies. The image of their weakness certainly created an incentive for the Russians to seek a better understanding with the most powerful European state. The military weakness of the Western democracies, a fact well-known to both Hitler and Stalin, gave them little to offer the U.S.S.R. at the bargaining table, and made them more of a burden than help as a military ally. The British and French ignored the impact of their own attitudes. Unlike Germany, they refused to send more important representatives to Moscow to negotiate with the Russians.

All of these factors should have activated red warning lights in the chancelleries of the Western democracies. This, however, did not happen. The democracies were in no hurry to conclude a political and military agreement with the Russians; they did nothing effective to counter a German-Soviet rapprochement and, in fact, helped to accelerate Russia's approach to Germany. When the Germans and Russians finally publicized their decision to sign a non-aggression treaty, the Western democracies were taken by surprise. How can we explain their surprise?

The first explanation is also the most important one. It is that of wishful thinking and of ignoring other partners or adversaries in the game of power politics; it is the projection of one's own interests onto other states and the substitution of ideology for realpolitik. For many years, the Western democracies were not sure whether Nazi Germany was serving as a buffer against Bolshevism and communism, or whether Germany itself was their most dangerous enemy. Similarly, they had always viewed the Soviet Union as a major ideological enemy and ostracized her. When they finally, and reluctantly, made up their minds that the Soviet Union could, after all, join a coalition against Nazi Germany, they could not understand why the Russians were not "overcome with joy." The Western democracies had adopted the paternalistic attitude of bestowing a great honor on the Russians.

They also failed to understand that what was good for them was not necessarily good for the Soviet Union. Given their long tradition of suspicion and hatred of communist Russia, their attitude during the negotiations was at best half-hearted. They sent low-level representatives to conduct the negotiations with the Russians;[119] they appeared to be stalling; they acted without determination and failed to reach any kind of effective decision. Most important of all, the Western democracies took the interests of their smaller allies—who were, in the context of an all-European conflict, less important than the Soviet Union—more into account than their own or Soviet interests.[120] In other words, they were not able to distinguish between major, dominant interests, and secondary, subordinate interests. (A similar inability to order priorities was demonstrated by the Allies in 1940, while they were already at war with the Germans, by their plans to aid Finland, which had been attacked by Russia.)

The Western democracies seemed to be unaware of the highly unfavorable impression their apparently unending series of concessions to Nazi Germany—beginning with the German remilitarization of the Rhineland, the Anschluss, and Munich—produced in other countries. Their desertion of Austria and Czechoslovakia obviously did not create an image of resolve and strength. They had, as already noted, nothing to add to Russian security—yet they were reluctant to collaborate with the Russians. The British offer to send, in case of a general European war, "two (divisions) and two more later" could not help but make a poor impression on the Russians who would have to commit "more than three hundred divisions." Had the Western democracies at least attempted to compensate for their military weakness by showing a genuine concern for Russia's security they might still have been able to interest the Russians in an agreement. They did not. As U.S. Ambassador Joseph Kennedy reported from London, the agreement they sought to reach with the Russians was "a negative agreement rather than a positive one. In other words, they would like to tie up Russia so that there is no possibility of the Russians considering a deal with Germany."[121] This "negative" policy was partially based on the information provided by all contemporary European intelligence estimates (including Germany and Poland) which vastly underrated Soviet military power. Hence, Russia was not considered a worthy military ally. (See also Appendix I to Chapter 2 above.)

In their negotiations, the French and British projected their own past experience with the Germans onto the Soviet Union. Their experiences with Nazi diplomacy had taught them that the Germans could not be trusted—treaties with Nazi Germany were usually broken before the ink was dry. They assumed that this lesson which was so obvious to them was equally evident to the Soviet Union. It was not, however, applicable to the Soviet Union because it had practically been excluded from the mainstream of European diplomacy since the end of World War I and had never been a direct victim of Nazi diplomatic practices. Moreover, even if the non-aggression treaty between Germany and the Soviet Union was not honored by the Germans, it could still provide the Soviet Union with precious time to rebuild its military strength. (The Western democracies, after all, had hoped to gain time when they signed the Munich agreement.)

In contrast to the Western democracies, the Germans had something positive to add to Russia's security. In the first place, an alliance with Germany reduced the immediate military threat to Russia. The Germans were ready to divide Poland, and recognize a Soviet sphere of interest in Eastern Europe. There was also the benefit to be derived from being a neutral country on good terms with the strongest side if a general European war should break out. If the Germans eventually attacked the U.S.S.R., the Western democracies would already be embroiled in the conflict and the U.S.S.R. would not have to bear the brunt of Germany's military power. In terms of "realpolitik," the British and French attitudes left the Soviet Union little choice.

Similarly, the Western democracies, despite their earlier experiences with him, failed to comprehend Hitler's determination to solve the Polish question. His readiness to disregard ideological barriers exceeded what

PUNCH OR THE LONDON CHARIVARI—JULY 12 1939

THE CALCULATING BEAR

they believed to be possible. Not only did the Western democracies overestimate the effectiveness of their military power while negotiating with
the Russians—they *underestimated* the combined deterrent power of
Britain, France, and the Soviet Union. In fact, the Western democracies'
lack of incentive in approaching the Soviet Union was partly based on
their serious miscalculation of Soviet military capabilities. (The Germans, who should have known better, committed the same mistake on
the eve of their invasion of the Soviet Union in 1941.)

A major impediment to Britain's ability to counterbalance Germany's
growing strength on the Continent was her reluctance to consider the
Soviet Union a worthy ally. Whatever the British military's perception of
the Soviets' real military strength, they apparently shared the attitude of
the British political establishment towards Russia—aversion. Nevertheless, they demonstrated a more realistic attitude. On March 18, 1939, the
British Chiefs of Staff, although they considered the Soviet Union "militarily an uncertain quantity," pointed out to their government the desir-
ability of a Russian alliance. "The possible advantages of a Soviet alliance
were that it would either deter Japan from entering the war or 'almost
certainly' prevent Japanese expeditions to Singapore or Australasia. It
would make Germany's general position in the Baltic difficult and specifically prevent the flow of Swedish iron ore to Germany."[122]

On April 24, the British military estimated Soviet military strength as
follows:

> They rated it low. Although they believed Russia possessed 9,000
> good but lightly armoured tanks, and could mobilise thirty cavalry
> divisions and a hundred infantry divisions after three months of
> war . . . the Russian aircraft industry was not much good. The state
> of Russian industry as a whole was so bad, so disorganised, that
> when taken together with poor rail communications, '. . . we con-
> sider it doubtful whether the national economy of the Soviet could
> deliver war stores at a greater rate than would suffice to keep in the
> field (on the Western Frontier) thirty divisions.'
>
> 'Russia, although a great Power for other purposes, was only a
> Power of medium rank for military purposes. . . . Her assistance
> would be of considerable, though not of great, military value . . .'[123]

Hitler probably would not have attacked Poland had the Western
democracies and the Soviet Union formed a military coalition. In Hitler's
opinion, there was no substitute for an agreement securing Russian
neutrality since he was afraid of waging a two-front war.

In addition, the British and French predicted the direction of German-
Soviet diplomacy on the basis of a faulty model that focused on the
German-Soviet ideological rivalry. The Western democracies over-
emphasized the intensity of ideological tensions between Nazism and

Communism. They—the British more than the French—had, in fact, created a rigid concept based on the Nazi-Soviet ideological rivalry that filtered out all contradictory evidence and *a priori* refused to consider seriously the possibility of a Nazi-Soviet rapprochement. The British were warned again and again that Soviet Russia and Germany might reach some kind of agreement; or at the very least, that Soviet Russia might sit back while the rest of Europe was propelled into war. They were warned by Sir William Seeds, their Ambassador in Moscow; they were warned by Daladier; they were even warned indirectly by Goering. Yet, Chamberlain, Halifax, and the Foreign Office remained obdurate. The warnings were dismissed time and again as 'inherently improbable.'[124] So confidently did the British count on the ideological estrangement between fascism and communism, that they imagined the Soviet government would be flattered at any nod of recognition.[125]

Actually, the easiest barrier for the Germans and Russians to overcome was their seemingly incompatible ideologies—the most difficult was to ascertain each other's intentions and determine their common interests. In the short run, *realpolitik* and compelling interests usually take precedence over ideology. As early as April 17, 1939, the Russian Ambassador in Berlin told Weizsaecker that, "Ideological differences had very little adverse effect on relations between Russia and Italy and need not disturb those with Germany either."[126] The differences between fascism and communism were perhaps less than those that existed between the Western democracies on the one hand, and Germany and the Soviet Union on the other. Under pressure, ideological principles could be adapted and bent. The Germans could therefore argue that despite the divergence in their views of life there was a common thread running through the ideologies of Germany, Italy, and the Soviet Union; that is, they opposed the capitalist democracies of the West. In brief, ideology was here converted from a barrier into a bridge. In his August 14 message to Molotov, Ribbentrop referred to the ideological dimension.

> The contradiction between the national idea, exemplified by National Socialist Germany and the idea of world revolution, exemplified by the U.S.S.R., has in the past years been the sole cause for the alignment of Germany and Russia in ideologically separate and hostile camps. The developments of the recent period seem to show that differing philosophies do not prohibit a reasonable relationship between the two States, and the restoration of new, friendly cooperation.[127]

As the British and French should have recalled, the Germans and the Russians had ignored their ideological differences in the past; both, on different occasions, had pursued policies contradictory to their ideologies. (This was easier for Nazi Germany, whose ideology was not as

THE HUMAN OSTRICHES

clearly defined as that of communism.) In the final analysis, almost every ideology, in order to survive, must be able to temporarily ignore its own doctrines to improve its long-term prospects. Such short-term deviations were certainly not new to any of the most fanatic and devout communist leaders.

The third explanation for the surprise achieved by both Germany and the Soviet Union is that of deception. In conducting negotiations, complete secrecy is impossible. The essence of deception is to help the enemy strengthen his existing conceptions, confirm his incorrect interpretations of the available information, and divert his attention from what is actually occurring.

Hitler's continuous declarations of Germany's peaceful intentions while he was planning his next war are a good example. All his speeches (such as his answer to Roosevelt's message on April 28) emphasized Germany's desire for peace. While at this stage hardly anyone could have been expected to believe Hitler, his speeches, nevertheless, helped him to gain time, divert attention, and disguise his real intentions. Until the last moment, he vociferously denied that he intended to use force to get what Germany wanted from Poland. He made demands and threats—but excluded any mention of the use of force.

The fact that the Soviet Union simultaneously conducted negotiations with the Western democracies and with Germany was deceptive. The British and French viewed such discussions as mutually exclusive. They believed that serious discussions between the Germans and Russians could only start *after* a complete and final collapse of negotiations with the democracies.[128] When one of the Kordt brothers came to London and informed Sir Robert Vansittart of the danger of a Nazi-Soviet rapprochement he refused to consider this information seriously and brushing it aside, answered that "we are . . . definitely concluding the agreement with the Soviet Union."[129] The Russians, for their part, followed a different path. According to their logic there was nothing wrong with pursuing serious discussions with two parties at once, and then choosing the highest bidder. For a long time the Russians could not decide which course to pursue, and they probably made their final decision only after the middle of August. What deceived the Western democracies was the genuine interest the Russians demonstrated in their negotiations. Thus, the Russian deception was all the more effective because it was not consciously planned.

A phenomenon mentioned before provides another explanation for the surprise achieved by the Ribbentrop-Molotov Agreement—the "cry wolf" syndrome, to which both the French and British governments fell victim. Since early May they had received numerous warnings of a forthcoming rapprochement, but none of the warnings had materialized. The repetition of similar warnings often dulls the decision-makers' attention to additional warnings. This is what Thomas Schelling refers to as "alert fatigue" in military preparedness.[130] "Alert fatigue" and the "cry wolf" syndrome should be simpler to deal with in the diplomatic sphere, at least in the sense that, unlike military warnings, they do not require a complicated and expensive partial mobilization of troops and a continued alert. In a diplomatic alert, the costs are primarily psychological. Therefore, political intelligence officers should be encouraged to be less hesitant in warning of an impending diplomatic surprise. This enables decision-makers to plan their countermoves according to political circumstances and react more effectively *if* the predicted event should take place. Such an alert need not involve the highest level decision-makers at all stages, although they should be informed of some of the projected countermoves.

One of the most frequent causes for military surprise is the attacker's inability until almost the last moment to make a clear-cut decision on questions such as which front to attack first, the direction from which to launch the attack, and the choice of targets.[131] What the attacker himself does not know until very shortly before his attack commences cannot be expected to be known by the opposing intelligence officers. A similar problem arises in regard to diplomatic surprise. Both Hitler and Stalin were not completely sure of their *own* intentions until the week prior to the signing of the non-aggression pact, to say nothing of the fact that they were not sure of *each other's intentions*. Therefore, "Those British and French statesmen and diplomats who were surprised can hardly be blamed; until almost the very end Hitler and Stalin also doubted the possibility of reaching an understanding."[132] In this respect many of the reports sent by the French Ambassador in Berlin, for example, were premature. Nevertheless, even if Hitler, who was constantly torn between, on the one hand, his hatred of communism and contempt for the Slavs, and, on the other, the dictates of *realpolitik*, finally made up his mind on a rapprochement with the Soviet Union only early in July—the growing number of warnings should have kept the French and British governments more alert to their significance.[133]

While the French and British diplomats cannot be blamed for failing to predict the exact timing and form of a German-Soviet rapprochement, they can be blamed for attaching such a low probability to this kind of agreement, and pursuing a policy which pushed the Soviet Union into the arms of Nazi Germany.

As has been noted, one of the basic problems in avoiding a surprise attack lies in the difficulty intelligence organizations have in distinguishing between signals and noise. The same problem also exists in attempts to avoid surprise in diplomacy, and the events leading to the Soviet-Nazi rapprochement are an excellent illustration of this point.

The head of the Northern Department of the British Foreign Office, when discussing the British Intelligence failure, gave a "classical," though somewhat naive, summary of the "signals vs. noise" problem in a memorandum written on August 25, 1939.

> In general, we feel ourselves, when attempting to assess the value of these secret reports, somewhat in the position of the Captain of the Forty Thieves when, having put a chalk mark on Ali Baba's door, he found that Morgiana had put similar marks on all the other doors in the street and had no indication to show which mark was the true one. In this case there were passages in many of our reports which told against the probability of a German-Soviet rapprochement. We had no indications that these statements were in general any less reliable than those in a contrary sense.[134]

THE COSTS OF DIPLOMATIC SURPRISE

Diplomatic surprise, unlike its military counterpart, often incurs heavy costs in addition to important benefits. The costs can usually be measured in terms of the loss of credibility with one's allies. In extreme cases, a former ally must be abandoned in the process of shaping radically new policies, and other allies must either adjust their policies or suffer the consequences.

The German-Soviet rapprochement and the resulting non-aggression pact involved long-range costs for both countries. The Germans humiliated and insulted the Japanese and the Italians by presenting them with a *fait accompli*.

The Germans did not inform the Japanese government of their talks with the Soviet Union despite the fact that the Japanese had joined the Anti-Comintern Pact.[135] As one of the prerequisites for concluding the non-aggression pact, the Soviet government asked the Germans to influence the Japanese to stop the war or "incidents" along the Soviet border. As the result of not being consulted on this matter, the Japanese learned a tough lesson in German-style realpolitik.

> Giving up on Japan temporarily, [Hitler] turned to Russia and concluded his startling non-aggression pact with Stalin on August 23, 1939. In the process he ignored some last-minute Japanese proposals and did not bother to inform Japan of his intentions. The pact . . . was a humiliating blow to Japan. Not only was it obviously an underhanded action and a direct violation of one of the secret provisions of the Anti-Comintern Pact, but it also completely upset the basis for Japanese foreign policy. Germany would be of no use to Japan in case of a Russo-Japanese conflict, which seemed more than barely possible in 1939. The Japanese Premier Baron Hiranuma resigned over the issue after making a protest to

Germany. Pro-Axis elements in Japan were for the moment discredited.[136]

Upon conclusion of the pact, Ribbentrop, to add insult to injury, did indeed advise the Japanese to come to an understanding with the Russians. He thus turned the Anti-Comintern Pact into nonsense, though he was the one who had initiated it.

The Japanese so-called Strike-North Faction, which had pressed for an attack on Russia, suffered a serious setback as a result of the German "surprise." This, in combination with the resounding Japanese defeat at the hands of Zhukov's tanks at Nomohon during the Russo-Japanese border conflict in the Far East, helped to divert Japanese attention to the south.[137] For their own reasons, the Japanese eventually followed Ribbentrop's advice and signed a neutrality pact with the U.S.S.R. on April 13, 1941.[138] The Japanese strictly observed this pact until the end of the war. They did not become involved in the Russo-German conflict even when the Soviet Union was hard pressed by the Germans; and they subsequently ignored Hitler's hints to join the war against the Soviet Union at a time when Germany could have used additional pressure on Russia from another front. If the Germans had not behaved so treacherously, the Japanese sense of honor and obligation as well as Germany's earlier success in "Operation Barbarossa" *might* have led the Japanese to attack the Russians in the Far East. Opening a second front would have forced the Russians to divide their forces, perhaps weakening them to the point of defeat. The reasons for Japanese neutrality in the war against Russia and their decision to turn south instead of north are, of course, more complex than can be related in this context.[139]

The Soviet Union, however, reaped a double profit. It acquired half of Poland and as a bonus a sphere of influence in Eastern Europe as well. More importantly, if Germany's actions did indeed alienate Japan, then the Russians unintentionally secured Japan's neutrality.

Hitler was not much more solicitous of his closer, Italian, ally. Problems arose between Germany and Italy not because the Italians lacked knowledge of the German-Soviet negotiations, but because the Germans informed them only selectively of their content. The resulting German-Soviet rapprochement far exceeded the scope which had been agreed upon with the Italian government.

Goering had already discussed *his* conception of a German-Soviet agreement with Mussolini in mid-April; Mussolini seemed to agree that *limited* German-Soviet detente was a good idea.[140] Unlike the Germans, Mussolini conceived of such a rapprochement in negative terms. In his view, the Germans should negotiate with the Soviet *solely* for the purpose of obstructing English and French efforts to reach agreement with the Soviet Union. Mussolini's instructions to Ciano who was to meet with Ribbentrop in Milan on May 6, 1939, summarize his policy.

Policy toward Russia? Yes to a policy that would prevent Russia from joining the anti-Axis bloc, but nothing more, since such a policy would be totally antithetic to present positions, completely incomprehensible internally, and would weaken the fabric of the Axis.[141]

The Germans had a different set of priorities; their agreements with Italy and Japan did not supersede all others. They were seeking, if only temporarily, a "positive" understanding that meant far-reaching collaboration with the Soviet Union. And, not sharing the Italian fear of risking a general European conflict, they continued to make preparations for the attack on Poland.

On May 26, Ribbentrop held separate conversations with the Italian and Japanese Ambassadors in Berlin in order to explore their views of a possible German-Japanese-Soviet agreement to prevent an Anglo-French-Soviet agreement. Both Ambassadors stated that their governments were unquestionably opposed to any such agreement.[142] Disappointed by the extremely negative response, Ribbentrop ceased to inform the Japanese of events pertaining to the German-Soviet dialogue, and simultaneously limited the information given to the Italians until mid-August 1939.

Through Ambassador Rosso in Moscow, the Italian government obtained reports on developments in the German-Soviet negotiations. Moreover, the Italian Ambassador directly contributed to the German-Soviet rapprochement on the instructions of Ciano: in an early July meeting with Vladimir Potemkin, the Deputy Commissar for Foreign Affairs, he had verified the German government's genuine interest in improving relations with the Soviet Union.[143]

When Hitler and Ribbentrop met with Ciano in Salzburg on August 11 and 12, they informed him of Germany's intention to reach a political understanding with the U.S.S.R. in the immediate future; they did not, however, tell him of the extent to which they had departed from the limitations agreed upon in the German-Italian meeting in Milan on May 6. According to this oral understanding, neither Germany nor Italy would go to war within the next three years. The combination of German disclosures and Rosso's reports should have at least given the Italians an inkling of the true nature of the German-Soviet accord. In the August meeting Hitler's and Ribbentrop's reports concerning an imminent agreement with the Soviet Union were premature. Reports from the Italian Ambassador in Berlin to Ciano and Mussolini on August 14 stated that the Germans had been overly optimistic concerning the conclusion of the German-Soviet treaty.[144]

After the August 11 and 12 meeting with Hitler and Ribbentrop, Count Ciano expressed his opinion of the German move in the following terms:

Germany was acting solely on her own initiative, without taking into account the interests and wishes of the other party to the treaty. It would, however, be a mistake to assume that the other party to the treaty would follow obediently and allow herself to be drawn blindly into such developments.[145]

In a report to Weizsaecker, Mackensen, the Ambassador in Rome, wrote: "The Duce has given Ciano the watchword: 'Friends and allies, yes; slaves, no.' "[146]

On August 16, the Italians received a report from Count Massimo Magistrati, the Italian Chargé d'Affaires in Berlin. He recounted a conversation with Astakhov, the Soviet Chargé d'Affaires in Berlin, who said that the German-Soviet trade agreement that was about to be signed would "serve as a good base for further developments."

On the whole, the Russians seemed to be optimistic concerning relations between Germany and Russia, and he stated that he is convinced that the Polish crisis will break out within approximately ten days.[147]

Nevertheless, the news of Ribbentrop's impending departure for Moscow to sign a political accord with the U.S.S.R. (telephoned to Ciano by the Nazi Foreign Minister himself) came as a great surprise to Ciano, Mussolini, and the Italian Embassy in Berlin.[148] Temporarily paralyzed by the news, Ciano and Mussolini were lulled into believing that German plans to attack Poland might not lead to a general European conflict.[149] Their surprise can be attributed to the contradictory reports arriving from the Embassies in Moscow and Berlin and their belief in Germany's adherence to the Milan understanding. But above all, the Italians, like the British and French, felt that traditional ideological rivalry between Germany and the Soviet Union was sufficient to prevent a comprehensive political agreement.

It was not until after the German-Soviet non-aggression pact was signed that Hitler found the time to send an apologetic note to the Duce. His excuse for keeping Italy in the dark was that "he had no idea" that the negotiations with the Soviet Union would proceed so quickly. He then tried to convince Mussolini that the treaty was the "greatest possible gain for the Axis." He hoped that the Italians would understand. They did understand—they understood the German contempt for Italian interests.

Obviously, the German attitude did not improve relations between the two states. This later cost the Germans dearly when Mussolini took his revenge. In October 1940, he did not inform the Germans of his plans to attack Greece because he feared that the Fuehrer would order him to halt the attack. He therefore presented Hitler with his own *fait accompli*. When he met with Hitler at Florence on October 28, he simply said,

"Fuehrer, we are on the march! Victorious Italian troops crossed the Greco-Albanian frontier at dawn today!"[150] in *The Rise and Fall of the Third Reich*, Shirer comments that Mussolini derived great pleasure in taking revenge on Hitler for all of his previous surprises. Hitler, of course, was furious.[151]

The Italian attack came at the worst possible moment for the Germans who were already in the process of planning their invasion of Russia. When it became clear that the Italians were being defeated by the Greeks, the Germans had to bail them out. This caused Hitler to postpone the beginning of "Operation Barbarossa" by about five weeks (from May 15, 1941 to June 22, 1941). The delay was fatal—it was one of Hitler's most catastrophic decisions.

The price the Soviet Union may have paid in the long run for its pact with Nazi Germany in terms of its control over European communist parties is difficult to evaluate, but it must have been considerable. After years of seeking the support of the communist parties in its conflict with Germany, the Soviet Union had suddenly made a 180° turn without consulting them. "Stalin's cynical deal with Hitler had thrown the French Communist Party into complete disarray. For three days after the announcement on the night of August 21 that the pact would be signed, the top Communist leaders . . . maintained an unaccustomed and embarrassed silence."[152] The French Communist Party was quick to come back into line, at least temporarily, and it welcomed the treaty as "saving the peace." A humiliating experience for the largest and most powerful Communist Party in Europe, the signing of the German-Soviet non-aggression pact proved that it had been serving Russia's national interests *more* than the cause of international communism. It has been said that the Communist International received its deathblow in Moscow on August 23, 1939, when it became clear that whoever served Stalin also served Hitler.[153]

CHRONOLOGY

Date	Event
October 1938	German Ambassador Schulenburg and Litvinov reach an oral agreement that German and Soviet mass media will henceforth refrain from attacking the other country.
	Ribbentrop applies first pressures on Poles with regard to Danzig.
	Hitler reassures Polish Ambassador of Germany's peaceful intentions.
November (approx.)	Hitler decides to incorporate Danzig without a general war.
End of December 1938–February/March 1939	First German-Soviet trade talks in Berlin and Moscow.
January 5, 1939	Hitler promises Polish Ambassador, "Danzig is German, but there will be no *fait accompli*."
January 12	Hitler has a long conversation with the Soviet Ambassador at the reception for the Diplomatic Corps. (This was a move carefully staged by Hitler to create an auspicious atmosphere in which, if necessary, a beginning could be made towards a rapprochement with Russia.)[154]
January 27	The London *News Chronicle* publishes an article (possibly inspired by Soviets) speculating on the possibility of a Nazi-Soviet rapprochement. This article was later reprinted in the Soviet press.
Early February	At a dinner party in the house of a prominent industrialist, General Keitel meets the Soviet Military Attaché who, alluding to Poland's condition, remarks that there is a

threat of revolution. If this should occur, Russia "could not remain indifferent." She would have to intervene to "reorganize those parts of the country adjoining her frontiers." Keitel immediately reports this conversation to Hitler.[154]

February 10	Talks open in Moscow.
March 10	Speech by Stalin before the Eighteenth Congress of the Communist Party. Leaves question of policy reorientation open.
March 15	Germany occupies Czechoslovakia.
March 18	Litvinov proposes a European Six-Power conference to halt further German aggression.
March 23	Partial mobilization of the Polish armed forces.
March 31	Britain's announcement of her unilateral guarantee to Poland.
April 1	The Soviet government denies that it has given its support to the British unilateral guarantee to Poland.
April 3	Hitler orders OKW and OKH to prepare plans for an attack on Poland.
April 6	Spain joins the Anti-Comintern Pact and Germany pushes for publication of that fact. Great Britain and Poland sign a provisional pact of mutual assistance.
	Last anti-Soviet cartoon appears in *Schwarze Korps*, the official S.S. paper.

April 7, 1939	Ribbentrop's special expert on Soviet affairs is instructed to improve his personal relations with members of the Soviet Embassy in Berlin.
April 16	Goering meets with Mussolini in Rome. Mentions Stalin's March 10 speech, possible rapprochement, and Hitler's omission of criticism of the Soviet Union.
April 17	Meeting between State Secretary Weizsaecker and Soviet Ambassador Merekalov in Berlin—supposedly to explore possibility of economic talks—but actually discuss political matters, among them Russia's desire to isolate itself from a general European war, and Germany's fear of another Triple Entente (Russia, England, France).
Approx. mid-April	Top Soviet agent in Japan, Richard Sorge, sends a warning to Moscow that Germany plans to attack Poland on September 1.
April 15	Roosevelt appeals to Hitler and asks for assurance that he will not attack any of a long list of states.
April 20	Ribbentrop indicates to the Japanese Ambassadors in Berlin and Rome that Germany will be compelled to sound out the Soviet Union on the prospects of a non-aggression pact.
April 28	Hitler answers Roosevelt in his Reichstag speech; he mentions all states except Poland in his pledge of peaceful intentions and omits the customary attack on the Soviet Union.
April 30	General Karl Bodenschatz of the German Air Ministry tells Captain Paul Stehlin, the French Assistant Air Attaché, that "something is go-

ing on in the East. Hitler is no longer thinking of regulating the German-Polish conflict without Russia. There have already been three partitions in Poland. Well, believe me, there will be a fourth." The Air Attaché gives a full report of this conversation to the French Ambassador in Berlin, Robert Coulondre. Coulondre takes the report seriously and forwards the details to Bonnet in Paris on May 7. Coulondre feels the matter is so urgent that he asks the Air Attaché to fly to Paris and report to the Foreign Ministry, but the Quai d'Orsay refuses to grant the Attaché an interview. Bodenschatz leaks the same information to the Polish Military Attaché on May 29.

Early May

General orders to the German press to exercise restraint toward the Soviet Union.

Hungarian Intelligence informs the Polish Ambassador in Berlin that Soviet-German contacts concerning a new partition of Poland have been made. This information is immediately sent by special courier to Warsaw.

May 1

Litvinov's book, *Notes for a Journal*, in which his ideas of collective security are set forth, is banned on Stalin's order.

May 3

Small item in "News in Brief" section of Soviet newspapers announces that Litvinov has been released from the position of Foreign Affairs Commissar. He is replaced by Molotov.

May 5

Litvinov's dismissal discussed by Astakhov and Schnurre in Berlin.

May 6, 1939

Hitler is briefed on German relations with the Soviet Union and discusses with Ribbentrop the possibilities of a rapprochement.

May 9

Coulondre wires Bonnet at the French Foreign Ministry: "For the last 24 hours Berlin has been full of rumors that Germany has made, or is going to make proposals to Russia leading to a partition of Poland."

May 12

The Reichs propaganda office asks the editors of German newspapers "not to occupy themselves in any way—therefore not even in the form of quotations from the foreign press —with the foreign rumors of a rapprochement between Germany and Russia."

May 17

Astakhov meets with Schnurre again to discuss "trade" matters. Again ends up discussing politics.

May 20

Schulenburg meets with Molotov "on resumption of trade talks." Molotov mentions the need for "political bases" before they can resume.

May 21

Schulenburg is told to freeze initiatives and adopt a "wait and see" attitude ("sit tight" order).

May 22

Italy and Germany conclude the so-called "Pact of Steel."

Coulondre sends a long telegram to Paris reporting that Ribbentrop regards a rapprochement with Russia as a prelude to the partition of Poland.

May 23

Hitler meets secretly with his military leaders. He states that further success in Europe can only be achieved through the use of force.

May 25

The editors of German newspapers are again advised that, "As long as the result of English-Russian negotiations is not known, a reserved attitude must prevail. Therefore no prophecies about their possible outcome. The press, can, however, hint in the commentaries at the threat created by this alliance of England with Bolshevism."

Ribbentrop instructs State Secretary Weizsaecker to deal with the problem of signaling and approaching the Soviet Union.

May 26

Ribbentrop hands Hitler a copy of the draft of his instructions to Schulenburg in Moscow, but Hitler, still influenced by Chamberlain's declaration in the House of Commons that a Soviet-British-French agreement is almost completed, considers these projected proposals to Molotov too bold and orders them held up.

May 29

Hitler approves the idea of a meeting between Weizsaecker and Astakhov on the pretext of trade in order to raise once more the issue of an agreement.

May 30

The German Economic Counselor in Moscow receives new instructions to resume economic negotiations.

Meeting between Weizsaecker and Astakhov (approved May 29) takes place.

Weizsaecker telegraphs Schulenburg in Moscow that, "contrary to the policy previously planned we have now decided to undertake definite negotiations with the Soviet Union."

May 31, 1939	Molotov responds positively in the Supreme Soviet to the German initiative of May 29.
June 1	Coulondre informs Bonnet "that Hitler will risk a war if he does not have to fight Russia. On the other hand, if he knows he has to fight her too, he will draw back rather than expose his country, party, and himself to ruin." He adds that Keitel and Brauchitsch told Hitler that if Germany had to fight Russia, she would have only a small chance of winning the war.
June 6	Hitler welcomes the 14,000 members of the Condor Legion returning from Spain and makes no mention in his speech of their fight against communism—a notable omission.
June 14	Astakhov hints at three Soviet options through the Bulgarian Minister in Berlin. Indicates preference for the option of a Soviet-German treaty.
June 14-29	Talks between a low-level British official and Moscow over guarantees to Poland and Rumania.
June 15	Hitler receives Army Commander-in-Chief Brauchitsch's plan for the attack on Poland.
June 22	General Keitel presents preliminary timetable for Case White (the attack on Poland) to take place on August 20.
June 28	Schulenburg meets with Molotov in Moscow for a discussion similar to that of May 20.
June 29	Hitler decides to halt talks with the Russians, and Schulenburg is told not to take any further political or

economic initiatives. An article by Politburo member Andrei Zhdanov accuses the British and French governments of using their talks with the Soviet Union as a bargaining chip to get a new deal from Nazi Germany.

July 2

In a speech to Party officials in Hamburg, Hitler tells his audience that an agreement with the Soviet Union would be reached soon and that he would settle the account with Poland once and for all.

July 4

The Italian Ambassador in Moscow relays a message from the German government to Deputy Commissar for Foreign Affairs Potemkin. The message is that Germany seriously wants to improve relations. He answers that improved relations would stabilize the area and safeguard peace.

July 7

The Soviet Chargé d'Affaires in Berlin denies categorically to French Ambassador Coulondre that there are any formal or informal negotiations going on between Berlin and Moscow.

July 8

The German economic representative in Moscow is instructed regarding further economic concessions which are submitted to Mikoyan on July 10. The Soviet answer is delayed for two weeks.

July 14

The French Consul in Hamburg repeats rumors that a German-Soviet pact will be completed if the British or French fail to complete one. Lt. Col. Count Gerhard Schwerin of the Abwehr meets in London with Admiral John Godfrey, Director of Naval Intelligence, and suggests to him measures that could deter Hitler

July 14, 1939 (cont'd)	from attacking Poland. These suggestions include: dispatching a battle squadron to the Baltic, two fully equipped divisions, and a group of heavy bombers to France, and inviting Churchill to join the Chamberlain government.
July 18	Babarin, the Soviet trade representative in Berlin, meets with Schnurre on the trade treaty.
	Weizsaecker wires Schulenburg to cancel the freeze orders (of June 29).
July 19	Czech Intelligence reports to President Benes that very far-reaching negotiations are taking place between Germany and the U.S.S.R.
July 21/22	The Soviet media announce resumption of economic negotiations with Germany.
July 22-August 13	Economic talks continue.
July 26	Schnurre, as instructed by Ribbentrop, sounds out Astakhov and Babarin about the Soviet Union's opinion regarding the improvement of relations with Germany.
July 31	Chamberlain announces in Parliament that an Allied military mission is being sent to Moscow.
	Schulenburg is instructed to see Molotov at once and "get down to business."
End of July	The Germans step up incidents along the Polish border and in Danzig.
August 2	Ribbentrop and Astakhov conduct more detailed talks.

August 3	Ribbentrop cables summary of talks to Schulenburg who is to meet with Molotov the same day. Schnurre meets with Astakhov to urge speed in economic talks so that quick political agreement will follow. Schulenburg meets with Molotov. Molotov expresses interest, but maintains a negative attitude, mentioning the Anti-Comintern Pact, Japan's opposition to the Soviet Union, and the Soviet Union's exclusion from Munich.
August 10	Astakhov meets with Schnurre to answer Ribbentrop's proposals of August 3 and to define the major problems.
August 11	The British-French military mission arrives in Moscow.
August 12	Astakhov and Schnurre meet again. It is suggested that the questions raised on August 10 can be treated in formal political discussions in Moscow. Russians emphasize desire for step-by-step talks.
August 13	Hitler tells Ciano that September 1 is the latest date for his attack on Poland.
August 14	Hitler is convinced that England and France will not fight.
	Ribbentrop sends two telegrams to Schulenburg through the Foreign Office.
	1) Counter any Russian-U.K.-French agreement with the argument that the British have nothing to offer.
	2) German counter-offer to the Russians.
	The British Consul in Danzig reports

August 14, 1939 (cont'd)

that "military precautions are substantially complete."

The British Military Attaché in Berlin reports that two million men are or will be very shortly under arms in the German Army.

August 15

German preparations for war are advancing rapidly. The Nuremberg party rally which was scheduled for early September is secretly cancelled.

Weizsaecker tells the British Ambassador that the Germans and Russians will definitely sign a non-aggression pact.[155]

Evening

Schulenburg delivers the message of August 14 to Molotov. In his answer, Molotov mentions the possibility of a non-aggression treaty.

August 16

Schulenburg's report on his discussion with Molotov reaches Ribbentrop and Hitler.

The American State Department receives reports on the German-Soviet negotiations from "certain members" of the German Embassy and forwards them to London through the British Ambassador in Washington.

August 17

Schulenburg meets with Molotov.

August 18

Ribbentrop sends Schulenburg another urgent telegram asking for another meeting with Molotov. Schulenburg is instructed to urge speed because of the question of possible conflict with Poland. The telegram includes a report that the trade pact has been concluded in Berlin. Late the same day, Sir Robert Vansittart, the Diplomatic

Adviser to the Government, calls on Sir Alexander Cadogan, the Permanent Under-Secretary of State, to tell him that reliable sources have informed him that Hitler has decided to go to war against Poland between August 25 and 28.

August 19

All German warships and submarines are ordered to sail to be at their stations by September 1.

Stalin briefs the Politburo on his decision to sign a non-aggression treaty with Nazi Germany. He explains that it would enable Russia to stay out of war for perhaps as long as a decade while the Germans, British, and French exhausted themselves in war. The Havas news agency sends a report on Stalin's briefing from Moscow via Geneva to Paris on the same day.

Soviets delay the signing of the trade pact in Berlin, say they want to wait for further instructions from Moscow.

In the first meeting of the day between Molotov and Schulenburg, Molotov insists that an immediate visit by Ribbentrop would be premature and that the trade and credit agreement must be completed first.

4:30 p.m.

In the second meeting, Molotov states that the Soviet government has reconsidered and that Ribbentrop can come to Moscow on August 26 or 27 if the trade agreement is signed on August 20. Molotov hands Schulenburg a draft of a non-aggression treaty.

August 20
2:00 a.m.

Trade agreement is signed in Berlin, with many details still unsettled.

August 20, 1939 (cont'd)
6:45 p.m.

Hitler sends a letter to Stalin in which he urges speed and accepts the Soviet draft of the non-aggression treaty. Asks if Ribbentrop can visit on August 22 or 23.

August 21
9:35 p.m.

Stalin's reply agreeing to Ribbentrop's visit on August 23 is received in Berlin.

10:30 p.m.

Hitler receives Stalin's reply.

11:00 p.m.

German radio announces plans for a non-aggression pact with the Soviet Union.

August 22

Russian press announces intention to sign the pact.

Hitler meets with his commanders-in-chief at Obersalzberg and orders attack on Poland for August 26. He also summarizes his view of the negotiations.

Ribbentrop leaves for Moscow.

The British Ambassador in Berlin informs Weizsaecker of Chamberlain's announcement that England will fulfill her obligations to Poland regardless of any German-Soviet agreement.

August 23
Noon

Ribbentrop's delegation arrives in Moscow.

3:30 p.m.

The German delegation is received in the Kremlin. Stalin is present at the talks. The major issues are settled in three hours.

At a later meeting, the secret protocol on Eastern Europe and the Baltic is agreed upon.

August 24

The treaty, dated August 23, is signed in the early morning hours of the twenty-fourth.

NOTES

1. Gerhard L. Weinberg, *Germany and the Soviet Union, 1939-1941* (Leiden: E. J. Brill, 1954), p. 15.

2. Adam B. Ulam, *Expansion and Coexistence: Soviet Foreign Policy, 1917-1973*, 2nd ed. (New York: Praeger, 1974), pp. 258-259.

3. Ernst von Weizsaecker, *The Memoirs of Ernst von Weizsäcker* (London: Victor Gollancz, 1951), p. 186.

4. Quoted in William L. Shirer, *The Rise and Fall of the Third Reich* (New York: Simon and Schuster, 1960), p. 458.

5. *Ibid.*, p. 463.

6. *Ibid.*, p. 454. Ulam claims that Chamberlain's declaration accelerated a Soviet-German rapprochement since the Germans now needed the Soviet Union as an ally. (Ulam, *Expansion and Coexistence*, pp. 267-268.)

7. *Documents on German Foreign Policy 1918-1945*, Series D (London: Her Majesty's Stationery Office, 1956), 6: 224-226. (Hereafter cited as *DGFP*.)

8. William L. Langer and Everett S. Gleason, *The Challenge to Isolation*, 2 vols. (New York: Harper Torchbooks, 1964), Vol. 1, p. 115. See also Weizsaecker, *Memoirs*, p. 186.

9. Shirer, *The Rise and Fall*, pp. 455, 467.

10. "The Polish Foreign Minister, Beck, for whom they [secret German pressures] meant a catastrophic bankruptcy of his foreign policy which was based on the fatuous assumption that Germany's previous pledges could be trusted, kept the facts of the German pressure secret both from the Polish public opinion and from Poland's allies. They were not to become public knowledge until April 1939." Ulam, *Expansion and Coexistence*, p. 260.

11. For a detailed discussion of the German-Soviet economic conversations and their coordination with the political intentions of both states, see Phillip Fabry, *Der Hitler-Stalin-Pakt, 1939-1941: Ein Beitrag zur Methode sowjetischer Aussenpolitik* (Darmstadt: Fundus Verlag, 1962), Chapters 1 and 2, especially pp. 35-38.

12. A. Rossi, *The Russo-German Alliance: August 1939-June 1941* (Boston: Beacon Press, 1951), pp. 4-5.

13. Weizsaecker, *Memoirs*, p. 119.

14. Weinberg, *Germany and the Soviet Union*, p. 12.

15. *Ibid.*, p. 12. Shirer, *The Rise and Fall*, p. 477.

16. *DGFP*, p. 1. Schulenburg wrote:

In that part of the speech devoted to foreign policy and in which was manifest unchanged adherence to the policy hitherto pursued, it was noteworthy that Stalin's irony and criticism were directed in considerably sharper degree against Britain, i.e., against the reactionary forces in power there, than against the so-called aggressor states, and in particular Germany. Moreover, this was also evident in Manuilski's report on the work of the Comintern. [Manuilski was a member of the Presidium of the Comintern 1924-1943].

17. It has usually been assumed that Stalin's speech was carefully analyzed by the Germans and especially Hitler, who did not miss Stalin's signals. There is, however, strong evidence to indicate that Stalin's speech was brought to Hitler's attention only much later than is usually assumed in the literature [the usual assumption was that Stalin's speech was immediately reported to Hitler. See below in this note.] The Germans and Russians later confirmed the effectiveness of this exchange of signals during the signing ceremony for the non-aggression treaty on August 23. Rossi has summarized this conversation as follows:

> When the non-aggression pact and the secret protocol were actually being signed in Moscow on 23rd August, 1939, Ribbentrop referred to Stalin's speech of 10th March. It included, he told Stalin, a phrase which Hitler had interpreted as expressing Stalin's desire for improved relations with Germany. To this remark Stalin replied: 'That was precisely my intention.' And Molotov confirmed this in the toast which he proposed immediately after the ceremony. Raising his glass to Stalin, he emphasized that 'it was Stalin himself who—by his speech of March, which was well understood in Germany—had brought about the reversal in political relations.' In his speech before the Supreme Soviet on 31st August, 1939, in support of the ratification of the pact concluded the previous week, Molotov also recalled that Stalin had wished to launch an appeal on 10th March for good-neighbourly relations with Germany, and he declared amidst the gratified laughter of the assembly (which was recorded in the official report), 'We see now that Comrade Stalin's declaration has on the whole been understood in Germany, and that it has produced practical results.' To Molotov's testimony can be added Ribbentrop's at the Nuremberg Trial: 'Marshal Stalin made a speech in March, 1939, in which he expressed a desire to foster better relations with Germany. I informed Adolf Hitler . . . I learned soon after through the negotiations of Minister Schnurre that Stalin had not used this phrase lightly.' (Rossi, The Russo-German Alliance, pp. 8-9). See the "Memorandum by an Official attached to the Staff of the Foreign Minister" (DGFP, 7:228).

In Der Hitler-Stalin-Pakt, 1939-1941 (Darmstadt: Fundus Verlag, 1962), Phillip W. Fabry claims that Stalin's speech was not brought to Hitler's attention (p. 18) and that he and Ribbentrop were first informed of Stalin's speech by Ambassador Schulenburg when Schulenburg met with Hitler on the 10th of May in Obersalzberg (after Litvinov's dismissal) (p. 22). Fabry bases his claim on the following book: Gustav Hilger, Wir und der Kreml (Frankfurt-Berlin: 1954), p. 13. Hilger, the German Economic Attaché in Moscow, claims in his memoirs that Hitler was surprised to hear of Stalin's speech. Upon hearing of the hints of a possible political understanding between the Soviet Union and Germany, Hitler asked Hilger to read the important passages twice in succession. If Hilger's claim is true, then two months elapsed before Hitler and Ribbentrop heard of Stalin's signals. Also, it would mean that Hitler did not respond to Stalin's signals in his April speech in the Reichstag (as is usually assumed), but rather that he *took the initiative prior to Stalin's dismissal of Litvinov. Hilger's evidence* (see Gustav Hilger and Alfred G. Meyer, *The Incompatible Allies: A Memoir History of German-Soviet Relations 1918-1941,* New York: Macmillan Co., 1953, p. 296) *seems reliable. Therefore we can conclude that both Hitler and Stalin started signalling each other at about the same time, and that Stalin's signalling in his March 10 speech was brought to Hitler's and Ribbentrop's attention only around May;* and that their intensified interest in contacts with Moscow came primarily as a reaction to Litvinov's dismissal. See also D. C. Watts, "The Initiation of the Negotiation Leading to the Nazi-Soviet Pact: A Historical Problem" in C. Abramsky, *Essays in Honour of E. H. Carr* (London: Archon Books, 1974), pp. 152-170.

18. Shirer, *The Rise and Fall,* p. 478. For an excellent analysis, see Mario Toscano, *Designs in Diplomacy* (Baltimore: Johns Hopkins University Press, 1970), Chapter II, Italy and the Nazi-Soviet Accords of August, 1939, pp. 48-124. Goering had not yet discussed his opinions on a possible rapprochement with the Soviet Union with Hitler (pp. 61-63).

19. See Weinberg, *Germany and the Soviet Union,* p. 23. In a message to Schulenburg in Moscow sent at the end of May, Ribbentrop indicated that the restraint of German newspaper attacks on the Soviet Union was due to careful control by the German government. See also Z.S.B. Zeman, *Nazi Propaganda,* Second edition, (New York: Oxford University Press, 1973), pp. 103-104. This German view had already found expression in certain respects in recent months. The earlier press polemics against Soviet Russia had been substantially toned down. (*DGFP,* 6:590) The change in tone of German newspapers was immediately noticed by the Russians, who were uncertain whether this was only a short-lived experiment or a real change in policy. See Raymond J. Sontag and James S. Beddie, *Nazi-Soviet Relations 1939-1941* (New York: Didier, 1948), pp. 4-5.

20. *DGFP,* 6:266-267.

21. Shirer, *The Rise and Fall,* p. 472.

22. Stalin's sudden dismissal of Litvinov and efforts to intensify political contacts with Germany beginning in mid-May in Berlin may have been triggered by a report by the German-born Soviet spy Richard Sorge in Tokyo. According to an article in the September 4, 1965, issue of *Pravda,* Sorge cabled Moscow "in the spring of 1939 . . . that the Hitlerite invasion of Poland would take place on September first." (See Louis Fischer, *Russia's Road From Peace to War: Soviet Foreign Relations 1917-1941,* New York: Harper and Row, 1969, p. 335). Later in the summer Sorge informed Soviet intelligence from the German Embassy in Tokyo that Russia was not on the target list of Germany. This clarification of German intentions made it easier for Stalin to proceed with the non-aggression treaty with Germany. See D. C. Watts, Introduction to David Irving's (ed.) *Breach of Security* (London, William Kimber, 1968), p. 36. In a letter Hitler sent Mussolini on August 25 to explain the German-Soviet Non-Aggression Pact, he stated that "the readiness on the part of the Kremlin to arrive at a reorientation of its relations with Germany became apparent after the departure of Litvinov." See Sontag and Beddie, *Nazi-Soviet Relations,* p. 81.

23. Quoted from the report of the German Chargé d'Affaires in Moscow

(*DGFP*, 6:419). The inconspicuous four-line notice on the last page of the Soviet dailies of May 4 announced that Litvinov was released at "his own request." On May 2, Litvinov had met as usual with the British Ambassador who later wrote, "He gave me no inkling of his intention to resign." (See Louis Fischer, *Russia's Road From Peace to War: Soviet Foreign Relations 1917-1941*, New York: Harper & Row, 1969, pp. 334-335).

24. Rossi, *The Russo-German Alliance*, p. 15.

25. *Ibid.*, p. 16. See also Shirer, *The Rise and Fall*, p. 531.

26. See Langer and Gleason, *Challenge to Isolation*, p. 369.

27. *DGFP*, 6:429.

28. Weinberg, *Germany and the Soviet Union*, p. 24.

29. *Ibid.*, p. 25. See also Langer and Gleason, *Challenge to Isolation*, p. 108.

30. Isaac Deutscher, *Stalin: A Political Biography* (New York, Oxford University Press, 1967); also Peter Kleist, *Zwischen Hitler und Stalin* (Bonn: Athenaeum Verlag, 1950), pp. 27-28.

31. *DGFP*, 6:536.

32. Schulenburg gave the complete details of this conversation with Molotov (as well as subsequent conversations) to Augusto Rosso, the Italian Ambassador in Moscow. Rosso in turn relayed the information on the progress of the German-Soviet contacts to his government. Unfortunately, most of the Ambassador's reports were sent directly to the area desks of the Italian Foreign Ministry rather than to the top decision-makers. As a result, many of his important reports did not receive the attention they merited. See Mario Toscano, *Designs in Diplomacy*, Chapter II, Italy and the Nazi-Soviet Accords of August 1939, pp. 48-124.

33. Weinberg, *Germany and the Soviet Union*, pp. 26-27. See also the instructions of Weizsaecker to Schulenburg "to sit tight and wait until the Russians will speak more openly." Sontag and Beddie, *Nazi-Soviet Relations*, pp. 12-15.

34. *DGFP*, 6:576.

35. *DGFP*, *ibid.*

36. Weinberg, *Germany and the Soviet Union*, p. 27. The Russians deliberately created an atmosphere that would keep the Germans on their toes. They led the Germans to believe that the Soviet-British-French conversations were making progress—they made the Germans feel that they had to outbid the Western democracies. "The two-track, two-train diplomacy" that the Soviets conducted deepened German concern. "The situation was somewhat reminiscent of Rapallo, where Chicherin and Litvinov created an impression of success with the British in order to induce the Germans to sign." Fischer, *Russia's Road From Peace to War*, p. 337. Fischer writes the best summary of the tactic the Russians employed to get the most out of the Germans. See Chapter 17, The Road to the Pact, pp. 322-349.

37. Shirer, *The Rise and Fall*, p. 489.

38. *DGFP*, 6:586-587.

39. See Fabry, *Der Hitler-Stalin-Pakt 1939-1941*, p. 27.

40. *DGFP*, 6:590-591. Also quoted by Shirer, *The Rise and Fall*, p. 491.

41. *DGFP*, pp. 591-592.

42. Shirer, *The Rise and Fall*, p. 492.

43. *DGFP*, 6:598. Weizsaecker's memorandum to Ambassador Schulenburg in Moscow on May 27, 1939.

44. Weinberg, *Germany and the Soviet Union*, p. 31.

45. Fabry, *Der Hitler-Stalin-Pakt 1939-1941*, p. 28.

46. *DGFP*, 6:606. See also Shirer, *The Rise and Fall*, p. 493. Weizsaecker's memorandum is one of the key documents for understanding the process of rapprochement between Germany and the Soviet Union. For the full document, see *DGFP*, 6:604-607. Or Sontag and Beddie, *Nazi-Soviet Relations*, pp. 12-15, and pp. 15-17.

47. Weinberg, *Germany and the Soviet Union*, p. 32.

48. *Ibid.*, p. 32.

49. *Ibid.*, pp. 34-35. See also Fabry, *Der Hitler-Stalin-Pakt 1939-1941*, pp. 32-33.

50. Sontag and Beddie, *Nazi-Soviet Relations*, pp. 20-21.

51. Fabry, *Der Hitler-Stalin-Pakt*, p. 39; Rossi, *The Russo-German Alliance*, pp. 19-20.

52. Weinberg, *Germany and the Soviet Union*, p. 35.

53. Fabry, *Der Hitler-Stalin-Pakt*, p. 40.

54. Shirer, *The Rise and Fall*, pp. 495-496.

55. Weinberg, *Germany and the Soviet Union*, p. 36.

56. *DGFP*, 6:936-938. See also Weinberg, *Germany and the Soviet Union*, p. 37.

57. *DGFP*, 6:995.

58. Sidney Aster, *1939: The Making of the Second World War* (New York: Simon and Schuster, 1973), p. 273.

59. *Ibid.*, pp. 273-274.

60. *Ibid.*, p. 274.

61. *Ibid.*, p. 274. See also Telford Taylor, *Sword and Swastika* (New York: Simon and Schuster), p. 311. For instance, General Gerd von Rundstedt described his reaction as follows: "This treaty made us, the old soldiers, very happy and satisfied us very much. Good relations with Russia were considered very important within the Reich's sphere."

62. Quoted in James E. McSherry, *Stalin, Hitler, and Europe: The Origins of World War II 1933-1939*, 2 vols. (Cleveland, Ohio: The World Publishing Co., 1968), pp. 182-183. See also Aster, *1939*, pp. 274-275; John Wheeler-Bennett, *The Nemesis of Power* (London: Macmillan Co., 1964), p. 444; Peter Hoffman, *The History of the German Resistance 1933-1945* (Cambridge, Mass.: The MIT Press, 1977), pp. 108-109.

63. Aster, *1939*, p. 275.

64. *Ibid.*, p. 275.

65. *Ibid.*, p. 277. For Hitler's decision, see a detailed discussion in Fabry, *Der Hitler-Stalin-Pakt 1939-1941*, p. 38.

66. Aster, *1939*, p. 276.

67. *DGFP*, 6:1006-1009.

68. *Ibid.*, pp. 1015-1016.

69. *Ibid.*, p. 1048.

70. *Ibid.*, pp. 1048-1049.

71. Shirer, *The Rise and Fall*, p. 506.

72. Weinberg, *Germany and the Soviet Union*, p. 48.

73. The Polish government was fully aware of German mobilization efforts and general preparations for war. (Since early June, Polish Intelligence had made weekly reports on German mobilization.) "The Polish generals and Beck still did not believe in a totally 'pessimistic' view of German-Polish relations . . . It was also hoped that important Nazi leaders such as Goering did not favor a Russo-German alliance because Poland served as a barrier, protecting Germany from the east." Richard A. Woytak, *On the Border of War and Peace* (New York: Columbia University Press, 1979), p. 86. This colossal misperception can to a limited degree explain—but not justify—Polish behavior that summer.

74. Rossi, *The Russo-German Alliance*, p. 22.

75. Ambassador Schulenburg on August 14 had no indication at all of the momentous events that were to begin unfolding that day. He wrote a letter to State Secretary Weizsaecker in which he discussed the possibility of leaving Moscow to attend the Nuremberg Party Day on September 1. See Sontag and Beddie, *Nazi-Soviet Relations*, p. 47, also Gregori Gafencu, *Last Days of Europe* (New Haven: Yale University Press, 1948), pp. 123-124.

76. Winston S. Churchill, *The Gathering Storm* (Boston: Houghton Mifflin, 1948), p. 391.

77. *DGFP*, 7:63-64.

78. Shirer, *The Rise and Fall*, p. 518.

79. *DGFP*, 7:77.

80. Aster, *1939*, pp. 316-317. See also McSherry, *Stalin, Hitler, and Europe*, p. 228, and John W. Wheeler-Bennett, *Munich: Prologue to Tragedy* (London: Macmillan, 1948), p. 410.

81. See Roberta Wohlstetter, *Pearl Harbor: Warning and Decision* (Stanford: Stanford University Press, 1962).

82. Aster, *1939*, p. 317n. In his book *Peace in Our Time* (London: Rupert Hart-Davis, 1971), Roger Parkinson claims that Halifax did receive Ambassador Lindsay's cable on the 18th of August. He bases his claim on *DBrFP* (Documents on British Foreign Policy), Vol. VII, pp. 41-42.

83. *DGFP*, 7:84.

84. *Ibid.*, 7:114-115.

85. *Ibid.*, 7:116.

86. *Ibid.*, 7:121-122.

87. *Ibid.*, 7:122.

88. Shirer, *The Rise and Fall*, p. 525.

89. *Ibid.*, p. 525.

90. *DGFP*, 7:134. It is interesting to note that Molotov, i.e., Stalin, now adopted the reverse condition for a successful rapprochement between Germany and the Soviet Union. His stand on May 20 was that a political basis must be created before economic negotiations could proceed. Now he seized the opportunity to insist that the economic treaty must be concluded before, and as a condition for, the signing of the non-aggression pact. See Hilger, *The Incompatible Allies*, p. 299.

91. See text in *DGFP*, 7:150-151.

92. *Ibid.*, 7:156-157.

93. *Ibid.*, 7:168.

94. Shirer, *The Rise and Fall*, p. 528.

95. *DGFP*, 7:200-204. A copy of this speech was passed to the British Embassy in Berlin by General Ludwig Beck and was received in London on August 25. Hoffman, *The History of the German Resistance*, p. 109. But according to Hans Hoehne in his book *Canaris*, the copy of Hitler's speech was given by Canaris to Colonel Oster who passed it to Hermann Maass, an anti-Nazi Social Democrat, who volunteered to give it to an American journalist, Louis P. Lochner, who finally passed it on to an official of the British Embassy in Berlin on August 25, p. 348. This is one of the most interesting of Hitler's recorded speeches. It was, on the eve of the war, a *tour d'horizon* of European politics and his evaluation of the outcome of the war against Poland. Clearly, he did not believe that the British and French would declare war on Germany, but he did correctly predict their lack of action *after* they had declared war. Hitler made a similar analysis during a military conference at Obersalzberg on August 14, which was recorded by Halder in his diary.

96. *DGFP*, 7:188-189.

97. Churchill, *The Gathering Storm*, p. 394.

98. So, by the way, were all Soviet ambassadors abroad. Fischer, *Russia's Road From Peace to War*, p. 344.

99. Quoted in Shirer, *The Rise and Fall*, p. 545, (from the British Blue Book, pp. 96-98).

100. Shirer, *The Rise and Fall*, p. 516.

101. *DGFP*, 7:203.

102. See Weinberg, *Germany and the Soviet Union*, p. 49.

103. Quoted in Shirer, *The Rise and Fall*, pp. 540-541. This problem was also recognized by the German Ministry of Propaganda which instructed all newspapers not to go suddenly overboard with praise of the Soviet Union, but only to "warm up the tone." See Zeman, *Nazi Propaganda*, p. 106.

104. See John Wheeler-Bennett, *The Nemesis of Power*, pp. 440-441.

105. See Aster, *1939*, pp. 314-315; also W. G. Krivitsky, *I Was Stalin's Agent* (New York: Harper & Brothers, 1939), especially after Chapter 1, pp. 17-42.

106. Woytak, *On the Border of War and Peace*, p. 86. See also Sven Allard, *Stalin und Hitler: Die sowjetrussische Aussenpolitik 1930-1941* (Berne: Franke Verlag, 1974), p. 190.

107. Shirer, *The Rise and Fall*, p. 482, quoting the French Yellow Book Dispatches Nos. 123, 125.

108. Woytak, *On the Border of War and Peace*, p. 86.

109. McSherry, *Stalin, Hitler, and Europe*, p. 182.

110. *Ibid.*, p. 182.

111. *Ibid.*, p. 182.

112. This report is quoted in Fischer, *Russia's Road From Peace to War*, p. 343, (quoting from the French Yellow Book, pp. 158-159).

113. *Ibid.*, p. 183. See also Aster, *1939*, pp. 274-275.

114. *DGFP*, 7:189.

115. *Ibid.*, 7:189. Also *DGFP*, Third Series, VII, p. 31; Allard, *Stalin und Hitler*, p. 185.

116. McSherry, *Stalin, Hitler, and Europe*, p. 227.

117. *DGFP*, 7:189.

118. Shirer, *The Collapse of the Third Republic* (New York: Simon and Schuster, 1969), p. 464.

119. "The governments whose prime ministers had not considered it beneath their dignity to fly to Munich almost at Hitler's nod, refused to send any officials of ministerial standing to negotiate the alliance with Russia. The servicemen sent for military talks were of lesser standing than those sent, for instance, to Poland and Turkey." Isaac Deutscher, *Stalin*, p. 434. Stalin, on the other hand, sent "his most important army chiefs and Voroshilov, the Commissar of Defence" to these conversations. *Ibid.*, p. 434.

120. In *Politics Among Nations* (5th ed.), Hans Morgenthau warns against situations in which weak states in effect make decisions for great powers (pp. 545-546).

121. Quoted in McSherry, *Stalin, Hitler, and Europe*, p. 187.

122. Robert Manne, "The British Decision for Alliance with Russia, May 1939," *Journal of Contemporary History*, Vol. 9, No. 3, July 1974, pp. 3-26.

123. The British and French could not contribute anything of value to Russian security nor recognize the Russian claim to an expanded "sphere of influence" because of their commitment to several East European states. Correlli Barnett, *The Collapse of British Power* (London: Eyre Methuen, 1972), p. 559, pp. 565-566. (See Appendix, Chapter 2.)

124. "Inherently improbable" quoted by A. J. P. Taylor from a Foreign Office minute concerning Nevile Henderson to Halifax on May 8, 1939, British Foreign Policy, Third Series, Vol. VII, p. 413 in A. J. P. Taylor, *The Origins of the Second World War* (New York: Atheneum, 1968), p. 229. See also Allard, *Hitler und Stalin*, p. 189.

125. *Ibid.*, p. 234.

126. *DGFP*, 6:266-267.

127. *Ibid.*, 7:62.

128. "Chamberlain himself not only shared the general shock in England and France that these two ferocious old enemies should sign a pact of friendship, but was also surprised and pained for another reason, for, as he confided to his Cabinet on 24 August: '*It appeared to be contrary to good faith that, while we were conducting negotiations with the Russians in all confidence, they should have been negotiating with Germany behind our backs.*' " (Emphasis added.) Quoted in Correlli Barnett, *The Collapse of British Power* (London: Eyre Methuen, 1972), pp. 571-572. Chamberlain's surprise can only be regarded as extremely naive. In diplomacy one *should* always assume that the other side will conduct negotiations with other parties according to its best interests. In addition, Chamberlain's negative attitude toward the negotiations with the Soviet Union pushed the Russians into Germany's arms. He could not alienate the Soviet Union and at the same time expect it to avoid any contact with the Germans.

129. Sven Allard, *Stalin und Hitler*, p. 185. This book includes the only attempt to evaluate whether or not the Western democracies had enough information to avoid being surprised (Chapter 17, pp. 184-192).

130. Thomas C. Schelling, *The Strategy of Conflict* (New York: Oxford University Press, 1969), pp. 244-245.

131. Michael I. Handel, *Perception, Deception, and Surprise: The Case of the Yom Kippur War* (Jerusalem: The Leonard Davis Institute for International Relations, Jerusalem Papers on Peace Problems, 1976, No. 19), pp. 12-13.

132. McSherry, *Stalin, Hitler, and Europe*, pp. 229-230. See also Deutscher, *Stalin*, p. 435.

133. See Allard, *Stalin und Hitler*, pp. 186-188.

134. Aster, *1939*, p. 318. For a similar comment, see the recently published official history of British Intelligence during World War II. The official history makes it clear that the British government did not obtain any "reliable and timely intelligence about the Russo-German negotiations in the summer of 1939." See F. H. Hinsley *et al.*, *British Intelligence in the Second World War*, Vol. 1 (New York: Cambridge University Press, 1979), p. 46. The first two chapters of the book (pp. 3-89) contain a devastating critique of the dismal performance of British Intelligence (both military and political) on the eve of the war. Unfortunately, the book does not discuss at all the Intelligence failures in giving advance warning before the reoccupation of the Rhineland in 1936 or the failure to anticipate the Soviet-German Nonaggression Pact in the summer of 1939. See also p. 430.

135. According to the Anti-Comintern Pact, Article II:

The High Contracting Parties will not during the period of this treaty sign political agreements of any kind with the U.S.S.R. which are contrary to the spirit of this agreement without mutual consent. (Quoted in Weinberg, *Germany and the Soviet Union*, p. 152.)

136. Paul W. Schroeder, *The Axis Alliance and Japanese-American Relations 1941* (Ithaca: Cornell University Press, 1958), p. 112. The only contradictory evidence is cited by Rossi, *The Russo-German Alliance*, p. 19, who claims that Ribbentrop told the Japanese Ambassador in Rome on June 16 that "Germany intends to sign a pact of non-aggression with the U.S.S.R." See also Johanna Menzel Meskill, *Hitler and Japan: The Hollow Alliance* (New York: Atherton Press, 1966), p. 30; Ernst L. Presseisen, *Germany and Japan: A Study in Totalitarian Diplomacy 1933-1941* (New York: Howard Fertig, 1969), pp. 223-225. Theo Sommer, *Deutschland und Japan zwischen den Maechten 1935-1945* (Tuebingen: J. C. B. Mohr, 1962), Chapter III-14, pp. 275-295.

137. The Soviet-Japanese Neutrality Pact, concluded after a prolonged process of mutual probing between the two countries, surprised the Germans. There is no detailed study of the process that preceded the Soviet-Japanese Neutrality Pact. See John Erickson, *The Road to Stalingrad* (New York: Harper and Row, 1975), pp. 76-78.

138. Robert C. Butow, *Tojo and the Coming of the War* (Stanford: Stanford University Press, 1961), p. 321.

139. See *Ibid.*, pp. 204-227.

140. Mario Toscano, *Designs in Diplomacy* (Baltimore: Johns Hopkins University Press, 1970), pp. 61-63.

141. *Ibid.*, p. 64.

142. *Ibid.*, pp. 75-76.

143. *Ibid.*, p. 94.

144. *Ibid.*, p. 111.

145. From a report by the German Ambassador in Rome, Hans Georg von Mackensen, to State Secretary Weizsaecker, in *DGFP*, 7:241.
146. *Ibid.*, p. 242.
147. Toscano, *Designs in Diplomacy*, p. 112.
148. *Ibid.*, p. 123.
149. *Ibid.*, p. 116.
150. Shirer, *The Rise and Fall*, p. 816.
151. *Ibid.*, p. 816.
152. Shirer, *The Collapse of the Third Republic*, p. 483.
153. Krivitsky, *I Was Stalin's Agent*, p. 38.
154. See David Irving, *The War Path*, p. 242.
155. See Guy H. Naylor, *The Secret War* (London: John Long, 1940), p. 44. This book was published during the war and may have damaged Weizsaecker's position.

BIBLIOGRAPHY

Allard, Sven. *Stalin und Hitler: Die sowjetrussische Aussenpolitik 1930-1941*. Berne: Franke Verlag, 1974.

Assman, Kurt. "Stalin and Hitler, Part I: The Pact With Moscow," *U.S. Naval Institute Proceedings*, June 1949. Vol. 75, no. 6, pp. 639-651.

Barnett, Correlli. *The Collapse of British Power*. London: Eryre Methuen, 1972.

Baumgart, Winifred. "Zur Ansprache Hitlers vor den Fuehrern der Wehrmacht im August 1939." *Vierteljahrshefte fuer Zeitgeschichte*, Vol. 16, 1968.

Bergamini, David. *Japan's Imperial Conspiracy*. New York: William Morrow, 1971.

Braubach, Max. *Hitlers Weg zur Verständigung mit Russland im Jahre 1939*. Bonn: Peter Hanstein Verlag, 1960.

Budurowycz, Bohdan B. *Polish-Soviet Relations, 1932-1939*. New York: Columbia University Press, 1963.

Bullock, Allan. *Hitler: A Study in Tyranny*. New York: Harper and Row, 1962.

Butow, Robert C. *Tojo and the Coming of the War*. Stanford: Stanford University Press, 1961.

Carr, E. H. "From Munich to Moscow," *Soviet Studies*, I (June, October 1949).
_____. *German-Soviet Relations Between the Two World Wars*. Baltimore: Johns Hopkins University Press, 1951.

Churchill, Winston S. *The Gathering Storm*. Boston: Houghton Mifflin, 1948.

Colvin, Ian. *The Chamberlain Cabinet*. London: Victor Gollancz, 1971.
_____. *Vansittart in Office*. London: Victor Gollancz, 1965.

Coulondre, Robert. *De Staline a Hitler: Souvenirs de deux Ambassades, 1936-1939*. Paris: Hachette, 1950.

Craig, Gordon A. and Felix Gilbert, eds. *The Diplomats 1919-1939*. Princeton, N.J.: Princeton University Press, 1953.

Crump, Hanson B. *American Diplomatic Reporting from the Soviet Union, 1934-1941*. (Unpublished Ph.D. dissertation, Columbia University, 1966.)

Dallin, A. "The Month of Decision: German-Soviet Diplomacy, July 22-August 22, 1939," *Journal of Central European Affairs*, IX (April 1949), 1-31.

Denicke, George. "The Origins of the Hitler-Stalin Pact," *Modern Review* (March-April 1948), 204-209.

Deutsch, Harold C. "Strange Interlude: The Soviet-Nazi Liaison of 1939-1941," *The Historian* (Spring, 1947).

Deutscher, Isaac. *Stalin: A Political Biography*, 2nd ed. New York: Oxford University Press, 1967.

Dilks, David, ed. *The Diaries of Sir Alexander Cadogan 1938-1945*. New York: G. P. Putnam's Sons, 1972.

Documents on German Foreign Policy, Series D, Vol. VI-VII.

Douglas-Hamilton, James. "Ribbentrop and War," *Journal of Contemporary History*, V, No. 4, 1970, pp. 45-63.

Erickson, John. *The Road to Stalingrad*. New York: Harper and Row, 1975.

Ernle-Erle-Drax, Admiral Sir A.R.P. "Mission to Moscow," *Naval Review*, XL: 3-4 (Nov. 1952), XLI: 1 (Feb. 1953).

Fabry, Philipp W. *Der Hitler-Stalin-Pakt 1939-1941: Ein Beitrag zur Methode sowjetischer Aussenpolitik*. Darmstadt: Fundus Verlag, 1962.

_____. *Die Sowjetunion und das Dritte Reich: Eine dokumentierte Geschichte der deutsch-sowjetischen Beziehungen von 1933 bis 1941*. Stuttgart: Seewald Verlag, 1971.

Fischer, Louis, *Stalin and Hitler: The Reasons for and the Results of the Nazi-Soviet Pact*. New York: The Nation, 1940.

_____. *Russia's Road from Peace to War: Soviet Foreign Relations 1917-1941*. New York: Harper and Row, 1969.

Fleming, Nicholas. *August 1939: The Last Days of Peace*. London: Peter Davies, 1979.

Ford, Franklin and Carl E. Schorske. "The Voice in the Wilderness: Robert Coulondre," in Craig and Gilbert, eds., *The Diplomats*, 555-578.

Hilger, Gustav and S. C. Meyer. *The Incompatible Allies: A Memoir-History of German-Soviet Relations 1918-1941*. New York: Macmillan Co., 1953.

Hilger, Gustav. *Stalin: Aufstieg der UdSSR zur Weltmacht*. Goettingen: Musterschmidt Verlag, 1959.

Hill, Leonidas. "Three Crises, 1938-39," *Journal of Contemporary History*, III, No. 1, 1968, pp. 113-114.

Hingley, Ronald. *Joseph Stalin: Man and Legend*. New York: McGraw-Hill, 1974.

Hinsley, F. H. *British Intelligence in the Second World War*. Vol. 1. New York: Cambridge University Press, 1979.

_____. *Hitler's Strategy*. Cambridge: Cambridge University Press, 1951.

Hoehne, Hans. *Canaris*. Garden City, N.Y.: Doubleday, 1979.

Hyde, H. Montgomery. *Stalin: The History of a Dictator*. New York: Farrar, Straus, and Giroux, 1971.

Ierace, Francis A. *America and the Nazi-Soviet Pact*. New York: Vantage Press, 1978.

Iklé, Frank William. *German-Japanese Relations 1936-1940*. New York: Bookman Associates, 1956.

Irving, David, ed. *Breach of Security*. London: William Kimber, 1968.

_____. *The War Path*. New York: Viking Press, 1978.

Kaiser, David E. *Economic Diplomacy and the Origins of the Second World War: Germany, Britain, France, and Eastern Europe*. Princeton: Princeton University Press, 1980.

Kleist, Peter. *Zwischen Stalin und Hitler*. Bonn: Athenaeum Verlag, 1950.

Krivitsky, W. G. *I Was Stalin's Agent*. New York: Harper and Brothers, 1939.

Langer, William L. and S. Everett Gleason. *The Challenge to Isolation*, Vol. I. New York: Harper Torchbooks. 1964, 105-121; 160-192.

Laqueur, Walter, *Russia and Germany: A Century of Conflict*. London: Weidenfeld and Nicolson, 1965.

Lukacs, John. *The Last European War: Sept. 1939-Dec. 1941*. Garden City, New York: Doubleday, 1976.

Manne, Robert. "The British Decision for Alliance with Russia, May 1939," *Journal of Contemporary History*, IX, No. 3, 1974, pp. 3-26.

McSherry, James E. *Stalin, Hitler and Europe, 1933-1939*, Vol. I. Cleveland: The World Publishing Co., 1968.

Meskill, Johanna Menzel. *Hitler and Japan: The Hollow Alliance*. New York: Atherton Press, 1966.

Middlemas, Keith. *Diplomacy of Illusion*. London: Weidenfeld and Nicolson, 1972.

Moravec, Frantisek, *Master of Spies*. London: The Bodley Head, 1975.

Morley, James William, ed. *Deterrent Diplomacy: Japan, Germany, and the U.S.S.R.-1935-1940*. New York: Columbia University Press, 1976.

Presseisen, Ernst L. *Germany and Japan: A Study in Totalitarian Diplomacy 1933-1941*. New York: Howard Fertig, 1969.

Rauch, Georg. "Der deutsch-sowjetische Nichtangriffspakt vom August 1939 und die sowjetische Geschichtsforschung" in Gottfried Niedhart, *Kriegsbeginn 1939*. Darmstadt: Wissenschaftliche Buchgesellschaft, 1976.

Ribbentrop, Joachim von. *The Ribbentrop Memoirs*. Translated by Oliver Watson. London: Weidenfeld and Nicolson, 1954.

Roberts, Henry C. "Maxim Litvinov," in Craig and Gilbert, eds., *The Diplomats*, pp. 344-377.

Rose, Norman. *Vansittart: Study of a Diplomat*. London: Heinemann, 1978.

Rossi, A. *The Russo-German Alliance: August 1939-June 1941*. Boston: Beacon Press, 1951.

Ruland, Bernd. *Deutsche Botschaft Moskau*. Bayreuth: Hestia Verlag, 1964.

Schorske, Carl E. "Two German Ambassadors: Dirksen and Schulenburg," in Craig and Gilbert, eds., *The Diplomats*, pp. 477-511.

Shirer, William L. *The Collapse of the Third Republic*. New York: Simon and Schuster, 1969.

_____. *The Rise and Fall of the Third Reich*. New York: Simon and Schuster, 1960.

Sommer, Theo. *Deutschland und Japan zwischen den Maechten 1935-1940*. Tuebingen: J. C. Mohr, 1962.

Sontag, R. J. and J. S. Beddie, eds. *Nazi-Soviet Relations: 1939-1941: Documents from the Archives of the German Foreign Office*. New York: Didier, 1948.

Tarulis, A. N. *Soviet Policy Toward the Baltic States, 1918-1940.* Notre Dame, Indiana: Notre Dame University Press, 1959.

Taylor, A. J. P. *The Origins of the Second World War.* New York: Atheneum, 1968.

Thompson, Neville. *The Anti-Appeasers.* Oxford: Oxford University Press, 1971.

Toscano, Mario. *Designs in Diplomacy.* Baltimore: Johns Hopkins University Press, 1970.

_____. *The Origins of the Pact of Steel.* Baltimore, Johns Hopkins University Press, 1967.

Toynbee, Arnold (ed.) *Survey of International Affairs, 1938.* London: Royal Institute of International Affairs, 1951.

_____. *Survey of International Affairs, 1939-1946: The World in March 1939.* London: Royal Institute of International Affairs, 1952.

Ulam, Adam B. *Expansion and Coexistence: The History of Soviet Foreign Policy, 1917-1967.* New York: Praeger, 1968.

Vnuk, F. "Munich and the Soviet Union," *Journal of Central European Affairs,* XXI: 3 (October 1961), 285-304.

Watt, D. C. "The Initiation of the Negotiations leading to the Nazi-Soviet Pact: A Historical Problem" in C. Abramsky (ed.) *Essays in Honour of E. H. Carr* (London: Archon Books, 1974), pp. 152-170.

Weinberg, G. L. *Germany and the Soviet Union, 1939-1941.* Leiden: E. J. Brill, 1954.

_____. *The Foreign Policy of Hitler's Germany: Starting World War II 1937-1939.* Chicago: Chicago University Press, 1980.

Wheeler-Bennett, John W. *Munich: Prologue to Tragedy.* London: Macmillan, 1948.

_____. *The Nemesis of Power: The German Army in Politics, 1918-1945.* London: Macmillan, 1964.

Williamson, Murray. *The Change in the European Balance of Power 1938-1939.* (Unpublished Ph.D. dissertation, Yale University, 1975.)

Woytak, Richard A. *On the Border of War and Peace: Polish Intelligence and Diplomacy in 1937-1939 and the Origins of the Ultra Secret.* New York: Columbia University Press, 1979.

Young, A. P. *The "X" Documents.* London: Andre Deutsch, 1974.

Zeman, Z. A. B. *Nazi Propaganda.* New York: Oxford University Press, 1973. Second edition.

4

THE U.S. AND CHINA:
THE GREAT DIPLOMATIC
LEAP FORWARD

When the moment comes to jump—leapfrog over the position immediately ahead.

William Safire describing Nixon's political philosophy.[1]

We took even ourselves by surprise. Originally we had not thought reconciliation possible. We were convinced that the Chinese were fanatic and hostile.

Henry Kissinger[2]

For over two decades after triumphant Communist revolutionaries proclaimed the establishment of the People's Republic of China in October 1949, Chinese-American relations were beset by ideological, economic, and military confrontations. To the United States, the emergence of a new Communist nation in 1949 meant that the West—the Free World—had lost an ally and acquired a dangerous antagonist. Until the mid-1960's, most Americans did not even begin to distinguish between the People's Republic of China and the rest of the Communist world—"they" simply belonged to a monolithic, centralized bloc that was dominated by the Soviet Union.

During the Korean War, American apprehensions about Communist China intensified: wasn't China aggressively trying to expand its borders and export the Communist ideology by force, if necessary? For their part, the Chinese were alarmed at the prospect of American military operations so close to their border and therefore chose to fight American troops in Korea. But neither side cared to indulge in, or indeed was capable of, the luxury of comprehending the other's perceptions. Determined to meet force with force, the United States encircled the PRC by signing a series of defense treaties with Asian states, of which those with the Republic of China (Taiwan), South Korea, and Japan were the most important. With the aid of its Western allies, the United States also continued to enforce an economic embargo on China long after the Korean

War came to an end and complemented the embargo by a political campaign to isolate the Chinese. And while the PRC demanded great power standing in the United Nations Security Council, the United States blocked even mere membership of the Communist Chinese in the United Nations.

Although the Korean and French Indo-China Wars were over by the mid-1950's and East-West relations had stabilized in the form of a bipolar world, based on a balance of terror, American-Chinese relations remained at a low ebb. Compelled by the zero-sum-game logic of a tight bipolar international system to support the staunchly anti-Communist Republic of China, America obviously could not even consider approaching the People's Republic of China. In the late 1950's this situation led the United States to commit an error which great powers are often liable to make: it allowed a weaker state to determine its foreign policy on issues that were primarily important to the weaker state. The Nationalist Chinese government capitalized on the fears of American politicians who did not want to be accused of a second "betrayal" of China and tried to strengthen the American commitment to the Nationalist cause by initiating the offshore islands crises (Quemoy and Matsu). The "tail wagged the dog," and, because of the Republic of China's brinkmanship policies, the United States found itself in a nuclear confrontation with the People's Republic of China and its ally, the Soviet Union. After the crisis was defused, the People's Republic continued to disseminate anti-American propaganda and to threaten the occupation of Taiwan, but contented itself with routine bombardment of the Taiwan-held offshore islands.

In the United States, the pro-Taiwan China lobby exerted heavy pressure on both public opinion and the Congress.[3] The State Department was sharply criticized for "the loss of China" to the Communists, and several middle-level policy-makers were purged during the Korean War and the McCarthy era. As a result, no American official dared to appear "soft" on Communist China by advocating a reversal of the anti-Peking policy.

Thus, the combination of the Cold War atmosphere, the possibly exaggerated perception of the power of the China lobby, and the influence of McCarthyism ruled out the possibility of any approach to China, let alone a rapprochement. John Foster Dulles' foreign policy precluded opening a dialogue with China or even responding to Chou En-lai's "Five Principles of Coexistence," enunciated during the Geneva Conference in 1954 and again at the Bandung Conference in April 1955. The logic of Dulles' policy had been weakened by the 1960's, but the forces of inertia and mutual misperception raised a formidable barrier to conducting a dialogue.[4]

Though in the early 1960's the cracks in the Soviet-Chinese alliance became increasingly evident, deeply rooted prejudices and preconceptions prevented early American recognition of the split. The U.S.S.R. and China had become bitter enemies who competed for the allegiance of other Communist and non-aligned states. But by the time the Soviet-Chinese rift had become an indisputable fact—which could have smoothed the way for a U.S.-Chinese reconciliation—the United States was heavily involved in the Vietnam War, and China was embroiled in the xenophobic, ideologically cathartic Great Proletarian Cultural Revolution. Hence a Chinese-American rapprochement seemed further away than ever.

Yet, as early as 1960, while he was still Vice-President, Richard Nixon attempted to visit the People's Republic of China. This unlikely voyage was, however, aborted when the State Department refused to grant permission to some Democratic Senators for a similar visit. The Senators, feeling that if they could not go, Nixon should not be allowed to go either, threatened to use the preferential treatment of the Vice-President for partisan political purposes. In the end, nobody went. Nevertheless, Nixon's interest in China did not prevent him from continuing to voice characteristically anti-Communist sentiments. During his presidential campaign against John F. Kennedy in October 1960, e.g., Nixon said: "Now, what do the Chinese Communists want? They don't want just Quemoy and Matsu. They don't want just Formosa. They want the world."[5]

Some analysts believe that an article published by Nixon in the October 1967 issue of *Foreign Affairs* marked a turning point in his basic position on the People's Republic of China. As the Johnson administration sank more and more deeply into the Vietnam quagmire, Nixon was supposedly contemplating radical changes in his article, "Asia After Vietnam."

> Any American policy toward Asia must come urgently to grips with the reality of China.
>
> Taking the long view, we simply cannot afford to leave China forever outside the family of nations, there to nurture its fantasies, cherish its hates and threaten its neighbors. There is no place on this small planet for a billion of its potentially most able people to live in angry isolation. But we could go disastrously wrong if, in pursuing this long-range goal, we failed in the short range to read the lessons of history.
>
> The world cannot be safe until China changes. Thus our aim, to the extent that we can influence events, should be to induce change. The way to do this is to persuade China that it *must* change: that it cannot satisfy its imperial ambitions, and that its own national interest requires a turning away from foreign adventuring and a turning inward toward the solution of its own domestic problems.[6]

Yet a careful reading of the entire article reveals that Nixon himself was then by no means certain of the best policy to adopt towards China.

In actual fact, "Asia After Vietnam" presents a largely negative picture of China. Nixon speaks of: the need to "recognize a common danger, and see its source as Peking" (p. 111); Peking's expansionist goals toward India, Thailand, and Malaysia (p. 111); the need to forestall the Chinese threat (p. 116): Chinese aggression (p. 123); China as "the epicenter of world revolution" (p. 123); and "the poison from the Thoughts of Mao" (p. 123). Throughout, Nixon refers to China as "Peking"—not as "the People's Republic." To him, it is China, not the United States, which must change and refrain from foreign adventures. At best, his attitude is contradictory; it is more positive than in the past, but it is also far from advocating a reversal of existing policies. As a shrewd politician, he is careful not to commit himself, lest a positive attitude toward China should evoke negative reactions at home. On the basis of this article he could always claim that he espoused a tough and immutable posture toward China. Commentators who chose the above quotation to prove that Nixon had already conceived of a new "grand design" that was later implemented as his China policy, have conveniently omitted an important part of the article. The missing section is tougher in tone.

> This does not mean, as many would simplistically have it, rushing to grant recognition to Peking, to admit it to the United Nations and to ply it with offers of trade—all of which would serve to confirm its rulers in their present course. It does mean recognizing the present and potential danger from Communist China, and taking measures designed to meet that danger. It also means distinguishing carefully between long-range and short-range policies, and fashioning short-range programs so as to advance our long-range goals . . .[7]

The practice of selective quoting that supports the theory on Nixons's early change of heart was probably encouraged by his own administration *only after* general support for his China policy had been secured. Evidently, Nixon had not completely formulated the 1969-1970 version of his China policy when he wrote the *Foreign Affairs* article, for he ignored all of the above-quoted caveats during his first term in office. "Asia After Vietnam" cannot be considered a serious signal to the Chinese. Nixon was advocating a policy of "firm restraint, of no reward, of a creative counterpressure designed to persuade Peking that its interests can be served only by accepting the basic rules of international civility." In his memoirs, Nixon devotes only one sentence to this article and in no way points to it as a signal to the Chinese.[8]

In *White House Years*, Henry Kissinger makes it clear that Nixon's China policy did not unfold according to a special plan.

Kissinger's assessment

In retrospect all successful policies seem preordained. Leaders like to claim prescience for what has worked, ascribing to planning what usually starts as a series of improvisations. It was no different with the new China policy. The new Administration had the general intention of making a fresh start. But in all candor it had no precise idea how to do this and it had to take account of domestic realities, not the least of which was Nixon's traditional support among the conservative "China lobby" that had never forgiven Truman and Acheson for allegedly betraying Chiang Kai-shek.[9]

Kissinger goes on to describe Nixon's early behavior toward China as schizophrenic: on the one hand, Nixon was interested in approaching China, but on the other hand he complained to Kissinger and Secretary of State Rogers about a certain U.S. Ambassador's failure to prevent the European nation in which he served from recognizing the People's Republic of China.[10]

It may be said, then, that when Nixon took office, his mind was not yet completely made up concerning this country's China policy. On the one hand, he was interested in seeking an opening towards China; on the other, he was sure neither of the Chinese response nor of the domestic support for such a move.

As a shrewd politician he therefore demonstrated much more caution in his early public statements than in his instructions to Henry Kissinger and the State Department. The danger in this policy was, of course, that in the early signaling stage the signals made in public may have *discouraged the Chinese* and given them the impression of a continuation of the old U.S. policy toward China, an impression which may not have been corrected by secret private messages.

As we shall see below, as Nixon crystalized his policy and became more confident, his tough public statements on China gave way to more positive public hints, while more daring moves were undertaken by secret diplomacy.[11]

The idea of moving toward China seemed more plausible as Nixon began to recognize opportunities for the United States in the growing Soviet-Chinese rift. Viewing the Soviet Union as the major adversary of the United States, he developed the concept of playing the Chinese off against the Soviet Union during the presidential election campaign of 1968. "Nixon's vision was an Asia where the Soviet and Chinese interests would cancel each other out, thereby requiring a permanent American presence, in one form or another, throughout the Pacific."[12] Nixon's attitude toward China was not so much the result of a change in his ideological world view as much as it was the product of his realistic assessment of global power politics and American national interests.

The Chinese government made the first move after Nixon's election, well before his inauguration. On November 26, 1968, Lei Yang, the Chinese Chargé d'Affaires in Warsaw, sent the American Ambassador, Walter J. Stoessel, a note proposing that they hold a formal meeting on February 20. (Such meetings between the American and Chinese Ambassadors in Warsaw, inaugurated by the PRC in 1955 in the spirit of "peaceful coexistence," had only taken place once or twice a year since the beginning of the Cultural Revolution.) The note came as a surprise to the Johnson administration because the last meeting with the Chinese had occurred on January 8, 1968. The delivery of the note was reported on Radio Peking, which in this connection referred to Chou En-lai's "Five Principles of Coexistence." This was the first time since the beginning of the Cultural Revolution that the "Five Principles," first enunciated by Chou En-lai in 1954 at the Geneva Conference leading to the French withdrawal from Vietnam, had been publicly mentioned. The Johnson administration decided to let the President-elect respond to the invitation when he took office.

The Nixon administration took its first hesitant steps toward the new China policy in 1969; but contradictory signals abounded on both sides, so the nascent rapprochement developed at a correspondingly hesitant pace. According to Kissinger, Nixon promptly signaled the Chinese in his Inaugural Address on January 20, 1969: "Let all nations know that during this administration our lines of communication will be open. We seek an open world—open to ideas, open to the exchange of goods and people—a world in which no people, great or small, will live in angry isolation."[13] But the Chinese did not respond to Nixon's "open lines of communication." In fact, the China News Agency denounced the new American President in flamboyant rhetoric as a "puppet" of the "monopoly bourgeois clique" which supported American expansionism all over the globe.[14]

The exchange of signals continued to proceed in this inauspicious fashion. During his first news conference on January 27, 1969, President Nixon was asked whether he had any plans for "improving relations with Communist China." His response in public was no more positive than the one he had given in the "Asia After Vietnam" article—he said that he saw "no immediate prospect of any change in our policy until some changes occur on their side."[15] This extemporaneous answer, given under the pressure of the news conference, seemed to reflect his traditionally-held views.

Five days later, on February 1, the President sent Kissinger, then Assistant to the President for National Security, a memorandum in which he suggested: "We should give every encouragement to the attitude that this Administration is exploring possibilities of rapprochement with the Chinese. This, of course, should be done privately and should under no circumstances get into the public print from this direction."[16] Moreover, Kissinger was to discreetly spread the idea among East European nations that the U.S. was moving toward China with the obvious goal of making the Soviet Union anxious to cooperate with the United States, particularly in ending the war in Vietnam.[17] In early February, Nixon also told Senator Mike Mansfield that he was convinced of the need to involve the Chinese in "global responsibility" before Sino-Soviet hostility erupted into open warfare.[18]

Meanwhile, China experts at the State Department and on Kissinger's staff had been evaluating the Chinese message of November 26. Finally, Nixon personally responded that his administration would welcome the proposed meeting in Warsaw, and both countries decided that the talks would resume on February 20. In early February, however, Chinese-American relations suddenly deteriorated: the Chinese Chargé d'Affaires in the Netherlands defected and was granted asylum in the United States. At first, the Chinese reaction was comparatively restrained. The PRC government sent a letter of protest to Washington on February 6, blaming the United States, the Chargé d'Affaires, and the Dutch government.[19] Things remained relatively quiet until the Chinese abruptly cancelled the Warsaw meeting on February 18, two days before it was to convene, ostensibly because the Americans had granted asylum to the defector and were supposedly plotting with the Nationalist government to send the defector to Taiwan. In *China-Watch*, Robert G. Sutter states: "In fact, the Chinese Nationalist Embassy on 9 February had predictably invited the diplomat to visit Taiwan, but the United States had remained silent on the issue, and the defector had remained in the United States." The actual reason for the cancellation was that the "ideologically pure" faction within the Chinese leadership vehemently opposed an approach to the United States.

> In a broad sense, the decision to cancel the Warsaw meeting was the work of Chinese leaders who favored a show of firm Chinese resolve against both the United States and the Soviet Union. These leaders, who seemed to center around Chiang Ching, had indicated that they viewed accommodation with the United States as a retreat from Chinese principles and as ideologically deviant behavior. Opposing them were leaders of the Chinese Foreign ministry under Chou En-lai, who had tried to . . . deal pragmatically with Peking's weak position in the balance of power in East Asia.[20]

This incident caused much suspicion on both sides, thus delaying the resumption of contacts for almost a year.[21]

By mid-February, the National Security Council was preparing a major study (NSSM-14) on the possibility of improving U.S.-China relations while the United States maintained relations with Taiwan. Nixon hoped that a two-China policy, if presented in mutually palatable terms, would be acceptable to the People's Republic of China.[22] He ordered the NSC and the China desk at the State Department to prepare studies, but did not inform them that he was considering a drastic reversal in American policy. Only Kissinger and Secretary of State Rogers knew of the President's plans. Since the smooth transition from one policy to another required secrecy, the number of participants during the first and second stages of exchanging signals with Peking was very small indeed. On February 18, the day the Chinese cancelled the talks scheduled for the 20th, the President instructed Secretary of State Rogers to declare that the United States wished to engage in a broad program of cultural and scientific exchange with China.

Three days later, while Kissinger was briefing newsmen on Nixon's upcoming visit to Europe, he was asked whether the President would be discussing China with European leaders. Answering positively, he said that the United States could not ignore the international role of a country of seven hundred million people. Kissinger then added that Nixon had always favored a policy of "maximum contact" with China. This seemed to be a signal to the Chinese, since Nixon had never publicly advocated such a policy.[23]

However, the sudden Chinese cancellation of the Warsaw meeting elicited a tough, pessimistic response from President Nixon. In this early stage of initiating the rapprochement with China, Nixon had not yet become accustomed to the ups and downs that are—as was demonstrated by the Nazi-Soviet negotiations—endemic to this type of signaling process. In a press conference on March 4, 1969, he said:

> Looking further down the road, we could think in terms of a better understanding with Red China. But being very realistic, in view of Red China's breaking off the rather limited Warsaw talks that were planned, I do not think that we should hold out any great optimism for any breakthroughs in that direction at this time.[24]

The prospects for the Chinese-American relationship did not look good, to say the least: the Chinese viciously attacked Nixon and the United States in their media while Nixon, in mid-March, described the "Safeguard" ABM program as a protection against the Chinese threat. Chinese fears of United States-Soviet Union collusion seemed to be materializing when Nixon said: "I would imagine that the Soviet Union would be just as reluctant as we would be to leave their country naked against a potential Chinese Communist threat. So the abandoning of the entire system, particularly as long as the Chinese threat is there, I think neither country would look upon with favor."[25]

The Chinese may have also perceived Nixon's remarks as expressing support for the Russians in the Sino-Soviet border clashes that had erupted along the Ussuri River on March 2, and again in mid-March. Each side claimed to have been the victim of the other's aggression and tension mounted. According to Kissinger, the administration was so pre-occupied with Vietnam that it did not even think of getting involved in Sino-Soviet troubles. "And while I favored establishing a triangular rela-tionship as a matter of theory, both Nixon and I still considered the People's Republic of China the more aggressive of the Communist powers."[26] These incidents were a turning point in the American-Chinese relationship, for the PRC was forced to think of ways to counter the very real Soviet threat.

Nevertheless, the desire of the Nixon administration to eventually establish a relationship with the Chinese was evident throughout the rather disharmonious month of March. Meeting with President de Gaulle in Paris on March 1, Nixon said that he was determined to open a dialogue with Peking "whatever the difficulties." (Earlier, the U.S. State Department had deplored de Gaulle's resumption of diplomatic relations with China.) Nixon indicated that he envisioned the eventual admission of Red China to the United Nations and the normalization of U.S.-China relations. Aware of "China's suspicions of the West and the United States," Nixon hoped to alleviate Peking's fears by ending the American involvement in Vietnam and initiating contacts with China.[27]

When de Gaulle attended Eisenhower's funeral a few weeks later, Nixon asked him to inform the Chinese government of the American desire to imporve U.S.-China relations. Accordingly, on April 23, 1969, de Gaulle instructed Etienne M. Manach, the newly appointed French Ambassador in Peking, to deliver Nixon's message to the Chinese leaders. As he transmitted the message in early May, the Ambassador also indicated that the United States would eventually soften its position on the Taiwan issue. Chinese leaders, including Chou En-lai, were skeptical—given Nixon's past attitude they did not see how such a change could be possible.

On March 28, Kissinger asked the NSC staff to prepare a study on "Trade with Communist China" (NSSM-35). The paper was written with the aid of State Department experts, the CIA, and the Treasury and Commerce Departments. Two possible approaches were discussed: (1) the "fell swoop" method—that is, the removal of all restrictions on the trade of non-strategic goods with China; (2) the gradual normalization of trade. Primarily for domestic political considerations, Nixon chose the second approach.[28]

On May 24, when Secretary of State Rogers visited President Yahya Khan of Pakistan in Lahore, he asked if Pakistan would be willing to help establish a secret diplomatic link with the Chinese government and in-form them that the United States was "serious and forthright" in its approach. President Khan agreed to deliver the message and serve as a go-between for the two countries.

In early June, Kissinger asked the State Department to propose gestures that the United States could make toward the People's Republic of China without simultaneously damaging U.S. relations with her allies in the Pacific. The Department suggested five possibilities, all of them economic. Of the five alternatives President Nixon selected two and also recommended some political and military moves, and late in July the United States unilaterally began to make the following friendly gestures.

(1)	July 21, 1969	Scholars, journalists, students, and Congressmen could now have their passports automatically validated for travel to Mainland China. In addition, American tourists could purchase in China goods in amounts up to $100 in value.
(2)	August 8, 1969	During his Asian tour, Secretary of State Rogers expressed the U.S. government's desire to resume the ambassadorial talks in Warsaw.
(3)	November 7, 1969	The United States decided to suspend routine naval patrols in the Taiwan straits which had been carried out since the Korean War by two destroyers of the Seventh Fleet.
(4)	December 15, 1969	The United States announced that it would remove all its nuclear weapons from Okinawa by the end of 1969. The weapons had reportedly been installed as a nuclear deterrent against Communist China.
(5)	December 19, 1969	The $100 limit on goods purchased in China by U.S. citizens was removed. Such goods could now be purchased in unlimited amounts. The Department of Commerce permitted foreign subsidiaries of American firms to trade freely with China in non-strategic goods.[29]

In order to ensure that these signals had been received and understood in the spirit intended, the United States used intermediaries such as France, Rumania, and Pakistan, since it had no direct diplomatic connections with China. In July and August of 1969, President Nixon embarked on a long tour of Asia during which he planned to signal the Chinese through friendly heads of state. It was no coincidence that the State

Department announced on July 21, on the eve of Nixon's departure, the decision to lift most travel restrictions on the People's Republic of China.

The President's tour began with a proclamation that was later dubbed "the Nixon Doctrine." The new policy, announced on July 25 during a stopover in Guam, helped to clear the air between the United States and China, although it was not exclusively a signal to China.

The United States would be ready, the President said, to support its Asian allies morally, financially, and materially, but would no longer send troops or engage in any type of direct military intervention. In most countries, the Nixon Doctrine was automatically interpreted as a direct reaction to the American experience in Vietnam. American allies in Asia would have to assume responsibility for their own defense. For Asian allies, the doctrine meant a watering-down of American commitments, but for the Chinese it meant a less threatening American posture in the future. The Nixon Doctrine provides a good example of the difficulty involved in transmitting signals across different cultures and political traditions.

> While the United States proposed to reduce its military commitments in the Pacific, it encouraged Japan and other countries to assume a larger military role. That, in turn, could lead to greater anxiety on the part of China.[30]

This is exactly what happened. In an August 5, 1969, interview with *New York Times* colummnist James Reston, Chou En-lai said that the doctrine was indeed contradictory and that there should be an effort at relaxation by *all* parties concerned.[31]

When President Nixon met with President Yahya Khan in Lahore on August 1, China was the major topic of their discussion. Khan told the President that the Chinese response to Pakistan's probing on behalf of the United States had been lukewarm. Nevertheless, they decided to maintain the Pakistani connection.[32]

On August 2, Nixon arrived in Bucharest to confer with a second important intermediary, President Nicolae Ceausescu of Rumania. The only public signal sent by Nixon during his trip was recognized by the Chinese—but not by independent observers. In the course of the formal banquet at the Council of State Palace in Bucharest, Nixon offered the following toast:

> Your country pursues a policy of communication and contact with all nations—you have actively sought the reduction of international tensions. My country shares those objectives. We are seeking ways of ensuring the security, progress, and independence of the nations of Asia, for, as recent history has shown, if there is no peace in Asia there is no peace in the world.[33]

A week later, on August 8, Secretary Rogers was much more explicit in his speech to the National Press Club in Canberra, Australia. The speech went unnoticed by the American press, but was reviewed with great interest in China.[34]

> We recognize, of course, that the Republic of China on Taiwan and Communist China on the mainland are facts of life. We know, too, that mainland China will eventually play an important role in Asian and Pacific affairs—but not as long as its leaders continue to have such an introspective view of the world. . . . Communist China obviously has long been too isolated from world affairs. This is the reason why we have been seeking to open up channels of communication. Just a few days ago, we liberalized our policies toward purchase of their goods by American travelers and toward validating passports for travel to China. Our purpose was to remove irritants in our relations and to help remind people on mainland China of our historic friendship for them. . . . We were prepared to offer specific suggestions on an agreement for more normal relations when the Chinese cancelled the scheduled resumption of the ambassadorial talks in Warsaw last February. None of our initiatives has met with a positive response. Apparently, the present leaders in Peking believe that it serves their purposes to maintain a posture of hostility toward the United States. They seem unprepared for any accommodation. Their central position is that they will discuss nothing with us unless we first abandon support of our ally, the Republic of China. This we do not propose to do. We nonetheless look forward to a time when we can enter into a useful dialogue and to a reduction of tensions. We would welcome a renewal of the talks with Communist China. We shall soon be making another approach to see if a dialogue with Peking can be resumed . . . in Warsaw or at any other mutually acceptable site.[35]

At the time he made this speech, Rogers was not aware of Nixon's talks with the leaders of Rumania and Pakistan.[36] Thus, the signal was not coordinated with President Nixon's feelers, although it probably appeared that way to the Chinese.

When the exchange of signals is presented in chronological order, the cumulative effect is impressive. In reality, the messages or moves of the respective sides were sometimes separated by more than a month, and their meaning was usually ambiguous. Despite the abundance of signals from the United States, the Chinese remained silent throughout the summer of 1969; nor did the signals seem to attract the attention of other states.

By the fall of 1969, there were indications that the Chinese were interested in resuming the Warsaw talks. Fear of a Soviet attack may have made them more responsive, since the United States was the only power that could match and possibly deter the forces of the Soviet Union. The serious Sino-Soviet border clashes that had broken out in March were only the beginning of smaller incidents that had occurred during the late spring and summer along the Amur River and the Sinkiang border. The Chinese may have felt that the Soviet Union was looking for an excuse to launch a preemptive attack, for such a possibility was implied by Russian diplomats who indicated that their country might decide to destroy China's nuclear force.[37] The clashes in Sinkiang also changed Kissinger's opinion of who was to blame for the military action. "Originally I had accpeted the fashionable view that the Chinese were the more militant country. But when I looked at a detailed map and saw that the Sinkiang incidents took place only a few miles from a Soviet railhead and several hundred miles from any Chinese railhead, it occurred to me that Chinese military leaders would not have picked such an unpropitious spot to attack. After that I looked at the problem differently."[38] Russian troop concentrations on the Chinese border had significantly increased to 25 fully equipped Soviet divisions. In such situations, the logic of realpolitik takes precedence over ideological concerns; thus, a common, though negative, interest was created between the United States and China.[39]

In October 1969, Nixon ordered Walter J. Stoessel, the American Ambassador in Poland, to contact Lei Yang, the Chinese Chargé d'Affaires, at the first suitable diplomatic function in order to inform him of the American desire to reopen the Warsaw talks. The American proposal was finally communicated to Lei Yang on December 3. The extraordinary delay was caused by the American Ambassador's reluctance to make such an unorthodox move, and the Chinese Chargé d'Affaires' similar reluctance to be contacted in such a manner.[40] Once more, a considerable period of time had elapsed between signals. However, shortly after Stoessel communicated his desire to meet with the Chinese Chargé d'Affaires to the Chinese interpreter, the American Ambassador received an invitation to come to the Chinese Embassy on December 11. At the meeting Stoessel proposed that the ambassadorial talks be resumed. At a follow-up meeting at the American Embassy on January 8, 1970, Lei and Stoessel set January 20 as the date for resumption of the Warsaw talks.[41] This was the first clear and positive Chinese response to the American signaling efforts of the previous summer. In his memoirs, Nixon says that "during 1969 the Chinese ignored the few low-level signals of interest we sent them, and it was not until 1970 that we began a serious approach to opening a dialogue. . . ."[42] Oddly enough, he describes all of the American signals in 1969 as "few" and "low-level." Naturally, people tend to remember their successes when writing their memoirs, and Nixon may be reluctant to reveal the extent to which his efforts in 1969 remained unrequited.

It is safe to assume that deteriorating relations with the Soviet Union played a very important part in the Chinese decision to resume the Warsaw talks. On January 8, Peking and Washington announced that the talks would begin on January 20 (Meeting No. 135). The U.S. State Department spokesman made reference to the discussions that would commence at "the Chinese Communist Embassy." A few hours later, the White House ordered that it be called "the Embassy of the People's Republic of China." Spokesman Robert McCloskey changed his terminology and repeated the reference to the People's Republic of China three times for emphasis. This was the first time that an official spokesman of the United States government had called China by its official name.

During the ambassadorial talks that resumed on January 20, Ambassador Stoessel read a carefully drafted statement which reassured the Chinese that "the United States did not seek to 'join in any condominium with the Soviet Union directed against China.' He added. . . : The United States 'would be prepared to consider sending a representative to Peking for direct discussions with your officials or receiving a representative from your government in Washington for more thorough exploration of any of the subjects I have mentioned in my remarks today or other matters on which we might agree.' "[43] Lei Yang then went on to read the moderately-worded statement of the Chinese government which also included a suggestion for the improvement of U.S.-China relations: "These talks may either continue to be conducted at the ambassadorial level or may be conducted at a higher level or through other channels acceptable to both sides."[44] According to a report published in the *Washington Post* on May 11, 1980, the first signals of U.S. readiness to change its position on the Taiwan issue were made at this meeting. The report stated that the Chinese Chargé d'Affaires had complained about continued U.S. silence regarding the issue of Taiwan. Ambassador Stoessel, after first paying lip service "to U.S. opposition to an armed attack on Taiwan," added that "[the] limited United States military presence on Taiwan is not a threat to the security of your government, and *it is our hope that as peace and stability in Asia grow, we can reduce those facilities on Taiwan that we now have.*"[45] (Emphasis added.) The channel of communication had been reestablished on a hopeful note, and the representatives of the two countries agreed to meet again in a month.

Shortly after the meeting in Warsaw, Nixon declared that a partial ABM system was needed to contain the Chinese. This contradictory signal echoed the themes which Nixon had used in his March 1969 announcement regarding the "Safeguard" ABM program. "[He] . . . indicated that the U.S. must be prepared to maintain a flexible defense program for the Pacific. The President predicted that within 10 years Communist China would have made significant strides in its nuclear delivery capabilities and that the U.S. must be ready to block any attempts by China of 'nuclear blackmail' against the U.S. or its Pacific allies. The President also said that the U.S. would seek some normalization of our relationship with Communist China.' "[46] This statement reflected Nixon's domestic problems. Though it could hardly be construed as an amicable gesture by the Chinese, they did not let it interfere with the meeting scheduled for February 20.

On February 18, the President sent a special report to Congress entitled, "U.S. Foreign Policy for the 1970's: A New Strategy for Peace." In the report, he spoke at great length about China.

> The Chinese are a great and vital people who should not remain isolated from the international community. The principles underlying our relations with Communist China are similar to those governing our policies toward the USSR. United States policy is not likely soon to have much impact on China's behavior, let alone its ideological outlook. But it is certainly in our interest, and in the interest of peace and stability in Asia and the world, that we take what steps we can toward improved practical relations with Peking.[47]

He explicitly reassured the Chinese that the United States would not take sides in the Sino-Soviet conflict.

> Our desire for improved relations is not a tactical means of exploiting the clash between China and the Soviet Union. We see no benefit to us in the intensification of that conflict, and we have no intention of taking sides. Nor is the United States interested in joining any condominium or hostile coalition of great powers against either of the large Communist countries. Our attitude is clear-cut— a lasting peace will be impossible so long as some nations consider themselves the permanent enemies of others.[48]

Nixon considers this report his first serious public signal to the Chinese.[49]

Although the report is generally regarded as a meaningful signal, it also includes a tough statement concerning the U.S. stand on China's acceptability to the United Nations. The issue of a U.N. seat for Communist China was not merely a question of becoming a member, but also one of "whether Peking should be permitted to dictate to the world the terms of its membership. The U.S. would continue to object to all attempts to deprive Nationalist China of its membership in the U.N."[50] But, beginning in April 1971, the American stance on China's admission to the United Nations underwent a gradual change.

As the United States continued to send largely favorable signals, the State Department and the White House staff (i.e., Kissinger) clashed over the wisdom of sending a special U.S. emissary to Peking. Fearing that a special envoy in China would jeopardize its authority and stir up trouble with U.S. allies, the State Department recommended that the subject not be brought up at the next meeting in Warsaw. Kissinger thought differently, and eventually won the day.[51]

As planned, the 136th meeting took place on February 20, 1970, and proved to be very successful. Encouraged by the tone of Nixon's foreign policy report (published two days before the Warsaw meeting), the Chinese said that the U.S. was welcome to send any representative, high or low ranking, to participate in talks in Peking. They did not state whether or not the talks were to remain secret.[52] This account of the February 20 Warsaw meeting is based on Kissinger's memoirs. A recent report states, however, that Kissinger's description minimized the importance of that meeting in order to emphasize his own contribution to the U.S.-Chinese rapprochement following his first secret visit to China.

According to this report, apparently leaked by a State Department official, Ambassador Stoessel stated during his conversation with Chargé d'Affaires Lei: "It is my government's position that the question of Taiwan . . . *is to be resolved by those directly involved.* . . . We do not intend to interfere in any peaceful settlement . . . It is my government's intention to reduce those military facilities which we now have on Taiwan as tensions in this area diminish." (Emphasis added.) This secret U.S. concession paved the way for the U.S.-Chinese rapprochement and can also be seen as the origin of the Shanghai communiqué released on February 27, 1972, at the conclusion of Nixon's visit to China, in which the U.S. affirmed "the ultimate objective of removing all U.S. forces and military installations from Taiwan."[53]

To Nixon and Kissinger, however, the Chinese offer appeared premature. In fact, it seemed too good to be true. "Adversaries for more than two decades, it seemed highly improbable that Mao Tse-tung, Chou En-lai, and the other PRC leaders would move so soon in the process."[54] An additional Chinese response to Nixon's foreign policy speech was the dispatch of an indirect message via the Pakistani channel on February 22. President Yahya Khan informed Washington through Pakistani Ambassador Hilaly that he believed recent U.S. actions had encouraged the Chinese.[55]

Though at this point President Nixon and Kissinger felt that they needed to resolve some doubts concerning Chinese intentions, the administration responded promptly by announcing a relaxation of most official restrictions on travel to China. Yet, wary of Chinese intentions, Washington feared that perhaps the Chinese only intended to drive a wedge between the United States and Taiwan. Talks in Peking, instead of in Warsaw, might also damage U.S. relations with Japan and the Soviet Union. In addition, some technical and logistical problems remained unanswered. Would the Chinese grant U.S. representatives diplomatic immunity? Would the U.S. be able to set up "secure communications channels" with Washington? Thus, the positive Chinese response did not mean that the pace of negotiations could suddenly accelerate. Even the most radical and dramatic changes in diplomacy often require an extended period of gestation—they involve the examination of all ramifications of the proposed new direction.

The next meeting was scheduled to take place in Warsaw on May 20 instead of in Peking, as the Chinese had suggested. At the last moment, on the 19th, the Chinese cancelled the meeting as a protest against the U.S. invasion of Cambodia—which had occurred three weeks earlier. This time, however, unlike at the occasion of the cancellation of the February 1969 meeting, the Chinese did not attack the Nixon administration or refer to the state of Sino-American relations; they criticized the action in more general terms and mentioned the possibility of rescheduling the meeting.[56] The United States tried to reassure the Chinese through third parties that it had no intention of either expanding its involvement in Indo-China or of perpetuating its presence in Cambodia or Vietnam. On the contrary, it wanted to withdraw from Vietnam and improve relations with Peking.

Some observers in Washington felt that the last-minute cancellation—like that of February 1969—was symptomatic of strong disagreement within the Chinese political elite. Chou hinted at this internal struggle in talks with Emil Bodnaras, a Deputy Premier of Rumania. In early June 1970 he told Bodnaras that he personally favored the improvement of relations with the Americans, but cautioned that he could not speak for the entire Chinese leadership. However, at a special meeting of the Chinese political and military elite that took place in Peking from August 23 to September 26, Chou's pragmatic policy which had received Mao's blessing, prevailed, thus clearing the way for rapprochement.[57] The signaling process that had virtually ended after the American invasion of Cambodia could now be resumed.

The first public indication of the new Chinese attitude occurred on October 1, 1970, when Edgar Snow (an American writer and long-time sympathizer of the Chinese Communists) was pointedly placed next to Mao in Tien An Men Square on China's National Day. In a conversation with Snow, Mao said that he was concerned about the Russians — Sino-Soviet differences were irreconcilable and would remain so for many years to come. At the same time, Mao's references to the United States were sympathetic.[58]

Curiously enough, at the time this signal went unnoticed by U.S. policymakers. In his memoirs, Kissinger explains what happened:

> Chou En-lai and Mao Tse-tung quite independently decided that the time had come to send us a signal. Unfortunately, they over-

estimated our subtlety, for what they conveyed was so oblique that our crude Occidental minds completely missed the point. On October 1 . . . Chou En-lai led the American writer Edgar Snow . . . and his wife to stand at Mao's side on Tien An Men (the Gate of Heavenly Peace) and to be photographed with Mao reviewing the annual anniversary parade. This was unprecedented; no American had ever been so honored. The inscrutable Chairman was trying to convey something. (As Snow himself later observed of the incident: 'Nothing China's leaders do publicly is without purpose.') Eventually, I came to understand that Mao intended to symbolize that American relations now had his personal attention, but it was by then a purely academic insight: we had missed the point when it mattered. Excessive subtlety had produced a failure of communication.[59]

Thus, signals transmitted across very different cultures and political systems are often misunderstood or not even noticed. It is therefore important to tailor signals to fit the quality and sensitivity of the intended recipient's intelligence service, his cultural background, and his political system as well as other factors that may have an undesired filtering effect on his perceptions.[60] The process is complicated because each side wants to signal the other without attracting the attention of third parties. In this case, the Chinese signals that were not understood until long after they had been sent only caused a brief delay in the American-Chinese road to rapprochement. The existence of strong common interests and other, more explicit signals eventually brought the two nations together.

In late October 1970, Nixon and Kissinger decided that the time was ripe to begin high-level talks in Peking. They thus informed the Chinese through two intermediaries—President Yahya Khan of Pakistan, and President Ceausescu of Rumania[61]—both of whom were visiting the United States to celebrate the 25th anniversary of the United Nations. Meeting with President Khan on October 24, President Nixon expressed his wish to send a representative to open the talks in Peking. There has been some speculation that Nixon also expressed his personal desire to visit China. Yahya, who was on his way to the People's Republic of China, agreed to brief the American government on the Chinese response as soon as he returned home. The Pakistani link was not entirely hidden from public view—during a White House press briefing, Press Secretary Ron Ziegler said that President Nixon and President Khan had discussed U.S.-China relations, and that President Khan would take an "unofficial" American message to the Chinese.[62] Two days later, Nixon met with the Rumanian President in the White House to discuss China. At an official dinner the same evening, Nixon mentioned (as he had during his visit to Bucharest on August 2) the fact that Rumania had good relations with diverse nations.

Edgar Snow and Mao in Tien An Men Square October 1, 1970 — the picture whose significance escaped the Nixon Administration

There are times when the leader of one nation does not have adequate communication with the leader of another. But as I was saying to the President earlier today, he is rather in a unique position. He heads a government which is one of the few in the world which has good relations with the Soviet Union and good relations with the People's Republic of China.[63]

Nixon's use of the term "People's Republic of China" was (in his own words) "a significant diplomatic signal."[64] It was the first time an American President had publicly used the term and thereby indicated his acceptance of the Communist government. Most diplomats and reporters paid no attention to the President's gesture, but Nixon's phraseology was not missed by Anatoly Dobrynin, the Soviet Ambassador in Washington. Later the same evening, he contacted Kissinger and inquired whether the President's unprecedented reference to the People's Republic had any hidden meaning. Kissinger replied that the choice of words had "no special significance and that after all, everybody, including the Soviet Union, uses the same phrase."[65]

Turning his attention to the "Rumanian channel," Nixon may have apprised President Ceausescu of United States willingness to deviate from its hitherto accepted policies and consider the relationship between the Republic of China on Taiwan and the People's Republic of China as an *internal* rather than an *international* problem. This would clarify a statement made by White House spokesman Ron Ziegler on the previous day. "The U.S. opposes the admission of the Peking regime into the U.N. *at the expense* of the expulsion of the Republic of China."[66] (Emphasis added.) The United States in fact adopted a two-China formula, as its later half-hearted support of Taiwan in the United Nations demonstrated. The shift in policy did not require any active change. It simply meant a lack of positive action on Taiwan's behalf. Nixon also requested that Ceausescu tell the Chinese that the United States "would like to exchange high-level personal representatives," even if full diplomatic relations would have to be delayed. He indicated, however, that the reestablishment of full diplomatic relations should be the long-range goal.[67]

Both messages were soon passed to the Chinese. President Khan visited Peking from November 9 and 14 and was received by Chairman Mao. Gheorghe Radulescu, a Rumanian Deputy Premier, went to China in the first week of November and was received by Chou En-lai.

A subtle change in American policy toward China took place in November 1970 when the issue of China's admission to the United Nations was the subject of a U.N. General Assembly debate. Instead of issuing its traditional objections to China's admission, the United States emphasized the injustice of China's demand that Nationalist China be expelled. (The resolution again failed to obtain the two-thirds majority needed to admit China under these conditions.) The significance of this change was lost on most political commentators, who considered it a mere tactical maneuver to combat growing support for China within the General Assembly.[68]

On December 9, Chou En-lai asked President Yahya to inform Washington that he would welcome the arrival of an American representative in Peking to discuss the Taiwan issue. Chou emphasized that the invitation had also been approved by Chairman Mao and Lin Piao. While Chou's invitation was welcomed in Washington, the United States proposed two changes in its reply which was sent via Pakistani Ambassador Hilaly: (1) the United States did not wish to limit the talks to the Taiwan issue; and (2) lower-level American and Chinese representatives should first meet in Pakistan to prepare for a subsequent higher level meeting in Peking.[69]

In mid-December, Premier Chou En-lai told Gheorghe Radulescu that China was interested in improving its relations with the United States, provided an adequate solution to the Taiwan problem could be found. Ceausescu forwarded the message to Kissinger through the Rumanian Ambassador in Washington.

> The communication from the U.S. President is not new. There is only one outstanding issue between us—the U.S. occupation of Taiwan. The P.R.C. has attempted to negotiate on this issue in good faith for fifteen years. If the U.S. has a desire to settle the issue and a proposal for its solution, the P.R.C. will be prepared to receive a U.S. special envoy in Peking. This message has been reviewed by Chairman Mao and by Lin Piao.[70]

In the course of his meeting with the Rumanian Ambassador, Kissinger asked if Chou's remarks meant that the U.S. must sever relations with Taiwan, or whether the Chinese would be willing to accept a compromise solution. The Ambassador felt that the Chinese would be open to some sort of compromise. This message and the Rumanian interpretation of it were of the greatest importance in encouraging Nixon's secret diplomacy.[71]

In the absence of direct contact for over 20 years, the United States and China needed the help of third parties who were familiar with *both* sides and could assist in interpreting their signals.[72] The rapprochement could have taken place without the help of these third parties, but the process would have been much slower and infinitely more complex. The Rumanians, and especially the Pakistanis, were aware of the delicacy of the messages they conveyed and both guarded the secrecy of the process. These intermediaries developed a personal interest in the success of the U.S.-China relationship, for their contribution could considerably enhance their prestige as well as gain the good will (which they hoped would eventually be translated into political and economic support) of the United States and China. Later, the Pakistanis did secure American and Chinese backing in the conflict with India.[73] For them, any move to strengthen China vis-à-vis the U.S.S.R. (which was supporting India) was a welcome move. For the Rumanians, an investment in the good will of the United States was politically and economically important; their participation in the rapprochement process was an assertion of neutrality and independence from the Soviet Union.

During December 1970 and January 1971, the Americans and Chinese conducted a serious exchange of messages through the good offices of the Pakistanis. Given the lack of certainty on both sides concerning the other's true intentions, neither side committed itself to a clear and binding position. As a result, the messages were sufficiently ambiguous to allow each side a plausible excuse for retreat. The Chinese (like the Germans in the negotiations leading to the Ribbentrop-Molotov agreement who instructed their Ambassador in Moscow to read their messages aloud in order not to give the Russians an official copy) did not even sign their notes.[74]

On December 18, Chairman Mao received Edgar Snow for an interview in yet another attempt to signal the United States. He went so far as to discuss the possibility of inviting President Nixon to China.

> The [P.R.C.] Foreign Ministry was studying the matter of admitting Americans from the left, middle, and right to visit China. Should rightists like Nixon, who represent the monopoly capitalists, be permitted to come? He should be welcome because, Mao explained, at present the problems between China and the U.S.A. would have to be solved with Nixon. Mao would be happy to talk to him, either as a tourist, or as a President. . . . What had Taiwan to do with Nixon? That question was created by Truman and Acheson.[75]

According to Snow, Mao preferred men like Nixon—men whose behavior was governed by pragmatism.

> Yes, Nixon could just get on a plane and come. It would not matter whether the talks would be successful. If he were willing to come, the Chairman would be willing to talk to him and it would be all right. It would be all right whether or not they quarrelled, or whether Nixon came as a tourist or as President. He believed they would not quarrel. . . . Discussing Nixon's possible visit to China, the Chairman casually remarked that the presidential election would be in 1972, would it not? Therefore, he added, "*Mr. Nixon might send an envoy first but was not himself likely to come to Peking before early 1972.*"[76]

This was an open invitation to President Nixon. From Mao's discussion, it is evident that he linked Nixon's wish to visit China with American domestic politics (i.e., Nixon's desire to remain in power led him to look for a master stroke that would enhance his popularity just before the upcoming election). As a matter of fact, Mao predicted that Nixon's trip to China would take place not too early to be forgotten by the voters and not too late for the full impact of the visit to be used in his campaign.

As requested by the Chinese, the publication of Snow's interview was delayed for a few months. The Chinese apparently assumed that Snow, like any Chinese newsman, would report the details of his conversation with Mao to U.S. officials as soon as possible. As it turned out, U.S. officials learned of the interview only when it was published after they had already received more explicit communications from Chou En-lai.[77]

The Chinese actually preferred to do business with Nixon who could "deliver the goods" since he had a reputation for being tough on Communism. A liberal would have been too weak to sell a radically new policy to Congress and the American public. Nixon's opportunism and "flexibility" were ideally suited to Chinese plans. If he had been too far to the right and dogmatic (like Vice-President Agnew, who objected to any approach to China and to sacrificing Taiwan in the process), he would not even have considered dealing with the PRC.

During February 1971, developments in Indo-China again interfered with the signaling process. This time, President Nixon's approval of the South Vietnamese invasion of Laos (which was supported by U.S. air power) led to a six-week halt in the exchange of messages through Pakistan. Worried about American intentions and the scope of operations in Laos, the Chinese were reported to have put 30 divisions on alert in the Yunan area.[78] The President tried to assuage Chinese fears on February 17 when he told newsmen that the Laotian operation "should not be interpreted by the Communist Chinese as being a threat to them." This statement attracted little attention at the time because it was not delivered at a televised news conference. During a television interview on February 26, Kissinger said that the events in Laos were "a temporary flare-up" that was "inseparable from the disengagement process" in Indo-China.[79] But the *People's Daily* lashed out at the United States. "By spreading the flames of war to the door of China, U.S. imperialism is on a course posing a grave menace to China. . . . Nixon has indeed fully laid bare his ferocious features and reached the zenith in arrogance."[80]

On February 25, 1971, Nixon spoke of expanding relations with China and of China's possible admission to the United Nations in his second "State of the World" message.

> In the coming year, I will carefully examine what further steps we might take to create broader opportunities for contacts between the Chinese and American peoples, and how we might remove needless obstacles to the realization of these opportunities. We hope for, but will not be deterred by, a lack of reciprocity.

We should, however, be totally realistic about the prospects. The People's Republic of China continues to convey to its own people and to the world its determination to cast us in the devil's role. Our modest efforts to prove otherwise have not reduced Peking's doctrinaire enmity toward the U.S.. . . . So long as Peking continues to be adamant for hostility, there is little we can do by ourselves to improve the relationship. What we can do, we will.[81]

The use of the name "The People's Republic of China" was another first—its first use in an official U.S. government document. This time, Dobrynin did not ask whether the reference was significant. The pessimistic tone of the report soon proved to be unfounded, because the Chinese stepped up the negotiations in April. Nevertheless, it may have unintentionally given political and foreign intelligence analysts the impression that a U.S.-China rapprochement was only a remote possibility.

The early months of 1971 yielded only vague and noncommital communications from the Chinese through the Pakistani channel. Nixon obliquely commented on this lack of progress in a March 4 news conference.

We would like to normalize relations with *all* nations in the world. There has, however, been no receptivity on the part of *Communist China*. But under no circumstances will we proceed with a policy of normalizing relations with *Communist China* if the cost of that policy is to expel Taiwan from the family of nations.[82] (Emphasis added.)

Nixon had reverted to the term "Communist China" as if to express his displeasure and frustration at the silence in Peking. This may have confused intelligence analysts in other countries, particularly the U.S.S.R.; his inconsistent terminology had diluted the impact of the earlier reference to "the People's Republic" in his report to Congress.

On March 14, Chou En-lai told a European diplomat in Peking that the PRC had finally decided to open a high-level dialogue with American leaders. Early that month the Chinese must have reached the conclusion that the U.S. no longer posed a serious threat, especially since it was in the process of withdrawing from Indo-China. Soon afterwards, more explicit messages began to flow through Pakistan.

The Chinese made their next move in the most unexpected way. On April 6, while attending the international table tennis competition in Nagoya, Japan, the Chinese team invited the American team to tour China for a week, with all expenses paid. Sung Chung, a spokesman for the Chinese team, said that the invitation had been extended "so that we can learn from each other and elevate our standards of play . . . [and also] . . . for the sake of promoting friendship between the peoples of China and the U.S."[83] The extraordinary invitation, which was immediately accepted by the Americans, was the first major public signal from the Chinese. The American Ambassador to Japan sent a top priority cable to the State Department, and Secretary Rogers passed the request for instructions on to Nixon and Kissinger. As often happens, even those who participate in a diplomatic surprise can themselves be taken by surprise.

> I was as surprised as I was pleased with the news [writes Nixon in his memoirs]. I had never expected that the China initiative would come to fruition in the form of a Ping-Pong team. We immediately approved the acceptance of the invitation. . . .[84]

This was the "Ping Heard Round the World," as a *Time* article breezily described it. State Department officials who had not been aware of Nixon's activities were startled and failed to recognize the significance of the event.

On April 10, the nine members of the American table tennis team, four officials, three journalists, and two wives left Hong Kong for the PRC. They were the first official American delegation to visit China since 1949. The Chinese accorded them a friendly reception and Chou En-lai was particularly warm when he greeted them on April 14 in the Great Hall of the People in Peking:

> You have opened a new page in the relations of the Chinese and American people. I am confident that this beginning again of our friendship will certainly meet with majority support of our two peoples.[85]

The United States responded with more than a reciprocal gesture. On April 14 the White House released the following statement from the President:

> I asked the Under Secretaries Committee of the National Security Council to make appropriate recommendations to bring this about. After reviewing the resulting study, I decided on the following actions, none of which requires new legislation or negotiations with the People's Republic of China:
> —The United States is prepared to expedite visas for visitors or groups of visitors from the People's Republic of China to the United States.
> —U.S. currency controls are to be relaxed to permit the use of dollars by the People's Republic of China.
> —Restrictions are to be ended on American oil companies providing fuel to ships or aircraft proceeding to and from China except on Chinese-owned or Chinese-chartered carriers bound to or from North Vietnam, North Korea, or Cuba.
> —U.S. vessels or aircraft may now carry Chinese cargoes between non-Chinese ports and U.S.-owned foreign flag carriers may call at Chinese ports.

—I have asked for a list of items of non-strategic nature which can be placed under general license for direct export to the People's Republic of China. Following my review and approval of specific items on this list, direct imports of designated items from China will then also be authorized.

—After due consideration of the results of these changes in our trade and travel restrictions, I will consider what additional steps might be taken. Implementing regulations will be announced by the Department of State and other interested agencies.[86]

President Nixon devoted much of the month of April to his China policy. While appearing before the American Society of Newspaper Editors in Washington on April 16, he said that he had recommended China as the best place for his daughters to go on their honeymoon trips when they got married later in the summer. He then expressed his own desire to visit China, hopefully while he was still in office. He added, "It is premature to talk about recognition. It is premature to talk about a change in our policy with regard to the United Nations. However, we are going to proceed in these very substantive fields of exchange of persons and also in the field of trade. That will open the way to other moves which will be made at an appropriate time.[87]

On April 21, Nixon promised the President of the U.S. Table Tennis Association that he would facilitate plans to invite the Chinese team to the United States.

On the 26th, a special presidential commission that included such conservatives as Henry Cabot Lodge (chairman), Cardinal Terence Cooke, Dr. Norman Vincent Peale, Senator Robert Taft, Jr., and Senator Bourke B. Hickenlooper, recommended that the United States adopt a two-China policy—that is, admit China to the United Nations as long as it did not mean the expulsion of Taiwan.[88]

The real breakthrough in this long and arduous signaling process came on April 27 when Pakistani Ambassador Hilaly presented Kissinger with a handwritten letter from Chou En-lai. (The note had no salutation.)[89] The message opened with what the Americans thought was a ritualistic reference to the need to solve the Taiwan question as a prerequisite to the improvement of U.S.-China relations.

Premier Chou en Lai thanked President Yahya for conveying the message of President Nixon on 5 Jan 71. Premier Chou en Lai is very grateful to President Yahya and he will be grateful if President Yahya conveys the following verbatim message to President Nixon:

"Owing to the situation at the time, it has not been possible to reply earlier to the message from the President of the USA to the Premier of People's Republic of China.

At present, contacts between the People's Republic of China and the United States are being reviewed. However, if the relations between China and the USA are to be restored fundamentally, the

US must withdraw all its Armed forces from China's Taiwan and Taiwan Straits area. A solution to this crucial question can be found only through direct discussions between high level responsible persons of the two countries. Therefore, the Chinese Government reaffirms its willingness to receive publically [sic] in Peking a special envoy of the President of the US (for instance, Mr. Kissinger) or the US Secy of State or even the President of the US himself for a direct meeting and discussions. Of course, if the US President considers that the time is not yet ripe, the matter may be deferred to a later date. As for the modalities, procedure and other details of the high level meeting and discussions in Peking, as they are of no substantive significance, it is believed that it is entirely possible for proper arrangements to be made through the good offices of President Yahya Khan. April 21, 1971."[90]

The Chinese were ready to surprise the world, but President Nixon wanted to wait for a more opportune moment. He explains his decision to maintain secrecy in his memoirs.

I felt that in order for the initiative to have any chance of succeeding, it would have to be kept totally secret until the final arrangements for the presidential visit had been agreed upon. With advance warning, conservative opposition might mobilize the Congress and scuttle the entire effort.[91]

There were other reasons for his decision. For one thing, it was not clear whether a direct meeting between high-ranking officials of both countries would be successful while the Vietnam war was still in progress; nor was it as yet certain whether a mutually satisfactory solution to the Taiwan issue could be reached. And in all probability Nixon wanted to reserve for himself the opportunity to announce his visit to China that was to usher in a new era in American-Chinese relations. After all, it was *his* policy; and with the presidential elections coming up in 1972 he was fully aware of the political advantages to be gained from a timely proclamation.

American-Chinese diplomacy from 1969 to the summer of 1971 is but one more proof of the naiveté of liberal Wilsonian objections to secret diplomacy. Contrary to Wilson's belief, secret diplomacy does not inevitably lead to war, but may in fact help to preserve the peace and ease tensions in the transition from a situation of conflict to one of friendship.

Nixon and Kissinger spent the next few days choosing the special emissary who would go to Peking. David Bruce (the U.S. negotiator with the North Vietnamese in Paris), Henry Cabot Lodge, and Secretary of State Rogers were among those mentioned—but the dice were loaded in Kissinger's favor from the beginning.[92]

On May 10 Kissinger handed Ambassador Hilaly the American reply to Chou's letter. The unsigned message was put in a sealed envelope and addressed to Pakistan's President Yahya. It read as follows:

President Nixon has carefully studied the message of April 21, 1971, from Premier Chou En-lai conveyed through the courtesy of President Yahya Khan. President Nixon agrees that direct high-level negotiations are necessary to resolve the issues dividing the United States of America and the People's Republic of China. Because of the importance he attaches to normalizing relations between our two countries, President Nixon is prepared to accept the suggestion of Premier Chou En-lai that he visit Peking for direct conversations with the leaders of the People's Republic of China. At such a meeting each side would be free to raise the issue of principal concern to it.

In order to prepare the visit by President Nixon and to establish reliable contact with the leaders of the Chinese People's Republic, President Nixon proposes a preliminary *secret* meeting between his Assistant for National Security Affairs, Dr. Kissinger, and Premier Chou En-lai or another appropriate high-level Chinese official. Dr. Kissinger would be prepared to attend such a meeting on Chinese soil, preferably at some location within convenient flying distance from Pakistan to be suggested by the People's Republic of China. Dr. Kissinger would be authorized to discuss the circumstances which would make a visit by President Nixon most useful, the agenda of such a meeting, the time of such a visit and to begin a preliminary exchange of views on all subjects of mutual interest. If it should be thought desirable that a special emissary come to Peking publicly between the secret visit to the People's Republic of China of Dr. Kissinger and the arrival of President Nixon, Dr. Kissinger will be authorized to arrange it. It is anticipated that the visit of President Nixon to Peking could be announced within a short time of the secret meeting between Dr. Kissinger and Premier Chou En-lai. Dr. Kissinger will be prepared to come from June 15 onward.

It is proposed that the precise details of Dr. Kissinger's trip including location, duration of stay, communication and similar matters be discussed through the good offices of President Yahya Khan. *For secrecy, it is essential that no other channel be used. It is also understood that this first meeting between Dr. Kissinger and high officials of the People's Republic of China be strictly secret.* (Emphasis in original.)[93]

The message was then taken to Islamabad by a special Pakistani diplomatic courier who handed it to President Yahya. Next, it was passed on to Pakistan's Foreign Minister Sultan Khan who forwarded it to Chang Tung, the Chinese Ambassador in Islamabad. Finally, it completed the last leg of the journey to Peking.[94]

In the meantime there had been additional public signals. On April 28 a State Department spokesman, in reply to a journalist's question, said that negotiations between the PRC and Taiwan would be the best solution to the Taiwan issue.

> This was a subtle departure from earlier policy: Washington was no longer saying that the Nationalists on Taiwan necessarily held legitimacy over the island, but, rather, that "sovereignty over Taiwan . . . is an unsettled question subject to a future international resolution."[95]

Nixon made another effort to send the Chinese a signal on the following day. In his memoirs, he recalls his hints.

> At my news conference on April 29, I gave another major clue to what was afoot. But once again even the most rigorous monitors and analysts of the Nixon rhetoric failed to pick up the point I was making.
> "What we have done is broken the ice, now we have to test the water to see how deep it is."
> Since none of the reporters had asked me anything about the specific possibility of a visit to China, I asked it of myself. At the end of my reply to a general question about our China policy, I said, "I would finally suggest—I know this question may come up if I don't answer it now—I hope, and as a matter of fact, I expect to visit mainland China sometime in some capacity—I don't know what capacity. But that indicates what I hope for the long term. And I hope to contribute to a policy in which we can have a new relationship with mainland China.[96]

On May 7, the U.S. Treasury Department formally lifted all restrictions on dollar transactions with China. This opened the way for the renewal of normal trade relations which had come to a halt in December 1950 after the Chinese intervention in the Korean War.

After sending the President's acceptance, Washington could only wait and hope. In Nixon's words, "the die was cast, there was nothing left to do not to wait for Chou's reply."[97] Nixon even prepared himself for "serious international embarrassment if the Chinese decided to reject my proposal and then publicize it."[98] But after three weeks he and Kissinger finally received a favorable message. On May 31, President Yahya informed the U.S. government via the Pakistani Ambassador that it could expect a positive reply.

> 1. There is a very encouraging and positive response to the last message.
> 2. Please convey to Mr. Kissinger that the meeting will take place on Chinese soil for which travel arrangements will be made by us.

3. Level of meeting will be as proposed by you.
4. Full message will be transmitted by safe means.[99]

The full message arrived by special diplomatic courier two days later. President Nixon had just finished entertaining President Anastasio Somoza of Nicaragua when Kissinger rushed in breathlessly, carrying two sheets of paper that had just arrived from the Pakistani Embassy. Nixon eagerly read the message:

> Premier Chou En-lai has seriously studied President Nixon's messages of April 29, May 17th and May 22nd 1971, and has reported with much pleasure to Chairman Mao Tse Tung that President Nixon is prepared to accept his suggestion to visit Peking for direct conversations with the leaders of the Peoples [sic] Republic of China. Chairman Mao Tse Tung has indicated that he welcomes President Nixon's visit and looks forward to that occasion when he may have direct conversations with His Excellency the President, in which each side would be free to raise the principal issue of concern to it. It goes without saying that the first question to be settled is the crucial issue between China and the United States which is the question of the concrete way of the withdrawal of all the U.S. Armed Forces from Taiwan and Taiwan Straits area.
>
> Premier Chou En-lai suggests that it would be preferable for Dr. Kissinger to set a date between June 15 and 20th for his arrival in China, and that he may fly direct from Islamabad to a Chinese airport not open to the public. As for the flight, he may take a Pakistan Boeing aircraft or a Chinese special plane can be sent to fly him to and from China, if needed. . . . Premier Chou En-lai warmly looks forward to the meeting with Dr. Kissinger in China in the near future.[100]

When the President finished reading, Kissinger said, "This is the most important communication that has come to an American President since the end of World War II."[101] For nearly an hour, the two discussed the meaning of the China initiative for America and the world. When they had finished it was close to midnight. The President was so moved by the occasion that he found an old bottle of Courvoisier brandy in the family kitchen and proposed a toast:

> Henry, we are drinking a toast not to ourselves personally or to our success, or to our administration's policies which have made this message and made tonight possible. Let us drink to generations to come who may have a better chance to live in peace because of what we have done.[102]

Since President Nixon was convinced that secrecy was essential in facilitating the historical change in American-Chinese relations, he and

Kissinger prepared an elaborate plan of deception to cover Kissinger's trip to Peking. (Appropriately enough, the code name of the plan was Polo, after Marco Polo.) To avoid any undue attention, it was decided to include the secret trip in a tour of Asia and Europe. The dates chosen for his trip (July 9-11) were confirmed with the Chinese about a week before Kissinger departed.

Kissinger left Washington on July 1, arriving in Vietnam the next day. He spent two highly visible and busy days in Saigon conferring with President Thieu on the American peace proposals before departing for Bangkok on July 4. He arrived in New Delhi on July 6, and by July 8 he reached Rawalpindi airport near Islamabad. The prolonged trip became very routine for the journalists, who saw little news in Kissinger's talks. By the time Kissinger arrived in Pakistan only three newsmen were left with him.[103] In Islamabad, Kissinger first paid a courtesy call on President Yahya with whom he discussed the final details of the secret trip. The manner in which Kissinger was to slip away had been carefully planned by the Pakistanis. A dinner scheduled for the same evening to which 90 (disappointed) local dignitaries had been invited was cancelled at five in the afternoon, purportedly because the guest of honor was "exhausted" and suffering from a slight stomach ailment. In order to maintain the authenticity of the cover, the food for the dinner was being prepared although the cancellation had, of course, been planned well in advance. This proved to be a shrewd move since one bored journalist did call the chef to ask about the menu. Journalists were told that Kissinger was leaving in the morning for a mountain resort outside Islamabad where he would be spending the next few days resting. The next day, a decoy convoy of limousines carrying American and Pakistani officials drove with an escort from Islamabad to the mountain resort. Suspecting that something was amiss, a few reporters were convinced that Kissinger was actually on the way to East Pakistan (Bangladesh) to mediate a solution to the crisis between East and West Pakistan. No one, however, guessed that he might be on his way to China. After President Nixon publicly disclosed Kissinger's trip on July 15, one journalist remarked:

The announced schedule of Kissinger's "fact-finding trip" to Asia and Paris was so vague and loose that any fool (I have myself particularly in mind) should have perceived, with all of the recent background at hand, that his main destination was Peking. Yet we of the Press and, it now turns out, the highest officials of immediately interested governments, notably those in Taiwan and Tokyo were simply not prepared that *this* President, this man who made a career of forceful anti-communism, was actually capable of so drastic and dramatic a break not only with past American policy but with his own pattern of attitude and behavior. More important aspects aside, it all provides a lesson in the folly of stereotyping Richard Nixon.[104]

In any event, the stage had now been set for "the greatest disappearing act in modern diplomatic history."

About the time that Kissinger was already in Peking, Nixon sent yet another signal in his address to a group of newspaper editors on July 10. He referred to mainland China as one of the most important countries in the world with a population of 800 million people and enormous economic potential.

> That is the reason why I felt [Nixon said] that it was essential that this administration take the first steps toward ending the isolation of mainland China from the world community. . . . What we see as we look ahead five years, ten years, perhaps it is fifteen years, but in any event within our time, we see five great economic superpowers: the United States, Western Europe, the Soviet Union, Mainland China and of course Japan.[105]

This speech, Nixon recalls in his autobiography, "received relatively little attention in Kansas City. As we were to learn later, however, it received a great deal of attention in Peking."[106]

While Kissinger was supposedly recuperating in the mountain resort, he had actually departed for Peking at 3:30 AM on a Pakistan International Airlines plane. The secrecy of the trip had been so well guarded that even the two security men accompanying Kissinger did not discover their destination until after they boarded the plane. Similarly, the American Ambassador to Pakistan, Joseph S. Farland, was not informed of Kissinger's whereabouts.[107] Only three of Kissinger's closest aides knew of the trip in advance. Since it was on an unscheduled flight, the plane had to take an uncharted route over the Himalayas in order to avoid detection by Soviet and Indian radar.[108]

Kissinger's plane landed at a military airfield near Peking at noon after a five and a half hour flight. He was greeted by the new Chinese military leader, Marshall Yeh Chien-ying, acting Foreign Minister Huang Hua, and two Foreign Ministry officials. Kissinger had been vested with unusual responsibility—he was on his own without direct contact with the White House. Now, on Chinese soil, he would be better able to gauge the sincerity of Chinese intentions and the feasibility of rapprochement.

By agreeing to hold the talks in Peking, the Americans had made a positive diplomatic gesture. Now it was China's turn. At 4 o'clock, Chou En-lai arrived at Kissinger's guest house. This was a remarkable sign of friendship for both Kissinger and his mission since, according to diplomatic protocol, a head of government is not required to call on a visitor who does not even have state rank.[109] Kissinger, Chou, and their staffs then sat down for talks which lasted for eight full hours. The rapport they established eased the initial tension—both Kissinger and Chou were in an accommodating mood. Their talks continued on a frank and businesslike basis for the next few days. Instead of stressing difficult current problems, the conversations focused on long-range developments. The Chinese did not insist on immediate American withdrawal from Vietnam, or termination of U.S. support for Taiwan as a precondition for rapprochement.[110]

In the first meeting, Chou indicated that he understood the limits on how far the Nixon administration could go in satisfying Chinese wishes. Uppermost in the minds of the two men was the need for a rapprochement in order to check the growing power of the Soviet Union. The second most important issue was the Taiwan problem. On June 21 Chou hinted to visiting American journalists that "a withdrawal of U.S. support for Taiwan would facilitate the solution of all other problems between the U.S. and the People's Republic of China."[111] Peking was pressing the United States to acknowledge that Taiwan was part of China and that its fate was an internal Chinese problem. The State Department had, on April 28, essentially accepted this interpretation. Kissinger could thus explain that the U.S. had already taken steps to fulfill China's conditions. Chou said that his country expected that the U.S. would, in due course, sever diplomatic relations with Taiwan, but he did not press for any specific date. (Chinese patience paid off when the U.S. moved its Embassy from Taipei to Peking in January 1979.)

The Nixon administration, Kissinger explained, would not break its relations with Nationalist China in the near future, though it was understood that full diplomatic relations with the PRC could only be established when the United States ceased to have diplomatic relations with Taiwan. The two men also discussed the problem of China's admission to the United Nations. China maintained its all-or-nothing position (i.e., China would enter the U.N. only as a full member that could take Nationalist China's place in the Security Council). The United States still objected to the expulsion of Taiwan. But it became clear in the course of the discussions that the People's Republic of China would be admitted to the U.N. and Taiwan would be expelled even if the United States did not support the move.

The Chinese did not make a central issue out of the U.S. military presence in Japan, South Korea, Taiwan, Thailand, and the Philippines. Since Chou only made a general reference to the issue, Kissinger and his aides suspected that the PRC was not averse to at least some American presence in Asia as a deterrent to the Soviet Union.[112]

It was also understood that the political future of South Vietnam should be settled by the opposing sides after a cease-fire went into effect, prisoners had been exchanged, and American forces had totally withdrawn. This understanding reflected the latest American proposals to the North Vietnamese, and the agreement was indeed implemented in this spirit two years later. Finally, they agreed that all Asian disputes should be settled by peaceful means only. This referred particularly to the conflict between North and South Korea, and the Soviet-Chinese border dispute.[113]

Kissinger and Chou decided that President Nixon's visit should take place no later than May 1972, that is, well before the beginning of the U.S. presidential election campaign.[114] Peking's decision to unconditionally invite President Nixon before the U.S. had withdrawn from Vietnam evinced the strong Chinese desire to break out of its political isolation and provide a counterbalance to Soviet power.

There is no doubt that the U.S.-Chinese rapprochement and Nixon's visit to China were meant to be the crowning achievements of the President's first term. The Chinese realized the impact that their decision to invite Nixon to the PRC would have on the election campaign. Until then, there had been a possibility that Mao and Chou would invite Senators McGovern and Kennedy to come to China in 1971; by inviting Nixon, the Chinese were speculating that he was in a better position to win the election.

During the last meeting on July 11, Chou and Kissinger decided that the services of the intermediaries—Pakistan and Rumania—were no longer necessary. All future contacts would be made directly through their embassies in Paris, Ottawa, and other cities. The announcement of President Nixon's upcoming visit was set for 10 PM Eastern Daylight time on July 15.

As soon as he returned to Islamabad, Kissinger cabled the codeword Eureka to the President—the signal that the trip had been a success.[115] Kissinger arrived back in the United States on July 13 and promptly flew out to San Clemente to brief Nixon on the details of his talks with Chou.

On July 14 Nixon met with Kissinger, Secretary of State Rogers, CIA Director Richard Helms, and General Alexander Haig. Newsmen were convinced that the meeting had something to do with the situation in Vietnam—but the subject was Kissinger's trip to China.

On the afternoon of July 15, President Nixon requested a few minutes from the networks to make a major announcement. At exactly 7:00 PM (California time) Nixon faced the television cameras in a Burbank studio and said:

> Good evening:
> I have requested this television time tonight to announce a major development in our efforts to build a lasting peace in the world.

As I have pointed out on a number of occasions over the past three years, there can be no stable peace and enduring peace without the participation of the People's Republic of China and its 750 million people. That is why I have undertaken initiatives in several areas to open the door for more normal relations between our two countries.

In pursuance of that goal, I sent Dr. Kissinger, my Assistant for National Security Affairs, to Peking during his recent world tour for the purpose of having talks with Premier Chou En-lai. The announcement I shall now read is being issued simultaneously in Peking and in the United States:

"Premier Chou En-lai and Dr. Henry Kissinger, President Nixon's Assistant for National Security Affairs, held talks in Peking from July 9 to 11, 1971. Knowing of President Nixon's expressed desire to visit the People's Republic of China, Premier Chou En-lai, on behalf of the Government of the People's Republic of China, has extended an invitation to President Nixon to visit China at an appropriate date before May 1972. President Nixon has accepted the invitation with pleasure.

"The meeting between the leaders of China and the United States is to seek the normalization of relations between the two countries and also to exchange views on questions of concern to the two sides."

In anticipation of the inevitable speculation which will follow this announcement, I want to put our policy in the clearest possible context.

Our action in seeking a new relationship with the People's Republic of China will not be at the expense of our old friends. It is not directed against any other nation. We seek friendly relations with all nations. Any nation can be our friend without being any other nation's enemy.

I have taken this action because of my profound conviction that all nations will gain from a reduction of tensions and a better relationship between the United States and the People's Republic of China.

It is in this spirit that I will undertake what I deeply hope will become a journey for peace, peace not just for our generation but for future generations on this earth we share together. Thank you and good night.[116]

The whole speech did not take more than 90 seconds, but its impact was stunning. The surprise was complete. "The moment the President completed his surprise announcement, the cameras switched to studio commentators for reaction. They were all flabbergasted, and one anchor man was literally speechless as he looked out into the living rooms of America."[117]

Nixon's declaration of his intention to visit the PRC had repercussions in the Soviet Union, Taiwan, Japan, and North and South Vietnam. As a meticulously prepared diplomatic surprise it had a major effect on the structure and power relations of the international system. The impact was immediate. Yet its effects have, if anything, become more important in the ensuing years.

The move gave the United States and China maneuverability by—in some respects—modifying the structure of the global system from a bipolar to a triangular system.[118] Before the U.S.-Chinese rapprochement, the Soviet Union was in a better bargaining position vis-à-vis the United States, since it had relations with both the U.S. and China and could serve as an important pivot in the international system. When the U.S. and China established direct contact, the United States became the pivot of a more complicated structure. China now had the option of collaboration with the United States against the U.S.S.R. The Russians felt less secure—and they may therefore have been willing to make a few diplomatic concessions to the United States during the summer and fall of 1971.

Ironically enough, it had been the U.S.S.R. which in 1950 temporarily left the U.N. Security Council in protest against American objections to China's admission. This time, it was the United States which had cleared the way for China's admission to the United Nations, while the Soviet Union was displeased with the prosepct.

Although Washington assured Taiwan of its support, Nixon's China diplomacy obviously heralded the end of a special U.S.-Taiwan relationship. Taiwan felt deserted. The United States was on the verge of accepting China's admission to the United Nations and the Security Council. For Taiwan that could only mean loss of prestige and influence, and, eventually, expulsion from the United Nations.

The United States paid a price for the rapprochement. In turning away from an old ally, the Americans undermined their credibility as reliable and trustworthy partners. The U.S. initiated the policy which ultimately enabled the PRC to obtain a Security Council seat; the U.S. was consciously sacrificing Taiwan's "automatically" supportive vote for that of a Communist country. (The vote at the U.N. occurred on October 25 and resulted in a resounding defeat for Taiwan. On November 30, 1971, Kissinger publicly declared for the first time that Washington believed "the ultimate relationship of Taiwan to the People's Republic of China should be settled by direct negotiations between Taiwan and the People's Republic of China."[119]) On the other hand, the United States had shed a commitment that might have dragged it into a conflict with the People's Republic at some future date.

The new American policy was a severe shock to the Japanese. They were worried that the expansion of American-Chinese relations would reduce Japan's value to the Americans and undermine U.S. security guarantees. The Nixon Doctrine, the American withdrawal from Vietnam, and now the secret U.S.-PRC rapprochement had caused the Japanese to lose much of their faith in the United States. As recently as 1969, President Nixon and Premier Eisaku Sato had reaffirmed the so-called "common-enemy thesis" (i.e., China).[120] Yet, as is typical of a patron-client relationship, the Japanese had no other choice but to accept the "insult" and trim their sails according to the U.S. policy shift. Accused of habitual subservience to American policies, the Sato government was sharply attacked from both ends of the political spectrum. Clearly, Japan was being treated more like a second-rate ally than the proud economic power that it was.[121]

Nevertheless, the Japanese could also capitalize on the new turn in U.S. policy. Japan now had long-range opportunities to improve its political and economic ties with the PRC; and Soviet-Chinese tensions would perhaps enhance Japan's security by reducing external pressures.

About a month after announcing the rapprochement, Washington administered its second "Nixon shock" to the Japanese government with its devaluation of the dollar—a move which had an adverse effect on Japanese exports. The two acts resulting in such unhappy consequences for Japan eventually led to the resignation of Sato's government. The price for the U.S. was, however, minimal. In view of Japan's economic and military dependence on the United States, it was in no position to do more than to protest.

Naturally, the U.S. and China had had to act with the utmost caution if their move was to succeed. The Soviet Union might have used advance knowledge of the new relationship to conduct an intensive public campaign against "hypocritical" Chinese collaboration with the Americans. Alternatively, the U.S.S.R., if it had guessed the intentions behind Nixon's early signals, might have attempted a rapprochement of its own with the PRC. That option was much less likely, but could not be totally discounted if the Russians had felt sufficiently outmaneuvered and desperate. Had they anticipated Nixon's visit, they would undoubtedly have done their best to disrupt the move by disclosing it beforehand. This argument holds for Taiwan as well.

Whether or not the Kremlin was literally stunned, as claimed by Western analysts, by the disclosure of Henry Kissinger's secret trip to the PRC and the accompanying announcement of Nixon's prospective visit to mainland China remains a debated issue. In theory, of course, the Russians ought to have received the news with equanimity, since for some time they had been dropping ominous hints concerning intensfied contacts between Peking and Washington and warned about the likely consequences of an impending Sino-American rapprochement. To be sure, the suddenness, speed, and magnitude of the unfolding events might still have caught the

Soviet leadership flatfooted, regardless of their belief in the accuracy of their own prognosis. Or the people involved could simply have been whistling in the dark, in the hope of exorcising the very specter that presently confronted them and whose appearance, which they had predicted in good faith . . . . would not materialize, now confounded all their real expectations.

When confronted with the *fait accompli*, Moscow greeted the news of Kissinger's expedition to Peking with stony silence. The reaction may very well have been due, as alleged by Western Kremlinologists, to the Russian leadership's sense of total bewilderment at such a rapid improvement in Sino-American relations. Not having foreseen this contingency, presumably the Soviet authorities had not formulated a suitable response and, unable to improvise on the spur of the moment, they chose after a brief initial delay to release a bare report of the event without speculating on its potential meaning.[122]

Thus, despite all their warnings concerning Chinese-American collusion, it must be assumed that the Russians refused to believe that it would actually happen. Their rigid conception of stubborn ideological differences between China and the United States, the long animosity between the United States and China, the war in Vietnam, U.S. support of Taiwan, Nixon's anti-Communist record, and other factors inhibited realistic evaluation of the situation.[123] It would perhaps be more accurate to describe the announcement of Nixon's visit—from the Russian point of view—as a *fait accompli* rather than as a total surprise, since the Russians must have expected such a move to take place sooner or later. The surprise therefore was more in timing than in the direction and shape that it took.

Thus, the remarkable secrecy that President Nixon and Kissinger were able to maintain despite the number of public signals exchanged was a crucial factor in the successful conclusion of the U.S.-China rapprochement. Kissinger describes the vulnerability of the process in his memoirs.

Some countries might have attempted to preempt our visit; others to thwart it. The tender shoot so painstakingly nurtured for more than two years might well have been killed. . . . I have no doubt now that the secrecy of the first trip turned into a guarantee of a solid and well-managed improvement of relations.[124]

The secrecy enabled either side at any point in the process to terminate the negotiations without a loss of face and without any other state being aware of the dialogue that had been taking place; and each side could, of course, resume contact at a later point in time.

The notes exchanged between the two sides were either oral and not binding (through the Rumanian channel), or in handwriting on paper without an official letterhead (through the Pakistani channel). Neither party trusted the security of cable communications, so all letters were hand-delivered by Agha Hilaly, the Pakistani Ambassador in Washington (and presumably by the same method in Pakistan or Peking). Moreover, at the beginning of the exchanges, Hilaly was instructed by the Chinese *not* to leave their documents with Kissinger—the messages were dictated instead.[125] Kissinger's replies likewise transmitted by Hilaly, were typed "on Xerox paper without a letterhead or a United States government watermark. They were not signed (and our bureaucracy was not informed)."[126]

This cumbersome procedure necessarily involved considerable delays. Some important Chinese messages took at least four days to reach the United States.[127]

Above all, secrecy was achieved by confining the number of participants to a bare minimum. Until the final stages, only President Nixon and his National Security Assistant had complete knowledge of the goal—only they knew the intentions behind the signals, the statements, the research papers, and so forth. Other participants were only privy to selected pieces of the Sino-American jigsaw puzzle. For example, Secretary of State Rogers was not aware of Nixon's and Kissinger's secret correspondence with the Chinese, and he was not briefed on the scope of their efforts to facilitate a rapprochement with China. As a result, in a London television interview on April 29, 1971, Rogers stated that Mao's invitation to Nixon as reported in a *Life* magazine article by Edgar Snow was "fairly casually made," was not "a serious invitation," and that the Chinese had a paranoid attitude and an "expansionistic" foreign policy. Rogers' statement came at a crucial point in the signaling process and might have caused serious damage to the precarious negotiation process. Nixon and Kissinger were thunderstruck, but could not blame anyone but themselves.[128] Rogers certainly added quite a bit of noise to the otherwise positive signals that had been directed at the Chinese. Ironically, he may have confused Soviet intelligence and unwittingly served better than any consciously designed deception plan. Similarly, Rogers was not told in advance of Kissinger's secret trip to the PRC and was notified by Nixon only when Kissinger had already reached his destination.

As any other operation of this scope, this, too, depended on a good portion of luck. According to Kissinger, "We received a great deal of credit afterward for our skill in keeping the information secret; as I review the exchanges, I am bound to thank our pure good fortune and the extraordinary discretion of the CIA, which was handling the exchanges."[129]

The ability of the United States to maintain secrecy came as a pleasant surprise to the Chinese, who since World War II had believed that Americans couldn't keep a secret.[130] (The publication of the Pentagon

Papers just before Kissinger left for China certainly did not add much to American credibility.)[131]

William Safire quotes President Nixon as saying that the U.S. government received no less than three messages from the Chinese about maintaining secrecy.[132] Kissinger does not, despite his sensitivity to the issue of secrecy, mention any such messages. There is, in fact, no evidence that the Chinese sent these messages. Possibly, Nixon's success in his China policy and his obsession with secrecy after the publication of the Pentagon Papers and after numerous other leaks, made him want to impress his close associates with the need to keep secrets in executing sensitive diplomatic maneuvers.[133] When Senator Ellender of Lousiana later remarked, "This was the best kept secret of the Administration." Nixon wryly replied, "It was the only secret."[134]

Secrecy was further guarded by diplomatic denials and deception, of which Kissinger's trip was the ultimate example. The long delays between each signal as well as the fact that there was no remarkable increase in the intensity and amount of signals emitted as the day of surprise approached only made the diplomatic maneuvering harder to detect.

Contradictory signals were always present—they were, for example, the breakdown of the Sino-American talks in Warsaw after the U.S. invasion of Cambodia; the American (public) position on the admission of the People's Republic of China to the United Nations; the continued U.S. support of Taiwan; the U.S. ABM policy; as well as Chinese newspaper attacks on the United States during the signaling process.

The difficulty in identifying a clear new trend in relations such as those that developed between the United States and China has been described by Robert Jervis.

> Actors can more easily assimilate into their established image of another actor information contradicting that image if the information is transmitted and considered bit by bit than if it comes all at once. In the former case, each piece of discrepant data can be coped with as it arrives and each of the conflicts with the prevailing view will be small enough to go unnoticed, to be dismissed as unimportant, or to necessitate at most a slight modification of the image (e.g., addition of exceptions to the rule). When the information arrives in a block, the contradiction between it and the prevailing view is apt to be much clearer and the probability of major cognitive reorganization will be higher.[135]

The problem is that by the time the information arrives in a block, it is already too late—because that information is the surprise itself.

CHRONOLOGY

Date	Event
1960	Vice-President Nixon attempts to obtain an invitation to visit the People's Republic of China. He is deterred when, after the State Department refuses several Democratic Senators permission to visit China, they threaten to make a public issue of preferential treatment for Nixon.
October 13, 1960	In the presidential campaign against Kennedy, Nixon adopts a sharply anti-Peking position, stating, e.g., that "The [Chinese Communists] want the World."
October 1967	*Foreign Affairs* publishes Nixon's article, "Asia after Vietnam," which is later used as evidence of a shift in his basic position toward Communist China.
Fall 1968	During the presidential campaign, Nixon begins to develop the idea of playing the Chinese off against the Soviet Union.
November 26, 1968	Through their Chargé d'Affaires in Warsaw, the Chinese propose the resumption of the Sino-American ambassadorial talks in Warsaw, which have been suspended since January 8. Peking Radio announces the proposal and mentions for the first time since the beginning of the Cultural Revolution, Chou En-lai's "Five Principles of Coexistence."
January 20, 1969	In his Inaugural Address, Nixon makes a veiled reference to the new administration's willingness to talk to China: "Let all nations know that during this Administration our lines of communication will be open. We seek an open world—open to

ideas, open to the exchange of goods and people—a world in which no people, great or small, will live in *angry isolation*."

January 24

Liao Ho-shu, a Chinese diplomat in the Netherlands, defects. (He is granted asylum in the United States on February 4, 1969).

January 27

At his first news conference as President, Nixon answers a question on plans for improving relations with China by saying that he sees "no immediate prospect of any change," unless there are changes on China's side.

January - June

During this period a substantial diminution takes place in the number of anti-American statements made by the Chinese as compared to the same period in 1968. Concurrently, the number of anti-Soviet statements increases considerably.

February 1

Nixon sends a memo to Kissinger (then head of the National Security Council), suggesting that they encourage the attitude "that this Administration is exploring possibilities of rapprochement with the Chinese." He warns that there should be no public evidence of this attitude.

Early February

Nixon tells Senator Mike Mansfield that he would like to "open the door" to China and is convinced that the Chinese must be involved in "global responsibility" in order to prevent open Sino-Soviet warfare.

The U.S. State Department deplores in strong language the French resumption of diplomatic relations with the PRC.

February 18, 1969

The Chinese suddenly cancel the Warsaw meeting with the United States scheduled for February 20, accusing the CIA of being responsible for the defection of their Chargé d'Affaires in the Netherlands. President Nixon instructs Secretary of State Rogers to declare that the U.S. wants to engage in a broad program of cultural and scientific exchange with China.

February 21

While briefing newsmen on Nixon's upcoming visit to Europe, Kissinger answers a question on whether Nixon will discuss China with European leaders: "The President has always indicated that he favors a policy of maximum contact with China."

March 1

Nixon tells President de Gaulle that he is determined to open a dialogue with Peking, "whatever the difficulties." He visualizes a place for China in the U.N. as well as normalized Sino-American relations.

March 2

A large-scale clash takes place between Chinese and Soviet troops on Damansky Island in the Ussuri River.

March 3

Ten thousand Chinese demonstrators attack the Soviet Embassy in Peking.

March 4

At a news conference, Nixon says: "But being very realistic, in view of Red China's breaking off the rather limited talks that were planned, I do not think that we should hold out any great optimism for any breakthroughs in that direction at this time." The State Department extends the long-standing ban on travel to mainland China.

March 7	One hundred thousand Russian demonstrators attack the Chinese Embassy in Moscow.
March 14	The President announces his decision to go ahead with the U.S. ABM Safeguard program mainly intended for use against China.
Mid-March	At Eisenhower's funeral, Nixon asks de Gaulle to act as a go-between and inform the Chinese government of the American desire to improve relations.
March 20	In an address to the National Committee on U.S.-China Relations in New York, Senator Edward M. Kennedy calls for a change in the American government's China policy. It should be a policy of peace which abandons old slogans and embraces current reality. The U.S. should unilaterally do away with restrictions on travel to China and nonstrategic trade. The Americans, according to Kennedy, should also discuss the possibility of full diplomatic relations with the PRC, and withdraw U.S. troops from Taiwan.
Early April	The State Department, presumably with the President's approval, criticizes Canadian moves to recognize the PRC.
April 18	At a press conference, President Nixon says American diplomacy would not be credible "unless we could protect our country against a Chinese attack aimed at our cities. The ABM will do that and the ABM Safeguard system has been adopted for that reason."
April 23	De Gaulle instructs the French Ambassador in Peking, Etienne M.

April 23 (cont'd)	Manach, to deliver Nixon's message to Chinese leaders.
Early May	Manach delivers the American message to the Chinese government. He also indicates that the U.S. will modify its Taiwan policy.
Mid-May	Clashes between Chinese and Soviet troops take place along the Amur and the Sinkiang borders.
Early June	Kissinger asks the State Department to propose steps which can be taken to "normalize" U.S.-China relations without damaging relations with allies in the Pacific.
July 16	Two Americans whose yacht has capsized near Hong Kong are taken prisoner by the Chinese.
July 21	The State Department issues a low-key statement easing, though not eliminating, U.S. restrictions on trade with, and travel to, the People's Republic of China.
July 24	The two American yachtsmen captured on July 16 are released.
July 25	While on a stopover in Guam, Nixon proclaims the "Nixon Doctrine." He announces that the U.S. will provide all aid *short of direct military intervention* for its Asian allies.
Early August	Nixon, during a tour of Asia and on his way back, meets with the leaders of two countries which have friendly relations with the People's Republic of China. Islamabad, Pakistan—Nixon meets with President Yahya Khan (August 1). Bucharest, Rumania—Nixon meets with President Ceausescu (August 2-3).

He asks both leaders to tell the Chinese government that the U.S. is interested in opening a serious dialogue.

August 8

In a major speech delivered in Canberra, Australia, Secretary of State Rogers expresses U.S. desire to resume the ambassadorial talks in Warsaw. He also emphasizes the relaxation of American restrictions on trade and travel to China.

A Soviet diplomat in a conversation with a middle-level State Department official inquires about the American reaction if the Soviet Union should attack Chinese nuclear facilities.

August 14

In a National Security Council meeting President Nixon expresses his opinion that the Soviets are the more aggressive party in the Sino-Soviet border clashes. He says that it is in the United States' interest not to allow the Soviet Union to destroy the PRC in a Sino-Soviet war.

Summer

Rumors of a possible Soviet preemptive attack on Chinese nuclear facilities circulate widely.

Fall

China and the U.S. exchange signals to try to reopen the Warsaw talks. Nixon orders the U.S. Ambassador to Poland to contact the Chinese Chargé at the first suitable diplomatic function and inform him of U.S. interest in resuming the talks. For various reasons, the message is not delivered until December.

October 10

Pakistani Air Marshal Sher Ali Khan visits Kissinger in the White House and reports that Nixon's mes-

October 10 (cont'd)

sage to the Chinese concerning the U.S. desire to improve relations has been delivered. He suggests that the Chinese would like to see some concrete evidence of U.S. intentions. Kissinger promises that U.S. destroyer patrols in the Taiwan straits will be stopped.

November 7

The U.S. suspends routine naval patrols by the Seventh Fleet in the Taiwan straits. As a gesture, this is leaked to Chinese officials in Hong Kong on November 26.

December

The U.S. Deputy Consul General in Hong Kong hears through a reliable intermediary the "private" view of a Chinese Communist official that some form of relationship between China and the U.S. could be established before 1973.

December 3

Nixon's message is finally given to the Chinese Chargé d'Affaires in Warsaw.

December 6

Two Americans who had been held in China since February 16, 1969, when their yacht strayed into Chinese waters off Kwantung province, are released. (This is a different incident than the one that occurred in July 1969.)

December 11

The U.S. Ambassador and the Chinese Chargé openly meet at the Chinese Embassy in Warsaw. The American Ambassador proposes that their talks be resumed and they agree to meet again within a month.

December 15

The U.S. announces it will remove all nuclear weapons from Okinawa by the end of the year.

December 19

The $100 dollar limit on the purchase of Chinese goods by Americans is lifted, allowing unlimited purchases.

The U.S. Commerce Department permits foreign subsidiaries of U.S. firms to trade freely with China in non-strategic goods.

January 8, 1970

The Chinese Chargé d'Affaires in Warsaw openly visits the U.S. Embassy. Peking and Washington announce resumption of the Warsaw talks on January 20. The intitial reference to the "Chinese Communist Embassy" by the American spokesman is, on orders from the White House, changed quickly to "the People's Republic of China's Embassy."

January 20

Talks in Warsaw resume. Diplomats of both countries establish a channel of communication and agree to meet again in a month. American Ambassador Stoessel in effect says that the United States is willing to send a representative to Peking or receive a Chinese representative in Washington. The Chinese proposal also suggests the possibility of talks at a higher level.

February 20

The Warsaw talks reconvene. The Chinese suggest moving the talks to Peking and say that they would welcome a U.S. representative of any rank.

March 16

The U.S. State Department continues the relaxation of the travel ban on Communist China. (It has officially been in force for over half a year.)

April 29

The U.S. authorizes the selective licensing of goods for export to the

April 29 (cont'd)	People's Republic and most other Communist countries.
April 30	U.S. invasion of Cambodia.
May 4-5	China strongly denounces the U.S. invasion of Cambodia as a "flagrant provocation."
May 18	Talks scheduled to begin the next day in Warsaw are cancelled by the Chinese to protest the invasion of Cambodia.
Early June	Chou En-lai tells Emil Bodnaras, a Deputy Premier of Rumania, that he favors a rapprochement with the U.S., but adds that he cannot pretend to speak for the entire Chinese leadership.
July 1	In a television interview with Howard K. Smith, President Nixon states that he wants to improve Sino-American relations as a means of coping with the Soviet Union.
July 2	The Chinese send up two MiG-19's in an apparently premeditated attempt to intercept and possibly shoot down a C-130 U.S. intelligence mission 100 miles off the Chinese coast.
July 10	The Chinese announce the release of Bishop James Walsh who had been arrested in 1958.
July 27	Chou En-lai appears on French television (recorded on July 16) and attacks both the U.S. and the U.S.S.R. and urges the U.S. to withdraw its forces from Indo-China, South Korea, and Taiwan.
July 28	The U.S. Department of Commerce approves an Italian company's sale to Communist China of 80 dump

trucks containing General Motors engines and parts.

August 23-Sept. 26

Special meeting of the Chinese military and political elite to resolve the U.S. question.

August 26

Restrictions prohibiting American oil companies abroad to allow foreign ships to use refueling facilities when going to and from mainland China are lifted.

October 1

On China's National Day, American writer and old friend of the Chinese Communists Edgar Snow is pointedly placed next to Mao on Tien An Men Square. In a conversation with Snow, Mao expresses dissatisfaction with "the present situation" with regard to the Soviet Union and appears sympathetic toward the U.S.

Early October

In a *Time* interview, Nixon says: "If there is anything I want to do before I die, it is to go to China. If I don't, I want my children to."

Late October

Nixon and Kissinger decide to go ahead with talks on a higher level.

October 25

Nixon meets with President Yahya Khan of Pakistan and asks him to convey to the Chinese the U.S. desire to send a high-ranking representative to Peking to open talks. The White House spokesman briefs newsmen and indicates that the two Presidents have discussed U.S.-China relations and that President Yahya will transmit an informal message from Nixon to the Chinese. However, on the same day a contradictory signal is given by Press Secretary Ronald Ziegler, who states that "the U.S. opposes the

October 25 (cont'd)

admission of the Peking regime to the U.N. at the expense of the expulsion of the Republic of China."

October 26

President Nixon meets with Rumanian President Ceausescu in the White House to confer about U.S.-China relations. They discuss the possibility of the U.S. viewing Taiwan as an internal Chinese problem. During an official dinner the same evening, Nixon becomes the first American President to refer to China as "the People's Republic." Anatoly Dobrynin, the Soviet Ambassador, later asks whether this reference has any significance, but Kissinger brushes his inquiry aside.

First week of November

Rumanian Deputy Premier Gheorghe Radulescu visits Peking and delivers Nixon's message regarding Taiwan.

November 10-15

President Yahya Khan visits Peking.

December 8

Pakistan's Ambassador to the U.S. delivers a message from Chou En-lai to President Nixon which includes an invitation to send a special American envoy to Peking.

December 16

Kissinger hands the reply to Chou En-lai's message to the Pakistani Ambassador. The United States expresses its readiness to hold high-level talks in Peking on a broad range of issues (not only Taiwan).

December 18

Edgar Snow has a five-hour interview with Mao Tse-tung in Peking which is published in the April 30, 1971 issue of *Life* magazine.

January 11, 1971

Rumanian Ambassador Corneliu Bogdan visits the White House to orally deliver a message that the

Chinese had transmitted via Deputy Premier Radulescu. Sent by Chou En-lai with the approval of Chairman Mao and Lin Piao, the note suggests that an American envoy would be welcome in Peking. Chou also hints for the first time that Nixon himself would be welcome to come to China.

January 29

Kissinger gives an oral message to the Rumanian Ambassador in Washington to the effect that the U.S. is prepared to discuss all international issues, including Taiwan, with the Chinese. (The message is given orally in an attempt to indicate preference for the Pakistani channel, the U.S. government being wary of possible Russian eavesdropping in Rumania.)

February

Nixon approves the South Vietnamese invasion of Laos and notifies Peking via the Pakistanis that it will only last six weeks.

February 4

China's *People's Daily* denounces U.S. operations in Laos. On the same day, though, Chiao Kuan-hua, the Chinese Deputy Foreign Minister, tells the Norwegian Ambassador in Peking that China is aware of a new trend in American foreign policy. He adds that sooner or later direct U.S.-Chinese meetings, presently hampered by the Indochina war, will resume. He asks the Ambassador to pass this message on to the Americans.

February 17

During a White House news conference, Nixon emphasizes that the Laotian operation presents no threat to the Chinese.

February 25

The State of the World message by

February 25 (cont'd)	Nixon to Congress refers for the first time in an official government document to "the People's Republic of China" and calls for the improvement of Sino-American relations.
February 26	Kissinger refers to events in Laos as a flare-up related to the Vietnam disengagement process.
Early March	Mao concludes that the U.S. is indeed disengaging from Indochina and that the Soviet Union is the major threat to China.
March 14	Chou En-lai tells a European diplomat that China has decided to open a high-level dialogue with U.S. leaders. The messages through Pakistan resume. On the same day, the telephone link between the U.S. and China is restored.
March 15	The U.S. State Department terminates all restrictions on American passports for travel to China.
March 26	The Soviet foreign affairs weekly *New Times* accuses the U.S. of conducting a "diplomacy of smiles" toward Communist China.
March	Chou En-lai meets with former Japanese Foreign Minister Aiichiro Fujiyama and tells him that "at some point a sudden dramatic improvement is possible in relations with the United States."
Early April	A message from China to the U.S. via the Pakistani Ambassador in Washington includes an invitation to send a high-level envoy to Pe-

king—it suggests Rogers or Kissinger.

April 6   The Chinese table tennis team, in Japan for an international tournament, invites the U.S. team to visit China.

April 10   The U.S. table tennis team plus four officials, three journalists, and two wives leaves Hong Kong for China. It is the first official U.S. delegation to visit China since 1949.

April 14   The U.S. table tennis team meets with Chou En-lai who refers to the reestablishment of mutual friendship. The U.S. embargo on trade with China is terminated after 21 years. Chinese can get visas to visit U.S., U.S. dollars can be used to purchase Chinese goods. U.S. oil companies can sell fuel to ships and planes en route to China, and U.S.-owned ships under foreign flags can visit China.

April 21   Nixon tells the head of the U.S. Table Tennis Association that he will help to invite a Chinese team to the U.S. The Soviet foreign affairs weekly *New Times* accuses Peking of playing diplomatic games with the U.S.

April 26   A presidential panel recommends that Peking be admitted to the U.N., but that Taiwan not be expelled.

April 27   The *New York Times* reports that administration officials have disclosed that Rumania was acting as an intermediary in communications between the U.S. and the PRC. The *Times* says that the Rumanian Deputy Premier informed Chou En-lai

April 27 (cont'd)

of the American desire for improved relations during meetings in November 1970 and again on March 22, 1971.

Pakistani Ambassador Hilaly delivers a message from Chou En-lai to Kissinger (in response to Nixon's message of December 16, 1970 which Chou received on January 5, 1971) inviting the U.S. to send a special envoy to Peking.

April 28

In an interview taped for British television, Secretary of State Rogers says that a visit to China by President Nixon might well be possible if relations continue to improve. Rogers says that he is "very much in favor of an exchange of journalists, students, and non-professional people with mainland China in the near future."

Charles W. Bray, a State Department spokesman, says that it might be possible to resolve the status of Taiwan by negotiations between Nationalist China and Communist China. Bray denies he is articulating a new policy of the administration. " . . . Mainland China," he says," has been controlled and administered by the People's Republic of China for 21 years and for some time we have been dealing with that government on matters affecting our mutual interests."

April 29

President Nixon expresses the hope that he will be able to visit Communist China "sometime in some capacity."

April 30

A *Life* article by Edgar Snow tells of Mao's positive attitude toward Nixon and says that he invited Nixon to come to China either as a

	tourist or as President. Mao also mentioned the problem of the U.S. elections and a target date for the visit (early 1972).
April-Early May	It is agreed that Kissinger will visit Peking (on a secret trip) between July 9 and 11.
May 4	The official Chinese newspaper, *Jenmin Jih Pao*, denounces Bray's statement (April 28) as "brazen interference in China's internal affairs." The article speaks of the continuing friendship between the Chinese and American peoples, but adds that Nixon's expressed desire for better relations with China has proven to be "fraudulent" in light of Bray's remarks. Peking also criticizes the Lodge Commission for recommending U.N. membership for *both* Taiwan and the PRC.
May 5	In an article in *New Times*, the Soviet Union accuses the Nixon administration of pursuing "anti-Soviet objectives in allowing the table tennis team to make its trip to mainland China."
May 20	The Chinese press continues its attacks on the United States despite American attempts to improve relations. An editorial in Peking's newspapers on May 20, the anniversary of Mao's first foreign policy speech, attacks the U.S. government, speaking of "U.S. imperialism" and "U.S. aggression, intervention, subversion and sabotage everywhere." (A standard criticism in Chinese rhetoric.) The editorial dismisses U.S. government overtures to China as "humbug."
June	The Pentagon Papers are leaked to the U.S. press, probably making the

June (cont'd)	Chinese more nervous about the ability of the Americans to keep a secret. The *New York Times* publishes the inside story of the U.S. government's involvement in the Indo-Pakistani War.
June 1	President Nixon announces that "a significant change has taken place among the members of the United Nations on the issue of admission of mainland China" and that the U.S. "is analyzing the situation." He says that the administration will announce its position at the fall session of the United Nations.
June 10	A list of 47 categories of items considered exportable to China is released by the U.S.
July 1	Kissinger leaves the United States to begin his trip to Asia (and his secret trip to Peking).
July 3	Kissinger arrives in Saigon.
July 4	He arrives in Bangkok.
July 6	He arrives in New Delhi.
July 8	He arrives in Islamabad, Pakistan, and meets with President Yahya Khan. Afterwards, according to the Pakistani plan, Kissinger cancels dinner due to "exhaustion" and announces that he will rest in a Pakistani mountain resort on his doctor's orders.
July 9	A decoy convoy heads into the Pakistani mountains. Kissinger flies to China shortly after 3 PM. One Pakistani newsman files a report of the detour and sends it to London, but he is not believed. Kissinger arrives in Peking at noon and is met by

	Chinese officials. At 4 PM Chou meets with Kissinger.
July 10	The talks continue successfully. Chou formally invites Nixon to visit China and Kissinger accepts on his behalf.
July 11	The last round of talks. The two sides decide against the further use of intermediaries. They plan a joint communiqué to be released by both countries on the fifteenth. Kissinger returns to Islamabad.
July 15	7 PM California time. Nixon announces Kissinger's trip and releases the communiqué.

NOTES

1. William Safire, *Before the Fall* (New York: Ballantine Books, 1977), p. 127.

2. Henry Kissinger, *White House Years* (Boston: Little, Brown, 1979), p. 163.

3. Ross Koen, *The China Lobby in American Politics* (New York: Macmillan, 1960).

4. Tad Szulc, *The Illusion of Peace: Foreign Policy in the Nixon Years* (New York: Viking Press, 1978), pp. 109-110. (Hereafter cited as Szulc, *Illusion of Peace*.)

5. Marvin Kalb and Bernard Kalb, *Kissinger* (Boston: Little, Brown, 1974), p. 218. (Hereafter cited as Kalbs, *Kissinger*.) See also *China and U.S. Foreign Policy*, 2nd ed. (Washington D.C.: Congressional Quarterly, 1973), p. 1. (Hereafter cited as *China and U.S.*)

6. Richard M. Nixon, "Asia After Vietnam," *Foreign Affairs*, Vol. 46, No. 1, October 1967, pp. 111-125.

7. In the 1968 presidential election campaign, Nixon made the following remarks on his intended policy toward China:

> I would not recognize Red China now and I would not agree to admitting it to the U.N. and I would not go along with those well-intentioned people that said, "Trade with them, because that will change them." Because doing it now would only encourage them, the hardliners in Peking and the hardline policy that they're following. And it would have an immense effect on discouraging great numbers of non-communist elements in Free Asia that are now just beginning to develop their strength and their own confidence. (*China and U.S.*, p. 89.)

This statement depicts more realistically than his article in *Foreign Affairs* Nixon's attitude toward China. It reveals the contradictory elements in his thought; he has not yet firmly decided what form his China policy will take. Thus far, it appears to be based on Cold War concepts of rapprochement because of the emphasis on U.S. deterrence, containment, and negotiation from a position of strength.

8. Richard M. Nixon, *The Memoirs of Richard Nixon* (New York: Grosset and Dunlap, 1978), p. 545. (Hereafter cited as Nixon, *Memoirs*.)

9. Kissinger, *White House Years*, p. 167.

10. *Ibid.*, p. 168.

11. See also Stanley Eugene Spangler, *The Sino-American Rapprochement, 1969-1972: A Study in Signaling.* Unpublished Ph.D. dissertation, University of North Carolina, 1978, chapter 3, pp. 30-72, and in particular, pp. 40-44.

12. Szulc, *Illusion of Peace*, p. 103.

13. Kissinger, *White House Years*, p. 168.

14. *Ibid.*, p. 168.

15. Kalbs, *Kissinger*, p. 221.

16. *Ibid.*, p. 220. In his memoirs, Kissinger describes the origins of the China initiative as follows: "But though I had independently come to the same judgment as Nixon, and though I designed many of the moves, I did not have the political strength or bureaucratic clout to pursue such a fundamental shift of policy on my own. Nixon viscerally understood the essence of the opportunity and pushed for it consistently. He had the political base on the right, which protected him from the charge of being soft on Communism." (Kissinger, *White House Years*, p. 163.) There is some doubt, however, that Kissinger independently realized at that early stage the need to change the China policy of the United States.

17. Kissinger, *White House Years*, p. 169.

18. Kalbs, *Kissinger*, pp. 219-220.

19. Robert G. Sutter, *China-Watch: Sino-American Reconciliation* (Baltimore: Johns Hopkins University Press, 1978), p. 79.

20. *Ibid.*, p. 81.

21. Sutter, *China-Watch*, pp. 78-109.

22. Szulc, *Illusion of Peace*, p. 114; also William Safire, *Before the Fall*, p. 368.

23. Kalbs, *Kissinger*, pp. 221-222.

24. Kissinger, *White House Years*, p. 169.

25. *Ibid.*, p. 170.

26. *Ibid.*, p. 172.

27. Kalbs, *Kissinger*, p. 222; also Kissinger, *White House Years*, p. 170.

28. Szulc, *Illusion of Peace*, pp. 113-115.

29. See *China and U.S.*, p. 22; Kalbs, *Kissinger*, p. 225; Szulc, *Illusion of Peace*, p. 117.

30. *China and U.S.*, pp. 18-19.

31. *New York Times*, August 5, 1969.

32. In his memoirs, President Nixon claims that he asked President Yahya Khan during Yahya's trip to Washington, D.C., in late October 1970 to help as an intermediary in the normalization of Sino-American relations. (Nixon,

Memoirs, p. 546.) Nixon mistakenly refers to his visit to Pakistan as taking place in July, whereas he only reached Pakistan in August. He does mention, though, that he had already discussed U.S.-China relations with President Ceausescu of Rumania.

33. Szulc, *Illusion of Peace*, p. 118.

34. *Ibid.*, p. 119.

35. *Ibid.*, p. 119.

36. *Ibid.*, p. 119.

37. This was also claimed by Haldeman in his memoirs, but was roundly denied by President Nixon and Kissinger. See Szulc, *Illusion of Peace*, p. 206; Kissinger, *White House Years*, p. 183. Kissinger reports that a Soviet embassy official approached a middle-level State Department official on August 18, 1969, and asked what the U.S. reaction would be to a Soviet attack on Chinese nuclear facilities.

38. Kissinger, *White House Years*, p. 177.

39. For Sino-Soviet relations, see *China and U.S.*, p. 66, p. 69, pp. 71-74, p. 76; A. Doak Barnett, *China and the Major Powers in East Asia*, Chapter 1, pp. 20-88; Sutter, *China-Watch*, pp. 83-103. For a detailed discussion, see also Kissinger, *White House Years*, Chapter 6, pp. 171-191. For a general background of Sino-Soviet relations, see O. Edmund Clubb, *China and Russia: The Great Game* (New York: Columbia University Press, 1971).

Professor Donald S. Zagoria of Columbia University testified on the development of the Sino-Soviet conflict at the House Foreign Affairs Subcommittee Hearings on China (September 16, 1970). He said:

> In fact, because of the Russian threat, China has demonstrated what may prove to be more than a passing interest in improved relations with the United States. . . . As a result of the split, China has completely reoriented its foreign policy away from the communist world and towards the West. . . . The three big powers—Russia, China, and the United States fear a combination of the other two against them. This provides the possibility of greater diplomatic flexibility for all three. . . . Out of fear, China will court better communications with the United States. While for the moment Peking's interest in reopening the Warsaw talks with the United States are guided largely by tactical considerations, they could develop into something more serious, provided the United States has a genuine willingness to reach such a detente. (*China and U.S.*, p. 72.)

See also Roger Morris, *Uncertain Greatness* (New York: Harper and Row, 1977), p. 204.

40. The need to maintain complete secrecy under the watchful eyes of the Poles (and hence the Russians) complicated and prolonged the process of establishing contact between the American Ambassador and the Chinese Chargé d'Affaires in Warsaw. All of the other 134 meetings between the Americans and the Chinese had taken place on Polish premises. This time, the meeting that followed between Stoessel and Lei Yang was held in the Chinese Embassy. (Szulc mistakenly refers to the date of this meeting as December 12 on p. 127.) (Szulc, *Illusion of Peace*, pp. 121-123; Kalbs, *Kissinger*, pp. 228-229.)

41. Kissinger, *White House Years*, pp. 188, 193.

42. Nixon, *Memoirs*, p. 545.

43. Kissinger, *White House Years*, p. 687.

44. *Ibid.*, p. 687.

45. Jack Anderson, "The China Opening," *Washington Post*, May 11, 1980, p. C7.

46. Lester A. Sobel, *Kissinger and Detente* (New York: Facts and Figures on File, 1975), p. 74.

47. Quoted in Nixon, *Memoirs*, p. 545.

48. Kissinger, *White House Years*, p. 689.

49. Nixon, *Memoirs*, p. 545.

50. Sobel, *Kissinger and Detente*, p. 84.

51. Kissinger, *White House Years*, p. 688.

52. *Ibid.*, p. 689.

53. Jack Anderson, "The China Opening," *Washington Post*, May 11, 1980, p. C7.

54. Spangler, *A Study in Signaling*, pp. 75-76.

55. Kissinger, *White House Years*, p. 689.

56. Sutter, *China-Watch*, p. 107.

57. Kalbs, *Kissinger*, pp. 231-232.

58. *Ibid.*, p. 232.

59. Kissinger, *White House Years*, pp. 685, 698-699. Spangler, in his dissertation, "*The Sino-American Rapprochement 1969-1972: A Study in Signaling*," written before Kissinger's memoirs were published, assigns a central role to this specific gesture. He writes, "The gesture was unprecedented—never before had a foreigner been invited to stand next to Mao on Tien an Men Gate to review the festivities. The signal to the U.S. was clear—China was prepared to move towards the U.S. and the plan was backed by no less a personage than Mao Tsetung," p. 91, also p. 100. As Kissinger makes clear, this signal was too subtle to be perceived by the U.S. Whatever the reason for this lack of perception, the incident demonstrates the danger of superimposing from hindsight elegant and rational explanations for ambiguous and complex communications across cultural barriers. As we have seen in Note 17, Chapter 3, it is dangerous to assume that what are considered obvious signals by the signaling party are automatically received and correctly interpreted by the other side. As noted above, Stalin's speech of March 10, 1939, was not immediately reported to Hitler. According to Gustav Hilger, the speech was brought to Hitler's attention by pure chance only two months later.

60. Robert Jervis, "Hypothesis on Misperception," *World Politics*, April 1968, pp. 474-475.

61. The Chinese did not have full confidence in the Rumanian channel perhaps because they were afraid of Soviet penetration; they therefore preferred to deal with the U.S. through the Pakistani channel. (Kissinger, *White House Years*, pp. 181, 704.)

62. Szulc, *Illusion of Peace*, p. 348.

63. *Ibid.*, p. 348.

64. Nixon, *Memoirs*, p. 546; see also Szulc, *Illusion of Peace*, p. 348.

65. Kalbs, *Kissinger*, p. 233.

66. *China and U.S.*, p. 22.

67. Nixon, *Memoirs*, p. 546.

68. Paul Y. Hammond, *Cold War and Detente* (New York: Harcourt, Brace, and Jovanovich, 1975), p. 271.

69. Nixon, *Memoirs*, p. 547.

70. *Ibid.*, p. 547.

71. *Ibid.*, p. 547; Szulc, *Illusion of Peace*, p. 350.

72. Both the Rumanian and Pakistani Ambassadors had, on delivering the Chinese messages, also tried to convey the attitudes of the Chinese and the atmosphere in which their messages had been given.

73. Szulc, *Illusion of Peace*, p. 405.

74. Kalbs, *Kissinger*, p. 234. Also Kissinger, *White House Years*, pp. 701-702; 724.

75. Quoted in Alan Lawrence, *China's Foreign Relations Since 1949* (London: Routledge and Kegan Paul, 1975), p. 210; see also Szulc, *Illusion of Peace*, pp. 350-351. The editors of *Life* magazine "didn't know what they had" in Mao's interview with Edgar Snow. Therefore, Mao's signaling in the interview only came to the attention of President Nixon and his aides when the article itself was published. (See Safire, *Before the Fall*, p.372.) Earlier knowledge of Mao's interview with Snow might have accelerated the American reaction and consequently, the whole signaling process. The Chinese, in considering the slow American response, must have assumed (projecting their own state control of the media on the United States) that Snow's interview had promptly been brought to the President's attention as soon as Snow returned to the United States.

76. Kalbs, Kissinger, p. 235. See Edgar Snow, "A Conversation With Mao Tse-Tung," *Life*, April 30, 1971, pp. 46-52. In retrospect, Snow's article was the clearest public signal reflecting China's desire for a rapprochement with the U.S.

77. Kissinger, *White House Years*, pp. 702-703. During the whole period Soviet intelligence experts carefully monitored the entire U.S.-Chinese exchange of public signals in these two countries' newspapers. See S. Sergeichuk, *Through Russian Eyes: American-Chinese Relations*. (Arlington, Virginia: International Library 1975).

78. Kalbs, *Kissinger*, p. 236.

79. *Ibid.*, p. 326.

80. Nixon, *Memoirs*, p. 548.

81. *Ibid.*, p. 548.

82. Szulc, *Illusion of Peace*, p. 396.

83. Sobel, *Kissinger and Detente*, p. 91.

84. Nixon, *Memoirs*, p. 548.

85. Quoted in Szulc, *Illusion of Peace*, p. 399.

86. Quoted in Szulc, *Illusion of Peace*, p. 399-400.

87. Nixon, *Memoirs*, pp. 548-549.

88. Szulc, *Illusion of Peace*, p. 403.

89. Kalbs, *Kissinger*, p. 237.

90. Kissinger, *White House Years*, p. 714; Nixon, *Memoirs*, p. 549; In *Illusion Of Peace*, Szulc mistakenly says that the Chinese wanted the visit to be kept secret (p. 400).

91. Nixon, *Memoirs*, p. 550.

92. *Ibid.*, p. 550. By his decision to send Kissinger rather than Secretary of State Rogers on the secret mission to China, Nixon "in effect declared Henry the winner in the jockeying between Kissinger and . . . Rogers." (Safire, *Before the Fall*, p. 372.) For Kissinger's version of the conversation, see Kissinger, *White House Years*, pp. 715-717. Kissinger says, "Nixon's overriding motive was undoubtedly that I understood our policy best, and that being familiar with my complicated chief [i.e., Nixon] I would be able to arrange the sort of Peking visit for him with which Nixon would be most comfortable. He could ask me without embarrassment to raise the public relations requirements of his insistently eager advance men. Another factor was undoubtedly that of all the potential emissaries I was the most subject to his control." (p. 717). It is certainly difficult to imagine hearing Kissinger say politely to Nixon, "No . . . no . . . We must send State Secretary Rogers," only in the expectation, of course, of having his suggestion brushed aside.

93. Kissinger, *White House Years*, p. 724.

94. Szulc, *Illusion of Peace*, p. 401.

95. *Ibid.*, p. 403.

96. Nixon, *Memoirs*, p. 550.

97. *Ibid.*, p. 551.

98. *Ibid.*, p. 551.

99. *Ibid.*, p. 551.

100. Kissinger, *White House Years*, pp. 726-727.

101. Nixon, *Memoirs*, p. 552.

102. *Ibid.*, p. 552.

103. Kalbs, *Kissinger*, p. 243. Kissinger gives a detailed account of his trip in his book, *White House Years*, pp. 733-755.

104. John Osborne, *The Third Year of the Nixon Watch* (New York: Liveright, 1972), p. 113.

105. Quoted in Szulc, *Illusion of Peace*, pp. 412-413; see also Nixon, *Memoirs*, pp. 552-553.

106. Nixon, *Memoirs*, p. 553.

107. The whole deception plan was almost shattered when a Pakistani journalist who worked for the London *Daily Telegraph* identified Kissinger on his way to the plane. A Pakistani official, who was unaware of the deception plan, told the journalist that Kissinger was headed for the PRC. The journalist immediately sent a report of his discovery to the *Daily Telegraph*, but luckily no one believed him. (Szulc, *Illusion of Peace*, p. 408.)

108. *Ibid.*, p. 407.

109. *Ibid.*, p. 410.

110. *Ibid.*, p. 411. For details of Kissinger's conversations in China, see *White House Years*, pp. 742-755.

111. Sobel (ed.), *Kissinger and Detente*, p. 95.

112. Szulc, *Illusion of Peace*, p. 412.

113. Kalbs, *Kissinger*, p. 249.

114. *Ibid.*, p. 249.

115. Nixon, *Memoirs*, p. 553.

116. Quoted in Szulc, *Illusion of Peace*, p. 417; see also Kissinger, White

House Years, pp. 757-759 for the formulation of Nixon's speech.

117. Kalbs, *Kissinger*, pp. 251-252.

118. This is Kissinger's evaluation of the consequences of the Sino-American rapprochement.

119. Kalbs, *Kissinger*, p. 255.

120. Fred Greene, *Stresses in U.S.-Japanese Security Relations* (Washington D.C.: The Brookings Institution, 1975), p. 12.

121. For the U.S. attitude toward Japan, see Kissinger, *White House Years*, pp. 761-762.

122. George Ginzburgs, "Moscow's Reaction to Nixon's Jaunt to Peking" in Gene T. Hsiao, *Sino-American Detente and its Policy Implications* (New York: Praeger, 1974), pp. 137, 141.

123. According to reports from Moscow in the *New York Times* on July 17, 1971, pp. 1, 2, the Soviets were stunned by Nixon's declaration of his forthcoming visit to China.

124. Kissinger, *White House Years*, p. 725.

125. *Ibid.*, p. 701.

126. *Ibid.*, p. 702.

127. *Ibid.*, p. 714.

128. *Ibid.*, p. 720.

129. *Ibid.*, p. 757.

130. *Ibid.*, p. 724.

131. *Ibid.*, pp. 729-730.

132. Safire, *Before the Fall*, p. 375.

133. Morris, *Uncertain Greatness*, p. 204.

134. Safire, *Before the Fall*, p. 489.

135. Jervis, "Hypothesis on Misperception," *World Politics*, April 1968, pp. 474-475.

BIBLIOGRAPHY

Anderson, Jack. The 'China Opening,' Washington: *The Washington Post*, May 11, 1980.

Barnett, A. Doak. *China and the Major Powers in East Asia*. Washington, D.C.: The Brookings Institution, 1977.

China and U. S. Foreign Policy, 2nd ed. Washington, D.C.: Congressional Quarterly, 1973.

Clubb, O. Edmund. *China and Russia: The Great Game*. New York: Columbia University Press, 1971.

Greene, Fred. *Stresses in U.S.-Japanese Security Relations*. Washington, D.C.: The Brookings Institution, 1975.

Hammond, Paul Y. *Cold War and Detente*. New York: Harcourt, Brace, Jovanovich, 1975.

Hsiao, Gene T. *Sino-American Detente and its Policy Implications*. New York: Praeger, 1974.

Kalb, Marvin and Bernard Kalb. *Kissinger*. Boston: Little, Brown, 1974.

Kissinger, Henry. *White House Years*. Boston: Little, Brown, 1979.

Koen, Ross. *The China Lobby in American Politics*. New York: Macmillan, 1960.

Kwan Ha Yim (ed.). *China and the U.S. 1964-1972*. New York: Facts on File, Inc., 1975.

Lawrence, Alan. *China's Foreign Relations Since 1949*. London: Routledge and Kegan Paul, 1975.

Morris, Roger. *Uncertain Greatness*. New York: Harper and Row, 1977.

Nixon, Richard M. "Asia After Vietnam," *Foreign Affairs*. Vol. 46, No. 1, October 1967, 111-125.

Nixon, Richard M. *The Memoirs of Richard Nixon*. New York: Grosset and Dunlap, 1978.

Osborne, John. *The Third Year of the Nixon Watch*. New York: Liveright, 1972.

Safire, William. *Before the Fall*. New York: Doubleday and Co., 1975.

Sergeichuk, S. *Through Russian Eyes: American-Chinese Relations*. Arlington, Virginia: International Library, 1975.

Sidey, Hugh, 'Thirsting to get into China' *Life*, April 30, 1971, p. 4.

Snow, Edgar. "A Conversation with Mao Tse-tung," *Life*, April 30, 1971, pp. 46-52.

Sobel, Lester A. *Kissinger and Detente*. New York: Facts and Figures on File, 1975.

Spangler, Stanley Eugene. *The Sino-American Rapprochement. 1969-1972: A Study in Signaling*. Unpublished dissertation, Chapel Hill: University of North Carolina, 1978.

Sutter, Robert G. *China-Watch: Sino-American Reconciliation*. Baltimore: Johns Hopkins University Press, 1978.

Szulc, Tad. *The Illusion of Peace: Foreign Policy in the Nixon Years*. New York: Viking Press, 1978.

Wich, Richard. *Sino-Soviet Crisis Politics: A Study of Political Change and Communication*. Cambridge: Harvard University Press, 1980.

5

SADAT AND THE "ELECTRIC SHOCK DIPLOMACY"

In the sphere of foreign policy, my "Peace Initiative" of February 4, 1971, was submitted less than four months after I had taken office. It had a tremendous impact both inside and outside Egypt. I believed that as military action was ruled out at the time, a diplomatic offensive had to be launched: the broad masses wanted to see action being taken all the time.[1]

Anwar el-Sadat

The world was stunned. Israel was in a tight corner, for there she was, confronting an Arab leader declaring for the first time ever that he was willing to conclude a peace agreement—the hardest thing in the world for her to predict or even dream of.[2]

Sadat on his first Peace Initiative

In Chapter I we observed that the combination of an authoritarian leader and a non-democratic system was most conducive to the employment of surprise tactics in diplomacy. It is hardly astonishing then, to find that the two preeminent authoritarian leaders of this century, Stalin and Hitler, whose careers confirmed the primacy of power and deceit in politics, were unsurpassed in the use of surprise to achieve their goals.

The brutal, lightning-like murder of Roehm—Hitler pretended to be his friend until almost the last moment—and the rest of the S.A. leadership during the "Night of the Long Knives" (June 30, 1934) is an extreme example of how a surprise blow can be used in domestic politics to liquidate the opposition. The pattern of behavior developed in the domestic arena was then applied in the conduct of Hitler's foreign policy.

Historians have looked back upon the mid-thirties with some vexation. This was the period in which Hitler repeated, on the plane of foreign policy, those same practices of overwhelming his opponents that had yielded him such easy triumphs at home. And he applied them in he same effortless manner and with no less success. In accord with his thesis that "before foreign enemies are conquered, the enemy within must be annihilated," he had behaved rather quietly in the preceding months. The reaction of European nations to Hitler's challenges is all the harder to understand because the process of seizing power, with its bloody end in the Roehm affair, had provided some inkling of the man's nature and politics.[3]

Surprise was a favorite gambit of Hitler's, in politics, diplomacy, and war: he gauged the psychological effect of sudden unexpected hammer-blows in paralyzing opposition.[4]

Stalin's ascent to power against the wishes of Lenin, and his eight-year struggle against the united opposition of Trotsky, Zinovyev, and Kamenev (and later against Bukharin, Rykov, and Tomsky) was "one of the most remarkable examples of self-assertion on the record."[5] Stalin proved himself to be a "determined power-seeking politician" who was "less hampered than his rivals by allegiance to principle."[6] In a struggle based on realpolitik, he continuously refined the techniques of accumulating power until, by 1928-29, he was the most powerful individual in the Soviet Union.

Sadat's road to power was a milder version of the Hitler and Stalin cases. Most of what we know about him has been gleaned from his own writings, speeches, and interviews. The shortage of information is due to the fact that during the Nasser period, Sadat, unlike Nasser himself, Mohamed Heikal, or Zakaria Mohieddin, did not have a significant impact on Egyptian thinking; hence, standard histories of the Nasser period only mention him in passing.[7]

Although Sadat was often at Nasser's side, he did not belong to his inner circle. After 1957, Nasser nominated him only to honorific posts such as President of the National Union, President of the Afro-Asian Conference, Speaker of the National Assembly, and Vice-President of Egypt—high-sounding posts without any important decision-making powers.[8]

Sadat exhibited many traits of the so-called *authoritarian personality*: he was extremely deferential to his superiors, but ruthless and dictatorial to his competitors and inferiors. Tiring of Sadat's excessive conformism, Nassar sometimes referred to him as *Bikbashi Sah Sah* (Colonel Yes-Yes) and complained, "If only Sadat would vary the way in which he agrees instead of always saying *sah* [yes] I would feel a lot better."[9]

When Nasser considered resigning in the aftermath of Egypt's defeat by Israel in 1967, he named Zakaria Mohieddin as his successor. But by 1970, Sadat had become his chosen successor for largely negative reasons; as a less threatening, seemingly docile candidate, Sadat was more acceptable to the Egyptian army whose support was crucial for the survival of any President.[10]

> It must have been his [Sadat's] consistent record of what he left unsaid and undone that did the trick. For eighteen years, he had never disagreed with anything that Nasser proposed; he had never taken an independent position after the revolution on any major question of domestic policy or foreign affairs. When on occasion he had marginally deviated . . . he quickly corrected his public posture and reentered the Nasser fold.[11]

Despite Nasser's tentative blessing, Sadat was far from an obvious choice. At the time of Nasser's death (September 1970), there were many other potential and no less powerful candidates—Zakaria Mohieddin, Abdul Latif Bagdadi, Ali Sabri, Kamal Al Din Hussein, and Sami Sharaf.

> These political rivals . . . came to see that a political compromise was necessary; and working the principle, somewhat akin to that which in arithmetic is called finding the lowest common denominator, they chose Sadat, a man without a power center of his own but with sufficiently close associations with Nasser to give the necessary public impression of continuity . . . What was not realized by some of those who put Sadat into office as a compromise candidate was that in a political system where almost all decisions emanate from the presidency, the man who sits in that seat has great powers, regardless of his personal characteristics.[12]

Chosen for his weakness, Sadat quickly demonstrated a facility for political maneuvering by attaining a virtual monopoly of power by 1971. (After returning from Nasser's funeral, Elliot Richardson reported to President Nixon that Sadat would probably not last more than six weeks in office).[13] Sadat gradually filled all cabinet, government, and mass media posts with loyal supporters, systematically ridding himself of potential opponents. For example, in February 1971, he introduced Sharawi Gomaa to Russian leaders as "my colleague and friend, whom I trust completely." But about two months later, Sadat became embroiled in a power struggle with his former colleagues, the so-called Nasser technocrats, and imprisoned Sharawi Gomaa, Minister of the Interior; Ali Sabri, Vice President; Sami Sharaf, Minister for Presidential Affairs; and Mohammed Faik, Minister of Information, for plotting to overthrow him.[14]

Since he had not inherited Nasser's charisma or political prestige, Sadat had to consolidate control over Egyptian politics the hard way. His strategy consisted of a series of interdependent moves, each of which could only succeed after the preceding move had been executed.

Sadat's main opponents were those people who had been closely associated with Nasser, many of whom were pro-Soviet leftists. In order to undercut them, Sadat first had to secure the support of the Egyptian

High Command and the Soviet Union—not an easy task, since Sadat had never been particularly pro-Russian; besides, the Soviet Union already had reliable supporters such as Ali Sabri. On the other hand, the Army had little sympathy for a pro-Soviet policy, thus making a coalition of contradictory elements, such as the Army and the Soviets, doubly difficult to establish. Rising to this challenge, Sadat squared the circle by promising everything to everyone.

> He went along with [General] Sadiq in the Army's interpretation of the cease-fire; and he said all the right things about the Russians, as Sabri had wanted. The chameleon had no difficulty making these adjustments, and thus he prepared to do on the home front what he was later to do to the Israelis on October 6, 1973. Sadiq and Sabri were content with Sadat's interpretation of his role as President; within two years Sadat had eliminated both of them.[15]

Once he acquired the *backing* of both the Soviet Union and the Army, Sadat was in a sufficiently secure position to dispose of his domestic opposition. The next step was to gain *control* of the Army which would ensure absolute control of Egyptian politics. This he accomplished by dissociating himself from Nasser's pro-Soviet policies and weakening Egypt's ties with the Soviet Union—acts which proved to be popular with the Army and the public in general.

Sadat's attempts to find a formula for unity between Egypt, Sudan, Syria, and Libya[16] caused his first open clash with the so-called chief power bloc (which included Ali Sabri, Sharawi Gomaa, and Sami Sharaf, who were all, according to Sadat, Soviet agents).[17] After a meeting between the four countries during the spring of 1971 had failed, Egypt, Syria, and Libya resolved to go ahead and hold the last round of talks which had been scheduled to take place in Benghazi, Libya. In Benghazi, the three countries managed to rescue the talks from failure by agreeing on a last-minute amendment. Upon his return to Egypt (Ali Sabri had accompanied him to the conference) Sadat submitted the agreement he had signed for Egypt to a meeting of the eight-member Supreme Executive Comittee of the Arab Socialist Union on April 21, 1971. During the debate that followed, Sadat found himself in the minority.

> Then the agreement was put to the vote. The result was that five out of eight—the Soviet agents in the leadership—were against it, and three—Dr. Mahmoud Fawzi, the Prime Minister; Hussein el-Shafei, the Vice-President, and myself—for it. Clearly, this was the climax of the conflict. They wanted to finish me off or, at least, to curtail my power so drastically that I would be incapable of taking any decision without their approval.[18]

Consequently, Sadat decided on a maneuver that Stalin and Hitler would have been proud of. Without losing the initiative, he proposed that the matter be submitted to the Central Committee.

They were surprised . . . . Taken unawares, and decidedly unprepared for this turn of events, they tried to play for time by calling for further studies to be made and for a reconsideration of the result of the voting. I insisted, however, that the entire subject be referred to the Central Committee. They tried desperately to win the Committee over, but to no avail. The agreement was ratified unanimously. So the first trial of strength ended in an absolute victory for me and they gave in . . . temporarily[19]

Sadat's power struggle with the Ali Sabri group was by no means over, nor was it as simple as he indicates.[20] He still had to carry out his own (milder) Night of the Long Knives or "the second revolution" as he calls it in his memoirs (otherwise euphemistically referred to as "the corrective movement").[21]

My timing, as the struggle against them intensified, was accurate. Zero hour was May Day 1971. They did everything in their power to make our celebration of the occasion a failure, but they were disappointed. . . . On May 2, I dismissed Ali Sabri from all the posts he held. It was a mere one-line report in the national papers.[22] [Sadat has always tried to maintain a facade of press freedom in Egypt, but the fact that such an important event in Egyptian politics received so little attention from the press proves the opposite.]

Little more than a week later, on May 10, 1971, a police officer informed Sadat of a plot to assassinate him on May 13 during his visit to al-Tahrir province.[23] Not unlike Hitler, who on the eve of his bid for political supremacy enlisted the support of the senior commanders of the Army, (the so-called *Deutschland Pact* of April 11, 1934)[24], Sadat now sought the backing of the Egyptian Army. Two key military officers, Generals Nassif and Sadiq, gave their tacit support. General Nassif, who was Commander of the Presidential Guard, had promised earlier in March to obey all orders issued to him by the proper constitutional authorities. After Sadat had delivered a speech at a military base near the Suez Canal on May 12, General Sadiq, who was Chief of Staff, indicated where he stood with the statement, "We understand your position."[25]

Proceeding to the next move, Sadat announced that he was tired, and postponed his scheduled trip to al-Tahrir. On May 13, he dismissed Sharawi Gomaa, Minister of the Interior and the supposed leader of the conspirators; then he ordered the new Minister of the Interior, Mamduh

Salem, to confiscate all of the incriminating tapes that were housed in the security section of the Ministry.

> Later that day—May 13—at precisely 10:57 P.M. (the time of the last full news bulletin on Cairo Radio's home service), Ashraf Marwan, Nasser's son-in-law, who was director of Sami Sharaf's office, called on me (Sadat) to submit the resignations of the Speaker of the National Assembly, the War Minister, the Information Minister, the Presidential Affairs Minister, some members of the Central Committee, and even a few members of the Supreme Central Committee as well.[26]

By their resignation en masse, the Ali Sabri Group hoped to paralyze Sadat's control of the armed forces, the intelligence services, the mass media, and general government operations. The conspirators underestimated Sadat's ability to turn the situation around. Accepting the resignations, he ordered the news to be broadcast immediately and the same night proceeded to reorganize the government.[27] Sadat nominated General Sadiq to be the new Minister of War, using the occasion to promote him to full general, and called General Ahmed Ismail out of retirement to be Director of Intelligence. The conspirators were promptly put under house arrest and formally arrested on May 16, thus enabling Sadat to assume full control of the Egyptian government.[28]

Apparently Sadat had laid a trap for his potential opponents; they had been followed by his secret police and their conversations taped. Sadat had planned his moves well in advance, and the conspirators unwittingly dug their own graves.[29]

On April 22, *two weeks before* he was informed of any conspiracy to assassinate him, Sadat notified the Soviet Ambassador that he intended to get rid of Ali Sabri. Being well-apprised of Soviet influence in Egypt, Sadat wanted to prevent Soviet intervention against himself on behalf of the conspirators. He therefore told the Soviet Ambassador that his move to get rid of Sabri was not directed against the Soviet Union (even though the conspirators were all identified as friends and sympathizers of the Soviet Union). Sadat said, "It is a purely internal dispute. If anyone suggests to you that what I am going to do is directed against the Soviet presence in Egypt you can tell them that I would be delighted if you would intensify your presence."[30]

To further assure the Soviet Union of his friendship, Sadat sent an important message to Brezhnev through Sami Sharaf, who attended the Twenty-Fourth Congress of the CPSU in Moscow on March 31, 1971, as the head of Egypt's Arab Socialist Union (ASU). In the message, Sadat proposed the consolidation of Egyptian-Soviet relations through a treaty of friendship and cooperation.[31] The Soviet Union eagerly accepted, and the treaty was concluded in Egypt on May 27, 1971.[32] In this manner, Sadat insured the continuation of Russian support for his regime while Soviet supporters in Egypt were being thrown in jail. In his memoirs, Sadat claims that the Soviet Union, not Egypt, proposed the treaty and that he personally was not in favor of it.[33] In *The Sphinx and the Commissar*, Mohamed Heikal contends that the idea was first suggested by Sadat himself in order to prevent Soviet opposition to his consolidation of power.[34]

Heikal's account is substantiated by an incident confirming Sadat's manipulation of the Soviet Union. In an attempt to improve Saudi-Egyptian relations, Kamel Adham, one of King Faisal's key advisers, came to Cairo in November 1971. During his visit he spoke to Sadat about "the Russian presence in Egypt, saying how much it alarmed the Americans, and pointing out that this was important at a time when the Saudis were trying to get the Americans more actively interested in the Middle East's problems."[35] Sadat replied that he was extremely dependent upon Russian assistance in the fight against Israel, but that once the first phase of Israeli withdrawal had been completed "he could promise that he would get the Russians out." With Sadat's consent, Adham transmitted this information to President Nixon. The news of this maneuver, which was apparently intended to "encourage" the United States to put pressure on Israel to withdraw from the Sinai, was then leaked by Senator Henry Jackson evidently in an attempt to sour Egyptian-Soviet relations.[36] When Sadat visited the Soviet Union in October 1971, he had the following words of reassurance for President Podgorny: "Our friendship isn't a question of tactics; it's a strategic concept."[37] Sadat's friendship for the Soviet Union certainly had strategic value—but once the strategic goal had been achieved in the 1973 war, the relationship turned out to be only tactical after all! In the aftermath of the Yom Kippur War, Sadat undermined the Soviet position in the Middle East by trading Soviet support for American support, and unilaterally cancelling the Soviet-Egyptian treaty of friendship and cooperation in March 1976.

Having eliminated the domestic opposition, Sadat was ready to tighten control over the Egyptian Army whose support was vital for his long-term survival.

> From the first. . . Sadat as the new President was very conscious of the fact that the decisive base for his authority and power was Sadiq and his officers. Sadat recognized this and, characteristically, went along with his military associates wholeheartedly and even with apparent enthusiasm. He said all the right things, did all the right things, and left unsaid and undone all the right things. . . . He did what he was told—and he did it well. . . . The Armed Forces were content and the Kremlin was satisfied.[38]

Sadat's major task, which he accomplished in yet another of his intricate moves, was to *neutralize* General Sadiq's power. During the "second revolution" Sadat had "thanked" Sadiq for his backing by promoting him to full general and nominating him to the position of War Minister (which had just been conveniently vacated by General Fawzi, one of the conspirators). In making an offer that General Sadiq could not refuse, Sadat had also taken the first step in weakening his influence.

Sadat proceeded to strengthen the position of the relatively young generation of Egyptian officers at the expense of the veteran Free Officers—the group that under Nasser had carried out the revolution in 1952. The field commanders of the Egyptian Army in particular supported changes in the structure of the High Command "in order to redress the balance against General Sadiq."[39] No sooner had Sadiq been kicked upstairs than Sadat formed an Armed Forces Council which excluded the Minister of War, but included "the Commanders of the First, Second and Third Armies, the Air Force, Navy and Army Commanders, the Chiefs of Air Defense and of Military Intelligence, and the Chief of Staff, General Shazli."[40] As an important base of support for Sadat, the Armed Forces Council henceforth made military policy.[41].

In the fall of 1972, long-standing disagreements between Sadat and Sadiq finally came to a head. Sadiq was using delaying tactics in carrying out Sadat's orders to prepare the Egyptian forces for war with the Israelis by mid-November because he did not agree that Sadat's idea of limited war would result in political gains for Egypt. On October 24, during a meeting of the Supreme Council of the Armed Forces, Sadiq vehemently opposed Sadat's plans and as a result was dismissed two days later. Sadat, who had always felt that Sadiq was too involved in politics for a military man, accused him of lacking offensive spirit, lying, and not following orders and appointed General Ahmed Ismail to take his place .[42]

To a certain degree, brutal determination and incessant maneuvering characterize many politicians in any type of political system. Nevertheless, a system which lacks institutionalized guidelines for the legitimate transfer of power encourages the indiscriminate use of force. A totalitarian government such as that of Hitler or Stalin recognizes no restrictions on the use of power—but a democratic system obliges even the most power-hungry politician to observe certain limits or else be forced out of office. The authoritarian leader in a non-democratic system, on the other hand, retains power *only* because he does not hesitate to make or break agreements and betray colleagues and supporters.

Hence, the difference between even the most ambitious politician in a democratic system and his authoritarian counterpart is qualitative. Although an elected politician can normally be assured of a minimum time in office, the authoritarian politician can, in a sense, never rest. By the time he has consolidated his position on the domestic front, his personality has been shaped in a Darwinian world where only the strong and ever-alert can survive; and he does not change his approach when it comes to foreign policy. Applying lessons learned in the domestic arena, the democratic leader also tends to view the world in terms of his own political system—that of compromise and limits on the exercise of power. Consensus and compromise are not only the means in a democratic system, they are also one of its principal goals. Therefore, the authoritarian leader is better equipped, at least in the short run, to capitalize on this wide conceptual gap in political culture and ethics. His presumably complete control over internal affairs renders him more capable of rapid changes in foreign policy; and because he can make major decisions alone and in secret, he is more likely to resort to surprise diplomacy.[43]

For example, Hitler hardly consulted any of his advisers prior to his decision to end the military restrictions of the Treaty of Versailles and reintroduce conscription.

> The generals. . .like everyone else. . .had been taken by surprise, for Hitler, who had spent the previous days at his mountain retreat at Berchtesgaden, had not bothered to apprise them of his thoughts. According to General von Manstein's later testimony at Nuremberg, he and his commanding officer. . .first heard of Hitler's decision over the radio. . . .[44]

> When Hitler was preoccupied with some plans or other, he often shut himself up alone in his room. You could hear him pacing restlessly up and down. He always took the really big decisions like rearmament, occupation of the Rhineland, etc., alone—mostly against the counsels of his staff and advisers.[45]

The same is true of Sadat, who decided to (1) announce his first peace initiative in February 1971, (2) expel the Soviet technicians from Egypt, and (3) make the unprecedented visit to Jerusalem in 1977, without consulting anyone.

> Later Tohamy was to tell an Israeli official how Sadat made up his mind to undertake the journey [to Jerusalem]. It took one minute between his voicing the idea and the decision to do it. The Egyptian government was stunned. . . .All of course was to no avail. Sadat does what Sadat does with the help of Allah and a strong army.[46]

In Stalin's Russia, the decision-making process could be equally swift and unimpeded. When Stalin decided to go ahead with the rapprochement with Nazi Germany, he simply decided (as early as

January 1939) that in the future, his office would issue instructions directly to the Soviet Ambassador and Chargé d'Affaires in Berlin.[47] On May 3, 1939, Stalin fired Foreign Minister Litvinov because he was too closely identified with a friendly policy toward the Western democracies and advocated the containment of Nazi Germany through collective security. In his place, Stalin appointed Molotov whose character was particularly suitable for negotiations with Germany. The reason for Stalin's choice becomes clear after reading the following description of Molotov's behavior during the final phase of Nazi-Soviet talks on the non-aggression treaty by a German diplomat.

> Molotov is a highly efficient administrator, a capable executive of policies that are handed down to him, and an experienced bureaucrat. In contrast to his predecessor. . .he has no creative mind. In negotiations which I witnessed or in which I took part, he never showed any personal initiative, but seemed to keep strictly to the rules laid down by Stalin. When problems came up, he would regularly say that he had to consult his "government." A typical example was Molotov's behavior in an important meeting with the German ambassador on August 19, 1939. Count Schulenburg called on him to transmit a communication to the effect that, if a non-aggression pact was concluded between the two powers, Ribbentrop would be in a position to sign a special protocol on the settlement of spheres of interest in the Baltic area. Although such a declaration was precisely what the Soviet government wanted, Molotov did not dare make a proper response by himself. The ambassador left without obtaining an answer; but he had not been back in the nearby embassy for ten minutes when the phone rang and he was asked to return to the Kremlin at once. He hurried back, and Molotov announced that he had meanwhile consulted his "government" (which could only mean Stalin), which had authorized him to hand the ambassador a draft of the non-aggression pact and which would be expecting the arrival of the German foreign minister at an early date for the conclusion of the pact.[48]

The author then compared the effect of Molotov's appointment to that of Ribbentrop in Germany on February 4, 1938. "Both shifts in personnel have in common that men of a certain intellectual integrity. . .were replaced by men whose outstanding trait was their loyalty to the leader."[49]

The problem posed for an authoritarian leader by an independent-minded foreign minister is strikingly illustrated by Sadat's experiences. Once Sadat decided to go to Jerusalem in late 1977, the Egyptian Foreign Minister, Ismail Fahmy, resigned in protest. Sadat then offered the position to Mohamed Riad (who was the Minister of State for Foreign Affairs), but Riad also resigned in protest. Finally, Sadat nominated

Butros Ghali, a man who had had little experience in foreign affairs but who could be relied on to carry out Sadat's orders as Acting Foreign Minister. Still searching for a Foreign Minister, Sadat nominated Egypt's Ambassador to Germany, Hassan Kamal, who later resigned in protest at Sadat's decision to sign the peace agreement with Israel in April 1979. Eventually, Sadat gave up. Butros Ghali became Acting Foreign Minister until Kamel Hassan Ali became Foreign Minister. In any case, Sadat, like Hitler or Stalin, makes all important foreign policy decisions.

Government control of the media obviously makes it much easier to implement a sharp reversal of earlier policies. When Hitler decided, in April 1939, on a policy of cautiously approaching the Soviet Union, the former vitriolic attacks on the Russians vanished from the German press. During the bargaining process with Israel after the Peace Initiative of 1977, Sadat continuously manipulated the Egyptian press; he orchestrated a campaign that directed signals at the United States, other Arab countries, and Israel. In Israel's case, he tried to isolate Begin among Israeli politicians as a villain, and build up Ezer Weizman who was more sympathetic to the Egyptian viewpoint.

Democratic governments, too, can influence the press, usually by selectively releasing information; but the press does not intentionally cooperate with these manipulative efforts. An even more crucial difference (as will be shown below) is that in an open society, the media can criticize government actions, whereas the media in a closed society represent only a Greek chorus of praise. This does not mean that policy reversals are easy even when the government controls the media. Because it has to take public opinion into account, an authoritarian government must usually introduce a radical change in policy by means of massive, well-coordinated doses of propaganda. When the Nazi-Soviet non-aggression pact was signed on August 23, 1939, the German newspapers naturally did not mention that only recently they had lambasted the Soviet Union as Germany's archenemy. Nor did the Soviet press point out that the new treaty in effect annulled the Soviet-Polish non-aggression treaty of 1934 and the Franco-Soviet treaty of 1936 or that Nazi Germany had been anathema to the Soviet leaders just a few weeks earlier.

Even authoritarian leaders should not try to offend public opinion more than is absolutely necessary; this rule was faithfully adhered to by Stalin when he bluntly rejected Ribbentrop's proposal that Germany and the Soviet Union issue a joint communiqué praising their newly formed friendship in "flowery and bombastic terms."

> Don't you think that we have to pay a little more attention to public opinion in our countries? For many years now we have been pouring buckets of slop over each other's heads, and our propaganda boys could never do enough in that direction; and now

all of a sudden are we to make our peoples believe that all is forgotten and forgiven? Things don't work so fast. Public opinion in our country, and probably in Germany, too, will have to be prepared slowly for the change in our relations this treaty is to bring about, and will have to be made familiar with it.

In any society, the leaders must demonstrate the advantages to be gained from a new policy direction. Following the Peace Initiative of 1977, Sadat had to make sure that the masses would be mobilized to cheer him on his "triumphant" return from Jerusalem, or he would have been in trouble; and he was indeed in a position to promise his cheering people that the move would bring Egypt peace and an improved economy. Hitler could boast that the non-aggression treaty with Russia in 1939 had broken the encirclement of Germany, enabled him to avoid fighting a war on two fronts, and secured raw materials and markets for Germany. Stalin could claim that the Soviet Union had gained time to strengthen its military forces, expanded its sphere of influence, and broken the *cordon sanitaire* surrounding it.

When two authoritarian leaders collaborate in the process of surprise diplomacy as in the Nazi-Soviet non-aggression pact, the change in policy can take place relatively quickly; the rapprochement between Germany and Russia took at most six months to accomplish, though negotiations in earnest took not much more than one month (from mid-July to the end of August 1939). If a democracy is involved, the process will take much longer: leaders must campaign for support and reach a compromise with some of those opposed to the new policy; they must at least to some extent take their country's allies into account; and live with the possibility that at any time the secret negotiations might be leaked to the press. President Nixon's announcement of his trip to Peking was the culmination of at least three years of signaling and negotiating. It took seven and a half more years until the process ended with the exchange of ambassadors in January 1979 and the termination of formal American relations with Taiwan. Even at that stage, President Carter's abrogation of the American treaty with Taiwan caused him many difficulties in Congress and with public opinion.[50]

Similarly, a year and a half elapsed between Sadat's visit to Jerusalem and the signing of the Egyptian-Israeli peace treaty in April 1979. Sadat was prepared to sign a peace agreement with Israel (on his terms) as soon as possible, for ratification by the Egyptian People's Assembly presented no problems whatever. Upon his return from Jerusalem in 1977, Sadat proposed to the People's Assembly that Egypt continue the peace negotiations. As he reports, "I was happy to get almost unanimous endorsement (with only 2 or 3 members, out of 360, objecting)."[51] Such a result (99.1% in favor) has probably never been recorded in a democratic system. The workings of Israeli democracy did not make for smooth sailing for Prime Minister Begin; he was fiercely attacked by many of the media and subjected to cross pressures both from the coalition parties and the opposition. Unlike Sadat, he could not present his policy to the Knesset to be more or less rubber-stamped, nor could he carry out his policy by fiat, firing inconvenient opponents as he pleased.

SADAT'S FIRST PEACE INITIATIVE: THE FAILURE OF A SURPRISE

Not since Hitler's series of *faits accomplis* in the mid-1930's has any statesman so systematically resorted to the use of the diplomacy of surprise as President Sadat of Egypt. Sadat has been able to capitalize on the twists and turns of his own policies primarily because he is not clearly identified with a single ideology such as Pan Arabism or Arab socialism. He is, of course, committed to an "Egypt first" policy, but this seems to be secondary to his guiding principle, the acquisition of power.*

Sadat has habitually kept options for action in different—even

---

* A look at some excerpts from Sadat's autobiography, *In Search of Identity*, leads one to believe that he is preoccupied with power. For example, "From the first day I assumed power" (p. 206); "When I took over power . . ." (p. 207); "Indeed, due to the inner power I had always felt, I had never been afraid to challenge existing conditions. And now that I was President, I felt I wielded tremendous *real* power, which had to be used in doing good." (p. 209, emphasis in the original); "The power-holders used, or rather abused, their power before my very eyes . . ." (p. 208); "When I took over power . . ." (p. 214); "I'm removing Ali Sabri because, although I accept differences of opinion, I cannot tolerate a power struggle." (p. 222); "I won't allow any 'spheres of influence' to come into being or any kind of power struggle to continue. Anyone who acts against the interests of Egypt will be made mincemeat of . . ." (p. 223). Conversely, in his memoirs Sadat does not admit to any weaknesses or faults. He ignores the fact that his repeated declarations to make 1971 the "year of decision" ended in no decision; he claims to have spoken from a position of strength during his peace initiative of 1971 (p. 281); and somehow translates an *almost* disastrous military defeat in October 1973 into a clear-cut victory over Israel. No politician can be expected to dwell on his failures or shortcomings, but the complete absence of self-criticism is highly unconvincing. Perhaps aware of his frequent use of the word power, Sadat summarizes his book in a modest tone. "I have never sought power, for early in my life, I discovered that my strength lies within me in my absolute devotion to what is right, just, and beautiful." (p. 314)

It is also worth mentioning that Sadat sees himself as the personification of the state ("l état c'est moi"). Examples from his memoirs will clarify this point: "The economic legacy Nasser left me . . ." (p. 213); "In January 1971, I had to take a decision on the Rogers Plan." (p. 218); ". . . to have my forces cross to the East bank." (p. 219); "The Soviet Union sent me the SAM batteries in April 1971." (p. 221); "This was how the Soviet Union always dealt with me." (p. 221); "My cease-fire decision was taken during the same night." (p. 263); "But my forces surrounded them on all sides. . . ." (p. 267); "It was at this point that my foreign minister felt himself unequal to the Initiative." (p. 309). It is difficult to imagine the President of the United States, the Prime Minister of Great Britain, or the leaders of the Soviet Union using this kind of phraseology. This is also noted by Raphael Israeli, editor of *The Public Diary of President Sadat*, Part I, *The Road to War* (Leiden: E. J. Brill, 1978), pp. 1-3. (To be cited hereafter as *Sadat's Diary*.)

contradictory—directions open at the same time. In order to enlist the assistance of key political and military leaders, he has been known to switch from a Pan-Arab to an Egypt-First policy, from a pro-Soviet to a pro-American stance, and from a radically anti-Israeli to a conciliatory approach. To Sadat, political loyalty is not necessarily an asset—he peremptorily dismisses those associates who do not strictly follow his orders and those whose services he no longer requires.

An example of his political expediency involves the Nasser legacy. Immediately after Nasser's death in September 1970, Sadat continuously praised Nasser's image and achievements in order to appear as the most suitable successor. But once he attained a modicum of security in the presidency, he leveled a vicious attack at that same regime. In his autobiography he points out the "worst and ugliest feature of Nasser's legacy," which was the "mountain of hatred" in a country where men "spied on their own kin just like in the Fascist regimes."[52]

This emphasis on power calculations, combined with the lack of a definitive ideology, has enabled Sadat to maintain maximum political flexibility—to rapidly shift directions in the best tradition of the balance of power theory. He does not abide by the rules—he creates them.

Sadat's first unexpected foreign policy move was the aborted "Peace Initiative" which he announced on February 4, 1971, only four months after assuming the presidency. The occasion of the speech was the expiration, on the following day, of the Egyptian-Israeli cease-fire agreement along the Suez Canal. During November and December 1970, Sadat had repeatedly threatened to renew the war unless Israel agreed to produce a timetable for withdrawal from all occupied Arab lands. The threats had been accompanied by the ominous warning that "a battle of destiny will follow the end of the cease-fire." But by the beginning of 1971, Sadat realized that the Egyptian armed forces were too weak to undertake such major military operations. Putting Israel on the defensive was his way of retracting the earlier, bellicose threats with a minimal loss of face. "My Peace Initiative of February 4, 1971, launched an Egyptian diplomatic offensive—the only alternative to a military one which I was, at the time, unable to undertake.'"[53]

The speech was primarily awaited for the sake of Sadat's decision on the future of the cease-fire agreement—a decision which he finally announced near the end of the 45 minute speech.[54] Other than reporting that Egypt would extend the cease-fire by another 30 days, until March 7, 1971, the media gave little coverage to the speech.

In his memoirs, Sadat portrays the speech as containing peace offers that were similar to, and as generous as, his Peace Initiative of November 1977. As will be shown, this is not really the case. Nevertheless, the first peace initiative is noteworthy because it contained, in a rudimentary form, many of the dramatic elements of the second, more successful initiative.

The presentation of the first peace initiative can be divided into two parts: (1) Sadat's announcement of his peace plan (in a general form) before the National Assembly on February 4, 1971, and (2) his interview with *Newsweek* magazine in which he further explained the peace proposal.[55] Sadat summarizes the announcement as follows:

> On February 4, 1971, I announced an *entirely new* "Initiative" in Parliament. The drift of it was that if Israel withdrew her forces in the Sinai *to the Passes*, I would be willing to reopen the Suez Canal; to have my forces cross to the East Bank; to extend the Rogers plan cease-fire by six, rather than three, months; to make a solemn, official declaration of a cease-fire; to restore diplomatic relations with the United States; and to sign a peace agreement with Israel through the efforts of Dr. Jarring, the representative of the Secretary of the UN. It was the first time an Arab leader had the courage to declare this in twenty-two years. None of my opponents had foreknowledge of my Initiative; they were surprised; indeed dumbfounded, to hear me declare it to the world in the course of my People's Assembly speech.[56] (Emphasis added.)

As it turned out, no one even considered the speech a *peace initiative*—the surprise was caused by Sadat's readiness to reopen the Suez Canal and station UN troops in the Straits of Tiran to guarantee the safe passage of Israeli ships, two conditions which Nasser had refused to even consider until Israel had completely withdrawn from all occupied territories.

As a matter of fact, Sadat's peace initiative of February 1971 was not as magnanimous as he would have us believe. He is trying to claim credit in retrospect by emphasizing the similarities between his two peace initiatives, whereas it is the differences between them which explain why the second one succeeded while the first failed at the very outset. Nevertheless, the first initiative was, given the circumstances, a bold and daring step.

Neither peace proposal was exclusively his own, as he claims in his autobiography. When Sadat took office, Israeli Defense Minister Moshe Dayan saw an opportunity to improve Egyptian-Israeli relations. Realizing that it would be very difficult for any Arab leader to sign a formal peace treaty with Israel, he advocated an incremental approach to peace, offering partial Israeli withdrawal for partial peace. He proposed that in return for a non-belligerency agreement, Israel withdraw its forces from the Suez Canal area and the Bar-lev line to the Western Passes of the Sinai (about 20 miles east of the Suez Canal); the area would be demilitarized and the Egyptians would be asked to make a reciprocal withdrawal from the West Bank of the Suez Canal or at least thin out their artillery. The Canal would then be cleared and reopened for international shipping (including Israeli ships) and Egypt would be able to rebuild its deserted and ruined cities along the Suez Canal. The implementation of this plan would lay the foundation for future negotiations and perhaps involve other Arab states as well.[57]

In late 1970, various versions of the "Dayan Plan", which was not very popular in Israel, were being discussed. The plan was sharply criticized by members of the cabinet and not formally acknowledged by the government. When asked, Dayan used to deny that such a plan even existed. His ideas were nevertheless communicated to Sadat through intermediaries such as the American Assistant Secretary of State Joseph S. Sisco and the UN mediator Dr. Gunnar Jarring. While insisting on a more comprehensive agreement, Sadat based many of the ideas of his initiative of February 1971 on Dayan's proposals. As *The Economist* commented after Sadat's speech, "Yesterday it was Israel's Moshe Dayan; today it is Egypt's Anwar Sadat."[58]

When Sadat first elaborated on his peace plan in an interview with his friend, *Newsweek's* senior editor Arnaud de Borchgrave, he demanded that Israel withdraw beyond El Arish—some 90 miles east of the Suez Canal—and not, as he claims in his memoirs, to the Sinai Passes.[59] Furthermore, the Suez Canal offer in his February 1971 speech was vague, for it did not specify whether Israeli ships would be allowed to use the waterway once it had been cleared and reopened. Sadat's statements in the *Newsweek* interview at least clarified this point.

Q. Does your proposal include free passage for Israeli ships?
A. Yes, we have agreed to this in our memorandum to Ambassador Jarring. Free passage is clearly spelled out. But first Israel must fulfill its obligations under the U.N. resolution [Resolution #242].[60]

This was understood to mean that even if Israel met Sadat's demands to withdraw from the Suez Canal, he did not propose to let it benefit from the reopening of the Canal as long as other provisions of the Security Council resolution had not been complied with (i.e., according to the Egyptian interpretation of U.N. Security Council Resolution 242, total withdrawal from all occupied territories).[61]

In addition, Sadat insisted that Egyptian troops cross the Canal following a partial Israeli withdrawal instead of demilitarizing the East Bank, as Dayan had suggested.[62] Sadat may have been so adamant on this point because it would have been a symbolic assertion of Egypt's full sovereignty over the Sinai. But the Israelis could not accept the demand to unilaterally relinquish the excellent defensive position along the Suez Canal—a position which they believed the Egyptians could not take by force.

When questioned on his readiness to normalize relations with Israel, Sadat replied:

> Golda Meir once said that peace will only come when she can drive her car from Tel Aviv to Cairo to do some shopping. That is a pipe dream based on the victory complex. America, for example, recognizes China's territorial integrity but does not have normal diplomatic relations with Peking. The exchange of ambassadors is a technicality . . . . Each nation decides for itself. But Israeli propaganda has used what I said to claim that I wouldn't recognize Israel's territorial integrity. That is absolute nonsense, designed to confuse American opinion.[63]

The Israelis suspected that if each nation were to decide for itself, they would decide to normalize diplomatic relations with Egypt—and Egypt would decide against it. Their suspicions might have stemmed from the kind of statements Sadat had made in a December 1970 interview with James Reston of the New York Times.

Reston: Will the Arabs be prepared to recognize Israel as a state?

Sadat: What we are prepared to do is specified in the Security Council resolution. Do not ask me to establish diplomatic relations with them; that will never happen.

Reston: Never?

Sadat: Never.

Reston: Not even if you are able to solve the problem of withdrawal to the pre-June 5th borders?

Sadat: Never, never, never! This is something nobody can decide. No one has the power to make such a decision. Our people here will crush anyone contemplating such a decision.[64]

What made the Israelis even more wary was the fact that Sadat's more liberal interpretation of his peace initiative in the *Newsweek* interview was not translated or published in Egyptian newspapers.[65] Sadat appeared ready to recognize Israel's sovereignty along its pre-June 5, 1967, borders, but he was not yet willing to normalize relations and *formally* recognize Israel's right to exist.

Above all, Sadat was only ready to negotiate a peace agreement through an intermediary such as Dr. Jarring. For Israel, readiness to negotiate directly was an important indicator of the sincerity of a peace initiative. Sadat's willingness to come to Jerusalem and negotiate directly with the Israeli government during his peace initiative in 1977 naturally evoked a more positive response. In the second peace plan, Sadat was also ready to normalize relations, agree to partial demilitarization of the Sinai, and open the Suez Canal to Israeli shipping before a comprehensive settlement had been reached.

Aside from the negative and ambiguous points, there were also some positive, even daring elements that resurfaced in the second peace initiative. Sadat was the first Arab leader to—de facto—recognize Israel's right to exist within its 1948-1967 borders without insisting on a return to the U.N. partition resolution of 1947.[66] In the *Newsweek* interview, Sadat described his conception of a peace treaty.

Q. I think it's important that you spell out as clearly as possible what you would be prepared to put in a peace treaty.

A. If Israel returns our land under the Security Council resolution, the inviolability and political independence of every state in the area, including Israel. We pledge our solemn word on this. We have no designs on Israel, it is Israel that has designs on us. The territorial integrity of Israel in secure and recognized borders will be guaranteed by the Big Four. . . . For all this to happen, however, there must be a just solution to the Palestinian problem.[67]

This statement was indeed recognized in Israel as a very important step forward. For the first time an Arab leader had publicly declared (though not yet to the Arab public in general or to his own people) that he was willing to recognize Israel on terms that were also basically acceptable to Israel. His final statement with regard to a just solution for the Palestinian problem, vague as it was, was commonly used by Arabs to mean the establishment of a Palestinian state in the place of, or at least alongside a shrunken Israeli state as outlined in the U.N. plan of 1947. Needless to say, this condition was not acceptable to Israel. Who would define the meaning of a just solution? This was an especially sensitive point because the Palestinian covenant called for the elimination of the state of Israel.

But even on this issue, President Sadat had demonstrated unusual flexibility. His ambiguity could also be interpreted positively from an Israeli point of view. When asked if he would agree to compensating the Palestinians for their losses, or to a referendum in the West Bank and the Gaza Strip to determine whether they wanted a separate, independent state or a confederation with Jordan he answered, "I'm not in the position to decide for the Palestinians, but this sounds like a reasonable way to solve the problem—compensation and referendum. They must decide by themselves."[68] By not rejecting such possibilities out of hand, as any PLO leader would have done, Sadat acknowledged, even encouraged, the exploration of solutions that might be acceptable to Israel and Jordan, but not to the PLO. In fact, the idea of a referendum was incorporated (in a slightly different form) into the Egyptian-Israeli peace treaty of March 26, 1979. Although Sadat did not yield on the Palestinian issue, he did not make the peace treaty contingent on its solution. In 1971 he relegated the Palestinian question to a less than primary position—he may have considered it of secondary importance when dividing the negotiations into more manageable segments. His attitude was not popular in the Arab world, but it was realistic.

The origins of the ideas which Sadat later brought to fruition were discussed in this interview. He considered the problem of mutual suspicion in these words: "Let's face it, I don't have faith in [the Israelis] and they don't have confidence in me. Let us try to restore confidence by testing their real intentions."[69] By 1977, he expressed the dilemma in more deliberate terms.

> I realized that we were about to be caught up in a terrible vicious circle precisely like the one we'd lived through over the last thirty years. And the root cause was none other than that very psychological barrier. . . . By a "psychological barrier" I mean that huge wall of suspicion, fear, hate, and misunderstanding that has for so long existed between Israel and the Arabs. It made each side simply unwilling to believe the other, and quite unprepared to accept anything transmitted through the U.S.A. (if channeled through other parties, a message from one side to the other would be viewed with even greater suspicion).[70]

Sadat also emphasized that the United States was the key to peace in the Middle East, implying that for a solution it was more important to approach the United States than the Soviet Union. This view was to prevail after the Yom Kippur War in 1973. Finally, he stressed the need for an overall settlement involving all the territories occupied in 1967—a point that was later included in the Egyptian-Israeli peace treaty.

The first peace initiative was, in Sadat's words, "a stunning surprise to the world at large. " No one had expected an obscure Egyptian President to take such a bold step. "There was no question but that Anwar Sadat had shaken up the Middle Eastern diplomatic scene in a way that no one—Arab or Israeli—had done in years."[71] The move put Israel "hotly on the defensive,'"[72] and resulted in intensified American pressure which in turn contributed to growing tension between Israel and the United States.

The Israeli reaction to Sadat's first initiative can be divided into two parts: (1) the immediate response to Sadat's speech in the National Assembly, and (2) the more reflective answer to his *Newsweek* interview. The first official reaction came from Israeli Prime Minister Golda Meir in an NBC interview on February 6, 1971. In a spontaneous and tough response, she stated that there was nothing innovative about Sadat's suggestions concerning the opening of the Suez Canal, and reiterated Israel's willingness to collaborate in the opening of the canal on condition that it would be open to Israeli ships. She asserted that Sadat was only interested in Israeli withdrawal, not formal peace.[73] Almost all observers, in Israel and abroad, interpreted the interview as a negative response—an interpretation that was strongly refuted by Mrs. Meir in the Knesset a day later. Yet Golda Meir's initial reaction represented the majority of Israeli public opinion. In its leading article on February 5, 1971, the liberal Israeli newspaper, *Haaretz*, claimed that Sadat was not ready for compromise since his 30-day extension of the cease-fire (and the demand for an Israeli timetable for withdrawal within that period) was essentially an ultimatum. The newspaper believed that Sadat's proposal to reopen the Suez Canal was simply a ploy to strengthen support for Egypt in shipping circles, particularly those of Western Europe. The article concluded with these comments:

> It is difficult to imagine that the Egyptian President believes that Israel would accept his demands. It could be claimed that yesterday Sadat presented himself as a moderate among the extremists—but that he did not remove himself from the basis of the extreme opinions, even though he avoided making threats as to what Egypt might do if its demands are not accepted.[74]

On February 9, 1971, after a long debate in the Israeli Cabinet, Prime Minister Meir gave a somewhat more cautious and detailed answer to Sadat's peace plan. Expressing the general Israeli feeling that Sadat's offers were too vague, she said that his phraseology had enabled him to avoid mentioning Israel by name when he had affirmed the "need to maintain the independence and integrity of all states in the area." "Israeli experience," she said, "has shown that the phrase 'all states of the region' is used by Arab governments to exclude, not include, Israel. When Egypt has declared on numerous occasions that the Suez Canal, for example, will be opened to 'all states' she has meant in theory as well as in practice all states except Israel." Similarly, she pointed to Sadat's use of the phrase "the legitimate rights of the Palestinians" as indicating his support of the Palestinian terrorist campaign to liquidate the State of Israel. And how could peace ever be established when his one-month extension of the cease-fire agreement was tantamount to an ultimatum, a threat to renew war after March 7? In view of Sadat's recent bellicose statements, the peace speech could hardly be considered a peace offer at all since he had at no point directly spoken of "peace between Egypt and Israel." Meir continued that Israel could not return to the June 4, 1967, borders because of its need for "secure and recognized borders"; but it was prepared to collaborate in the reopening of the Suez Canal, discuss the normalization of civilian life along the canal, and reduce its military presence in the area if Israeli ships would benefit from the reopening of the canal. Finally, she maintained that in order to resolve all the problems and suspicions between Israel and Egypt, the two countries would certainly have to conduct *direct negotiations*. At that time, she felt that Sadat's offer as presented in the speech meant that he aspired to achieve a strategic advantage without making real progress towards peace. "It seems to me strange," said Meir, "to suggest that we should withdraw from the canal in the absence of any authoritative agreement on the absolute termination of war."[75]

The speech was immediately rejected by Egypt, a spokesman of the Egyptian government stating that the opening of the Suez Canal for Israeli shipping depended on Israel's readiness to solve the Palestinian refugee problem. One week after Sadat's speech, the Egyptian representative to the United Nations, Dr. Zayat, said that his country would formally recognize Israel provided Israel put a limit on Jewish immigration. This proposal and the knee-jerk response to Mrs. Meir's speech perhaps even strengthened "the vicious circle of suspicion," causing many political observers in Israel to conclude that Sadat's peace offer had been just another political maneuver.

President Sadat explained his peace plan in more detail in the February 14 interview with *Newsweek*. It is not known whether his explanation was planned or whether it was a spontaneous reply to Mrs. Meir's speech. Be that as it may, his *Newsweek* interviewer, Arnaud de Borchgrave, later arrived in Jerusalem to discuss Sadat's unprecedented contribution to peace with any Israeli who would listen. In an interview with the Israeli evening paper, *Maariv*, he emphasized that Sadat had gone over the text of the *Newsweek* interview and made sure that it accurately represented his ideas on peace. (Again, it is unclear whether de Borchgrave went to Israel on his own initiative or with Sadat's blessing—but his appearance was probably more than mere coincidence.)[76] Whatever the purpose of his mission, de Borchgrave did not have much luck. In *The War of Atonement*, Chaim Herzog describes an unsuccessful interview with Golda Meir.

> With this interview [Sadat's] in hand, de Borchgrave flew to Jerusalem and met a number of people who were impressed by this new development. He was received by Prime Minister Golda Meir and related to her the details of his interview with Sadat. Mrs. Meir listened with ill-concealed impatience and stopped him in the middle, saying, "If I am not mistaken you have come to interview me, so please pose your questions." At the end of the interview, de Borchgrave said, "Madame Prime Minister, I fear that your remarks will be out of date when they are published, because in the meantime Sadat will respond to an overture by Ambassador Jarring and will announce that he is prepared to make peace!" At this point, Mrs. Meir reacted sarcastically. "That will be the day. I don't believe it will happen." De Borchgrave flew back to New York via Zurich. At Zurich airport he was paged and called to the telephone: it was the *Newsweek* representative, relaying a request from Jerusalem that the text of the interview with Golda Meir be returned for amendment,

because in the meantime Sadat had made the declaration which de Borchgrave had forecast. The fact that Mrs. Meir did not amend the text, but merely brought it up to date, confirmed de Borchgrave's opinion that Mrs. Meir here missed the greatest opportunity to prevent war.[77]

The Israeli response to Sadat's *Newsweek* interview was mixed, though clearly more positive than to his earlier National Assembly speech. On the negative side, Sadat's insistence on Israeli withdrawal to a line east of El Arish was considered unacceptable as the basis for only a partial interim agreement—though not for a full peace treaty. Israelis also rejected the possibility that the Palestinian refugees would be able to choose between reparations and a return to Israel since the latter choice was not regarded as feasible.[78] Others saw a hardening of Sadat's position in that he would only discuss the reopening of the Suez Canal as part of a general settlement of the Arab-Israeli conflict, and not as a separate problem. The withdrawal of Israeli troops as far back as the eastern Sinai—almost to the pre-1967 border—without allowing Israeli use of the Canal in return was not acceptable. [79]

Israeli political and intelligence analysts also scrutinized every word of Sadat's interview and then monitored the versions reported in the Egyptian media in order to pinpoint any differences in emphasis. Arabic translations in the Egyptian newspapers spoke about a condition of peace, not a peace agreement. They attached more significance to Sadat's commitment to the Palestinians and omitted the part of the interview in which he expressed his readiness to allow the presence of U.N. peacekeeping troops as a guarantee for free passage through the Straits of Tiran. In the original text, Sadat had said that the U.N. force, once brought in, could only be withdrawn by a unanimous agreement of the Big Four, but the Egyptian newspapers which did mention this proposal implied that the force would be subordinated to the instructions of the U.N. Security Council.[80]

On the positive side, Sadat's interview reflected a new flexibility; unlike Nasser, he had at least expressed Egypt's readiness to station an international peacekeeping force adjacent to the Straits of Tiran and said that negotiations could begin on the basis of a partial Israeli pullback in the Sinai. (Nasser had always insisted that Israel must withdraw from the West Bank and East Jerusalem even before it withdrew from the Sinai.) Although he still felt that a final peace agreement could only be worked out after *all* issues had been solved, Sadat was willing to approach the final goal on a piecemeal basis. Moreover, Israeli commentators realized that Sadat had spoken of Israel in an unprecedentedly positive manner, exposing himself to domestic pressures and the attacks of other Arab countries such as Syria and Libya.

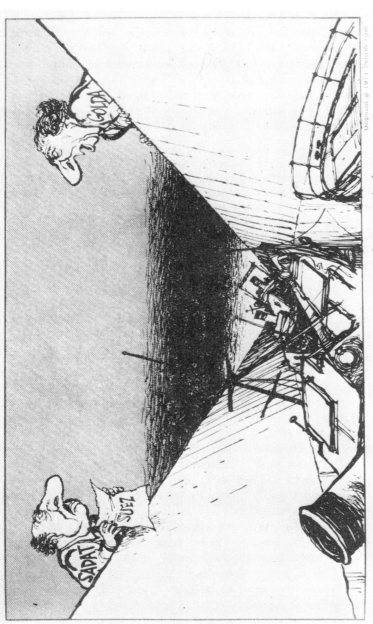

'The answer is "no"—now, let's hear the suggestion'

In an interview with *Maariv*, Mrs. Meir's confidant, Israel Galili, conceded that it was difficult to know what Sadat actually had in mind due to his contradictory statements. However, he conceded that for the first time formal Egyptian expressions towards Israel had changed for the better. This was an important change in itself—a step forward from the 1967 Khartoum decisions which declared that there would be no peace, no recognition, and no negotiations with Israel.[81] In a public debate, Israelis tried to ascertain whether Sadat's latest declarations were diplomatic bluff or an indicator of a genuine change in his position. In a *Maariv* article published on February 26, 1971, Chaim Herzog wrote:

> The Arabs have built themselves a few sacred cows that have guided their way. These sacred cows were exemplified by the three "no's" agreed on in the Khartoum Conference in 1967. While deep in their hearts many of the Arab leaders knew that this policy was impractical, they adhered to it in public. The debate continued and Arabs insisted on no negotiation, no recognition, and no peace with Israel. Israel on its part kept insisting on peace negotiations, but the two sides did not get any closer . . . . Suddenly, the situation has changed and an Arab leader, Egypt's president, crossed the Rubicon, ignored all the sacred cows, and announced his readiness to make peace with Israel under certain conditions. And as a result, the wide gap, the gap of suspicion that separates us and the Arabs was discovered. Not because Israel does not want peace, but because no one can say what is the meaning of peace with the Arab world.[82]

Herzog then concluded that the Sadat move had to be an honest attempt to reevaluate Egypt's position in the conflict.

Despite Israel's acknowledgement that Sadat had made a remarkable move, his peace initiative became the topic of endless discussions between Israel and Egypt through the mediation efforts of Dr. Jarring and the United States, gradually losing its momentum until it faded away like so many other diplomatic efforts before the 1973 war.

Why did the "first peace initiative" fail? In many ways, it was premature. Since Sadat had not yet firmly consolidated his own political power, he was considerably limited in his ability to make concessions that extended beyond the bounds of Nasser's legacy. Four months after becoming president, he was in no position to shatter 20-year-old policies and antagonize the Soviet Union and its supporters or the army.

Admittedly a step in the right direction, his plan contained too many contradictions: he offered to recognize Israel's right to exist *de facto* but refused to refer to it by name; he offered to normalize diplomatic and other relations after peace had been established, but would not negotiate directly with Israel to reach that goal; he wanted to reopen the Suez Canal but refused to let Israel use it; he demanded that Israel withdraw its forces from the canal, but refused to demilitarize the Sinai once Israel pulled back; he was prepared to negotiate separately with Israel, but not to conclude a separate peace treaty; and finally, he spoke one language to the international mass media, and another to the Egyptian public.

Only after he had proved his dedication to the Arab cause during the Yom Kippur War in 1973, could Sadat afford to negotiate on equal terms. By 1977, he had released himself from Nasser's excessive dependence on the U.S.S.R. (which had never encouraged a peaceful solution to the Middle Eastern conflict) and strengthened his power base within Egypt. Having succeeded in the war against Israel to a higher degree than Nasser ever had, Sadat was now in a better position vis-à-vis the Egyptian army which opposed a "premature" or "humiliating" peace with Israel. His increasingly powerful position enabled him to undertake bolder decisions in 1977 that were less popular with a considerable number of Egyptian politicians and military men.

From a practical as well as a psychological point of view, the timing of the first peace initiative was also poor because with the memory of the 1967 war, the War of Attrition, and the PLO terrorist campaign fresh in their minds, the Israelis were *militarily* too strong and sure of themselves. In addition, the first Sadat offer came too soon after the Soviet Union and Egypt had flagrantly violated the cease-fire agreement during the summer of 1970,[83] whereas the peace initiative of 1977 followed three years of a successful separation agreement in the Sinai—an agreement that had contributed to an atmosphere of mutual trust.

Israel's response to Sadat's peace initiative was that while it was willing to negotiate withdrawal from most of the Sinai and occupied territories, it would not pull back behind the June 4, 1967, borders even in return for a comprehensive peace treaty. This was totally unacceptable to Sadat in 1971—as it was in 1977. But by 1977, Israeli military thinking had changed considerably as a result of the 1973 war. Secure borders were still considered vital, but it was recognized that dynamic and mobile warfare could to a large extent compensate for natural borders; besides, "secure borders" were—and are—by no means the panacea for Israel's security problems.

And as a result of less steadfast American backing, Israel's bargaining position also changed between 1971 and 1977. In 1971, Israel could implicitly count on American support because of the Soviet presence in Egypt, especially along the Suez Canal. (In addition, opening the Suez Canal would have.substantially shortened the Soviet Union's supply route to North Vietnam.) Moreover, the American President was preoccupied with domestic issues and the war in Vietnam as well as the progress of his China policy, and therefore had little time or inclination to wield the power and prestige of his office for mediation in the Middle

East.[84] Six years later, the Vietnam War was over, the Suez Canal was open, and the Soviet presence in Egypt had practically been eliminated. Under these circumstances, Israel's bargaining position was weakened by the Carter administration's more sympathetic policy toward the Arab states and Egypt in particular.

Thus, conditions in the Middle East were radically different in 1977. Israel's confidence had been shaken while that of Egypt had been bolstered, so both sides were able to negotiate on a more equal basis; a new Israeli government had been elected; Sadat had improved his image and strengthened his credibility. Having consolidated his power, he could present his earlier ideas in a more coherent form to serve as the basis for negotiations—and the United States could take a more active, forceful part in advancing the cause of peace.

A COMPARISON OF SADAT'S FIRST (FEBRUARY 1971) AND SECOND (NOVEMBER 1977) PEACE INITIATIVES

Sadat's Peace of Separation Proposals of 1971	Sadat's Peace Initiative 1977
No direct negotiations.	Direct negotiations.
Sadat's move was *not* preceded by earlier direct negotiations to assure the success of his move.	Sadat's move was preceded by direct contacts between Israeli and Egyptian representatives. He made his move only after a positive Israeli response was assured.
No diplomatic recognition of, or normalization of relations with, Israel—only non-belligerency agreements with the possibility of normalization in the next generation.	Sadat offers full peace, including normalization of relations, in exchange for Israeli concessions.
Promise to open Suez Canal to Israeli shipping only *after* complete Israeli withdrawal.	Suez Canal will be opened to Israelis after their partial withdrawal (actually the Suez Canal was supposed to be open to Israeli shipping following the 1975 disengagement agreement).
No agreement to demilitarize the Suez Canal. The emphasis is on allowing Egyptian troops to cross the Canal.	Demilitarization of the Sinai. A small number of Egyptian forces will cross the canal. Airfields will be demilitarized.

Sadat calls for a referendum by the Palestinians to decide on unification with Jordan or autonomy.

Sadat formulates similar position. Will agree to Palestinian unity with Jordan or Palestinian autonomy. For Sadat, Palestinian issue is secondary in importance to Egyptian interests.

Israeli answers were vague. No constructive counter-proposals were made.

Constructive Israeli counter-proposals followed by negotiations.

Little awareness of Israeli perceptions and insecurity.

Sadat shifts his political concepts and gains insight into Israeli point of view.

A strict time limit offered for Israeli withdrawal. Sadat extends cease-fire for only 30 days and talks about the "year of decision."

Pressure for quick Israeli moves, but no specific time limit or ultimatum.

Perceptions of Israeli military superiority.

Egypt's honor has been restored by Sadat in the 1973 war. Israel is still militarily stronger, but Sadat can claim that he is now negotiating on an equal footing.

Timing is bad: (1) too soon after the War of Attrition; (2) old-guard Israeli leadership highly suspicious of Egypt's intentions; (3) U.S. still involved in the Vietnam War; (4) Sadat is an unknown leader with little or no credibility; (5) U.S. not enthusiastic about opening the Suez Canal because such a move would facilitate Soviet transport of supplies to North Vietnam.

New leadership in Israel, including Dayan who has an innovative approach to the Arab-Israeli conflict. The United States has withdrawn from Vietnam and is anxious to become involved in Middle East mediation efforts.

THE DECISION TO EXPEL THE SOVIET MILITARY ADVISERS FROM EGYPT, JULY 1972: A SURPRISE WITH LIMITED GOALS

Sadat's first big surprise—the February 4, 1971, Peace Initiative—ended in failure, but his unexpected decision to expel Soviet military advisers was a successful unilateral move designed to achieve limited goals. By endangering its position in Egypt and the Middle East, Sadat hoped to blackmail the Soviet Union into closer collaboration with

Egypt. Instead of weakening his country's relations with the U.S.S.R., Sadat was actually interested—for the time being—in forcing the reluctant Russians to strengthen their commitments. In *The Sphinx and the Commissar*, Mohamed Heikal refers to this move as telling the Russians to "double your stakes or quit."[85]

Prior to the first peace initiative, Sadat attempted to develop an effective Egyptian military option against Israel. After Israel's *de facto* rejection of the peace offer, he redoubled his efforts to improve Egypt's capacity to wage war. Unfortunately, the Soviet Union, Egypt's weapons supplier, refused to cooperate. Between the time Sadat took office (October 1970) and expelled the Soviet advisers (July 1972), he made no less than four visits to the Soviet Union attempting to procure weapons. (His visits took place on March 1, 1971; October 12-13, 1971; February 2-4, 1972; and again at the end of April 1972; not to mention many other ministerial-level visits.) The Egyptians were primarily interested in sophisticated offensive (what they, however, referred to as deterrent) weapons, such as the MiG-25, a Mach 3 high-altitude interceptor and surveillance aircraft.[86] (At the time, the plane was referred to as the MiG-23, its NATO code name is Foxbat, and the Russians call it the X-500.) This aircraft was considered the perfect weapon with which to neutralize Israeli air superiority and intercept low-level deep penetration raids by Israeli F-4 Phantoms and A-4 Skyhawks. (In reality, the MiG-25 is not very effective against the Israeli type of low-level penetration, nor is it suitable for air-to-ground attacks.)[87] In addition, the Egyptians asked for medium-range conventional ballistic missiles (Scuds) in order to be able to retaliate against targets in Israel in return for any Israeli deep penetration bombing of Egypt*; large quantities of the more sophisticated Soviet ground-to-air missiles, the SAM-3 and the SAM-6; heavy artillery; anti-tank missiles; bridging equipment necessary for crossing the Suez Canal; and various counter-electronic devices.[88] Both Sadat and Heikal vividly recall Egypt's frustration in trying to obtain these weapons from the Soviet Union.[89]

---

* It has been argued that Sadat's request for offensive weapons (e.g., the Scud missile) was immaterial to Egyptian offensive capability because even a very large number of the conventional warhead missiles would have little impact as compared with a small number of fighter bombers. [See, for example, Alvin Z. Rubinstein, *Red Star on the Nile* (Princeton: Princeton University Press, 1977), p. 192.] While the claim is technically correct, it misses the point. Sadat wanted the Scud missiles, as he himself said, as a deterrent weapon—not as an offensive weapon. It is true that while Israeli fighter bombers made many raids against strategic targets in Syria in 1973, (targets such as fuel depots, electrical facilities, etc.) no such attacks were made against Egypt in the same war. The reason could very well have been that the Israelis wanted to avoid incurring civilian casualties from the Scud missiles. If so, Sadat's request for "deterrent weapons" did prove to be a wise move. [See Chaim Herzog, *The War of Atonement* (Tel Aviv: Steimatzky, 1975), pp. 24-26.]

For almost two years, the U.S.S.R. evaded Egypt's requests. Without directly refusing to supply the weapons and equipment, they simply claimed that they did not possess certain items (such as counter-electronic devices, submarine detection equipment, or heavy artillery).[90] Reluctant to equip the Egyptians with the most advanced weapons which they had not even supplied to their Warsaw Pact allies, the Soviets probably recalled the fate of their weapons in past Middle Eastern conflicts. During the Six Day War in 1967 and the subsequent War of Attrition, large amounts of Soviet equipment fell into Israeli hands (such as during the Israeli raid on Ras Arab on December 26, 1969, in which top-secret Soviet radar was captured). Feeling that their concern was justified, the Russians often stationed their latest equipment in Egypt on the condition that only Soviet crews would operate the equipment. Under this type of agreement, the Soviets let their pilots fly reconnaissance missions for the Egyptian armed forces using MiG-25s; they further added to Egyptian humiliation by asking them to publicly announce that Egyption pilots were flying the MiG-25s (which Sadat reluctantly consented to do).[91] A similar problem arose when the Russians agreed to supply Egypt with SAM 3 anti-aircraft batteries and train Egyptian crews, who, when they became sufficiently qualified, could take over operation of the missiles. The anti-aircraft batteries arrived in Egypt in April 1971; by May 1972, 18 crews were capable of assuming control of the SAM-3s. (The Israelis, by the way, under-estimated the speed with which the Egyptian crews learned to operate these weapons. They calculated that the crews would require at least three years, whereas it took them less than two.) The Russians, however, refused to turn over the missile batteries to the Egyptians until a compromise was reached and the Egyptians were given control of 12 batteries.[92]

Another confrontation over the control of equipment and weapons occurred during Sadat's secret visit to the Soviet Union in March 1971. After "sharp exchanges" between Sadat, Kosygin, Marshal Grechko, and Brezhnev, the Soviets indicated that they would supply the Egyptians with missile-equipped planes and train the crews *if* the Egyptians would use them only after Soviet permission had been granted. Sadat rejected the deal on the spot.

> I was livid with rage at this. . . . "Nobody," I said, "is allowed to take a decision on Egyptian affairs exept the people of Egypt itself—represented by me, the President of Egypt! I don't want the aircraft."[93]

After Sadat's outburst, Brezhnev adopted a more conciliatory tone and promised to deliver 30 MiG-25s to Egypt. The aircraft never arrived, and

Sadat ordered the four Soviet-operated MiG-25s in Egypt to be grounded indefinitely.[94]

All of these incidents aggravated relations between the Egyptian Army and its Soviet advisers who numbered at least 15,000 by 1972. Another Russian ploy was to promise the Egyptians certain sophisticated equipment, but to deliver different and inferior equipment. They once promised to send Sadat some MiG-23's for which he was prepared to pay in hard currency obtained from Libya. But when General Hassan, the Deputy Minister of War, went to Moscow when delivery was due, the Soviets reneged on the original deal and offered to supply the Egyptians with modfied MiG-21's instead.[95] Needless to say, very little of the equipment that the Egyptians wanted had arrived by the spring of 1972.

Apart from being afraid that their top-secret equipment would be compromised by the Egyptians, the Russians were apparently also worried that Egypt would start a war prematurely and force the Soviet Union to come and bail it out, thus endangering the new Soviet-American detente policy and risk a direct confrontation with the U.S.[96] The Russians were particularly concerned about such a possibility in the spring of 1972 because of President Nixon's scheduled visit to Moscow in May. Sadat's assurances that the Egyptians did not want the Russians to fight for them did not assuage Soviet anxiety; in fact, such assurances may have had the opposite effect, since the Soviet Union was certain that without its help the Egyptians would lose the war even more quickly, and badly damage Soviet prestige in the Middle East.

Whatever the reasons for the Russian stalling tactics, Sadat began to lose patience. The Egyptians suspected that the Soviet Union preferred to maintain a "no war, no peace" situation which would leave Israel in occupation of the Sinai and keep Egypt indefinitely mobilized for war. Army and student pressure on Sadat to "do something" (i.e., to attack Israel) grew during the winter of 1972.

When Sadat went to Moscow on February 1, 1972, and asked why the weapons promised to him on his previous visit in October 1971 had not been delivered, Brezhnev said that he was to blame because the whole matter had become snarled in red tape. Sadat vehemently rejected the excuse.

> "I am not convinced of that," I said, "and if this is repeated I will have to act—a decision will have to be taken." I was beside myself with rage.[97]

The Soviet response was to placate the Egyptians by sending them other, non-essential weapons.

In April 1972, Sadat made a final attempt to effect a change in the Soviets' attitude. He urged them to send him the necessary weapons so that Egypt would be able to go to war in case the American presidential election in November 1972 did not improve the chances for a peaceful solution.[98] The Soviet Union agreed and furthermore promised to send Sadat a detailed report of their conversations with President Nixon in May because Sadat was apprehensive that the United States and the Soviet Union, in order to strengthen their newly-forged détente, might agree to contain the Middle Eastern conflict by reducing arms sales to both Israel and Egypt.

In the meantime, reports from Egypt revealed the growing number of incidents between the Egyptian Army and its Soviet advisers. Most Egyptians, both military and civilian, were offended by the arrogant and patronizing Soviet attitude. As early as February 1972, *Newsweek* published a long article on the tension between the Egyptian Army and its advisers.[99]

In May 1972, Mohamed Heikal, editor-in-chief of Egypt's leading newspaper, *Al Ahram*, published a series of articles in which he argued that the Soviet Union had a vested interest in the "no war, no peace" situation which worked against Egyptian national interests.[100] In one of the articles, Heikal quoted an interview with Luigi Longo, the head of the Italian Communist Party, who suggested that with Egypt in political and military limbo, all of the progressive elements in Egypt would have "the opportunity to intensify the class struggle and the education of the masses. This would enable you [the Egyptians] to carry out the social revolution and the national revolution simultaneously.[101] These hints that the Soviet Union was interested in the perpetuation of the Egyptian-Israeli conflict did not go unnoticed in Moscow where *Pravda* attacked Heikal for his audacious slandering of Russian motives.

Sadat used the occasion of President Podgorny's visit to Egypt in late April 1972 to explain that in particular he needed the means to neutralize the Israeli Air Force so that a crossing of the Suez Canal might be possible. He tried to convince the Soviet Union that this was an urgent need because the United States and its "agent" Israel were gradually gaining control over the Middle East. No mention was made of the problems related to the Soviet experts in Egypt.[102]

Following Nixon's visit to Moscow on May 20, 1972, the Soviet Union and the United States issued a joint communiqué advocating the relaxation of military tensions in the Middle East. This came as a "violent shock" to President Sadat, confirming his suspicions that the Soviet Union, in contradiction of its promises to him, was ready to freeze the situation in the Middle East while Egypt lagged at least twenty steps behind Israel; in this context, military relaxation meant nothing but capitulation to Israel.[103]

On May 26, after the Brezhnev-Nixon meeting that so infuriated him,

Sadat nevertheless sent a message to the leaders of the Soviet Union commemorating the first anniversary of the signing of the Soviet-Egyptian treaty of friendship, "the language of which cannot have given those to whom it was addressed any inkling of what was to come. Sadat sent congratulations 'from the bottom of my heart.' He called the treaty 'a wonderful reflection and firm confirmation of the deep and friendly ties between us,' and so on."[104]

An equally amicable letter addressed to Brezhnev was delivered by General Ahmed Sadiq, the Minister of War, who visited Moscow in early June. In the letter Sadat thanked Brezhnev for his defense of Egypt's position in the recent talks with President Nixon but went on to complain that public statements made by leading American officials after the Moscow talks hinted at agreements contrary to those reached between Sadat and Brezhnev the previous April. Finally, Sadat again pressed for the speedy implementation of the training programs and the supply of arms.[105]

One can only speculate what went on in Sadat's mind in June 1972; there were many considerations which ultimately forced on him the conclusion that shock treatment was the appropriate remedy for Soviet indifference. Sadat himself may not be fully aware of how he finally arrived at his decision. Soon after he announced it he told Heikal that "for a month he had been unhappy, with a feeling that something was brewing at the back of his mind and yet being unable to decide exactly what it was."[106] The decision was made by Sadat alone and "whether his colleagues agreed or disagreed with it, there was nothing they could do about it."[107]

The first person to be apprised of his decision was Egypt's Vice President, Dr. Mahmoud Fawzi. On Thursday, July 6, President Sadat "told him in an almost casual way that he was thinking of asking the Soviet Union to withdraw its military personnel from Egypt because they had become a burden. . . ."[108] The next day, Sadat summoned General Sadiq, the Minister of War, and said, "I am going to tell you something that will make you smile all over your face. [General Sadiq strongly favored an anti-Soviet line.] I have decided to ask the Russians to get out."[109] Completely surprised, Sadiq played the devil's advocate, but to no avail. The third person to be informed was the Soviet Ambassador, Vladimir Vinogradov, who heard the news on Saturday, July 8. (Vinogradov had asked to see Sadat on July 6 to hand him Brezhnev's letter reporting on Nixon's Moscow visit. By that time Sadat had already decided to expel the Soviet experts in anticipation of Brezhnev's report which he thought would only be another evasion of Egypt's request for weapons; he therefore informed the Ambassador that he would receive him on July 8.)[110]

When the Soviet Ambassador met with Sadat on July 8, he first handed him Brezhnev's letter which stated that the Soviet Union had presented Egypt's position to President Nixon, but that no real progress had been made on matters involving the Middle East. The long letter made no mention of the weapons shipments promised in April 1972 and implied that Egypt was not ready to open a war against Israel. This sketchy and vague report on the conversations with Nixon was far from the detailed analysis that the Soviets had promised to send to Sadat soon after the talks ended. Sadat gives a lively account of the exchange that followed in his autobiography.

> I asked the Soviet Ambassador: "Is this *the* message?"
> "Yes," he said.
> "You were, weren't you, with us in Moscow last April," I said, "and you did hear us agree that the weapons should be sent to us before the U.S. elections took place?"
> "Yes," he replied.
> "Well," I continued, "this message doesn't mention that."
> "This is the message I have received."
> "Well," I said, "I cannot accept it, and indeed reject the Soviet leaders' method in dealing with us. Please convey all I am going to tell you to the Soviet leaders as an official message.
> "One. I reject this message you've transmitted to me from the Soviet leaders, both in form and content. It is unacceptable. I reject, too, this method in dealing with us.
> "Two. I have decided to dispense with the services of all Soviet military experts (about 15,000) and that they must go back to the Soviet Union within one week from today. I shall convey this order to the War Minister.
> "Three. There is Soviet equipment in Egypt—four MiG-25s, and a Soviet-manned station for electronic warfare. You should either sell these to us or take them back to the Soviet Union.
> "Four. No Soviet-owned equipment should stay in Egypt. Either you sell it to us or withdraw it within the fixed date.
> "Five. All this should be carried out in a week from now.
> The Soviet Ambassador didn't believe it. He thought it was an attempt at blackmail.[111]

Sadat reminded the bewildered Vinogradov that Egypt was anxious to maintain its friendship with the Soviet Union, but that the problem of broken promises with regard to the timetables for weapons deliveries had to be solved.[112]

The Ambassador answered sheepishly that Brezhnev's letter was to be regarded only as an interim report, not as a final one. The Soviet Union, which had full confidence in the Egyptian leadership, did admit that it was having problems with weapons deliveries due to transport difficulties. He denied Sadat's accusations of a change in Soviet policy towards Egypt resulting from détente with the United States.

Sadat's decision was kept secret until the Russians were already leaving the country. He tried to assuage Soviet anger by sending Egypt's Prime Minister, Dr. Aziz Sidqi, to Moscow on July 13 to do what he could to soothe "hurt feelings" and possibly arrange for the purchase of more military equipment. He offered to buy the four MiG-25s stationed in Egypt as well as the Soviet Quadrant missile batteries (SAM 6) stationed around the Aswan High Dam, apparently hoping to cash in on his blackmail attempt before it was made public. Sadat also hoped that by keeping the move secret, he could convince the Russians to supply Egypt with the weapons it requested in return for the cancellation of the expulsion order.

Not wishing to push the Soviet Union too far, Sadat proposed to Brezhnev that they publish a j   communiqué announcing that the Soviet experts had completed their ..ork in Egypt, so that the Western press would not be able to declare with *Schadenfreude*, as it later did, that the Russians had been asked to leave.

But Brezhnev was in no mood to conceal Sadat's move. "He said: "You asked for the experts. If you want them to leave that is your decision, and we will comply with it. But we are never going to be party to a cover-up story and will not take the responsibility before history of suggesting that they are being withdrawn at our request.' "[113]

General Okunev, an air defense expert who headed the Soviet military mission in Egypt, had immediately contacted Marshal Grechko in Moscow after hearing of Sadat's meeting with the Ambassador, and by early Monday morning he had received instructions to comply with Sadat's demands. A few hours later he presented General Sadiq with a plan for the evacuation of the experts (who by then numbered 21,000); the evacuation was quietly and efficiently completed within the seven-day deadline.[114]

On July 17, Egyptian newspapers reported that Sadat would make an important statement before the ASU (Arab Socialist Union) the next day. This was a major understatement. "By the time Sadat had finished his 90-minute speech, he had drastically changed the course of Egyptian policy and altered the entire Middle East equation."[115] The long-term impact of Sadat's stunning announcement to expel the Russians was hard to predict, but it was nothing less than the Soviet Union's biggest setback in the Middle East since it had first made friends with Gamal Abdul Nasser in 1955.[116]

For Western, Arab, and Israeli intelligence and political analysts, Sadat's decision seemed to shatter the concept that Egypt must, regardless of the tensions, cultivate good relations with the U.S.S.R. This conception of Egypt as an obedient Soviet client state had previously prevented all observers from even speculating on the possibility that Egypt might ask the Soviet Union to withdraw its military advisers. Many perhaps even believed that with the presence of close to 20,000 military experts in Egypt, the Soviet Union would simply refuse to leave if asked.

Speculation was rife as to Sadat's intentions. Optimists suggested that the move was intended to facilitate a separate peace with Israel: pessimists believed that Sadat had kicked the Russians out in order to free Egypt for a renewed offensive against Israel.[117]

Others developed what can be termed the domestic pressure theory; the move, they said, had nothing to do with Sadat's military or foreign policy, but instead stemmed from domestic pressure to get rid of the unpopular Soviet military advisers. Perhaps Sadat had been presented with an ultimatum by Egypt's leading army officers who were anxious to limit Soviet interference in Egyptian affairs.[118] A more extreme theory believed by some to this day, is that Egypt and the Soviet Union collaborated in a move to deceive Israel and the United States—that is, Egypt only pretended to expel the Russians in order to conceal its preparations for war and put Israel off guard.[119] The fact of the matter was that most of the Soviet Union's "military advisers" did leave Egypt, and as a result Israeli Military Intelligence underestimated Egypt's capacity to wage war, thus contributing to the Israeli lack of preparation on the eve of the Yom Kippur War.

Not all observers discarded the original concept. *Newsweek* wrote:

> What really brought things to a head, however, was Sadat's growing conviction that the Soviets were not about to help Egypt build a military force capable of challenging the Israelis. Twice this year, the Egyptian president traveled to Moscow to demand a Soviet pledge to provide such offensive weapons as MiG-23 fighters.[120]

In an interview with *U.S. News & World Report*, Israeli officials speculated that Sadat had made his move with three major goals in mind: (1) to relieve the growing tension between Egyptians, particularly the Army, and the Soviet advisers; (2) to "blackmail" the Soviet Union into supplying Egypt with more weapons and equipment with which to defeat Israel; (3) to signal the United States that Egypt was capable of casting off Russian influence if the Americans agreed to pressure Israel into relinquishing the occupied territories.[121] As far as the Israelis were concerned, the original concept of Egypt's desire to go to war was not completely demolished—but it had been weakened. Although all of the evidence relating to Sadat's true intentions was available to the readers of any major weekly magazine, it was, at that time, shrouded in contradictory evidence and "noise."

In retrospect, the evidence conclusively demonstrates that the original concept of Egypt's dependence on Soviet aid was correct after all. Sadat's dramatic surprise and the ensuing Soviet exodus caused observers to think that a major change had taken place, when in fact it was only a surprise with very limited goals. Sadat wanted the Russians to supply him with large quantities of modern weapons; he was trying to *increase*, not decrease Soviet involvement in Egypt.

Sadat met with Egyptian newspaper editors two weeks after his ASU speech and briefed them on the considerations involved in his decision. According to Sadat, the Soviet refusal to sell certain types of equipment to Egypt, the long delays in delivery, and the conditions placed on the operation of the equipment all contributed to his final decision.[122] There were, however, more important indicators which showed that he had not severed all ties with the Soviet Union.

Sadat's speech on July 18 had implied that *all* Soviet experts would have to leave Egypt. But an article in the July 29, 1972 issue of *The Economist* noted: "True, the Soviet military experts attached to Egyptian units, probably around 4,000-5,000, have left or are going. But about twice this number of Russian military men are believed to be in Egypt, engaged mainly, though not necessarily exclusively, on anti-Nato operations."[123] On July 22, Mohammed Zayat, the Minister of State for Information, further diluted the meaning of the withdrawal order when he told a press conference that the decision to expel the advisers would not affect the facilities used by the Soviet Navy in Mersa Matruh, Alexandria, Port Said, and Ras Banas in the Red Sea. Furthermore, Sadat's order had distinguished between Soviet *advisers* and Soviet *instructors*. The former had to go; the latter were to remain until they had "fulfilled their contracts."[124] In fact, many of the Soviet experts either never left Egypt or else returned after a few months.

Both Cairo and Moscow were careful not to let the incident escalate. As mentioned above, Sadat had "generously" offered to "cover" for the Soviet Union by releasing a communiqué announcing that the Soviet experts had completed their work rather than been expelled. In sending Premier Sidqi to Moscow on July 13 before the decision had been made public, Sadat indicated to the Russians that his primary purpose was to procure more weapons for the fight against Israel.

Sadat did not use the opportunity to turn to the United States for help. As Heikal writes in *The Sphinx and the Commissar*, "The main cause for surprise was that Sadat had apparently made no effort to extract some concessions from the Americans for his action. Surely, it was argued, if he had told Washington that he was seriously contemplating getting rid of all his Soviet advisers, the Americans would have been eager to offer him something in exchange."[125] A few days after Sadat's decision had been made public, Henry Kissinger reportedly told one of his assistants: "I don't understand President Sadat. If he had come to me before this happened and told me about it, I should have felt obliged to give him something in exchange. But now I've got it all for nothing."[126]

Had Sadat made contact with the United States, he would have lost the Soviets' military support and thus would have been forced to delay his attack on Israel indefinitely. What Sadat wanted was to *strengthen*, not weaken his country. If he planned to go to war against Israel, he was in the short run completely dependent on the Soviet Union. The United States could not be expected to supply him with weapons on a massive scale, and even if it had wanted to, the switch from Soviet to American equipment would have delayed any war against Israel by many years. Once he had achieved whatever goals he set for himself in the Ramadan War in 1973, he quite abruptly deserted the Soviet Union for the United States.

How did the Soviet Union arrive at its decision to give in to Sadat's "blackmail"? In the Politburo, Marshal Grechko, representing the military point of view, argued that if the Soviet Union did not want to suffer a similar blow elsewhere in the Middle East, it must give the Arabs enough weapons to take the offensive against Israel. If the Arabs were victorious, they would be obligated to the U.S.S.R. for the arms received from them; if they were defeated, they would have to turn to the Soviet Union for help.[127] When Dr. Sidqi visited Moscow again to make amends to the Russians, he found that they were ready to accelerate the flow of arms. In February 1973, the Minister of War, Marshal Ismail, left for Moscow to sign the biggest arms deal ever concluded with the Soviet Union.[128] "SAM-3 and SAM-6 missiles, the latest anti-aircraft and anti-tank weapons (Strellas and Molutkas), tanks with infra-red range-finding aids, bridging equipment, all started pouring into Egyptian ports in vast quantities. It was, as Sadat said, as if all taps had been fully turned on. 'It looks as if they want to push me into a battle,' he added."[129] Between December 1972 and June 1973, Egypt received more arms from the Soviet Union than it had in the previous two years.[130]

Sadat's and Heikal's memoirs, corroborated by other available evidence, prove that Sadat's decision was mainly intended to pressure the Soviet Union into increasing its military support, but he was motivated by other considerations as well. In the first place, Egyptian national pride had long been bruised by the massive presence of Soviet military advisers—a constant reminder of dependence, weakness, and inferiority. The prolonged presence of these advisers, combined with the humiliating memories of the 1967 defeat and the frustration following the failure of Nasser's war of attrition (1968-1970), constantly reminded the Egyptians of their need for foreign help. These feelings were exacerbated by the

Russians who made it clear that the Egyptians were not ready to go to war, especially without Russian aid, and that Egyptians were no match for Israelis. As Sadat explains in his autobiography, the Soviets were seen as the "new pashas"—just a different version of the old imperialists.

A further reason for the expulsion of the Soviet experts was that the Soviet Union had begun to feel that it enjoyed a privileged position in Egypt—so much so that the Soviet ambassador had assumed a position comparable to that of the British High Commissioner in the days of British occupation of Egypt . . . Yet another reason for my decision was that I wanted to put the Soviet Union in its place—its natural position as a friendly country, no more, no less. The Soviets had thought at one time that they had Egypt in their pocket and the world had come to think that the Soviet Union was our guardian. I wanted to tell the Egyptians that the will of Egypt was entirely Egyptian; I wanted to tell the whole world that we are always our own masters. Whoever wished to talk to us should come over and do it, rather than approach the Soviet Union.[131]

Sadat was determined to prove that Arabs could fight too. "They all said that without Soviet advisers I could not go to war. . . . If Arab victory there was to be, it had to be clearly Arab. A victory that the world would describe as a non-Arab victory would clearly have defeated my strategic object."[132] This also explains why, soon after the Soviet experts left Egypt, Heikal made a special point in *Al Ahram* (August 11, 1972) to disclose an incident in which the Israelis had shot down five Russian pilots in a few seconds on July 30, 1970. He then went on to tell his readers that this proved that Russian accusations as to the incompetence of Egyptian pilots were untrue—and that in fact, Russian pilots were no better than Egyptian pilots.[133]

Sadat's move was enthusiastically welcomed by the Egyptian public; he became more popular than ever before and strengthened his position within the ranks of the Egyptian army.[134] There were other side benefits as well. Sadat could openly blame his failure to keep his promise to make 1971 "the year of decision" on the Russians—after all, they had refused to supply Egypt with the necessary arms.

While Sadat did not contact the United States, his move was of value for future relations with the Americans because it demonstrated that if Egypt so desired (and was sufficiently tempted) it could leave the Soviet sphere of influence. Furthermore, although Sadat may not have consciously planned for the expulsion of the Soviet experts to deceive Israel and the United States concerning his determination to go to war, it did to some degree have that effect.

The Soviet Union, the West, and Israel misinterpreted my decision to expel the military experts and reached the erroneous conclusion which in fact served my strategy, as I had expected—that it was an indication that I had finally decided not to fight my own battle. That interpretation made me happy; it was precisely what I wanted them to think.[135]

Sadat's decision to expel the Soviet military experts is an unusual and interesting example of the successful use of surprise as an instrument in foreign policy. He shocked the Soviet Union into concessions it would not otherwise have made, while deceiving his adversaries and strengthening his position within Egypt.

CHRONOLOGY

Date	Event
December 1969	Sadat is nominated Vice President of Egypt.
January 1970	During a secret visit to Moscow, Nasser asks for large quantities of new Soviet military equipment, particularly anti-aircraft missiles and fighter aircraft.
February	Massive air and sea lift of Soviet military equipment to Egypt.
June	Nasser visits Moscow and requests more Soviet military aid.
August 7	The war of attrition between Israel and Egypt is ended by an Israeli-Egyptian cease-fire agreement. The Egyptians immediately breach it by moving ground-to-air missiles to the Suez Canal area.
August 13	Israel complains to the U.S. that Egypt has violated the cease-fire agreement by moving forward no less than 34 anti-aircraft missile batteries.
September 3	The Israeli government announces that, in response to the Egyptian violation of the cease-fire agree-

September 3 (cont'd)	ment, it will not consider itself bound by it, nor continue to take part in the U.N.-initiated Jarring peace talks.
September 28	Nasser dies.
October 7	In his first public speech as Provisional President of Egypt, Sadat pledges to continue the fight against Israel and Zionism and to strengthen Egypt's friendship with the Soviet Union.
October 17	Sadat is sworn in as Egypt's new President.
November 7	In a speech in Haifa, Defense Minister Dayan informally suggests that Israel must renew its efforts to seek a partial agreement with Egypt.
November 9	Sadat extends the cease-fire agreement with Israel by three months.
November 17	Dayan's suggestion concerning a new partial agreement and further conversations with Egypt is discussed by members of the Government party, Maarach ("The Alignment"), in the Knesset.
November 22	Dayan's proposals are discussed by the Israeli government.
December 11	Dayan visits Washington and discusses his suggestions for a new partial separation agreement.
December 24	In a message to President Nixon, Sadat claims that Egypt is not a Soviet satellite.
December 29	Israel agrees to the renewal of the Jarring mediation efforts.
February 4, 1971	Sadat announces his first "peace initiative": Egypt is prepared to nego-

tiate a separation agreement and open the Suez Canal provided Israel withdraws from all of the Sinai. Sadat extends the cease-fire agreement for 30 days.

February 8 — Jarring presents Israel and Egypt with a series of questions concerning a peace agreement. He asks Israel to withdraw to its 1967 border in return for a full peace agreement, recognition by Egypt, and the opening of the Suez Canal to Israeli ships.

February 9 — In a firm reply to Sadat's proposals, Prime Minister Golda Meir asserts that Sadat simply wants unilateral withdrawal from the Sinai—not peace.

February 15 — Sadat's answers to Jarring's initiative are basically positive, but he continues to insist on a total Israeli withdrawal to the 1967 borders and the fulfillment of Palestinian rights.

February 21 — The Israeli Alignment Party discusses the Egyptian reply. Its partly positive character is recognized.

February 26 — Israel replies positively to Jarring's questions but states that it will not make a complete withdrawal to the 1967 borders.

March — Sadat questions General El-Leithy Nassif, Commander of the Presidential Guard, regarding his loyalty. Nassif says that as a professional soldier he will obey any orders given by President Sadat.

March 1-2 — During one of Sadat's secret visits to Moscow, the Russians promise to supply Egypt with sophisticated military equipment—a promise which is not kept.

March 7   Sadat decides that Egypt will not re-
                       new the cease-fire agreement.

March 22   Defense Minister Dayan suggests to
                       Prime Minister Meir that Israel
                       make the following offer to Egypt:
                       a unilateral Israeli withdrawal to the
                       Sinai Passes (about 20 miles from
                       the Suez Canal); the demilitarization
                       of the area vacated by Israel; nor-
                       malization of life in the area by
                       opening the Suez Canal and rebuild-
                       ing the cities along the Canal. The
                       Israeli government accepts a slightly
                       modified version of Dayan's pro-
                       posal the same day.

March 31   Aware of the necessity to assure the
                       Soviet Union of his friendship,
                       Sadat sends an important message
                       to Brezhnev through Sami Sharaf,
                       who attends the Twenty-Fourth
                       Congress of the CPSU in Moscow
                       on March 13, 1971, as head of Egypt's
                       Arab Socialist Union (ASU). In the
                       message, Sadat proposes the con-
                       solidation of Egyptian-Soviet rela-
                       tions through a treaty of friendship
                       and cooperation.

April 4   Sadat declares that Egypt will open
                       the Suez Canal if Israel withdraws
                       to the El Arish-Ras Mouhamed line.

April 21   Sadat faces opposition from the Ali
                       Sabri faction during a meeting of the
                       Supreme Executive Comittee of the
                       Arab Socialist Union. He decides to
                       refer the debate to the Central Com-
                       mittee where he is sure of obtaining
                       a majority.

April 22   Sadat informs the Soviet Ambassa-
                       dor to Egypt of his intention to dis-
                       miss Ali Sabri, making it clear that
                       this is a purely internal Egyptian
                       move which is not directed against
                       the Soviet Union's interests.

May 1	Soviet leaders inform Sadat that they are "prepared to sign such a treaty [a treaty of friendship and cooperation] any time [he wishes] . . ."
May 2	Sadat dismisses Ali Sabri from all of his posts.
May 10	A police officer shows Sadat tapes of telephone conversations which prove the existence of a plot to assassinate him.
May 12	Sadat obtains the backing of Generals Fawzi and Sadiq.
May 13	Sadat dismisses Sharawi Gomaa from his post as Minister of the Interior. In the early evening, Sadat orders the new Minister of the Interior to seize all tapes kept in the Security Section of the Ministry. Late in the evening, Sadat is notified that the Ali Sabri group has made its move: five key ministers resign, hoping to hamstring Sadat. But Sadat quickly accepts their resignations and nominates new ministers.
May 15	"Popular demonstrations" in support of Sadat. Sadat declares he will uphold Nasser's original policies.
May 16	Ali Sabri and friends are arrested.
May 25	Soviet President Podgorny visits Cairo to discuss the draft text for the treaty of friendship and cooperation, insisting that prompt conclusion of the treaty is essential. In return, he promises Sadat immediate delivery of new weapons including the latest Soviet aircraft.
May 27	The Egyptian-Soviet Treaty of Friendship and Cooperation is signed.

July

An attempted coup d'état by Communists in the Sudan ends in failure. In condemning the coup, Sadat says that he cannot accept having common borders with a communist regime.

October 12-13

On a visit to Moscow, Sadat again explains his desire to be on an equal footing with Israel and asks the Russians to show more confidence in Egypt. According to Sadat, the Soviet leaders again promise to send him the requested missile-equipped aircraft and experts to train Egyptian crews.

November

The Indo-Pakistani war breaks out. The Russians divert weapon shipments intended for Egypt to Pakistan and also remove some weapons stationed in Egypt.

In an attempt to improve Saudi-Egyptian relations, Kamel Adham, one of King Faisal's key advisers, visits Cairo. He warns Sadat of American alarm at the Soviet presence in Egypt at a time when the Saudis are trying to encourage active American interest in the Middle East's problems. Sadat replies that he needs Russian help in the fight against Israel, but that once the first phase of Israeli withdrawal has been completed he will evict the Russians.

December 11

Sadat asks the Soviet Ambassador to arrange for him to visit Moscow as soon as possible.

December 27

Sadat is informed that the Soviet leaders will be able to receive him in Moscow on February 1 and 2, 1972.

February 1-2, 1972

Sadat visits Moscow and asks about the extremely long delay in the shipment of the promised Soviet arms. The Russian promise to send some arms (not the ones Sadat wants most) immediately.

April

Rumanian President Ceausescu visits Egypt. Sadat mentions the possibility of arranging a meeting with Golda Meir through the good offices of the Rumanians. He later backs out of this suggestion.

Late April

Sadat's fourth visit to Moscow. The Soviet leaders agree (1) to send Sadat a "detailed report" on Nixon's scheduled May 20 visit to Moscow and (2) to start sending Egypt the promised weapons.

May 20

Following President Nixon's visit to Moscow, the Soviet Union and the United States issue a joint communiqué advocating the relaxation of military tensions in the Middle East.

May 26

Sadat sends the Soviet leaders a telegram commemorating the first anniversary of the Egyptian-Soviet Treaty of Friendship and Cooperation.

June 1

Sadat sends Brezhnev a letter which includes seven points concerning Soviet policies toward Egypt.

June 15

Sadat sends Brezhnev another letter inquiring about his June 1 letter.

July 6

Vladimir Vinogradov, the Soviet Ambassador in Cairo requests an interview with President Sadat.

July 8

Vinogradov meets with Sadat and relays Brezhnev's answer, which is evasive and does not even mention the long-awaited arms shipment. Sadat rejects the message and de-

July 8 (cont'd)	mands that the Soviet Union, within the next week, withdraw all of its military experts and equipment not sold to Egypt.
July 13	Egyptian Prime Minister Dr. Aziz Sidqi visits Moscow with instructions to (1) soothe the Soviet's hurt feelings, and (2) try to obtain more weapons.
July 17	Sadat publicly announces his decision to expel the Soviet experts from Egypt.
July	Sadat instructs General Sadiq to prepare a limited paratrooper operation against Israel in Sharm el-Sheikh for November 1972.
July 27	Sadat rejects Israel's renewed call for direct negotiations following the ouster of the Soviet advisers from Egypt.
Early August	Brezhnev sends Sadat a personal letter which explains Soviet policies and essentially asks for an explanation of current Egyptian policies. Sadat is angered by certain parts of the letter but refrains from replying immediately.
Late August	Sadat's reply to Brezhnev's letter expresses his frustration at being unable to obtain sufficient weapons to "deter" Israel. Sadat reiterates the importance of receiving the necessary military equipment by October 1972.
October 16	Egyptian Prime Minister Sidqi visits Moscow again.
October 24	At a meeting of the Supreme Council of the Armed Forces, Sadat ar-

gues in favor of a limited war against Israel, but is opposed by General Sadiq.

October 26

General Sadiq is dismissed. General Shazli, the Chief of Staff, is appointed Commander-in-Chief of the Army; General Ahmed Ismail, former Director of Intelligence, is appointed Minister of War.

October 27

Sadat also fires the Deputy Minister of War, the Commander of the Navy, the General commanding the Central Military Area and the (nonmilitary) Director of Intelligence.

November

General Ahmed Ismail reports the completion of defensive plans and begins drawing up plans for an offensive against Israel.

December

As a good will gesture Sadat asks General Ismail to inform the Soviet Ambassador that Egypt is prepared to grant a five-year extension to the agreement concerning naval facilities for the Soviet Mediterranean Fleet.

December 1972-June 1973

Egypt receives a flood of weapons from the Soviet Union.

January 27, 1973

The Paris agreement ending the war in Vietnam is formally signed. Kissinger orders the National Security Council to prepare a special extensive study on the Arab-Israeli conflict which now occupies more of his and the Administration's attention.

January 31

A unified Egyptian-Syrian armed forces command is set up.

April

In the April 9 and 23 editions of *Newsweek*, Sadat unveils his war plans against Israel in an interview with Arnaud de Borchgrave.

April-May	Major military mobilization exercises are held in both Egypt and Syria.
May 19	Sadat visits Damascus.
May 25	Plans for the combined Egyptian-Syrian military operations are outlined.
August	Extensive political activity takes place between Syria, Jordan, and Egypt.
August 22	At the naval headquarters in Alexandria, top Egyptian and Syrian military officers coordinate final plans for war against Israel.
August 28	Sadat visits Syria and Saudi Arabia.
September 12	Syria, Jordan, and Egypt conclude an agreement for cooperation. Egypt renews its diplomatic relations with Jordan.
September 13	In a lengthy dogfight between Israeli and Syrian aircraft, 13 Syrian fighters are shot down. Tension increases on the Syrian-Israeli border.
September 22	Henry Kissinger replaces William Rogers as U.S. Secretary of State.
October 1	Sadat makes his final decision to attack Israel on October 6.
October 3	The Egyptian War Minister visits Damascus to check last minute preparations.
October 4	Sadat informs the Soviet Union of his decision to launch a war against Israel on October 6.
October 5	The Soviet Union begins to evacuate its advisers and their families from Egypt and Syria.

October 6	Total surprise is achieved in Egyptian-Syrian attack on Israel.
	The Syrians want to end the war as soon as possible, while Sadat wants to prolong it.
October 13	President Nixon decides to start a weapons airlift to Israel.
	Sadat rejects a British proposal to initiate a debate in the U.N. Security Council on a cease-fire.
Ocober 14	Arab oil ministers meet in Kuwait and decide to impose a selective oil embargo, reducing oil output by five percent.
	Egypt launches a major armored offensive south east of the Suez Canal and is defeated.
October 15	Israeli forces cross the Suez Canal.
October 16	In a speech to the Egyptian National Assembly, Sadat announces his willingness to convene an Arab-Israeli peace conference on condition that Israel agrees to completely withdraw to its 1967 borders. President Assad of Syria attacks Sadat's proposals.
October 16-17	Kosygin arrives in Egypt and urges Sadat to accept a cease-fire.
October 19	Sadat decides to accept an immediate cease-fire.

NOTES

1. Anwar el-Sadat, *In Search of Identity: An Autobiography* (New York: Harper and Row, 1978), p. 208. (To be cited as Sadat, *In Search of Identity*.)

2. *Ibid.*, p. 280.

3. Joachim Fest, *Hitler* (New York: Harcourt Brace Jovanovich, 1974), pp. 483-484; see, for a similar comment, E. M. Robertson, *Hitler's Pre-War Policy and Military Plans 1933-1939* (New York: Citadel Press, 1967), p. 1.

4. Allan Bullock, *Hitler: A Study in Tyranny* (New York: Harper and Row, 1962) p. 378.

5. Ronald Hingley, *Joseph Stalin: Man and Legend* (New York: McGraw Hill, 1974), p. 168.

6. *Ibid.*, p. 173.

7. Jon Kimche, "The Riddle of Sadat," *Midstream*, April 1974, pp. 7-8.

8. *Ibid.*, p. 13.

9. *Ibid.*, p. 12. Sadat was referred to by his colleagues as "Nasser's poodle." (*Time*, January 2, 1978, p. 27.) The "poodle" turned out to be a cunning fox in the game of political survival. Sadat once explained his behavior by saying, "If you showed ambition with Nassar that was the end." (*Time*, January 2, 1978, p. 27.) For a long time Nasser had a low opinion of Sadat. He has been quoted as characterizing Sadat by saying that "Sadat's greatest ambition is to own a big automobile and have the government pay for the gasoline." Quoted in Pedro Ramet, *Sadat and the Kremlin*, "The California Seminar on Arms Control and Foreign Policy," Santa Monica, February 1980, No. 85, p. 9. (Hereafter cited as Ramet, *Sadat and the Kremlin*.)

10. Kimche, "The Riddle of Sadat," *Midstream*, April 1974, p. 16.

11. *Ibid.*, p. 13.

12. R. Michael Burrell and Abbas R. Kelidar, *Egypt: The Dilemmas of a Nation—1970-1977*. (Beverly Hills: Sage Publications, 1977), The Washington Papers, Vol. 5, No. 48, p. 14. For a similar opinion, see Walter Laqueur, "On the Soviet Departure from Egypt," *Commentary*, December 1972, p. 62.

13. Sadat, *In Search of Identity*, p. 215. This was also Henry Kissinger's opinion. He viewed Sadat as "an interim figure who would not last more than a few weeks," and adds, "That was among my wildest misjudgments!" (Henry Kissinger, *White House Years* (Boston: Little, Brown, 1979), pp. 1276-1277.

14. Mohamed Heikal, *The Sphinx and the Commissar: The Rise and Fall of Soviet Influence in the Middle East* (New York: Harper and Row, 1978), p. 220. (To be cited as Heikal, *The Sphinx and the Commissar*.)

15. Kimche, "The Riddle of Sadat," *Midstream*, April 1974, p. 17.

16. Sadat's attempt to find a formula for political unity between Egypt, Syria, Libya, and Sudan, cannot have been very seriously intended in light of his history. In 1957, he published a book on Arab unity in which he sharply criticized the Arab League and the lack of Arab aid to Egypt during the Sinai (Suez 1956) campaign. The book proved to be popular in Egypt, but was quickly withdrawn because of Nasser's pan-Arab aspirations. Sadat was denounced by Heikal as a defeatist and subsequently lost his position as editor of *al Goumhouria*. (See Kimche, "The Riddle of Sadat, *Midstream*, April 1974, p. 8.) Sadat's peace

initiative in 1977, and his verbal attacks on other Arab countries before and after the signing of the Egyptian-Israeli peace treaty, clearly indicate that he subordinates pan-Arab interests to Egypt's interests.

17. Sadat, *In Search of Identity*, p. 216.

18. *Ibid.*, p. 218.

19. *Ibid.*, p. 218. For the most detailed discussion of this episode, see also Mohamed Heikal, *The Road to Ramadan* (New York: Quadrangle Books, 1975), "The Downfall of the Ali-Sabri Group" in Chapter 3; see also Heikal, *The Sphinx and the Commissar*, pp. 224-225.

20. See Heikal, *The Road to Ramadan*, pp. 122-139. According to John Barron in *KGB: The Secret Work of Soviet Secret Agents* (New York, N.Y.: Readers Digest Press, 1974), pp. 51-59, the central figure in the plot against Sadat was Sami Sharaf, Minister of Presidential Affairs and a KGB operative, and not Ali Sabri. See also Ramet, *Sadat and the Kremlin*, p. 1n.

21. See Alvin Z. Rubinstein, *Red Star on the Nile: The Soviet-Egyptian Relationship since the June War* (Princeton, N.J.: Princeton University Press, 1977), p. 181.

22. Sadat, *In Search of Identity*, p. 223.

23. In his memoirs, Sadat gives a different date, saying that he was informed of the conspiracy on May 11. (*In Search of Identity*, p. 223; see also Heikal, *The Road to Ramadan*, pp. 133-134.)

24. See Shirer, *The Rise and Fall of the Third Reich* (New York: Simon and Schuster, 1960), pp. 214-215.

25. Heikal, *The Road to Ramadan*, p. 134. Sadiq was interested in weakening the pro-Soviet opposition to Sadat not only because of the Army's dislike of the Soviet Union's patronizing attitude, but also because he thought he had a better chance of influencing Sadat than the Ali Sabri group. It was soon obvious that he was wrong. Kimche claims that General Sadiq planned and executed the coup, or what Sadat calls the second revolution. (See Kimche, "The Riddle of Sadat," *Midstream*, April 1974.) This is contradicted by the Heikal and Sadat versions, which seem to be more reliable. The Army remained benevolently neutral and thus played a passive though major role in the so-called second revolution.

26. Sadat, *In Search of Identity*, p. 224.

27. *Ibid.*, p. 224.

28. Heikal, *The Road to Ramadan*, p. 135.

29. The extent of the conspiracy is not clear. Most of the evidence comes from Heikal's book, *The Road to Ramadan*, and Sadat's autobiography, *In Search of Identity*. There was also a lot of "indiscreet talk" by men like Gomaa and Sharaf. They did not (as far as we know) have concrete plans for a coup d'état. Sadat, in fact, preempted a potential rather than an immediate threat against his rule. Some observers doubt that such a conspiracy existed at all, since the evidence presented during the "trials" was not very convincing. (See Kimche, "The Riddle of Sadat," *Midstream*, April 1974, p. 24.)

30. Heikal, *The Road to Ramadan*, p. 129.

31. Heikal, *The Sphinx and the Commissar*, p. 227. Raphael Israeli in *The Public Diary of President Sadat*, p. 73, contends that President Podgorny was the one who talked Sadat into signing a 15-year Treaty of Friendship with the Soviet

Union. This may be the version Sadat would like to disseminate, but it contradicts Heikal's testimony. The Soviet-Egyptian Treaty of Friendship and Cooperation had lasted less than five years, when on March 14, 1976, the Egyptian People's Assembly unceremoniously voted 307-2 to abrogate it. Needless to say that no attention was paid to the clause in the treaty calling for a year's notice before terminating it.

32. *Ibid.*, p. 227.

33. Sadat, *In Search of Identity*, p. 225.

34. Heikal, *The Sphinx and the Commissar*, p. 227.

35. Heikal, *The Road to Ramadan*, pp. 119-120.

36. *Ibid.*, p. 120.

37. Heikal, *The Sphinx and the Commissar*, p. 235.

38. Kimche, "The Riddle of Sadat," *Midstream*, April 1974, p. 18.

39. *Ibid.*, p. 24.

40. *Ibid.*, p. 24.

41. *Ibid.*, p. 24-25.

42. Sadat, *In Search of Identity*, pp. 234-236; also Heikal, *The Road to Ramadan*, pp. 180-181.

43. For a similar discussion of the problems involved in projecting one's own experience in the process of evaluating an opponents' behavior, see Robert Jervis, "Hypotheses on Misperception," *World Politics*, Vol. 20, No. 3, April 1968, pp. 466-472.

44. Shirer, *The Rise and Fall of the Third Reich*, p. 284; see also John Wheeler Bennett, *The Nemesis of Power*, pp. 338-339n.

45. David Irving, *The War Path*, p. 48. (Quoting Hitler's adjutant, Wiedemann.)

46. Sidney Zion and Uri Dan, "The Untold Story of the Mideast Talks," *New York Times Magazine*, January 21, 1979, pp. 47-48.

47. Montgomery Hyde, *Stalin: The History of a Dictator* (New York: Farrar, Straus, and Giroux, 1971), p. 383.

48. Gustav Hilger, *The Incompatible Allies: A Memoir-History of German-Soviet Relations 1918-1941* (New York: Macmillan, 1953), pp. 290-291, also p. 300.

49. *Ibid.*, p. 292n; on Ribbentrop's character, see also Paul Seabury, *The Wilhelmstrasse: A Study of German Diplomats under the Nazi Regime* (Berkeley: California University Press, 1954), p. 50; Robertson, *Hitler's Pre-War Policy and Military Plans 1933-1939*, p. 50; Gordon Craig and Felix Gilbert (eds.), *The Diplomats: 1919-1939* (Princeton: Princeton University Press, 1953).

50. John Tierney (ed.), *About Turn: The China Decision and its Consequences* (New Rochelle, N.Y.: Arlington House, 1979).

51. Sadat, *In Search of Identity*, p. 311.

52. Sadat, *In Search of Identity*, pp. 208-210; also Alvin Z. Rubenstein, *Red Star on the Nile*, pp. 316-320. When Sadat came to power, he publicly revered Nasser's memory and described his death as a national disaster (address of October 19, 1970), swore to follow Nasser's footsteps (in his speech accepting his presidential candidacy, October 8, 1970), and continued later to refer to Nasser in flowery language as "The Commander of our Revolution and our Nation's

Teacher" . . . "The Hero of July 23," . . . "the creative architect who constructed Arab-Soviet friendship bridges" (in a speech given May 26, 1971), "The standard-bearer, the loyal son of his nation, and the admired father of his people." (Radio address, July 23, 1971). Sadat began to attack Nasser only much later.

53. Sadat, *In Search of Identity*, pp. 221-222, pp. 278-281.

54. *New York Times*, February 5, 1971, p. 3.

55. *Newsweek*, February 22, 1971, pp. 40-41. The choice of an American magazine as a major platform for an important policy announcement was highly unusual, to say the least, especially when both the United States and the United Nations were trying to mediate between the two sides. See *The Economist*, February 20, 1971, p. 33.

56. Sadat, *In Search of Identity*, p. 219.

57. For Dayan's plan, see *The Economist*, February 13, 1971, pp. 30-31; Kimche, "The Riddle of Sadat: *Midstream*, April 1974, p. 21; *Newsweek*, February 15, 1971, p. 37; Shmuel Segev, *Anwar Sadat's Road to Peace* (in Hebrew) (Tel Aviv: Massada, 1979), pp. 198-205; William B. Quandt, *Decade of Decisions: American Policy Toward the Arab-Israeli Conflict 1967-1976* (Berkeley: University of California Press, 1977), pp. 136-137; Henry Kissinger, *White House Years*, p. 1280; Abba Eban, *An Autobiography*, (New York, N.Y.: Random House, 1977) pp. 470-476.

58. *The Economist*, February 13, 1971, p. 30.

59. *Newsweek*, February 22, 1971, pp. 39-40.

60. *Ibid.*, p. 39.

61. *The Economist*, February 13, 1971, p. 33.

62. Sadat, *In Search of Identity*, p. 219.

63. *Newsweek*, February 22, 1971, p. 41.

64. Kimche, "The Riddle of Sadat" *Midstream*, April 1974, pp. 21-22. (Quoted from the *New York Times*, December 28, 1970.) See also text in Israeli, *Sadat's Public Diary*, pp. 14-15.

65. There were some significant differences between the text of the interview given to *Newsweek* and the Arabic version as distributed by the Egyptian news agency MENA on February 16, 1971. In the Arabic version, instead of talking about a peace treaty, reference was made only to "peace conditions." The passages in which Sadat referred to Israel's inviolability and political independence as well as to its right of navigation through the Suez Canal were completely omitted. In his *Newsweek* interview Sadat's condition for peace with Israel was the total withdrawal from all occupied Arab territories. The Arabic version also included the vague demand to restore the Palestinian rights. See Israeli, *The Public Diary of President Sadat*, p. 32.

66. *Newsweek*, February 22, 1971, pp. 40-41.

67. *Ibid.*, p. 41.

68. *Ibid.*, p. 41.

69. *Ibid.*, p. 40.

70. Sadat, *In Search of Identity*, pp. 302-303.

71. *Newsweek*, March 1, 1971, p. 34.

72. *The Economist*, February 20, 1971, p. 34.

73. For the text of Meir's interview with NBC, see *Haaretz*, February 7, 1971, pp. 1, 3.

74. *Haaretz*, February 5, 1971, p. 1.

75. *Haaretz*, February 11, 1971, p. 9.

76. *The Economist*, February 20, 1970, p. 34.

77. Chaim Herzog, *The War of Atonement* (Jerusalem: Steimatzky's Agency Ltd., 1975), p. 18.

78. *Haaretz*, February 16, 1979, p. 9.

79. *Maariv*, February 16, 1971, p. 8.

80. *Maariv*, February 18, 1971, p. 12.

81. *Maariv*, February 26, 1971, p. 16.

82. Chaim Herzog in *Maariv*, February 26, 1971, pp. 9-16.

83. It must be remembered that only a short time before the Israeli Government had had a very negative experience regarding Egyptian observance of agreements. On August 8, 1970, a cease-fire *in place* agreement was signed between Israel and Egypt. It was agreed that *no* additional troops, military installations, and above all, anti-aircraft missile batteries would be brought into the cease-fire area. Israel reluctantly accepted the terms of the agreement under U.S. pressure; at the time, Israel had gained the upper hand by its attacks along the Suez Canal front, and had successfully prevented the Egyptians from installing or bringing forward more missile batteries. As soon as the cease-fire went into effect, the Egyptians (with the aid of the Soviet Union) broke the agreement by installing many anti-aircraft missile batteries along the Suez Canal. This breach of the agreement was even admitted by President Sadat in a speech on January 2, 1971, when he said, "The cease-fire was a wonderful opportunity for us to build and reinforce all our positions along the entire battle front . . . . . Our forces did not lose a moment in the first cease-fire period." (Rubinstein, *Red Star on the Nile: The Soviet-Egyptian Relationship Since the June War*, see pp. 124-126.) The Egyptian move negated all the costly and lengthy military operations which the Israelis had conducted along the Suez Canal (and considerably improved Egypt's military position at no cost to the Egyptians).

After the Israelis complained, the United States was, as an agreed trustee of both sides, at first very reluctant to admit that such a flagrant breach of the agreement had taken place. The American attitude further reduced Israel's willingness to put its trust in diplomatic accords that were guaranteed by others. Given this experience and Sadat's open insistence on moving Egyptian troops into the Sinai following a partial Israeli withdrawal—before a formal peace treaty had been signed and the Suez Canal opened to Israeli shipping—it is not surprising that the Israeli government was reluctant to put faith in Sadat's promises. It should be noted that Israel had considered the possibility of attacking the new Egyptian anti-aircraft missile bases that had been moved forward. This was not done. Israel paid dearly for its acceptance (under U.S. pressure) of the Egyptian breach. In October 1973, the same Egyptian anti-aircraft missiles covered the Egyptian crossing of the Suez Canal and took a heavy toll in Israeli aircraft. (For a detailed account of the American side which confirms the Israeli complaints, see: Kissinger, *White House Years*, pp. 582-593).

84. Quandt, *Decade of Decisions*, pp. 129, 142-143. For the continued nego-

tiations between Israel and Egypt through the good offices of the United States, see *Decade of Decisions*, Chapter 5.

85. Heikal, *The Sphinx and the Commissar*, p. 242. For a systematic presentation of possible explanations for the Egyptian-Soviet rift in 1972, see the pyramidologist (as distinguished from an Egyptologist, who deals with ancient Egyptian history) Ramet, *Sadat and the Kremlin*, pp. 3-24.

86. *Ibid.*, pp. 248-249.

87. Israeli Phantom jets acquired something of a mythological aura in Sadat's eyes—almost to the point of obsession. No doubt this helped him to excuse and explain the poor performance of the Egyptian Air Force. As a matter of fact, the MiG-21, and its later versions, is an excellent fighter-interceptor, which is simpler to operate and maintain than the F-4 Phantom, and hence more suitable to the requirements of the Egyptian Air Force. In October 1979 Sadat finally got his F-4 Phantoms from President Carter. According to recent reports, the Egyptian Air Force finds these planes difficult to maintain and operate. Only 9 out of 35 F-4's supplied are operational at any given time. See "Washington Star," July 8, 1980, p. D-6.

88. Heikal, *The Sphinx and the Commissar*, p. 220.

89. See Heikal, *The Road to Ramadan*, pp. 160-165; Sadat, *In Search of Identity*, pp. 220-221. pp. 225-231.

90. Heikal, *The Sphinx and the Commissar*, pp. 229, 250. Sadat described the Soviets' delaying tactics in one of his speeches as follows, "The Soviet Union calms us down and never says no . . . they let us calm down . . . , but since no implementation is in sight, I am swept by the whirlwind and I cannot control events any longer . . . This is one aspect of our differences . . . Our strategies are different. They believe that this problem can be placed at spot No. 3, 4, or 5, but for me it is top priority, it means everything for us: life, death, sleep, awakening, food and beverage. . ." Israeli, *The Public Diary of President Sadat*, p. 238, (from a speech delivered on July 24, 1972.)

91. Sadat, *In Search of Identity*, pp. 220-222; Heikal, *The Road to Ramadan*, p. 163.

92. *Ibid.*, p. 161.

93. Sadat, *In Search of Identity*, p. 220.

94. *Ibid.*, pp. 220-221.

95. Heikal, *The Road to Ramadan*, p. 162.

96. Sadat's repeated emphasis on his desire to avoid an American-Soviet confrontation indicates that this possibility must have been frequently mentioned to him by the Russians. See Israeli, *The Public Diary of President Sadat*, p. 213 (speech delivered on May 14, 1972) and p. 238 (speech given on July 24, 1972.) 1972.)

97. Sadat, *In Search of Identity*, p. 228.

98. *Ibid.*, p. 229.

99. *Newsweek*, "Cairo Puts the Chill on Russia," February 28, 1972, pp. 32-35. (This article may have been inspired or leaked by the Egyptian government as a warning signal to the Soviet Union to mend its ways.)

100. Heikal, *The Road to Ramadan*, p. 164; Heikal, *The Sphinx and the Commissar*, p. 238.

101. Heikal, *The Sphinx and the Commissar*, p. 238.

102. *Ibid.*, p. 240.

103. Sadat, *In Search of Identity*, p. 229.

104. Heikal, *The Sphinx and the Commissar*, p. 241.

105. Heikal, *The Road to Ramadan*, p. 170; Heikal, *The Sphinx and the Commissar*, p. 241.

106. Heikal, *The Road to Ramadan*, p. 170. Sadat described his decision to expel the Russian advisers as one of the most difficult of his life. Israeli, *President Sadat's Public Diary*, p. 240 (speech on July 24, 1972).

107. Heikal, *The Sphinx and the Commissar*, p. 292.

108. Heikal, *The Road to Ramadan*, p. 170.

109. *Ibid.*, p. 171.

110. *Ibid.*, p. 171.

111. Sadat, *In Search of Identity*, pp. 229-230.

112. Heikal, *The Road to Ramadan*, p. 171.

113. *Ibid.*, p. 176. For the official Soviet version of their withdrawal from Egypt, see Ramet, *Sadat and the Kremlin*, pp. 12-17.

114. *Ibid.*, p. 115; The ouster of the Soviet Union's experts from Egypt fits perhaps the definition of a *fait accompli*—that is, it was more of a surprise in terms of timing than in terms of the substance of the decision itself. The Russians were, after all, aware of the tension that their presence in Egypt had created since they had already been kicked out of Indonesia and Ghana. Heikal can therefore justifiably say, ". . . the Soviets were shocked by the President's decision but not surprised. They were deeply annoyed and hurt, but had prepared themselves in advance for something of the sort." (Heikal, *The Road to Ramadan*, p. 175.)

115. *Newsweek*, July 21, 1972, p. 26.

116. *Ibid.*, p. 26.

117. See for example, *U.S. News and World Report*, August 7, 1971, pp. 38-39.

118. Walter Laqueur, "On the Soviet Departure from Egypt," *Commentary*, December 1972, pp. 61-68.

119. Uri Ra'anan, "The Soviet-Egyptian Rift," *Commentary*, Vol. 61, No. 6, June 1976, pp. 29-35. In 1976, Uri Ra'anan still believed that the expulsion of the Soviet Union's experts from Egypt was part of a deception plan despite the evidence presented in Heikal's book, *The Road to Ramadan*, (published in 1975), and the evidence of Sadat's rapprochement with the United States. He omits references to Heikal's book which was already available when he wrote his article. Heikal's evidence would have refuted his argument. For a critique of Ra'anan's "theory," see Ramet, *Sadat and the Kremlin*, pp. 17-22.

120. *Newsweek*, July 21, 1972, p. 27.

121. *U.S. News and World Report*, August 1972, p. 39.

122. *Newsweek*, August 7, 1972, pp. 28-29.

123. *The Economist*, July 29, 1971, pp. 31-32.

124. *Ibid.*, pp. 31-32; see also Rubinstein, *Red Star Over the Nile*, p. 191.

125. Heikal, *The Sphinx and the Commissar*, pp. 242-243.

126. Heikal, *The Road to Ramadan*, p. 184.

127. Heikal, *The Sphinx and the Commissar*, p. 253.

128. Sadat, *In Search of Identity*, p. 238.

129. Heikal, *The Sphinx and the Commissar*, p. 253-254.

130. Heikal, *The Road to Ramadan*, p. 181.

131. Sadat, *In Search of Identity*, p. 231.

132. Sadat in an interview with Arnaud de Borchgrave, March 18, 1974. Quoted in Rubinstein, *Red Star on the Nile*, p. 195.

133. *Ibid.*, p. 204. Heikal, *The Road to Ramadan*, p. 162.

134. See Rubinstein, *Red Star on the Nile*, p. 191. Walter Laqueur interpreted Sadat's position after the expulsion of the Soviet experts as "weaker than it has ever been before; the military men who had backed him are gone and it is by no means certain he can trust their successors. His eventual fall from power now seems only a question of time." (*Commentary*, December 1972, p. 66.)

135. Sadat, *In Search of Identity*, p. 230. The Israelis were misled to a large degree. The ouster of the Soviet experts further strengthened their concept that Egypt would not be ready to go to war in 1973.

"Sadat's move against the Soviets . . . was received with satisfaction too in Israel, although Sadat's purpose was completely misunderstood. The various Israeli announcements were of relief and gratification at the removal of the Soviet from this front of Israel. Not appreciating the true reasons for Sadat's move, motives which were far removed from the true one were read into it, a fact that contributed in no small measure to the strengthening of the 'concept' which played such a vital part in misleading Israel." (Herzog, *The War of Atonement*, p. 22.)

6

THE CONTINUATION OF WAR
BY OTHER MEANS

Soon we encountered a methodological problem—we had no established procedures telling us how to seek out and examine signals indicating a movement toward peace. We had had much experience involving war—we knew what signals to search for. But what indicated peace? We had seen a form of Arab expression that was different in both form and content. But could we ignore the possibility that such talk might be Arab propaganda intended to dull our senses and deceive us?[1]

Major General Shlomo Gazit, Director of Israeli Intelligence, 1974-1979

One of the most dramatic diplomatic surprises of the 20th Century was President Sadat's so-called Peace Initiative of 1977. Early in October 1977 the likelihood of peace in the Middle East seemed more remote than ever. The Arabs and Israelis were becoming entrenched in extreme positions even as the Carter administration made extraordinary efforts to bring them together at a Geneva peace conference before the year's end. Rejecting the approach of the step-by-step diplomacy as practiced by Kissinger under Presidents Nixon and Ford, the Carter team had opted for an overall solution. But by the end of October it was evident that even if the Geneva conference could be convened in accordance with the American timetable, a comprehensive peace treaty and a solution to the Middle East conflict would never be the result. Then, on November 9, President Sadat of Egypt dropped a bombshell: he announced his readiness to go to Jerusalem and negotiate directly with the Israelis. Thus the Geneva deadlock was overcome, and it looked as if peace in the Middle East was at least a possibility again.

Sadat's decision to break the impasse in Arab-Israeli negotiations by going to Jerusalem was the result of four distinct though interrelated factors. The first factor concerned developments within Israel: Menachem Begin, a long-time leader of the opposition with the reputation of a powerful hawk, was elected Prime Minister in May 1977; moreover, Israel expressed a willingness to negotiate with Egypt, although it stubbornly resisted all pressure to negotiate with the Palestinian Liberation Organization. During the summer and autumn of 1977, the Israelis had secretly approached Egypt and offered to make considerable concessions in the Sinai in return for a peace or non-belligerency agreement resulting from direct Israeli-Egyptian talks.

The second factor was the influence of the two superpowers and the radical, uncompromising stance of other Arab states. Sadat realized that there was a limit to the amount of pressure that the United States could productively exert on Israel. Furthermore, Soviet backing of the extreme Palestinian and Syrian positions rendered success at Geneva an impossibility. In adopting a position somewhere in between those of Israel and the other Arab participants, Egypt therefore had most to lose since it would be unable to take advantage of Israeli offers at such a conference.

Sadat's perception of Egypt's role in the Arab world was the third factor; he felt that Egypt should turn inward and grapple with its economic problems instead of exhausting its resources in endless wars with Israel. So he pursued a policy in which Egyptian interests took precedence over all other Arab concerns.

The fourth and final factor was Sadat's own personality. The astonishing visit to Jerusalem allowed him to indulge his flair for drama and political creativity, whereas the laborious, unpromising pre-Geneva talks did nothing to encourage a man who was known for his impatience with details and lengthy negotiations. Moreover, even had Begin rejected his offer to come to Jerusalem, he would have scored high in world public opinion and further isolated Israel.

It is difficult to pinpoint the specific train of events which prompted Sadat to undertake his peace initiative, but it *is* possible to examine some of the circumstances that encouraged and influenced his decision. The Israeli national election on May 17, 1977, was one of those events. After a close race, Israeli citizens ousted the coalition of Labor parties that had enjoyed 30 years of uninterrupted rule, and elected instead a coalition of right-wing parties headed by Menachem Begin. The unexpected change in voting behavior was the result of (1) demographic changes within Israel; (2) the voters' displeasure with economic problems and political corruption; (3) the identification of the Labor Party with Israel's lack of preparedness for the Yom Kippur War; (4) the seeming weakness of the Labor Party in the face of American pressure;[2] (5) the desire to see new faces and new ideas in power. The trend reflected a more intransigent and belligerent mood—a signal to the United States that Israelis were opposed to the establishment of a Palestinian homeland (i.e., state) and that they were not going to make unilateral concessions to neighboring states. Not long before the Israeli elections, President Carter had irritated Israelis when he advocated the establishment of a Palestinian homeland during his visit to a town meeting in Clinton, Massachusetts. Carter's remarks as well as mounting American pressures on the Israeli government on the eve of the elections inadvertently aided the right-wing opposition in its campaign against the "soft" Labor Party.

The outcome of the elections was described as "a swing towards right-wing and religious nationalism" and "the day of the hawks"; and Begin was called a terrorist, an authoritarian zealot, a primitive ideologue, and a Zionist fundamentalist. While most of these descriptions contained a grain of truth, they were obviously much exaggerated and reflected considerable ignorance of Israeli politics. Begin was labeled a super hawk, but after being a loyal member of the opposition for 30 years and serving as a minister without portfolio in the Eshkol and Meir national unity governments for almost four years, he could at best be described as a vegetarian hawk whose talons had been drawn.

More than a little surprised by his own victory, the Prime Minister-elect formed his new coalition government. As if to validate his reputation as a hawk, he chose no less than three well-known ex-Generals for his cabinet: Moshe Dayan was named Foreign Minister (Begin lacked Dayan's experience in dealing with foreign policy, defense problems, and the Arabs); Ezer Weizman, the flamboyant, outspoken Air Force General, became Minister of Defense; and "Arik" Sharon, a daring commando officer who was known for his crossing of the Suez Canal during the Yom Kippur War, was chosen as Minister of Agriculture. In October 1977, after lengthy negotiations, two Generals who were members of the Democratic Party for Change joined the government (partly at the encouragement of American officials) in order to exert a moderating influence: Yiegael Yadin became Vice Premier, and Meir Amit, Minister of Transport.

Begin's election caused considerable consternation in the Arab world, where he was famous as the fanatical Zionist terrorist responsible for the Dir Yassin Massacre. Arab radio and newspaper commentators concluded that the chances of a settlement through negotiations had been ruined while the probability of a new war had increased. In Beirut, a PLO spokesman proclaimed, "The Zionists have shot the first round of the next war."[3] A Radio Bagdad commentator said, "What we claimed all along has now become clear to all Arabs; any attempt to negotiate with the Zionists is ridiculous and is bound to fail—the only solution is war."[4] The leaders of Syria, Saudi Arabia, and Egypt—Assad, Khalid, and Sadat—hastily met in Riad, Saudi Arabia, on May 19, 1977, in order to coordinate their strategies. Reports claimed that the three leaders "reached the conclusion that a military confrontation . . . [was] inevitable and that they . . . [had] decided to accelerate their preparations for war." Radio Damascus stated: "Now there is a 100 percent chance of war". An Egyptian spokesman declared, "We don't see how it is possible to negotiate with Begin. Only military action can help."[5] King

Hussein of Jordan warned that the probability of war had increased. "The smallest border incident could explode the whole region. Israel's new leaders are looking for an excuse for war."[6] Ignorance of Begin's current ideas and policies fueled dire predictions about the new, supposedly "trigger-happy" Israeli government.

When Begin spoke of the need to expand Jewish settlements in Judea and Samaria during his first interviews with the foreign press, he certainly did nothing to dispel his image as a fanatic.[7] But other, more optimistic voices heralded his election as a positive event. One of President Carter's aides was quoted as saying, "It took a hard-liner like Nixon to go to China."[8] Senator Jacob Javits of New York added, "The victory of the right will help the United States in its efforts to bring stability to the area. This is because a more hawkish government will be able to neggotiate with the Arabs from a more uniform position concerning the desired solution."[9] Austrian Chancellor Bruno Kreisky said that regimes which were not suspected of intending to make concessions could better impose such concessions on public opinion.[10] In other words, a right-wing government is frequently in a better position than any other government to take a turn to the left in its foreign policy.

In the long run, Begin's government *did* reflect more continuity than change. Begin, Dayan, Weizman, and others had served in earlier Labor governments, and Begin's own ideas had inevitably changed since the late 1940's and early 1950's. As the leader of the opposition Begin had frequently expressed his opinions in Israeli newspapers, so his ideas were certainly not unknown. As a matter of fact, he was a prolific writer whose column appeared regularly in every second or third weekend edition of the Israeli evening newspaper *Maariv*.* A content analysis of his articles would show that while some of the assumptions about him were right, many others were outdated.[11] In articles published between 1974 and 1977, Begin *does* exhibit symptoms of the "Munich syndrome": he does not believe in unilateral concessions or appeasement; his experiences in Russia during World War II made him staunchly anti-communist, and perhaps even more, anti-Russian; and he would resist at any cost the establishment of an independent Palestinian State in the West Bank or the halting of Jewish settlements there. On the other hand, a careful reading of his—very repetitive—articles indicates that he had no sentimental or other ties to the Sinai or the Golan Heights, and that under mutually satisfactory agreements he would return those areas to

* I have counted no less than 71 full-length articles by Begin which appeared in *Maariv* between January 1974 and May 1977. But almost no one outside of Israel (as well as many commentators in Israel) paid systematic attention to his articles. When Begin was in contradiction to the CIA forecast elected in May 1977 and high U.S. officials asked for his file, they found that the file was based on the analysis of a book entitled *The Revolt*—a book that Begin had written in the late 1940's.

Egypt and Syria. His strong anti-Soviet attitudes are certainly shared by Sadat, and most of the ideas expressed in his articles were not so different from those of the Labor government. Moreover, he appeared to be *more* flexible than the Labor government concerning the Sinai Peninsula and the Golan Heights.

Where foreign policy and security are concerned, the major difference between Begin and his predecessors is more a matter of style than of substance. Begin's old-fashioned, sentimentalist style contrasts sharply with that of the more experienced Labor government leaders (such as Golda Meir, ex-Foreign Minister Abba Eban, ex-Prime Minister Rabin, ex-Foreign Minister Yigal Allon, etc.) who were less openly anti-Soviet and used a more "rational" vocabulary.

Like every Israeli Prime Minister before him, Begin wasted no time after his election in declaring his willingness to negotiate directly for peace with the Arabs. When presenting his government in the Knesset on June 20, 1977, he declared:

> Our prime concern is to avoid another war in the Middle East. I am calling upon King Hussein, President Sadat, and President Assad to meet me whether in our own capitals or on neutral territory, either in public or out of the limelight, to discuss the establishment of real peace between them and Israel. Too much blood, Jewish and Arab, has been shed in the region. Let's put an end to this hated bloodshed and seriously and sincerely sit by the negotiating table. If this call is rejected, we shall take note of Arab intransigence, which will be nothing new. Five prime ministers that have preceded me—David Ben-Gurion, Moshe Sharett, Levi Eshkol, Mrs. Golda Meir, and Yitzhak Rabin repeatedly called for such meeting, but the other side has either avoided a response or answered in the negative. . . .[12]

Begin then presented his government's platform for a vote of confidence. It contained no less than five guidelines pertaining to the future of peace negotiations with Israel's neighbors.

> 5. The Government will place the aspiration for peace at the forefront of its concerns, and will strive actively and constantly to achieve permanent peace in the region.
>
> 6. The Government will invite Israel's neighbors, jointly and severally, either directly or through a friendly state, to conduct direct negotiations towards the signing of a peace treaty, without prior conditions on the part of anyone and without formulation of a solution drawn up from outside.
>
> 7. The Government announces its readiness to take part in the Geneva conference, at such time as it shall be invited to do so by the United States and the Soviet Union on the basis of Security Council resolutions 242 and 338.

8. In preparation for the Geneva conference and direct negotiations, the Government announces Israel's readiness to conduct negotiations in order to achieve true, contractual, and effective peace that will lead to normalization of life in the region.

26. The Government will honor the international agreements signed by previous governments.[13]

Behind the scenes, Begin did more than just talk about peace. Using a variety of secret communication channels provided by Morocco, Rumania, and apparently also Iran and India, he tried to signal Sadat that Israel was ready to negotiate directly with Egypt and make generous territorial concessions in return for a full-fledged peace agreement.

The Israeli government had maintained secret contacts with Arab governments for many years. (Among the better known were Golda Meir's travels in Arab dress and veil to meet King Abdullah of Jordan in Amman and elsewhere; and King Hussein's meetings with Israeli leaders in Israel as well as in several other locations.)[14] One channel that became very active during 1975 was King Hassan of Morocco, who served as a constructive, highly secret contact and mediator between Israel, Egypt, and Saudi Arabia.[15] In October 1976, King Hassan invited Prime Minister Rabin for a secret three-day visit to Rabat. Accepting the invitation, Rabin flew to Paris where he boarded King Hassan's private plane and completed the trip to Morocco.[16] During the meetings, King Hassan suggested that Rabin meet Saudi Crown Prince Fahd in Morocco in January 1977. Rabin agreed and the meeting was scheduled, but Prince Fahd cancelled at the last moment.[17] While in Morocco, Rabin also discussed the possibility of negotiating with the Egyptian government and asked King Hassan to explore the Egyptian terms for a possible agreement, but the Egyptians never responded to this inquiry. Nothing concrete resulted from Rabin's visits to Morocco, yet the contacts he made there eventually led to a series of meetings in Rabat between top-level Egyptian and Israeli intelligence officials after Begin's election. The rapport established in these meetings later contributed to Sadat's decision to visit Jerusalem.[18]

The next step in the process of communicating Israel's desire to reach an agreement with Egypt was Begin's trip to Rumania on August 25, 1977.[19] Upon the invitation of President Ceausescu who had tried to mediate between Israel and Egypt for some time,[20] Begin spent three days in Bucharest and had two long conversations with the Rumanian President. During their first meeting on August 26, Ceausescu said he felt that an Egyptian-Israeli meeting would take place soon, although he did not know at what level. He simply assured Begin, "We [the Rumanian Government] are working on it."[21] From Sadat's autobiography[22] it is clear that Prime Minister Begin convincingly expressed his desire for peace and his willingness to make meaningful concessions to Egypt in the Sinai, for he impressed Ceausescu as a sincere leader who could deliver what he promised. By the time Sadat visited Rumania in early November, Begin had sent another message to Ceausescu in which he again expressed his readiness to meet with Sadat in Jerusalem, Cairo, or some neutral place without any formalities.[23] (When Sadat officially announced his decision to come to Israel on November 17, Begin sent a message of thanks to President Ceausescu for his contribution to the Egyptian-Israeli dialogue.)[24]

Just before Sadat visited Rumania, President Ceausescu gave him a very positive report of the conversations with Begin, saying that he felt the chances for peace were good with such a "strong" Israeli prime minister. This convinced Sadat that even an "extremist" like Begin might genuinely desire peace, thus encouraging his feeling that the time for an initiative had come.[25] In a *Time* interview, Sadat recalled his conversation with Ceausescu:

> So I first wanted to make sure of one thing. Does Begin really intend to establish peace or not? Is Israel genuine in its demand for peace talks? I started my journey to Rumania. I had a very long talk with [President Nicolae] Ceausescu—tête-à-tête. . . . I asked, is Begin genuine in his will for peace? He said yes. . . . The second question that I wanted to know was this: Is Begin strong enough or not, because I can't deal with a weak government or a weak leader, like Rabin? We had a talk before that, Ceausescu and I, about Rabin, and both of us reached the consensus that he was weak. I like to deal with a strong government and a strong man. In this respect I have to mention that I would have preferred to deal with the old lady [Golda Meir]. She has guts! Really! Well, Ceausescu told me what he discussed with Begin, and we reached the conclusion that the man is strong.[26]

Prime Minister Begin was not the only Israeli official trying to communicate with Sadat. During the summer Foreign Minister Dayan (on his own initiative and with Begin's approval) attempted to send similar messages to President Sadat and King Hussein through different channels. The full story of Dayan's secret diplomacy will probably not be published for a long time, but it is possible to reconstruct a general sketch of his contacts with Egyptian representatives through the information that was leaked to the press. According to Israeli newspapers, Dayan made four secret trips during August, September, and October, of which three were for meetings with close aides of Sadat. On August 22, Dayan secretly met with King Hussein of Jordan while on a public visit to England. It is not clear whether this is included among Dayan's secret trips, since only the meeting and not the trip was secret. Apparently the

Shah of Iran was also acting as a go-between for the Israelis and Egyptians. In early August, Dayan had gone on "vacation" for a week. He went on a secret trip to India, and probably to Teheran, in an attempt to establish direct negotiations with Egypt. It is almost certain that Dayan had extensive conversations with the Shah of Iran during the first half of August, though this has not been officially confirmed, nor were there any "leaks" on the subject.[27] What is beyond doubt is that Dayan visited Morocco twice before Sadat came to Jerusalem. The first visit took place on September 16 and 17, 1977. En route to the United States, Dayan slipped away in Paris where a plane of Morocco's King Hassan II whisked him off to Tangier to talk with Egypt's Deputy Prime Minister, Hassan el-Tohamy, one of Sadat's closest confidants.[28] The exact content of the conversations is not known, but Dayan reportedly promised that the Begin government would be prepared to withdraw from *most* of the Sinai, let Egypt restore its complete sovereignty over the Sinai, put Israeli settlements in the Rafah-El Arish area (Yamit) under the Egyptian flag, transfer Israeli military air bases to the United Nations, and create an enlarged buffer zone between Israeli and Egyptian forces in the Sinai to avoid future confrontations.[29] Tohamy did not give Dayan a clear-cut answer concerning Sadat's plans and a possible meeting with Begin. Before leaving, Dayan asked Tohamy whether they would meet again and Tohamy replied that he was not sure. Israeli journalists reported that Tohamy knew Sadat was planning the peace initiative and had deliberately misled Dayan. If this report is correct, then Sadat was considering a bold peace initiative as early as September 1977.[30] Yet, from what is known of Sadat's habit of not informing *anyone* (especially not that far in advance) when he is planning an audacious move, it can be assumed that even Tohamy did not know what Sadat had in mind—even supposing that Sadat himself had already arrived at a decision.

The discussions concerning a meeting between Begin and Sadat focused on arranging such a meeting in secret and on neutral territory. Dayan went to Morocco again later in October, a month before Sadat's visit to Jerusalem, and met with a senior Egyptian politician in order to coordinate a secret meeting between Begin and Sadat, perhaps even in Israel.[31] This explains why the Israelis, having initiated the contacts and collaborated with the Egyptians to bring about a secret meeting between Begin and Sadat, were surprised when Sadat decided to turn the proposed talks into a public event.

*   *   *   *   *

The first disclosures concerning earlier Israeli meetings with Egyptians in Morocco appeared in Israeli newspapers toward the end of December 1977. Most of these initial accounts were very general, simply reporting that Israeli representatives had made generous promises to the Egyptians prior to Sadat's decision to come to Jerusalem. These reports originated with Israelis who opposed Begin's "concessions"—they worried that Begin had gone too far without informing the Israeli public. After the appearance in the May 1978 issue of *Jeune Afrique* of a report that Dayan had met with one of Sadat's close aides during the previous fall, Israeli newspapers started carrying general accounts of Dayan's meetings in Morocco. These accounts were probably based on leaks from Dayan and his supporters, since they were intended to refute accusations and complaints that were coming from two opposing sources. The Egyptians claimed that Dayan had promised concessions which Israel (now that Sadat had come to Jerusalem) was trying to disavow; and the Israeli opposition complained that Dayan had exceeded his authority and "given everything away" to the Egyptians. Dayan's story, as leaked to the press, was that while he had told the Egyptians that Israel would be generous, he had not made any specific promises.[32]

Obviously, the Israeli government, because of its repeated offers to make substantial concessions to Egypt in return for a peace agreement, does deserve some credit for the realization of Sadat's peace initiative. Begin's and Dayan's promises certainly produced inordinate expectations in Sadat, exaggerated perhaps by Tohamy's perception of what Dayan had told him in Morocco. In addition, it may never be known whether Sadat's claims at the bargaining table that the Israelis had promised him more in return for his dramatic and courageous move were simply tactics or the truth. Nevertheless, after the peace agreement was finally signed, it was clear that Sadat had obtained much more than any Israeli government, including Begin's, had ever said that it was willing to concede even for a full-fledged peace treaty.

The misunderstanding over what promises were made in the meetings that took place before Sadat's visit to Jerusalem demonstrates the dangers involved when two leaders who know exactly what they want send close aides to negotiate in their name. The aides may promise more (or less) than their leader intended, or perceive the position of the other side in a different way. Subsequently, the leaders do not necessarily feel themselves bound by the promises made, and the whole cycle of bargaining can become immensely complicated. When diplomacy depends on the decisions and will of one person rather than on a larger forum such as a cabinet, all negotiations are only a prelude to the final and binding decisions that are taken by the leader himself.

To better understand the context on which President Sadat decided to launch his peace initiative it is necessary to examine the prolonged and tortuous indirect negotiations between Israel, Egypt, and Jordan following the 1973 war. This is not the place to go into a detailed discussion of these intricate and nerve-wracking negotiations.[33] My intention here is to briefly summarize some of the major prolems which plagued the negotiating process by the autumn of 1977 and examine their impact on Sadat's decision to launch his peace initiative.

In the absence of direct negotiations between Israel and the Arabs, the American government acted as a mediator even before the 1973 war had ended. While the United States had, in the years between 1969 and 1973, repeatedly presented plans (e.g., the Rogers Plan) for mediation in the Middle East, these efforts had never wholly occupied Washington's attention. Following the 1973 war, the Arab oil embargo, and the end of American involvement in the Vietnam War, the Middle East negotiations soon occupied center stage. Their importance was enhanced by President Nixon's need to divert attention from his domestic difficulties. Finally, under the Carter administration, they became the most important U.S. foreign policy issue.

During the Nixon and Ford administrations, Secretary of State Henry Kissinger pursued a limited and cautious policy of *partial* and *separate* agreements between Israel and its neighbors. The short-range American goal was to stabilize the volatile situation in the Middle East; but, mainly in order to safeguard the supply of oil to the U.S., Western Europe, and Japan, the ultimate aim was to use the American role as mediator to improve American relations with the Arab states—even if this meant a gradual reduction in commitment and aid to Israel. But in order to improve relations with the Arab states, the United States had to convince Israel to relinquish some of the territory it had conquered in 1967 and 1973; Israel, however, would only make such concessions if it was assured of increased American military and economic aid. Paradoxically, while it was trying to gradually back out of its special relationship with Israel, the United States was actually stepping up aid to Israel. After each round of talks, Israel grew stronger (at least militarily) and was in a better position to withstand American pressure.[34] Naturally, the closer Israel was in the process of negotiation pushed toward its 1967 borders, the more it resisted making concessions. By playing a central role in the peace-making process, the United States hoped to exclude the Soviet Union and thus undermine Russian influence in the region. The inevitable result of this policy was to give the Soviet Union even more reasons to support the radical Arab states.

The first in the series of agreements negotiated by Kissinger through the long process of shuttling between Cairo and Jerusalem was the Egyptian-Israeli disengagement treaty of January 14, 1974.

This agreement disengaged the forces of Egypt and Israel, involved the first significant Israeli withdrawal from occupied territories, and saw the first formal and partial Egyptian commitment to a process of peace-seeking. It definitely established the concept of step-by-step movement toward peace even while retaining the framework of the Geneva Peace Conference, and it definitely established Kissinger as an effective peace broker between Israel and its neighbors.[35]

Aside from reducing tensions and establishing a demilitarized zone, the agreement led to the termination of the Arab oil embargo that had gone into effect during the opening phases of the 1973 war. In addition, the United States agreed to increase economic and military aid to Israel while it also improved its relations with Egypt.

The second agreement negotiated by Kissinger was the Syrian-Israeli disengagement agreement of May 31, 1974. Because of the intense animosity between the parties involved, Kissinger had to work much harder and shuttle almost daily between Jerusalem and Damascus. The wearisome horse-trading finally ended with the Israeli agreement to withdraw from Syrian territory that had been occupied during the Yom Kippur War and make a small symbolic pullback from territory occupied in the 1967 war. Under this agreement, the United States promised to undertake a long-range plan of supplying Israel with arms.[36]

Another American attempt to negotiate a similar understanding between Israel and Jordan during the summer of 1974 ended in failure. Since Jordan had not taken a very active part in the 1973 war, it had not made enough sacrifices to present any claims as a result of involvement in that war. This failure reflected the much greater difficulties involved in determining the future of the West Bank. The Golan Heights and the Sinai Peninsula are sparsely populated areas that do not strategically threaten the most vulnerable parts of Israel. The West Bank, on the other hand, is densely populated by Palestinian Arabs who could harbor a sizable guerrilla or terrorist force; therefore, the West Bank could serve as a springboard against the most populated and strategically important narrow waist of Israel. During their October 1974 summit meeting in Rabat, the heads of the Arab states decided that only the PLO and the Palestinians—not Jordan—could negotiate with Israel on the future of the West Bank. This decision immediately weakened Israeli and Jordanian incentive to conclude an agreement on the West Bank.

Kissinger tried to negotiate still another Israeli-Egyptian separation agreement in the winter of 1975. This time, Israel was asked to make concessions (withdrawal from the Sinai Passes and the oil fields of Abu Rodes) that were more vital to its interests. Faced with heavy American pressure, Rabin's government rejected both Egyptian and American demands. The Israelis insisted on a non-belligerency agreement, an American guarantee of their oil supply, and an increase in military aid from the United States. After the talks broke down in March 1975, the United

States declared that it was reassessing its policy in the Middle East (implying, of course, that it was considering the reduction of political, economic, and military support to Israel). Another reason for the reassessment process was to explore the possibility of substituting the Geneva peace conference—where Israel would be isolated and outnumbered—for the step-by-step diplomacy. The Israeli government ultimately accepted most of the conditions it had rejected earlier and signed a second disengagement agreement in Geneva on September 4, 1975. The agreement was to be valid for three years unless it was extended or superseded by another agreement.

In a special memorandum, the United States agreed, in exchange for Israel's withdrawal from the Sinai passes and oil fields, to guarantee Israel's normal oil supplies in the event of an embargo.[37] It also promised to sympathetically consider Israel's "long-term military supply needs . . . and requests for advanced and sophisticated weapons.[38] Further American commitments concerned the possibility of convening the Geneva conference.

1) The Geneva Peace Conference will be reconvened at a time coordinated between the United States and Israel.

2) The United States will continue to adhere to its present policy with respect to the Palestine Liberation Organization, whereby it will not recognize or negotiate with the Palestine Liberation Organization so long as the Palestine Liberation Organization does not recognize Israel's right to exist and does not accept Security Council Resolutions 242 and 338. The United States Government will consult fully and seek to concert its position and strategy with Israel with regard to the participation of any additional states. It is understood that the participation at a subsequent phase of the conference of any possible additional state, group, or organization will require the agreement of all initial participants.

3) The United States will make every effort to insure at the conference that all the substantive negotiations will be on a bilateral basis.

4) The United States will oppose and, if necessary, vote against any initiative in the Security Council to alter adversely the terms of reference of the Geneva peace conference or to change Resolutions 242 and 338 in ways which are incompatible with their original purpose.[39]

It was this commitment to Israel that later hampered—among other factors—American attempts to find a peace formula for convening the Geneva conference. The conference was delayed so long and looked so hopeless, that it convinced President Sadat to pass up Geneva and negotiate directly with Israel.

The so-called step-by-step diplomacy had served to reduce tensions in the Middle East, but as a long-range policy it had exhausted itself with the last Egyptian-Israeli disengagement agreement in September 1975. The only area where it was still possible to arrange one more separation agreement between the two countries was the Sinai, where the large, uninhabited territory enabled Israel, in Rabin's words "to trade a little territory for a little peace."

In the course of his "shuttle" diplomacy, Kissinger negotiated the agreements for both sides. When in Israel, he represented the Egyptians (or Syrians) and told the Israelis how far they could go. Conversely, when in Egypt, he represented Israel's position. As the broker holding both the carrot and the stick, he artificially bridged the gap. Israel paid the Egyptians in territory, and Egypt paid the United States by helping to strengthen the American position in the Arab Middle East and lifting the Arab oil embargo. The United States then compensated Israel (and also Egypt to a lesser extent) with political, military, and economic support. After the 1975 separation agreement, the Israelis began to fear that if the process of making incremental agreements continued, they would run out of territory before a genuine peace treaty could be concluded. The Egyptians, on the other hand, were apprehensive not only that the Israelis would become more obstinate, but also that by continuing to make separate agreements with Israel they would be ostracized in the Arab world. As 1975 came to a close, all parties involved in the negotiations realized that a different and more comprehensive approach to peace must be attempted. Step-by-step diplomacy was in the final analysis unsatisfactory because it did not solve the Palestinian problem or lead at any stage to *direct* Arab-Israeli talks. Therefore, Egypt, Israel, and the U.S. turned to the only immediately obvious alternative, which was to reconvene the Geneva conference.

Soon after taking office as President of the United States in January 1977, Jimmy Carter came out in favor of the comprehensive approach to peace in the Middle East. Carter's approach was based on a study which his foreign policy adviser and National Security Council head, Zbigniew Brzezinski, had obtained from the prestigious Brookings Institution in Washington, D.C. This study, which was written in 1975 by several distinguished Middle East experts, was contained in a pamphlet entitled "Toward Peace in the Middle East"; it was a rational report that carefully took the positions of all parties into account. There is, however, a difference between a balanced, scholarly plan for peace and a practical policy. A compromise that seems fair to the disinterested observer may be a question of life and death for others; therefore, one or more of the sides involved usually find it impossible to compromise on certain issues.

Brzezinski slightly modified the Brookings study and presented it to

Carter who approved its adoption as the American approach for peace in the Middle East. The plan proposed that the comprehensive solution to the Middle East conflict be based on peace treaties between Israel and its Arab neighbors according to the following terms: the normalization of relations through tourism, trade, and the like; Israel's withdrawal to the June 4, 1967, borders with only minor adjustments; and a homeland or independent state as a possible solution to the Palestinian problem. While the first recommendation that relations between Israel and its neighbors be normalized was continuously advocated by Israel, the last two recommendations were totally unacceptable to Israel.[40] For strategic reasons Israel refused to withdraw to its pre-1967 borders; it was willing to modify its position in the Sinai and maybe even the Golan Heights, but not on the vulnerable West Bank.

The proposal for the establishment of a Palestinian state (referred to in the Brookings report as a "homeland")[41] was anathema to the Israelis who felt that the primary Palestinian goal was to destroy Israel and establish their own state in its place. Since the PLO had attacked Israeli territory *before* 1967—and therefore *before* Israel occupied the West Bank—the Israelis were certain that the goal of the PLO was not simply the liberation of the occupied territories but the liquidation of the State of Israel. The Palestinian goal was clearly set forth in the Covenants of 1964 and 1968, which, as of today, remain unchanged. They state that there is no place for an independent Jewish state alongside an independent Palestinian state.* Obviously, no Israeli government would agree to

---

* The Palestinian National Covenant of 1968 is the only basic political document accepted by all of the PLO's factions. The following excerpts express the tenor of the document.

Article 2: Palestine, with the boundaries it had during the British Mandate, is an indivisible territorial unit.

Article 9: Armed struggle is the only way to liberate Palestine. Thus, it is the overall strategy, not merely a tactical phase. The Palestinian Arab people assert their absolute determination and firm resolution to continue their armed struggle and to work for an armed popular revolution for the liberation of their country and their return to it. . . . [This article rules out the possibility of a political solution which by definition is one of compromise.]

Article 15: The liberation of Palestine from an Arab viewpoint, is a national duty and it attempts to repel the Zionist and Imperialist aggression against the Arab homeland and aims at the elimination of Zionism in Palestine. . . .

Article 19: The partition of Palestine in 1947 and the establishment of the State of Israel are entirely illegal, regardless of the passage of time, because they were contrary to the will of the Palestinian people and their natural right in their homeland, and inconsistent with the principles embodied in the Charter of the United Nations, particularly the right to self-determination.

Article 20: . . . Judaism being a divine religion is not an independent nationality. Nor do Jews constitute a single nation with an identity of its own: they are citizens of the states to which they belong.

(As of today, the Covenant remains unchanged.)[42]

supinely accept its own destruction. The PLO's indiscriminate terror campaign against Israel—hijacking, the Munich Olympics massacre, the Ben Gurion airport massacre, to mention only a few of the more glaring instances—only reinforced the Israeli conviction that the Palestinians intended to implement their covenant.

An overall peace settlement at Geneva required the consent of Egypt, Israel, Syria, Jordan, and the PLO. Israel refused to negotiate with the PLO, while the Arab governments insisted that a peace settlement was not possible without the PLO. For its part, the United States had, as part of the September 1975 Egyptian-Israeli Disengagement Agreement, promised not to negotiate with the PLO until it recognized Israel's right to exist and accepted Security Council Resolutions 242 and 338. The catch was that the only way for the Americans to persuade the PLO to recognize Israel (and thus be able to convene the Geneva conference) was through direct talks between American and Palestinian representatives. The United States finally decided to break its promise to Israel; it allowed secret meetings with Palestinians during the Nixon, Ford, and Carter administrations.[43]

The PLO refused to recognize Resolution 242 because it only discussed the refugee problem and did not mention the Palestinian right to self-determination. Without referring directly to Israel, the resolution speaks of the rights of all Middle Eastern countries (and by implication, Israel) to secure and recognized borders. This, of course, contradicts the Palestinian Covenant of 1968. The Palestinians therefore adamantly refuse to recognize Resolution 242 as long as it does not explicitly acknowledge their right to self-determination and statehood. This demand is unacceptable to Israel and in violation of the United States-Israel memorandum of September 1975. Moreover, even if the PLO recognized United Nations Resolution 242 as the other Arab states have, the Israeli government would probably insist that the Palestinians formally revise many of the articles in their covenant. Given the dynamics and political views of most factions in the PLO, this would be an impossible task.

The Carter administration therefore pursued a policy of amending U.N. Security Council Resolution 242 (which was originally drafted with American support.)[44]

The Israeli government also had other reasons to be worried about the Geneva conference; at Geneva, it would always be in the minority. There was no doubt that the Soviet Union, which had severed diplomatic relations with Israel in June 1967, would consistently side with the radical Arab position. Such backing would make Arab negotiators more intransigent and either isolate the more moderate Arab governments (i.e., Egypt and Jordan) or force them to accept extreme policies. Once at Geneva, the United States—Israel's only ally—might find it difficult to support

Israel. The Israeli government realized that it would be forced to adopt a stubborn position and perhaps leave the conference. Ultimately, Israel felt that it would be blamed for the breakdown of a conference which was doomed to fail from its inception.

During the summer and fall of 1977, the United States invested much time and effort in trying to convene the Geneva conference by December 1977. The fact that the debate was procedural did not mean that it could be more easily resolved. As usual, the United States was looking for a compromise, trying hard to convince the Israelis to negotiate with non-PLO Palestinians. The PLO announced that *any* Palestinian who planned to attend the Geneva conference must receive its permission; dissenters would be assassinated as traitors. This did not prevent the State Department from proposing that the Palestinian representatives at Geneva need not be formal PLO members. Israel, however, still refused to deal with any independent Palestinian delegation, insisting on bilateral talks with all Arab delegations as a bloc (in order to avoid complications and being outvoted all the time).

At that point, the United States committed a serious tactical error. Instead of cautiously following Kissinger's "success syndrome" foreign policy, the Carter administration adopted an all-or-nothing Middle Eastern policy that was bound to be self-destructive.[45] Apparently as an additional way to pressure Israel, the United States recruited the support of the Soviet Union for a moderate amendment to Resolution 242. On October 1, the United States and the Soviet Union issued the following joint statement:

Having exchanged views regarding the unsafe situation which remains in the Middle East, United States Secretary of State Cyrus Vance and member of the Politburo of the Central Committee of the Communist Party of the Soviet Union, Minister for Foreign Affairs of the USSR A. A. Gromyko, have the following statement to make on behalf of their countries, which are co-chairmen of the Geneva peace conference on the Middle East:

1. Both governments are convinced that vital interests of the peoples of this area as well as the interests of strengthening peace and international security in general urgently dictate the necessity of achieving as soon as possible a just settlement of the Arab-Israeli conflict. This settlement should be comprehensive, incorporating all parties concerned and all questions.

The United States and the Soviet Union believe that, within the framework of a comprehensive settlement of the Middle East problem, all specific questions of the settlement should be resolved, including such key issues as withdrawal of Israeli armed forces from territories occupied in the 1967 conflict, the resolution of the Palestinian question including ensuring the legitimate rights of the Palestinian people, termination of the state of war and establishment of normal peaceful relations on the basis of mutual recognition of the principles of sovereignty, territorial integrity, and political independence.

The two governments believe that, in addition to such measures for ensuring the security of the borders between Israel and the neighbouring Arab states as the establishment of demilitarized zones and the agreed stationing in them of UN troops or observers, international guarantees of such borders as well as of the observance of the terms of the settlement can also be established, should the contracting parties so desire. The United States and the Soviet Union are ready to participate in these guarantees subject to their constitutional processes.

2. The United States and the Soviet Union believe that the only right and effective way for achieving a fundamental solution to all aspects of the Middle East problem in its entirety is negotiations within the framework of the Geneva peace conference, specially convened for these purposes, with participtipation in its work of the representatives of all the parties involved in the conflict including those of the Palestinian people, and legal and contractual formalization of the decisions reached at the conference.

In their capacity as co-chairmen of the Geneva conference, the U.S. and the USSR affirm their intention through joint efforts and in their contacts with the parties concerned to facilitate in every way the resumption of the work of the conference not later than December 1977. The co-chairmen note that there still exist several questions of a procedural and organizational nature which remain to be agreed upon by the participants to the conference.

3. Guided by the goal of achieving a just political settlement in the Middle East and of eliminating the explosive situation in this area of the world, the U.S. and the USSR appeal to all the parties in the conflict to understand the necessity for careful consideration of each other's legitimate rights and interests and to demonstrate mutual readiness to act accordingly.[46]

The Israeli government totally rejected the Soviet-American statement. For one thing, the United States had broken its promise contained in the September 1, 1975 American-Israeli memorandum to obtain Israeli consent before calling for the participation of Palestinian representatives at the Geneva conference.

The official Israeli reaction, drafted by Prime Minister Begin, was published on October 2.

1. The Soviet Union's demand that Israel withdraw to the pre-June 1967 borders—a demand which contravenes the true meaning of Security Council Resolution 242— is known to all.

2. Despite the fact that the Governments of the U.S. and Israel

agreed on July 7, 1977 that the aim of the negotiations at Geneva should be "an overall peace settlement to be expressed in a peace treaty," the concept of a "peace treaty" is not mentioned at all in the Soviet-American statement.

3. There is no reference at all in this statement to Resolutions 242 and 338, despite the fact that the U.S. Government has repeatedly affirmed heretofore that these resolutions constitute the sole basis for the convening of the Geneva Conference.

4. There can be no doubt that this statement, issued at a time when discussions are proceeding on the reconvening of the Geneva Conference, cannot but still further harden the positions of the Arab states and make the Middle East peace process still more difficult.

5. As the Prime Minister has stated, Israel will continue to aspire to free negotiations with its neighbours with the purpose of signing a peace treaty with them.[47]

To the governing coalition as well as the opposition in Israel, the joint Soviet-American statement was the first step of an imposed settlement favoring the Arab position. Foreign Minister Dayan announced that the declaration meant "the end of the road" for Israeli-American contacts concerning Geneva. In a radio interview in Israel, former Prime Minister Rabin recommended that Israel refuse to attend the Geneva conference under those conditions, adding that the Soviet-American joint statement had created an unprecedented lack of confidence in American intentions. The Chairman of the Israeli Labor Party, Shimon Peres, voiced a similar opinion and former Foreign Minister Yigal Allon said that the statement was "unnecessary, ill-timed, and ill-phrased."[48] In an interview with the Israeli newspaper *Maariv*, Allon accused Begin's government of incompetence and suggested a return to step-by-step diplomacy. Attacked from both ends of the political spectrum, Begin's government had to adopt a firmer stance, and the new American initiative resulted in a unified negative reaction from all Israeli parties.

The declaration also caused a private confrontation between Israel and the Carter administration. The vehement Israeli reaction, the American Jewish community's sharp protest, the criticism of U.S. labor leaders, members of Congress, and the mass media brought the Carter administration under heavy fire.

Rabbi Alexander Schindler, chairman of the Conference of Presidents of Major American Jewish Organizations, declared: "We are profoundly disturbed by the joint U.S.-Soviet statement which, on its face, represents an abandonment of America's historic commitment to the security and survival of Israel."[49] Many, including former Secretary of State Henry Kissinger, claimed that the Carter administration had committed a serious mistake by introducing the Soviet Union back into the Middle

East talks after the Nixon and Ford administrations had successfully excluded it since December 1973.[50]

Within a few days, Israel and the United States realized that they must make an effort to avoid further deterioration in their relations. On the evening of October 5, Foreign Minister Dayan met with President Carter and Secretary of State Vance at the United Nations Plaza Hotel for what Dayan later described as a "brutal conversation." Much of this conversation can be reconstructed from Dayan's leaks to the press.

The President admitted that he was surprised by the intense criticism of the joint Soviet-American statement. Nevertheless, he is said to have delivered a virtual ultimatum to Dayan. The Palestinians, Carter said, would be represented at the Geneva conference, and Israel would eventually have to accept a Palestinian entity or "homeland" on the West Bank and Gaza. If Israel refused to go along with this, the President would appeal to American Jews ("the friends of Israel") and warn them that Israeli intransigence was obstructing the attainment of peace and endangering vital American interests. If Israel was not prepared to make further concessions for peace, it would remain isolated in the world.

Dayan replied that Israel would never accept an independent Palestinian state in any guise, nor would it sit with PLO representatives in Geneva. (In September, the Knesset had passed a resolution by a vast majority—92 to 4—forbidding the Government to negotiate with the PLO.) Dayan made it clear that if the United States insisted on either a separate PLO delegation or on inclusion of PLO representatives in other Arab delegations, Israel would not participate. Dayan then protested the U.S. initiative of introducing the Soviet Union into the negotiations at that stage. At one point in the conversation, the President told Dayan that "not all the American promises to Israel are in the box." Dayan answered [according to his version] that there were certain historical situations when the leaders had to decide whether they preferred promises to their deepest beliefs . . . particularly when there was reason to suspect that the promises would not be honored. Dayan then summarized the many critical occasions in which the United States had not come to Israel's aid. Israel, he said, would rather be internationally isolated than yield on issues such as the establishment of a Palestinian state or negotiations with the Palestinians. Carter did not seem to be convinced by Dayan's arguments but nevertheless wanted to avoid a break with Israel and the American Jewish community.

They therefore compromised on a "working paper," which in fact modified the language and content of the joint Soviet-American statement. Yet the working paper, couched in terms of what former Prime Minister Rabin described as "constructive ambiguity," undoubtedly represented an erosion of the previous Israeli position. In his attempt to improve relations with Israel President Carter had agreed on the working paper, but he still regarded it as only an intermediate agreement that was subject to modification at a later stage. The following is the text of the working paper as it was read to the Knesset on October 13.

1. The Arab parties will be represented by a unified Arab delegation which will include Palestinian Arabs. After the opening sessions, the conference will split into working groups.

2. The working groups for the negotiation and conclusion of peace treaties will be formed as follows:

    A. Egypt-Israel;
    B. Jordan-Israel;
    C. Syria-Israel;
    D. Lebanon-Israel.

3. The West Bank and Gaza issues will be discussed in a working group to consist of Israel, Jordan, Egypt, and the Palestinian Arabs.

4. The solution of the problem of the Arab refugees and of the Jewish refugees will be discussed in accordance with terms to be agreed upon.

5. The agreed basis for the negotiations at the Geneva peace conference on the Middle East are U.N. Security Council Resolutions 242 and 338.

6. All the initial terms of reference of the Geneva peace conference remain in force, except as may be agreed by the parties.[51]

Dayan felt that the working paper was making the best of a bad situation. He pointed out that most of the negotiations would be bilateral; the PLO and the "legitimate rights of the Palestinians" (i.e., a Palestinian political entity) were not mentioned; Resolutions 242 and 338 were again established as the sole basis for the Geneva peace conference; and, in addition to the Arab refugees, the Jewish refugees from Arab countries were mentioned. The working paper also implied that the United States would not force Israel to take a position without its consent. The paper was presented as if the principles established during the first Geneva peace conference in 1973 had not been modified (paragraph 6), but in fact, Dayan's agreement to include Palestinian Arabs in the United Arab Delegation (UAD) was a significant concession on Israel's part. Now Begin's government was accused by both the opposition and the government coalition parties of attempting to bring the Palestinians into the Geneva conference through the back door.

Heavy criticism followed Dayan's report to the Knesset on his talks with President Carter. Former Defense Minister Peres argued that because the working paper essentially granted political status to the Palestinians in the Geneva conference, it was a de facto amendment of

Resolution 242. In a *Maariv* interview, former Prime Minister Golda Meir said that Israel should not, under the circumstances, go to Geneva. She felt that the working paper was worse than surrender—Israel had endangered itself and encouraged the Arabs to adopt an extreme and uncompromising attitude.[52]

The subsequent actions of the United States proved that it did not see the working paper as a final and binding document. American officials soon proposed that Palestinians invited to the conference be able to come from neighboring Arab countries as well as from Gaza and the West Bank. Many Israelis realized that the United States was trying to bring representatives of the PLO to Geneva in a carefully disguised way. During October 1977, Israeli officials repeatedly emphasized that they would not go to Geneva if members of the PLO were included in the United Arab Delegation.

The Arab states and the PLO on the whole welcomed the joint Soviet-American declaration as a significant step in increasing the pressure on Israel. Although the Soviet Union seemed to have modified its support of the Arab interpretation of Resolution 242 by agreeing to include the term "withdrawal of Israeli forces from territories occupied in the 1967 conflict" (as opposed to "withdrawal of *all* Israeli forces . . ."), the joint declaration was closer to the Arab rather than the Israeli position: it omitted any reference to Resolutions 242 and 338, neglected to mention the need for a formal peace agreement, and spoke of "ensuring the legitimate rights of the Palestinian people." As the Soviet-American joint statement had been tempered by the American-Israeli working paper, so the Arabs wanted to modify the American-Israeli working paper. It seemed as if the Geneva conference would be delayed forever by procedural matters; and even if the conference was eventually convened, it was almost certain that the presence of the Palestinians and Israelis under one roof would quickly lead to an insoluble impasse. While the majority of Arab states reacted favorably to the Soviet-American joint declaration, perhaps because they hoped to convene the Geneva conference and then outmaneuver Israel (and Egypt) with the support of the United States and the Soviet Union, this was not true of Egypt. On the surface the Egyptian reaction was mild, but Sadat was actually alarmed.[53]

This was the complex backdrop against which Sadat made his unexpected decision to circumvent the Geneva peace conference and instead go directly to Jerusalem. Like the Israelis, Sadat found it hard to reject the Geneva conference outright. Sadat is known to have little tolerance for "petty" procedural or organizational details; as a poor administrator who is impatient with staff work, he detests reading reports and prefers to have them delivered orally.[54] If it took so much time to "inch along" toward an agreement on the pre-Geneva procedural matters, the conference was bound to be even more nightmarish. Moreover, Sadat (unlike the Carter administration) knew from his secret contacts with the Israeli government that he could obtain substantial territorial concessions in the Sinai in return for a peace agreement. For Sadat, Geneva did not add anything that Egypt could not obtain directly from Israel: worse still, the conference might have ruined the embryonic understanding which existed between Israel and Egypt. At Geneva, the dynamics of the conference might have forced Egypt to either adopt a radical stance in accordance with the Syrian and Palestinian position which was backed by the Soviet Union, or else to be labeled a traitor to the Arab cause. If Egypt should, by some chance, reach agreement with Israel in the bilateral negotiations at Geneva, it would be very difficult to ratify and implement such an agreement if the other Arab participants—Jordan, Syria, and the Palestinians—failed in their talks with Israel. To return and negotiate separately with Israel after the collapse of the peace conference would have made Sadat look even more opportunistic to his fellow Arabs.

Nor was Sadat keen on having the Soviets present at Geneva. After he had finally succeeded in reducing Egypt's dependence on Soviet political and military support, the Carter administration by inviting the Soviets to Geneva naively helped to expand their influence in the Arab world. Sadat knew as well as the Israelis that Russian participation in the Geneva conference would undermine if not destroy the chances of reaching a comprehensive agreement. Sadat summarized the situation in a *Time* interview on January 2, 1978.

> I suddenly found all the parties concerned—Egypt, Jordan, Syria, Israel—starting to quarrel and differ on the procedural papers. Syria said that if this is an American paper [the U.S.-Israel working paper] it is a colonial and imperialist paper. If it is an American-Israeli paper, well, it is colonial, Zionist, imperialist—all these descriptions. I felt also, when President Assad sent a special envoy to me, that Syria was not serious about going to Geneva. The Soviet Union was starting its own tricks with the Syrians and with the Palestinians.[55]

Sadat was not convinced that the Soviet Union was genuinely interested in establishing peace in the Middle East, since the very existence of a continued conflict was the best guarantee for the continuation of Soviet presence in the area. He also observed the American failure to convince Israel to attend the Geneva conference on the basis of the joint Soviet-American declaration and the successful Israeli counterpressure that resulted in President Carter's quick retreat from his new Middle Eastern policy. The only possible conclusion was that the American ability to pressure Israel—and get results—was limited, and would be further curbed by American domestic support for Israel.

Ironically enough, Israel and Egypt had a common interest in *not* attending the American-initiated Geneva peace conference. For Sadat, the almost certain failure of the Geneva conference would further complicate Arab-Israeli relations, increase the probability of renewed war for which Egypt was not prepared, push Egypt into dependence on Soviet military aid in the event of war, and obstruct a possible rapprochement with the United States. Therefore, he chose to pass up "the Geneva syndrome" of sluggish, fruitless talks and decided to get down to business with the Israelis.

In addition to Israeli promises, Sadat's pessimistic assessment of the Geneva peace conference, and Sadat's own personality, a fourth factor, namely, Sadat's perception of what was best for *Egypt*—inspired his journey to Jerusalem.

From a military point of view, Egypt's strength had declined in both absolute and relative terms following the 1973 war because of the deterioration of Egyptian-Soviet relations. Meanwhile, Israel's military strength had increased on both counts: just before Sadat's visit to Jerusalem, experts in the Pentagon estimated that Israel's military strength had increased 160% relative to its condition during the Yom Kippur War, while that of Egypt had decreased to 90% of its power in 1973.[56]

Despite Sadat's public statements that Egypt was victorious in the October 1973 war, he knew perhaps better than even his generals how close Egypt had come to a military disaster worse than that of 1967.[57] He knew that Israeli troops came to within 60 miles of Cairo and that without American intervention, the surrounded Egyptian Third Army would have collapsed. It was clear that if Egypt could not win a war against Israel under the ideal conditions of total surprise, it could not expect better results under less favorable circumstances. First of all, Egypt had replaced only part of the arms it lost during the October 1973 war. And in order to fight Israel, Egypt would need military support on Israel's eastern border from the large Syrian army. The Syrians, however, had become deeply involved in the civil war in Lebanon in 1976 and were not available for a war effort against Israel.

Aware that he had no viable military option at least in the short run, Sadat preferred to perpetuate his image as the victorious leader of the October 1973 war. Why should he risk military defeat or the territories regained through the October war and the ensuing disengagement agreements?[58] Excluding military conflict, Sadat was faced with two options: the first was to maintain the "no war, no peace" situation, hoping that American pressure and incremental diplomacy would eventually lead to the recovery of territory that Egypt had lost in the 1967 war; the second option, which no other Arab leader had dared to consider, was to "make peace, and make it quickly."[59] Military conflict or the first option would have hampered any efforts to solve Egypt's economic problems, so the most rational choice was the road to peace.

Unlike Hitler and Napoleon (but like Bismark, Churchill, or Stalin) Sadat knew when to abandon the military arena and return to the political. Though he was no doubt influenced by Egypt's near defeat in 1973, he must be given credit for possessing more political maturity than most other leaders in modern history. Sadat, like the Israelis, must also have realized that prolonged modern conventional war was beyond the military and economic capacity of all but the superpowers. Therefore, even if a conventional war were to end in overwhelming victory for one side, Egypt (or Israel) would ultimately find itself more dependent on one of the superpowers; and perhaps the superpowers would intervene in order to prevent a decisive victory by either side. The situation in which the United States (and the Soviet Union) saved the Egyptian Third Army which was trapped on the east bank of the Suez Canal during the 1973 conflict, might be reversed the next time. This view, which undermined the logic of resorting to war, may explain why Sadat decided that the October 1973 war was to be the last military conflict while he was President.[60]

Another important but largely ignored consideration in Sadat's calculations was his belief that Israel had acquired nuclear weapons. (This is also the opinion of the CIA.)[61] During the visit to Jerusalem, members of Sadat's entourage said that they knew Israel possessed nuclear weapons; and the subject was again broached by the Egyptians during military conversations with Israel, when they indicated that they would be pleased to see Israel sign the non-proliferation treaty (NPT). Its dependence on the Aswan High Dam and the Nile as well as the concentration of its population in Cairo and Alexandria, makes Egypt the most vulnerable of all Arab states to a nuclear attack.

Of prime importance in Sadat's calculations, however, was his realization that it was the United States, and only the United States, that could make Israel withdraw from the territories occupied in 1967 and furnish Egypt with the necessary economic aid.[62] At least two major obstacles prevented Egypt from gaining American support: (1) As long as the Soviet Union was Egypt's closest ally and the source of large-scale military aid, rapprochement with the United States was not feasible; (2) The United States was committed to Israel's survival.

Sadat overcame the first obstacle by reorienting Egyptian foreign policy after the October War toward the United States and the West. Once Egypt's ties with the USSR had been weakened, Sadat could approach the United States.[63] Convinced that only the United States and Saudi Arabia could rescue the Egyptian economy from collapse—Saudi economic and military aid was already flowing into Egypt—Sadat wanted to attract private American investors and obtain extensive U.S. economic assistance in the form of an Egyptian "Marshall Plan."[64] To gain the confidence of American investors, Egypt needed stability and a better economic infrastructure, conditions which were impossible to realize as long as it was at war with Israel.

Having resolved to reduce Egypt's ties to the USSR, Sadat had to find another weapons supplier for his country's army. His almost mystical belief in the superiority of American technology and military hardware, combined with his conviction that the Soviet Union had always withheld its most modern equipment from Egypt at a time when the United States was showering Israel with arms[65]—meant that the United States appeared to him as the only alternative weapons supplier. But since the United States was committed to Israel's security, it was highly unlikely that Egypt would receive a significant amount of weapons until it ceased to be at war with Israel.[66]

The most obvious step was to proclaim Egypt's desire for peace with Israel, thus making it easier for the United States to increase its political, economic, and military support of Egypt and the Arab cause. By coming directly to Jerusalem, Sadat could dramatically prove Egypt's sincere desire for peace and, in his own words, "put the ball in Israel's court."[67] If Israel was not ready to make the necessary concessions, Egypt would earn American sympathy. In a *Time* magazine interview published on January 2, 1978, Sadat said: "I put everything before them [the Knesset] to decide, and whatever happens after that, they will be guilty, not me again."[68] With a single bold stroke, the Egyptian president hoped to secure American economic and military support and drive a wedge between the United States and Israel (or at least induce the United States to adopt a policy that was more favorable to Egypt).[69]

The Egyptian economy was in a dismal state, suffering from chronic problems, such as one of the fastest growing populations in the world (its population today is 41 million and expanding at a rate of 2.8% a year);[70] a high rate of illiteracy; a weak economic infrastructure; unproductive agriculture; and an inefficient industry. Between 1960 and 1966, Egypt's economy grew at the reasonable rate of 4% per annum: between 1966 and 1976 the GNP growth slowed to a mere 1.2% primarily because of the increased war effort. After the 1967 war, Egypt chose to invest more in guns than in butter, with military expenditures climbing from about 9% of the GNP in 1960 to more than 25% in 1967.[71]

By the autumn of 1977, Egypt's national debt was 13 billion dollars and its annual economic support from Saudi Arabia and the United States amounted to 5.4 billion dollars.[72] This enormous burden on the already faltering economy approached the point of no return, for investments in the productive civilian sector dropped each year by 2 to 4 percent. The per capita income that had been growing at the respectable pace of 4% a year from 1960 to 1966 grew by only 2% after 1967. Productivity dropped because already scarce skilled and educated manpower was transferred to the Army; and the increased military expenditures fueled inflation. During the same period, Egypt lost its income from the Suez Canal and the oil wells in the Sinai while continuing to shoulder the burden of the Arab military effort against Israel. The once flourishing Egyptian cities along the Suez Canal were completely destroyed—while Israel and the other Arab confrontation states (Syria, Jordan, Iraq) did not suffer any similar damage. Growing weary of the endless war with Israel which actually only marginally affected their interests at its inception in 1948, the Egyptians became disgruntled that they alone had sacrificed more for the Arab cause than all of the other Arab states combined.

In January 1977, the Egyptian government tried to save about half a billion dollars annually by reducing food subsidies. This measure, which would have added about five dollars a month to the average family's expenditures on flour, oil, and fuel, sparked large-scale riots in Cairo and Alexandria during which at least 79 people were killed. The largely anti-Sadat demonstrations subsided only after the price increases had been rescinded.[73] In fact, after the 1973 oil embargo caused oil prices to rise, the Egyptians felt frustrated because they were making sacrifices and growing poorer as other Arabs were accumulating vast wealth.[74] The contributions of other Arab countries, in particular Saudi Arabia, defrayed some of Egypt's military expenditures but they were not enough to compensate for the long-run losses.

When questioned about the peace initiative's effect on the Egyptian economy, Sadat replied:

Enormous! Enormous! Do you know that there are two big powers in the world now that have standing armies of 700,000? The U.S. and the Soviet Union. And Anwar Sadat also has 700,000! Can you imagine? For sure, the impact on our economy, on our reconstruction, on our rebuilding would be tremendous. Tremendous![75]

Sadat and the Egyptian people realized that the time had come to turn inward and tend their "sick economy" before it was too late. Another war with Israel would only perpetuate Egypt's economic backwardness. The Egyptian President decided to put Egypt first without, if possible, deserting Arab interests. "This time [he said] I am going to treat them [the Syrians and the Palestinians] according to their size."[76] He was interested in increasing the amount of aid that Egypt was receiving from the Arab oil-producing nations, assuming (incorrectly) that whatever course of action he took towards Israel, Egypt would still be backed by its Arab allies. After all, the other Arab nations were, to a large extent, dependent on Egypt's military strength as a stabilizing element in the region. Sadat underestimated the power of the PLO and the radical Arab states to blackmail and threaten the vulnerable oil-rich countries; nor, of course, did he foresee the impact of the revolution in Iran, which demonstrated that many countries in the region might be vulnerable to relatively small groups of political and religious fanatics. After Egypt signed the peace agreement with Israel, much of its economic support from the Arab oil-producing countries was diverted to Jordan.

An additional factor of great importance is, of course, Sadat's own personality and style of leadership. Unfortunately, he is essentially an enigma. As he once said to a magazine interviewer, "No one ever knows what I am thinking, not even my own family."[77] "The President keeps the important decisions secret; his ministers, and even his wife, usually hear about them the same time the public does. When Sadat finally does arrive at a decision, it is usually irreversible."[78] He speaks and writes often, but never discusses his inner self or his true goals; these can only be deduced from his actions. The decision to go to Jerusalem and negotiate with the Israelis was no exception—it was taken alone and, in fact, in disregard of his ministers' opinions.

Arriving at key decisions by himself is what makes Sadat's "electric-shock" diplomacy so successful. When everyone else was still thinking of the consolidation of Egypt's friendship with the Soviet Union, Sadat was already considering a shift toward the United States (though he knew he needed Soviet support for his war against Israel). When, after the 1973 war, most Egyptian officials were planning the next war, Sadat was planning for some type of accommodation with Israel. While the government implements existing policies and manages day-to-day matters, Sadat is busying himself with grand strategy.

Differences between Sadat and his predecessor, Gamel Abdul Nasser, are instructive. Nasser was an idealist, loyal to friends or causes long after they had become irrelevant or burdensome. Relying on charisma and intuition to bring him success, Nasser often impulsively committed his country to actions on a grand scale. His arms deal with the Soviet Union, the nationalization of the Suez Canal, the construction of the Aswan High Dam, the unification with Syria, involvement in the war in Yemen, the Six Day War in 1967, and the subsequent War of Attrition— all ended in failure, or in Phyrric victory at best. Sadat operates in almost the opposite way; he is cautious and pragmatic, devoting considerable thought to the formulation of a workable strategy. If Nasser was, in Machiavelli's typology of leaders, a charismatic, heroic lion, then Sadat is a shrewd and rational fox.

True to his style, Sadat carefully weighed Egypt's position in the Arab-Israeli conflict and its policy toward Israel. The origins of his policy of accommodation with Israel can be found in his unsuccessful peace initiative in 1971 and his decision not to resort to war again after 1973. The

circumvention of the Geneva conference was not an impulsive decision—
it was the outcome of much deliberation.[79]

It is worth emphasizing that the traditional Arab attitude toward Israel
does not even allow for incremental changes in policy. Therefore, the
only way for Sadat to overcome or avoid Arab opposition to direct
negotiations with Israel was to make an unexpected move before they
had time to react. While it was a daring and imaginative move, it was
also a rational one designed to achieve certain long-range goals. The surprise put Sadat two steps ahead of Israel and the United States, and three
steps ahead of other Arab states. Anything less than an action that would
radically change the nature of the Egyptian-Israeli relationship would
have been a complete waste of time from Sadat's point of view. In a sense,
it may be said that he was doing the thinking and taking the initiative for
all parties concerned; and though his courage and vision cannot be over-
emphasized, it must also be remembered that as the leader of one of the
largest and most powerful Arab states, he was the only one who could
make such a completely unorthodox move. Israeli offers to negotiate had
been continuously rebuffed since 1948. Thus, Israel could aid and
support such a move but had to be reactive. The United States did not
have the power to convince the Arabs to alter their stance and no other
leader of an Arab state was sufficiently powerful to break out of the
mold.

On November 9, 1977, Sadat was ready to launch one of the most sensational diplomatic surprises of the century. Upon opening the new
session of the Egyptian National Assembly that day, he complained of
the procedural problems that Israel was creating in order to cause the
Arab states to refuse to participate in the Geneva peace conference. He
stated that he, however, did not attach any importance to procedural
matters and was willing to accept whatever formula would unravel the
procedural snarls since he would in any case demand the return of all the
occupied territories and the rights of the Palestinians. Furthermore, all
prospective participants must thoroughly prepare for the conference in
order to avoid it deteriorating into a forum for the fruitless exchange of
accusations. The peace conference was not to be considered a goal, but
simply the means to force Israel to choose between a just peace or a
dangerous confrontation.

> . . .It is Israel which fears the Geneva conference. Why? It is because
> we have exported to the Israeli society the division, fear, defeatism,
> doubt and suspicion and everything which we suffered from in the
> past.
> Why should we return to this state? No, never. I am ready to go to
> Geneva. I will not hide it from you as representatives of the people
> and I say it for all our people here and our Arab nation to hear—and

you have heard me say it—I am ready to go to the ends of the earth if this will prevent a soldier or an officer of my sons from being wounded—not being killed, but wounded. (Applause.)

I say now that I am ready to go to the ends of the earth. Israel will be astonished when it hears me saying now before you that I am ready to go to their house, to the Knesset itself and to talk to them. (Applause.)

Thank God, brothers and sisters, members of the People's Assembly, there is no time to lose and there is no loss since we are the masters of our own decision.[80]

At first, Sadat's unprecedented statement was explained away as a rhetorical device: it was not taken too seriously by anyone except Prime Minister Begin and some top Israeli government officials who understood that this was Sadat's response to the earlier secret contacts in Morocco and elsewhere.

On the following day, on November 10, Begin publicly welcomed Sadat's initiative and reminded journalists that immediately upon taking office, he had offered to meet the Egyptian President anywhere, including Cairo, if it would further the cause of peace in the Middle East. He then rejected Sadat's demand that Israel pull back to its pre-June 1967 borders and establish a so-called Palestinian state.[81] Later that day, Defense Minister Ezer Weizman met with members of the United States Congressional Armed Services who were scheduled to leave for Egypt on November 11, and asked them to convey a message of welcome to President Sadat.

On Friday, November 11, Prime Minister Begin recorded a direct appeal to the Egyptian people which was to be broadcast in Egypt the next day. The speech was typically sentimental and bombastic in tone.

Citizens of Egypt: This is the first time that I address you directly, but it is not for the first time that I think and speak of you. You are our neighbors and always will be.

For the last twenty-nine years, a tragic, completely unnecessary conflict continues between your country and ours . . . . Much blood was shed on both sides. Many families were orphaned and bereaved, in Egypt and Israel. In retrospect, we know that all those attempts to destroy the Jewish State were in vain . . . [and] so it will be in the future.

You should know that back we came to the Land of Our Forefathers, that it is we who liberated the country from British rule, and we established our independence in our Land, for all generations to come.

We wish you well. . . . In ancient times, Egypt and Eretz Israel were allies, real friends and allies, against a common enemy from the north. Yes, indeed, many changes have taken place since those days, but perhaps the intrinsic basis for friendship and mutual help remains unaltered.

We, the Israelis, stretch out our hand to you. Ours is not, as you know, a weak hand. If attacked, we shall always defend ourselves as our Forefathers, the Maccabees did—and won the day.

. . . Your President said, two days ago, that he will be ready to come to Jerusalem, to our Parliament—the Knesset—in order to prevent one Egyptian soldier from being wounded. It is a good statement. I have already welcomed it, and it will be a pleasure to welcome and receive your President with the traditional hospitality you and we have inherited from our common Father, Abraham. And I, for my part, will, of course, be ready to come to your capital, Cairo, for the same purpose: No more wars—peace—a real peace, and forever . . . .[82]

Begin's speech did not include a formal invitation, but it was certainly an encouraging response; and it was of course front-page news in the United States where it was hailed as an act of statesmanship. American government officials optimistically (and as one-track-minded as ever) stated that Sadat's move and Begin's response augured well for the Geneva conference. Egypt welcomed Begin's appeal but criticized the fact that it was addressed only to Egypt, and not to all Arab states; this was regrettable since Egypt was an integral part of the Arab world, and if Begin thought that he could drive a wedge between Egypt and the rest of the Arab world, he was bound to fail. Sadat complained that Begin had completely ignored the problem of the occupied territories as well as the rights of the Palestinians and made it clear that he would never sign a separate peace treaty with Israel.

In the meantime the Begin-Sadat dialogue continued. In the course of a meeting with the 13 members of the U.S. Congressional Armed Services Committee, Sadat reiterated his readiness to appear before the 120 members of the Knesset and spend three or four days, if necessary, discussing peace in the Middle East. Asked when he would be prepared to go on such a journey, Sadat said that he would go whenever the Israelis were ready to formally invite him. In the evening of the same day, Begin announced that he would invite President Sadat of Egypt to come to Jerusalem in order to discuss a permanent peace between Israel and Egypt.

To most Israeli political and military observers it seemed as if an event in a novel was unfolding before their eyes. Israeli military experts advanced the suggestion that Sadat might actually be preparing for war.[83] Others speculated that he was devising an alibi for rejecting the American-Israeli working paper, which was drafted by Dayan, Carter, and Vance, setting the conditions (which were partly deliberately ambiguous) under which Israel would be prepared to go to Geneva. However, most Israelis saw positive elements in Sadat's move, whatever his intentions, since he was the first Arab leader to break the taboo against talking directly with Israel. While U.S. State Department officials evaluated the chances of a Begin-Sadat meeting as no better than "fifty-fifty,"[84] the dialogue between them continued.

The dialogue was now transferred to the arena of American television; it became what has since been referred to as "television diplomacy." All major U.S. television networks competed for Sadat and Begin to appear either together or consecutively and repeat their declarations on the national news. On Monday, November 14, Walter Cronkite of CBS taped an interview with President Sadat who said that he was ready to visit Israel within one week after receiving an appropriate invitation.[85] He said that he would consider an invitation issued through American channels to be appropriate. A few hours later, Cronkite taped an interview with Prime Minister Begin who said that he would transmit an invitation to Cairo and cancel his scheduled trip to England if Sadat was indeed prepared to visit the Knesset.[86]

Cronkite then broadcast Sadat's statement and Begin's reply on the evening news; and now that both leaders had irrevocably committed themselves to their historic meeting in Jerusalem, the pace of events accelerated. On the same day, a controversial statement was released in the name of the Chief of Staff of the Israeli Defense Forces (IDF), Lieutenant General Mordechai Gur. It pointed to the possibility that Sadat's intended visit might be a ploy to divert Israeli attention from the extensive Egyptian maneuvers which were taking place at the time, and a potential Egyptian attack. Israeli newspapers sharply criticized Gur's statement as detrimental to the delicate dialogue; they said that even if Sadat had intended to deceive Israel, there was no need to make public statements about it. Dayan, too, had warned of the possibility of deception during a Cabinet meeting on Sunday, November 13. What Dayan had in mind was perhaps more related to political deception, but the Egyptian military disposition as observed by Israeli intelligence had drawn much attention and aroused suspicion.[87] (On November 18, the day before Sadat's visit, Israeli newspapers still published numerous articles that speculated on the chance that Sadat was preparing for a military move.[88])

On November 16, Sadat visited President Assad of Syria in an apparent attempt to neutralize Syrian objections and assure Assad of Egypt's continued fidelity to the Arab cause. Assad violently opposed the move, warning Sadat of its dangerous long-term consequences. In the meantime, Arab reactions were relatively calm, perhaps because they could not believe that Sadat was really serious about going to Jerusalem. It was assumed that Sadat had the support of Saudi Arabia and Jordan.

Radio Moscow asserted that Sadat's planned visit to Israel was part of an Israeli plot to divide the Arab world and exclude the Soviet Union from the Middle East peace talks.

Later the same day, Sadat received Begin's formal invitation which had been forwarded by the United States.

Jerusalem, November 15, 1977

His Excellency
Mr. Anwar Sadat
President of the Arab Republic of Egypt
Cairo

Dear Mr. President,

On behalf of the Government of Israel I have the honour to extend to you our cordial invitation to come to Jerusalem and to visit our country.

Your Excellency's readiness to undertake such a visit, as expressed to the People's Council of Egypt, has been noted here with deep and positive interest, as has your statement that you would wish to address the members of our parliament, the Knesset, and to meet with me.

If, as I hope, you will accept our invitation, arrangements will be made for you to address the Knesset from its rostrum. You will also, if you so desire, be enabled to meet with our various parliamentary groups, those supporing the government as well as those in opposition.

As to the date of the proposed visit, we shall be glad to meet with your convenience. It so happens that I am scheduled at the invitation of Prime Minister Callaghan to leave for London on Sunday, November 20, on an official visit to Great Britain. Should you advise me, Mr. President, that you would be ready to come to Jerusalem on Monday, November 21, I would ask Prime Minister Callaghan's indulgence and arrange to postpone my visit to Britain, so as to be able to receive you personally and to initiate together with you talks on the establishment of peace, for which, as we both know, the peoples of the Middle East yearn and pray.

Alternatively, should you decide to come here on Thursday, November 24, or thereafter, I would be back from London by Wednesday afternoon and greet you upon your arrival.

May I assure you, Mr. President, that the parliament, the Government and the people of Israel will receive you with respect and cordiality.

Yours sincerely,

Menachem Begin[89]

Sadat's affirmative answer came in the form of a long official announcement.

President Muhammad Anwar as-Sadat has agreed to visit Jerusalem. His Excellency will perform the blessed 'Id al-Adha prayers in Al-Aqsa Mosque. The visit will begin on Saturday evening, 9 Dhi al-Hujjah 1397, corresponding to 19 November 1977, on the basis of the letter he has received from President Carter to which the Israeli Government's invitation was attached.

On Sunday morning, 10 Dhu al-Hijjah 1397, corresponding to 20 November 1977, his Excellency will perform the blessed 'Id al-Adha prayers in Al-Aqsa Mosque together with the sons of the Palestinian people.

His Excellency the President has been accustomed to performing the 'Id prayers in the Sinai Peninsula, following its liberation during the triumphant October war, with the heroic soldiers and the valiant officers as well as with the people of the Sinai Peninsula. However, the call of peace based on justice has prompted President as-Sadat to go this year to perform the blessed 'Id al-Adha prayers in Al-Aqsa Mosque. He has responded to the call.

When the President of the Arab Republic of Egypt answers the call of peace and decides to go to Jerusalem, he does so in the name of the legitimate and just demands of all the Arab people and the Palestinian people, to ward off dangers which threaten the inhabitants of the regions and all mankind—dangers of calamities—to spare the blood of possible victims and martyrs and to stop the waste of sacrifices, efforts and energy.

President Sadat, who believes in the justice of the Arab cause, is answering the invitation to visit Jerusalem in the name of the pan-Arab responsibility which he shoulders, overcoming any sensitivity in facing his enemy. At the same time, he believes that presenting the facts directly, as President as-Sadat will do during his meeting with the Knesset on Sunday afternoon, is better than dealing with them in long and circuitous methods.

When the peace journey takes place in the atmosphere such as that in which it is taking place, after the Arabs regained their glory with the October war, it takes place under circumstances not governed by the spirit of defeat nor restricted by fear of misinterpretation, especially since its aim is to achieve an overall solution for the Arab cause.

The historic responsibility which the leaders of the Arab nation should shoulder now makes it incumbent upon them to work for peace in the area as long as it is a just peace aimed at liberating the Arab territory occupied after the 1967 defeat and the fulfillment of the legitimate rights of the Palestinian Arabs.

President as-Sadat today shoulders his pan-Arab responsibility. He lets no opportunity pass without seeking this just peace. May God grant the Arab nation success in achieving its objectives.[90]

On November 17, Israeli newspapers still reported that Sadat's visit would take place a week later. Sadat, however, maintained the accelerated tempo. On Friday, November 18, a group of 60 Egyptian security men and other officials arrived in Jerusalem, for the first time in Israel's 30-year history, on a direct flight from Cairo to Ben Gurion Airport in order to lay the groundwork for Sadat's visit on the following day. Israeli officials were under extreme pressure to make all the necessary security arrangements, set up the timetable for the visit, provide for the unprecedented number of journalists that were expected to flood Israel, and establish special international communication centers (including direct lines to Egypt) at Ben Gurion Airport and in Jerusalem. Hotel rooms had to be found for the journalists, and the IDF orchestra worked hard to learn the Egyptian national anthem.

As it became evident that Sadat's plan to talk directly with the Israelis was indeed materializing, radical Arabs viciously attacked the Egyptian President. They declared that his move was a blow to the Arab nation and called on the Egyptian people to carry out their national responsibility (i.e., overthrow Sadat). The Libyans demanded that all other Arab states impose a boycott on Egypt. In a more reserved tone, Jordanian newspapers expressed the fear that Sadat intended to make a separate deal. The Saudis cautiously adopted a wait-and-see attitude, while the so-called moderate Arab states like Tunisia, Morocco, and Sudan indicated their support.

Within Egypt, Foreign Minister Fahmy resigned, perhaps more because he was insulted at not being consulted on, or at least apprised of, Sadat's plans, than because of his opposition to direct negotiations with the Israelis. Sadat nominated Mahmoud Riad to take Fahmy's place, but he too resigned after a few hours. Finally, Sadat nominated Butros Ghali, one of his loyal aides, as a temporary Foreign Minister.

American officials were not happy that Sadat's initiative brought Egypt and Israel into direct contact, for it seemed to endanger American leverage in the Middle East and wreck the American plan to prepare for the comprehensive approach at Geneva. Informallly they voiced doubts that the trip was too dangerous for Sadat's personal safety and that while he was away in Israel, a coup d'état might take place in Egypt; they warned that if Sadat's mission failed, it would be next to impossible to resume the peace negotiations.

On Saturday, November 19, at exactly 7:59 P.M., Sadat landed at Ben Gurion Airport near Tel Aviv. In one swift move, Sadat had dissolved the diplomatic stalemate on the road to Geneva and revolutionized the course of history in the Middle East.

Sadat's November 9 announcement of his readiness to go to Jerusalem as well as the rapid materialization of his plan, stunned all nations in the Middle East, including Israel (despite its partial, though not always conscious role in contributing to his plans). In Israel, Sadat's move was referred to as the political Ramadan, i.e., comparable to Sadat's military surprise during the Ramadan (Yom Kippur) War in 1973. Sadat's diplomatic surprise was so effective because he did what can so rarely be done by well-established politicians; he defied an entrenched political concept, namely, that no Arab leader would negotiate, especially in public, directly with Israel and thereby acknowledge its right to exist. In fact, a leader must always be ready to change an accepted political concept if he wants to achieve a first-rate diplomatic surprise. Unlike the military arena in which surprise is considered part of the planning process, political surprise is not part of routine diplomatic or political behavior and therefore requires the readiness to alter established concepts.

Like most of his other surprises, Sadat's peace initiative was intended to bring immediate and concrete results. As opposed to most of the diplomatic surprises and *faits accomplis* discussed in this book, the Sadat Peace Initiative of 1977 was not just a by-product of secrecy—it was of intrinsic value, calculated to shock and prod others into action. Indeed, during his visit to Israel, Sadat repeatedly emphasized the need to sustain the momentum in the Egyptian-Israeli negotiations—otherwise, he warned, the peace initiative might fail as a result of Arab opposition. Concrete results should be continuously achieved to validate the success of his initiative and its contribution to the Arab cause. This was, among others, recognized by Israeli Foreign Minister Dayan, who urged the Israeli government to quickly take a stand on the basic issues between itself and Egypt, and to follow up Sadat's bold move with its own proposals.

Sadat maintained the momentum by using his favorite shock tactics. On November 26, 1977, a week after his trip to Jerusalem, he called on all the relevant parties to the Middle East conflict (including the PLO, the Soviet Union, and the Secretary General of the U.N.) to attend an international conference in Cairo "to hammer out a settlement so that a reconvened Geneva Middle East peace conference lasts for months rather than years."[91] In announcing that the purpose of the proposed Cairo conference was to prepare for the Geneva talks, Sadat was more than likely trying to placate the United States which had invested so much effort in the idea of a comprehensive settlement. The actual purpose in calling for a preparatory conference was to keep up the pace of events and weaken the leadership role of the United States and the Soviet Union in the Middle Eastern negotiations. Of all the parties invited to the Cairo conference, only Israel and the United States agreed to send representatives. Soon after it convened in Cairo on December 13, 1977, the conference lost its momentum in routine discussions.

This was by no means Sadat's last surprise following the trip to Israel.

On January 16, 1978, a conference for the discussion of the political aspects of Sadat's peace initiative by the Egyptian and Israeli Foreign Ministers and the American Secretary of State opened in Jerusalem. After three days of difficult negotiations, Sadat decided (again without any warning or consultation) to recall Egyptian Foreign Minister Ibrahim Kamel (who had been appointed only a few days earlier), even though some progress was being made. Everyone, including the members of the Egyptian delegation, was surprised. The news of the decision was announced on Radio Cairo.

> Bargaining, auctioneering, and attempts to waste time and energy are no longer acceptable methods for realizing the principles of peace . . . . If Israel believes that a settlement here and a settlement there or an airfield here and an airfield there are more effective for its security than the conviction of her neighbours to live with her peacefully, Israel is opting for a peace imposed by force of arms.[92]

By launching successive surprises after the dramatic peace initiative, Sadat hoped to impose an accelerated timetable on the other partners—and to induce them to recognize the need for concessions worthy of his grand strategy. Whether or not progress was being made at the political conference in Jerusalem, President Sadat would have recalled Foreign Minister Kamel to emphasize the need for speedy and fruitful talks. It is interesting to note that during the Jerusalem conference, Kamel could not make any decisions without consulting Cairo, i.e., Sadat, by telephone on every issue, however small.

Why was Sadat's strategy of shock diplomacy so successful? As regards the Israelis, they very understandably did not place much hope in either the mediation efforts of Rumanian President Ceaucescu or the Israeli-Egyptian contacts prior to Sadat's peace initiative of 1977—simply because similar talks had been held year after year without yielding results. The most the Israelis expected was a lower-level secret meeting. The Egyptian representatives who had previously met with the Israelis certainly had no idea of what Sadat had in mind (nor for that matter, did Sadat know in September what shape his initiative would take). This does not detract from the importance of the Israeli attempts to contact Sadat, for it at least provided him with the assurance that he would get a positive response from Israel if and when he decided to make his move.

Most Israeli politicians and intelligence officers had maintained that no Arab leader could openly make such a bold move; and, as far as other Arab leaders were concerned, they were proved to be correct. During the time Sadat was busy rethinking the old political concepts, Egypt continued to emit signals indicating its adherence to the traditional line. Sadat's declarations and interviews all pointed to a desire to reconvene the Geneva peace conference even against the wishes of other Arab countries. In October, he tried to convince the PLO to accept Resolution 242 so that it could open a dialogue with the United States and thus join the Geneva conference. Later that month, he suggested that a working group from Arab countries and Israel prepare for the conference by dealing only with questions of substance; and another of his proposals compromised between the American, Israeli, and PLO positions by suggesting that the PLO be represented at Geneva by an American professor of Palestinian origin who was not a member of the PLO.

Earlier in October, during the ceremonies commemorating the fourth anniversary of the October War, Sadat and the Egyptian Chief of Staff had threatened that if attempts to reach a just peace failed, Egypt would not hesitate to resort to war. Even after Sadat's declaration of his willingness to visit Israel and Begin's direct appeal to the Egyptian people, Radio Cairo compared Begin to Hitler, saying that the only language Israel understood was that of guns. Egypt was seen as part of the Arab confrontation states—more moderate than Syria and the PLO, but not substantially different from Jordan. Therefore, given the available evidence, the Israelis reached the correct conclusion—they obviously could not have known what the Egyptian ministers did not know. In diplomacy, unlike in war, once in a while an occasion arises where only one person knows a plan—and total secrecy is guaranteed.

At the time of Sadat's announcement American diplomatic efforts were directed toward reconvening the Geneva conference for a comprehensive peace settlement. The United States was still trying to convince Sadat to accept the American-Israeli working paper as the basis for convening the conference. Sharing Israel's perceptions concerning the unwillingness of Egypt (and the Arab world in general) to negotiate directly with Israel, American officials were surprised by a move which they had considered impossible. Obviously, there were no contingency plans for such an event. President Carter's announcement and the official but unenthusiastic blessing of the State Department did not disguise American apprehension about being forced out of the negotiations—the most important U.S. lever in the Middle East. And what if Egypt and Israel should sign a separate agreement, thus ruining the chances of concluding the much-wanted comprehensive peace treaty? Fortunately for the Carter administration, the competitive tensions between Sadat and Begin as well as American financial leverage caused both men to laud Carter's contribution to Sadat's peace initiative and allow him to pay the costs of the resulting accord.

Begin and Sadat vied in their praise for Carter, who was desperately in need of a quick foreign policy coup. Each hoped to get Carter's support for the ensuing negotiations and in addition to acquire American political, economic, and military backing. When the U.S. was brought back into the picture, it was forced to support a new course of action which contradicted its own original plan. Only later in the talks was the United States able to reintroduce some elements of a comprehensive plan into the partial peace agreement.

Sadat's peace initiative of November 1977 was indeed unique—it was the most dramatic unilateral diplomatic surprise of this century. It transformed the Middle Eastern regional system and its links to the global system. The Soviet Union was once again excluded from the Middle Eastern negotiations while the United States enlarged its role in the area and moved closer to the Egyptian and Arab position. Israel became more isolated, though the direct threat to it decreased as a result of the split in the Arab camp. Sadat also laid the foundation for a Palestinian state by accepting Israel's recognition of the Palestinian right to autonomy. Regardless of whether Sadat only intended to benefit Egypt or whether his intentions were more selfless, he was the first Arab leader to make the daring conversion from military to peaceful means.

Sadat has achieved one political and diplomatic surprise after another as President of Egypt. Given his style of making all major decisions alone and informing his aides only at the last moment, if at all, he can maintain total secrecy. He has, indeed, perfected the use of surprise as a tool in diplomacy. As long as he remains Egypt's President, his friends and foes alike must expect the shock of a dramatic surprise.

In the final analysis, it is, however, too early to tell whether Sadat's peace initiative is just one step in a gigantic plan of deception (such as Hitler's 1934 Treaty of Non-Aggression with Poland) or a sincere expression of his desire for peace. The safest assumption probably is that he will "play it by ear," changing his position according to changing circumstances. His cancellation of the Soviet-Egyptian Treaty of Friendship and Cooperation, as well as his precarious and isolated position in the Arab world and his tendency to abruptly change course may all indicate that his peace initiative is only one more in a yet incomplete chain of events that may yet be undone.

CHRONOLOGY

Date	Event
October 21, 1973	Meeting in Moscow, Kissinger and Brezhnev agree to an immediate cease-fire on the basis of U.N. Resolution 242.
	Cease-fire agreed upon at U.N. Security Council is to take effect on October 22.

November 8	Israel and Egypt conclude a six-point agreement concerning the question of getting supplies to the beleaguered Egyptian Third Army and the exchange of prisoners of war.
January 18, 1974	The first Egyptian-Israeli disengagement agreement.
May 31	Syrian-Israeli disengagement agreement.
October 25-29	The heads of the Arab states meet in Rabat, Morocco. They announce that only the PLO, not Jordan, can negotiate with Israel on the future of the West Bank.
March 8-22, 1975	Collapse of Israeli-Egyptian negotiations conducted with the help of Secretary of State Kissinger concerning a new disengagement agreement. The United States holds Israel responsible and declares that it will reassess its Middle Eastern policy.
June 5	Sadat reopens the Suez Canal.
September 4	A new Egyptian-Israeli disengagement agreement is signed in Geneva. The U.S. promises not to negotiate with the PLO as long as it refuses to accept Resolution 242 and acknowledge Israel's right to exist. The U.S. also guarantees weapons supplies for Israel as well as oil, if necessary. Israel withdraws from the oil fields in the Sinai.
December	The Brookings report, "Toward Peace in the Middle East," is published.
March 14, 1976	Egypt terminates the Soviet-Egyptian treaty of friendship and cooperation of May 27, 1971.

October	Israeli Prime Minister Rabin secretly visits Morocco for three days as King Hassan's guest.
January 20, 1977	Carter is inaugurated as President of the United States.
March 16	At a town meeting in Clinton, Massachusetts, Carter talks about "a homeland for the Palestinians."
May 17	Begin becomes the new Prime Minister of Israel.
June 26	Begin presents his government's program to the Knesset. He calls for Arab-Israeli negotiations and for peace in the Middle East. Dayan gives Begin a memorandum including his proposals for peace.
July 19-24	The Egyptian-Libyan border war.
Early August ?	Dayan visits Iran and meets with the Shah. He also visits New Delhi.
August	President Carter, National Security Adviser Zbigniew Brzezinski, and Secretary of State Cyrus Vance meet for a three-hour strategy session on American policy in the Middle East. They decide to seek the active participation of the Soviet Union in the Arab-Israeli peace-making process and to convene the Geneva Peace Conference by the end of 1977.
August 22	Foreign Minister Dayan meets with King Hussein of Jordan in London. Hussein suggests he would be ready to sign a peace treaty with Israel in return for a complete Israeli withdrawal from the West Bank including East Jerusalem and on condition that the West Bank would not be demilitarized.
August 25-29	During an official visit to Rumania, Begin expresses his desire for peace,

End of August (cont'd)

readiness to make concessions, and willingness to meet Sadat if such a meeting can be arranged. He asks President Ceausescu to help establish contacts with Egypt.

Early September

Israel presents a proposal for a peace treaty to the United States.

September 4

Dayan meets with the King of Morocco in Fez.

Sadat receives a personal letter from President Carter suggesting that the situation calls for a bold move. This letter contributed to Sadat's decision to plan his visit to Jerusalem. The contents of this letter has not been made public so far.

September 16

Foreign Minister Dayan meets with Egyptian Vice Premier for Presidential Affairs Tohamy in Morocco.

September 18

Dayan returns to Israel to report to Prime Minister Begin.

October 1

Joint American-Soviet declaration on the Middle East.

October 4

Carter makes a cautious speech on the Middle East situation at the U.N.

Sadat and Arafat decide to adopt a common strategy concerning the U.S.-Soviet stand.

October 5

President Carter and Foreign Minister Dayan meet in New York. They agree on an American-Israeli working paper to set the framework and conditions for the Geneva peace conference. The working paper, in essence, modified the American-Soviet statement on the Middle East from October 1.

October 10

President Sadat states in Cairo that if the current peace efforts (i.e., the

Geneva Peace Conference) fail, a new Arab-Israeli War will be inevitable.

October 14

In reaction to the Soviet embargo on weapons shipments, Sadat suspends Egypt's repayment of debts to the Soviet Union for ten years.

October 15

Administration spokesman Hodding Carter states that the United States did *not* agree to exclude the PLO from the Geneva peace conference. He does not rule out the discussion of a Palestinian state on the West Bank and Gaza.

The U.S. knows that the PLO cannot be a party to the Geneva conference because Israel would refuse to attend the conference.

Sadat favors the Geneva peace conference pending clarification of the American-Israeli working papers.

Golda Meir warns that the American-Israeli working paper is a trap.

October 17

Egypt demands far-reaching changes in the American-Israeli working paper.

October 18

Sadat warns that he will boycott Geneva if it is going to be based on an unacceptable formula for the Arabs.

October 24

In a speech, Sadat threatens to resume war with Israel. He demands total Israeli withdrawal and the establishment of a Palestinian state.

October 25

Begin issues a tough reply to Sadat's speech. He states that Israel will not be intimidated by warlike acts "and sometimes self-defense is achieved

October 25 (cont'd)	by a counterstrike." He adds that Israel will defend itself with a preemptive strike and reminds Sadat that "all was ended with your defeat."
October 30	During Sadat's visit to Rumania, President Ceausescu briefs him on the Ceausescu-Begin conversations. The Rumanian President is convinced that Begin genuinely desires peace.
November 1	Sadat arrives in Iran for talks with the Shah.
November 3	Sadat returns to Egypt. Radio Cairo announces that Sadat will deliver a speech to the new Egyptian Parliament on November 9 in which he will discuss the Middle East situation and problems related to the Geneva peace conference.
November 7	Sadat convenes Egypt's National Security Council and presents his idea of visiting Jerusalem.
November 9	In a speech before the Egyptian National Assembly, Sadat declares his readiness to go to Jerusalem and speak to the Knesset, if necessary, to achieve peace.
November 10	Prime Minister Begin asks the American Ambassador in Israel to deliver a message to Sadat through the American Embassy in Cairo. The message states that Sadat is welcome to visit Israel.
November 11	In an unprecedented speech, addressed directly to the Egyptian people, Begin calls for "no more wars, no more bloodshed, and no more threats." He again invites Sadat to come to Jerusalem.

November 12

Sadat tells a member of the House of Representatives Armed Services Committee that he looks forward to visiting Jerusalem at the earliest possible date but that he must first receive a formal invitation from Israel.

November 13

Begin informs the Israeli cabinet of his intention to send Sadat a formal invitation and recommends that the Knesset allow President Sadat to deliver his speech in a special session.

November 14

The U.S. Embassy in Israel transmits Begin's invitation to Sadat to the U.S. Embassy in Egypt.

In an interview with CBS, Sadat reiterates his readiness to visit Israel. This interview is broadcast alongside another interview in which Begin invites Sadat to Jerusalem.

November 15

Begin informs the Knesset that he has formally invited Sadat to visit Israel.

Israeli Chief of Staff Lieutenant General Mordechai Gur warns of an Egyptian deception plan to cover a possible military surprise attack.

Sadat receives Begin's invitation.

November 16

Sadat visits President Assad in Damascus in an attempt to gain Syrian support for his planned visit to Israel. Israeli Defense Minister Ezer Weizman rebukes Chief of Staff Gur for his unauthorized public statement.

Sadat sends a cable (via Cyprus) to the dovish New Outlook Symposium on the Middle East in Tel Aviv and urges the participants to discuss the Palestinian problem.

November 17   It is officially announced in Jerusalem and Cairo that Sadat will arrive in Israel on Saturday, November 19.

                              Egyptian Foreign Minister Fahmy resigns.

                              Syria, Iraq, Libya, and the PLO sharply attack Sadat for his plans to visit Israel.

November 18   An advance Egyptian team arrives at Ben Gurion airport by direct flight from Cairo to prepare for Sadat's visit.

November 19   Sadat arrives in Israel at Ben Gurion airport at 8 P.M.

November 20   Sadat addresses the Israeli Knesset.

November 21   Sadat speaks to members of the Knesset.

                              Sadat leaves Israel for Egypt.

November 26   Sadat makes another unexpected move. In a speech to the Egyptian National Assembly, he proposes that a conference to advance the preparations for the Geneva peace conference be held in Cairo beginning, if possible, as early as December 3. He invites the United States, Israel, the Soviet Union, the PLO and all other Arab countries.

November 27   Egypt's Ambassador to the United Nations transmits to Israel an official invitation to the Cairo conference. Israel accepts the invitation. All Arab states and the PLO reject the invitation.

November 28   The Soviet Union also rejects Sadat's invitation.

November 29

President Carter announces that the United States will send a representative to the Conference.

December 3

Dayan meets Tohamy again in Morocco.

December 7

Sadat closes all Soviet and East European cultural centers in Egypt.

December 8

Sadat sharply attacks the Arab heads of state at the Tripoli Conference convened to attack his Peace Initiative.

Secretary of State Vance arrives in Cairo.

December 9

Vance visits Jerusalem.

December 13

The official Israeli delegation leaves for the Cairo Conference.

December 14

Opening ceremony of the Cairo Conference.

December 15-17

Prime Minister Begin pays an official visit to Washington.

December 20

Israeli Defense Minister Weizman arrives in Egypt for talks with General Gamasy.

December 21

Weizman meets with Sadat in Ismailia.

December 25

Sadat and Begin meet in Ismailia. Little progress is made.

December 26

The Cairo Conference ends.

January 4, 1978

Carter and Sadat meet in Aswan. In a joint statement, they declare that a real peace must be based on normal relations; Israel must withdraw to its 1967 borders and the le-

January 4 (cont'd)	gitimate rights of the Palestinians must be recognized.
January 11	The Israeli-Egyptian Military Committee meets in Cairo.
January 13	The deliberations of the Military Committee are delayed.
January 15	Egyptian Foreign Minister Kamal arrives in Israel for talks to implement Sadat's Initiative.
January 15-18	No progress is made in the political meeting in Jerusalem.
January 18	At 6:50 PM. Radio Cairo stops its transmissions and announces that President Sadat has decided to recall the Egyptian delegation from the Jerusalem conversations.
Janaury 20	Secretary of State Vance arrives in Egypt.
January 22	In response to Egypt's recall of its delegation, Israel delays Defense Minister Weizman's departure for Cairo.
	Sadat breaks diplomatic relations with the Arab countries participating in the Tripoli Conference.
February	Sadat meets with the head of the Israeli opposition, Shimon Peres, in Salzburg, Austria.
July 24	The Foreign Ministers of Israel and Egypt meet in Leeds Castle in England.
	Begin declares that Israel will not give something (i.e., withdraw) for nothing (i.e., no real peace).
July	Sadat orders the Israeli military mission in Egypt to leave Egypt.

| July | Sadat decides to suspend peace negotiations with Israel. |

September 5 — The Camp David discussions begin between Israel and Egypt with Carter as mediator.

September 10 — An agreement for a framework to sign a peace treaty between Israel and Egypt is signed.

NOTES

1. Major General Shlomo Gazit, *The Arab Israeli Conflict after the Camp David Agreements*, (Mimeo) Notes for a lecture given by the former head of Israeli Intelligence as part of his farewell speech to his staff, p. 6.

2. This was Prime Minister Rabin's opinion. He stated that President Carter's declarations on the Palestinians during April 1977 and Carter's cancellation of certain weapons shipments promised to Israel by the Ford administration caused damage to his party's election campaign. See *Maariv*, June 16, 1967, pp. 1, 3. See also Yitzhak Rabin, *Pinkas Sherut* (Tel Aviv: Maariv Library, 1979), Vol. 2, p. 519. The English translation of Rabin's autobiography, *The Rabin Memoirs* (Boston: Little, Brown Co., 1979), is a highly condensed version of the two-volume Israeli edition.

3. *Yediot Aharonot*, May 19, 1977, p. 1.

4. *Ibid.*, p. 1.

5. *Ibid.*, May 20, 1977, p. 1.

6. King Hussein quoted in *The London Times*, May 26, 1977.

7. For example, in *Newsweek*.

8. *Newsweek*, May 30, 1977, p. 11.

9. *Yediot Aharonot*, May 1977, p. 2.

10. *Haaretz*, May 25, 1977, p. 3, quoting Sulzberger in the *New York Times*.

11. See Michael Handel, *World Reaction to Begin's Election* (Mimeographed unpublished paper in Hebrew, 1978).

12. Quoted in *Maariv*, June 21, 1977, p. 4.

13. For the full text, see *Jerusalem Post*, June 21, 1977, p. 2.

14. See Golda Meir, *My Life* (New York: G. P. Putnam's Sons, 1975)., pp. 214-221.

15. King Hassan of Morocco believed and still believes that Israeli collaboration with moderate Arab governments would help to contain the radicalization of the Arab world and the Soviet Union's influence in the region. See Eitan Haber, Zeev Schiff, and Ehud Yaari, *The Year of the Dove* (New York: Bantam Books, 1979), p. 9. This is a journalistic account of the Sadat Peace Initiative and the negotiations that followed his initiative. Another journalistic account is Shmuel Segev, *Sadat's Road to Peace* (Hebrew) (Tel Aviv: Massada, 1978).

16. Yitzhak Rabin, *The Rabin Memoirs* (Little, Brown), pp. 320-321.

17. *Time* Magazine, August 14, 1978, p. 18.

18. See *Time*, August 14, 1978, pp. 17-18; also *The Year of the Dove*, Chapters 1-2.

19. A widely circulated story, published first in the Israeli weekly *Haolam Ha'ze*, No. 2124, of early May 1978, and later in August 14, 1978, in *Time* magazine, indicates that during the hectic summer of 1977 other secret contacts took place between Israel and Egypt. In this note I shall recapitulate the story for the benefit of readers unfamiliar with it, though it is impossible to verify the authenticity of this cloak-and-dagger episode. Senior Israeli Intelligence sources claim that the story *as told* was nothing but the fabrication of a creative journalist. It appears, however, that a different type of warning that affected Egyptian-Libyan relations was given to Egypt by the Israelis. The following story must therefore be taken with a large grain of salt.

In August 1978, *Time* published the fairly detailed account supposedly based on leaks from Israeli Intelligence services concerning Israel's secret contacts with Egyptian officials in Morocco in 1977 (and Rabin's visit to Morocco in 1976). Another important disclosure was that Israel had informed Egypt of a plot against it by a leftist organization supported by Libya. Sometime in early July 1977, the Israeli Mossad (the equivalent of the American CIA) obtained information that an extreme leftist Arab group was training in Libya with Colonel Quadaffi's knowledge and support to overthrow the moderate pro-Western governments in the Sudan, Saudi Arabia, and Egypt. When Prime Minister Begin was told about it, he asked what was usually done with such information. The answer was that if it was in Israel's interest to inform the governments involved, the normal procedure was to pass the information to the United States and let the United States inform the governments concerned. Begin then suggested that it would be better to forward the information directly to Egypt and thus perhaps earn the gratitude of the Egyptian government. He instructed the head of the Mossad, Major General Yitzhak Hofi to arrange a meeting with his Egyptian counterpart and deliver the information in person. A meeting took place in Rabat in mid-July with General Mohammed Shoukat of Egypt. (According to the account by Sidney Zion and Uri Dan in the *New York Times* Magazine of January 21, 1979, p. 22, Hofi met with Lieutenant General Kamal Hassan Ali in Casablanca.) After the Egyptians investigated the Israeli information and found it to be correct, Sadat was quick to signal his appreciation, when on July 16, he announced that Egypt was prepared to sign a peace treaty with Israel and "guarantee her place in the area." Three days later, following some border incidents which were used as a *casus belli*, the Egyptians made a preemptive strike on terrorist training camps in Libya, as well as against radar installations, airfields, and other military targets along the Egyptian-Libyan border. At the time, political observers found it difficult to explain the motive behind Egypt's punitive expedition against Libya. Sadat's explanation was not believed. "Mr. Sadat's own explanation —that it was Colonel Quadaffi who had been trying to overthrow the Egyptian regime—is not a sufficient answer." (*The Economist*, July 30,

1977, p. 11) A number of other explanations, all of them unconvincing, were put forward. For example, (1) the containment of Libya's involvement in Chad; (2) Egypt's own involvement in Chad; (3) Sadat wanted to demonstrate to the United States that he could fight radical elements in the Arab world; (4) diverting the energy and frustration of the Egyptian army against an easy target; (5) diversion from Egypt's own economic problems; (6) President Sadat was trying to silence Libyan opposition to a peace gesture toward Israel, etc. (See for example *The Economist*, July 30, 1977, pp. 11-12, p. 52; and *Maariv*, translations of an article from the *Los Angeles Times*, July 25, 26, 27, 1977) In his autobiography, *In Search of Identity*, Sadat does not mention the Egyptian-Libyan border war. The "border war" as it later became known, lasted until July 25 and was stopped by the Egyptians. While the Egyptian army was involved in raids on Libya, Prime Minister Begin took the unusual step of reassuring Egypt and declared in the Knesset that Israel would remain neutral and not take advantage of the situation. This may have been another signal of good will to Sadat from Israel.

20. In early 1972, the Deputy Foreign Minister of Rumania visited Israel and asked to see Prime Minister Meir alone. He brought a secret message from Rumanian President Ceausescu who had just returned from a visit to Egypt. Ceausescu invited Meir to Bucharest in order to give her a message from Sadat. When Mrs. Meir arrived in Bucharest, she received a briefing on Ceausescu's conversations with Sadat. "Ceausescu told me," Mrs. Meir recalls in her memoirs, "that he understood from Sadat himself that the Egyptian leader was ready to meet with an Israeli, maybe with me; maybe not; maybe the meeting would be on a slightly lower level than the heads of state. But a meeting of some sort could take place. I said, 'Mr. President, this is the best news I have heard in many years,' as indeed it was. We talked for hours about it, and Ceausescu was almost as excited as I was. There was no question in his mind that he was delivering a historic and absolutely genuine message. He even talked to me about details. 'We won't work through ambassadors or foreign officers,' he said, 'not mine, not yours.' He suggested that his Deputy Foreign Minister maintain personal contact with me through Simcha Dimitz, then my political secretary, who had come with me to Bucharest." (Meir, *My Life* p. 401) Nothing came of that meeting, which Sadat does not mention in his autobiography.

In the Hebrew edition of his memoirs, Rabin also reports that in one of his conversations with Secretary of State Kissinger, Kissinger mentioned Sadat's desire to know whether the Israelis really wanted peace and a genuine solution to their security problems. Kissinger suggested that Prime Minister Rabin send a letter to Sadat explaining Israel's desire for peace. Rabin wrote the letter, and Kissinger took it to Sadat, later reporting to Rabin that Sadat had been very moved by the letter. However, nothing came out of this attempt and Rabin never received a reply to his letter. (Rabin, *Pinkas Sherut*, Vol. II, p. 458.)

21. *Maariv*, November 18, 1977, p. 15.

22. Sadat, *In Search of Identity*, pp. 305-306.

23. *Maariv*, November 18, 1977, p. 15.

24. *Ibid.*, p. 3. Begin seems to have overestimated the Rumanian role in Sadat's decision to launch his peace initiative.

25. Sadat, *In Search of Identity*, p. 306.

26. *Time*, January 2, 1978, p. 30.

27. See also *Newsweek*, October 3, 1977, p. 43, "Dayan's Secret"; also Segev, *Sadat's Road to Peace* (Hebrew), pp. 42-43.

28. The October 3, 1977, editions of both *Time* and *Newsweek* reported that Dayan had made some mysterious visits to meet Arab leaders in September. *Newsweek* mentioned that such visits were made in order to meet with Sadat's representatives (which we know was correct) but did not identify Dayan's destination (p. 43). *Time* reported only one visit, but correctly identified Tangier, Morocco, as the location. ("The Minister and His Mystery Trip," p. 34).

29. See Eitan Haber, Zeev Schiff, and Ehud Yaavi, *The Year of the Dove* (New York: Bantam Books, 1979) Chapter 2, pp. 9-14. See also *Maariv*, August 4, 1978, p. 15.

30. Sadat, *In Search of Peace*, p. 305.

31. This has been suggested by Israeli Minister of the Treasury Simcha Ehrlich. See *Maariv*, March 3, 1978, p. 2.

32. In order to facilitate an agreement between Israel and Egypt, Dayan may have promised the Egyptian representative in this and other meetings more than Begin actually had in mind. In the version he leaked to the press, Dayan claimed that he had made only promises of a general nature, assuring the Egyptians that every subject was open to negotiation. Dayan maintained that Tohamy insisted that prior to any meeting between Sadat and Begin, Israel must withdraw from all of the Sinai—to which Dayan answered that "it may be that Sadat would convince Begin when they meet to withdraw from all the Sinai, but this can only be the result of an agreement—not a condition for such a meeting." Tohamy relayed the spirit and contents of this conversation to Sadat. According to Dayan, the only operative subject on the agenda was to plan a meeting between Begin and Sadat which Begin had already proposed to Ceausescu during his visit to Bucharest in August. See *The Year of the Dove*, Chapter 2, pp. 9-14.

33. The Arab-Israeli negotiations after the 1967 war and the Yom Kippur War of 1973 are very interesting examples of international bargaining and diplomacy. Given the immense complexity of the subject, the intense bargaining involved, and the secrecy surrounding much of the negotiations, it is easy to understand why a detailed study has not yet appeared. Concerning the Arab-Israeli-American negotiations after the 1973 war, the following accounts are useful.

Dayan, Moshe. *Moshe Dayan: The Story of My Life.* New York: Warner Books, Inc., 1977. Part VIII, Aftermath 1973-1975, pp. 659-746.

Golan, Matti. *The Secret Conversations of Henry Kissinger: Step by Step Diplomacy in the Middle East.* New York: Quadrangle, The New York Times Books, 1976. (A good journalistic account of Kissinger's shuttle diplomacy.)

Perlmutter, Amos. *Politics and the Military in Israel 1967-1977.* London: Frank Cass, 1978. Chapters 5-7.

Quandt, William B. *Decade of Decisions*. Berkeley: University of California Press, 1977.

Rabin, Yitzhak. *Pinkas Sherut*, Vol. II Chapters 5-10 are excellent. In the abbreviated American edition, his account is to be found in Chapter 13, pp. 253-276. The second volume of Kissinger's memoirs will also shed more light on this period.

Rubinstein, Alvin Z. *Red Star on the Nile*. Princeton: Princeton University Press, 1977. Chapter 9.

Safran, Nadav. *Israel, The Embattled Ally*. Cambridge, MA: Harvard University Press, 1978.

Sheehan, Edward F. *The Arabs, Israelis and Kissinger*. New York: The Reader's Digest Press, 1976. (A journalistic pro-Arab account.)

34. This explains why, after every agreement to supply Israel with American weapons, the United States found excuses to slow down or delay the supply of weapons already promised in order to use them as leverage for Israeli "cooperation" in the next round of talks. The Israelis justifiably complained that they were being made to pay twice for each American promise. For example, much of the military aid and material promised to Israel in return for its agreement to make concessions to the Syrians in the Israeli-Syrian disengagement agreement in May 1974, was only delivered to Israel after it made further concessions to Egypt in 1975. The best discussion of these U.S. bargaining tactics is included in a long article by Yuval Neeman entitled "Surrendering the Future" in *Haaretz*, February 6, 1976; see also Rabin, *Pinkas Sherut* (Hebrew) Vol. II, p. 465.

35. Nadav Safran, "American-Israeli Relations: An Overview," *Middle East Review*, Winter 1977/78, p. 39. For details of the negotiations leading to the first disengagement agreement, see Golan, *The Secret Conversations of Henry Kissinger*, Chapter 5, pp. 144-179; Quandt, *Decade of Decisions*, Chapter 7, pp. 207-253; Safran, *Israel the Embattled Ally*; Rabin, *Pinkas Sherut*, Chapter 4, pp. 442-460. For the full text of the agreement, see Golan, *The Secret Conversations of Henry Kissinger*, Appendix, pp. 259-260.

36. For details, see Golan, *The Secret Conversations of Henry Kissinger*, Chapter 6, The Damascus Shuttle, pp. 179-212. The text of the agreement and the attached protocols can be found in Golan, *Ibid*. Appendix, pp. 261-264.

37. See Sheehan, *The Arabs, the Israelis and Kissinger*, p. 256.

38. This was orally promised to Israel by the United States in the process of negotiating the Israeli-Syrian Disengagement Agreement of May 1974, but the promise was not kept and Israel had to pay a second time for the same promise. This time the Israelis demanded that the promise be explicitly included in the American-Israeli memorandum. See Sheehan, *The Arabs, the Israelis and Kissinger*, pp. 245-259, for the full text of the Egyptian-Israeli agreement and the American-Israeli memorandum and secret memorandum.

39. For the full text, see Sheehan, *The Arabs, the Israelis and Kissinger*, pp. 256-257.

40. See *The Rabin Memoirs* (American edition) for a brief summary of Carter's policy at that time (p. 316).

41. See *Toward Peace in the Middle East* (Washington, D.C.: Brookings Institution, December 1975). For the Israeli reaction to the Brookings plan, see Shlomo Aronson, "Israeli Views of the Brookings Report," *Middle East Review*, Vol. 10, No. 1, Fall 1977, pp. 19-26. See also Rabin, *The Rabin Memoirs*, (American edition), p. 294.

42. For a detailed discussion, see Y. Harkabi, *The Palestinian Covenant and Its Meaning* (London: Valentine Mitchell, 1979). The articles cited here can be found on pp. 33, 61, 74, 76, and 78.

43. See Amos Perlmutter, "Begin's Strategy and Dayan's Tactics: The Conduct of Israeli Foreign Policy," *Foreign Affairs*, Vol. 56, No. 2, January 1978, p. 364.

44. See Arthur J. Goldberg, "The Meaning of 242," *Jerusalem Post*, June 10, 1979, Supplement, pp. 2-3. For an interesting exchange on the meaning of Resolution 242, see also an exchange of letters in the *Economist*, October-November 1979.

45. Rabin, *The Rabin Memoirs* (American edition), pp. 201-202. For that very reason, Kissinger was reluctant until the Yom Kippur war to get involved in the "hopeless" Middle East problems.

46. *Jerusalem Post*, October 2, 1977, p. 1.

47. *Ibid.*

48. *The New York Times*, October 3, 1977, pp. 1, 6.

49. *Ibid.*, p. 6.

50. *Ibid.*, p. 6.

51. *Jerusalem Post*, October 14, 1977, p. 1.

52. *Maariv*, October 14, 1977, p. 15.

53. Sadat, *In Search of Identity*, p. 302.

54. *Time*, January 2, 1978, p. 22.

55. *Ibid.*, p. 30.

56. Syria's strength was estimated at 110% of its strength in October 1973. See a report in *Maariv*, November 8, 1977, p. 2. Anthony Cordesman, "How Much is Enough?", *The Armed Forces Journal*, October 1977; and Gazit, "The Arab-Israeli Conflict Following the Camp David Agreements," pp. 1-2.

57. This is by no means reflected in his account of the war in his memoirs. See Sadat, *In Search of Identity*, Chapter 9, The October War, pp. 232-276.

58. Gazit, "The Arab-Israeli Conflict Following the Camp David Agreements," p. 4.

59. *Ibid.*, p. 5.

60. Mohamed Hassanein Heikal, "Egyptian Foreign Policy", *Foreign Affairs*, July 1978, Vol. 56, No. 4, pp. 714-728.

61. For the CIA's assumption that Israel has acquired nuclear weapons, see *The New York Times*, August 9, 1972 (Hedrick Smith, "Israel has an Atomic Bomb"), p. 1. See also Gazit, "The Arab-Israeli Conflict Following the Camp David Agreements," p. 2; Muhammad Hasanayn Haykal (sic), "Frankly Speaking: The Israeli Atomic Bombs—Why Was Israel Obliged to Make the Bomb?" translated from Amman's *Ar-Ra'y*, January 20, 22, 24, 26, 1976 in translations in *Near East and North Africa*, No. 1471, JPRS 66788 February 13, 1976.

62. Heikal, "Egyptian Foreign Policy", *Foreign Affairs*, July 1978, Vol. 56, No. 4, pp. 725-726.

63. *Ibid.*, pp. 725-726.

64. *Ibid.*, p. 725.

65. *Ibid.*, p. 725.

66. From a military point of view, Egypt may in fact have made a bad deal, since the Soviet Union has a much larger weapons industry and could, in times of emergency, supply Egypt (and other Arab countries) from its weapons depots. In recent years, the Soviet Union began producing much more sophisticated weapons in quantities that could easily compete with the United States. For example, the Egyptians have been complaining for years that the Soviet Union does not produce medium and long-range fighter bombers such as the U.S. Phantom F-4, or even the Skyhawk A-4. The Soviet Union has recently started to develop sophisticated long-range attack fighters such as the Sukhoi Su-19 (Fencer), the Sukhoi Su-17 (Fitter C), the MiG-27 (Flogger D and F), the MiG-23 (or Flogger B), attack anti-tank helicopters, excellent tanks like the T-72, and so forth. Most of these modern weapons are less expensive and as effective as those produced in the United States, and probably can be supplied on better economic terms than those offered by the United States. But if Sadat did in truth decide that the October 1973 war was the last war, this becomes a less important consideration.

67. Sadat, *In Search of Identity*, p. 308.

68. *Time*, January 2, 1978, p. 31.

69. Sadat, *In Search of Peace*, p. 304; Gazit, "The Arab-Israeli Conflict Following the Camp David Agreement," p. 4.

70. *The Economist*, July 14, 1979, p. 62.

71. For 1967 estimate see William A. Dellalfar and Howard Pack, "Economic Benefits of Peace in the Middle East: Some Cautionary Notes—Some Potential Benefits," *Middle East Review*, Spring 1979, Vol. 11, No. 3, pp. 10-17.

72. *Time*, November 28, 1977, p. 41.

73. *The Economist*, January 1977, pp. 59-60.

74. Heikal, "Egypt's Foreign Policy", *Foreign Affairs*, July 1978, Vol. 56, No. 4, pp. 725-726, Gazit, "The Arab-Israel Conflict Following the Camp David Agreement," pp. 2-3; Sadat also mentioned in the *Time* interview that ". . . Syria always wants Egypt to do the dirty work for them." *Time*, January 2, 1978, p. 32.

75. *Time*, January 2, 1978, p. 32.

76. *Ibid.*, p. 32.

77. *Time*, January 2, 1978, p. 22.

78. *Ibid.*, p. 22.

79. See also Heikal, "Egypt's Foreign Policy" in *Foreign Affairs*, July 1978, Vol. 56, No. 4, p. 726.

80. *Foreign Broadcast Information Service [FBIS] Daily Report, Middle East and North Africa*, November 10, 1977, Vol. 5, No. 217, p. D-18.

81. *Maariv*, November 10, 1977, p. 1

82. Release of Document, Israeli Government, November 16, 1977.

83. *Maariv*, November 11, 1977, p. 1.

84. Rabin, *The Rabin Memoirs* (American edition), p. 321.

85. Sadat also described his decision: "I did not tell anything to any of my colleagues and did not ask them to agree or disagree on this matter. I think that

my responsibility as the President of Egypt is to try and attain peace by all means. I have made this decision. Certainly there are people who object to it, but as long as I am convinced that this is the right way and that my people support me, I will execute the whole plan." (Sadat in an interview with Walter Cronkite quoted in *Maariv*, p. 12, November 15, 1977.)

86. For the role American television networks played in Sadat's peace initiative, see: *Maariv*, November 15, 1977, pp. 1-2; *Time*, Time essay, "T.V. Goes Into Diplomacy" December 5, 1977, p. 44; *Time*, "Behind Cronkite's Coup" November 28, 1977, p. 47.

87. *Maariv*, November 18, 1977, p. 15.

88. For example, *Maariv*, November 18, 1977, p. 23.

89. See text in *Jerusalem Post*, November 17, 1977, p. 3.

90. *Foreign Broadcast Information Service [FBIS] Daily Report, Middle East and North Africa*, Friday, November 18, 1977, Vol. 5, No. 223, p. D-1.

91. *Jerusalem Post*, November 27, 1977, p. 1.

92. *Ibid.* January 19, 1978, p. 2.

BIBLIOGRAPHY

Books:

Burrell, R. Michael and Abbas R. Kelidar. *Egypt: The Dilemmas of a Nation—1970-1977*. Beverly Hills: Sage Publications, 1977. The Washington Papers, No. 48, Vol. 5.

Dayan, Moshe. *The Story of My Life*. New York: Warner Books, 1977.

Eban, Abba. *An Autobiography*. New York: Random House, 1977.

Eidelberg, Paul. *Sadat's Strategy*. Dollard des Ourmeaux, Quebec: Dawn Books, 1979.

Golan, Matti. *The Secret Conversations of Henry Kissinger: Step By Step Diplomacy in the Middle East*. New York: Quadrangle, The New York Times Books, 1976.

Haber, Eitan, Zeev Schiff, and Ehud Yaari. *The Year of the Dove*. New York: Bantam Books, 1979.

Harkabi, Y. *The Palestinian Convenant and its Meaning*. London: Valentine Mitchell, 1979.

Heikal, Mohamed. *The Road to Ramadan*. New York: Quadrangle Books, 1975.
_____. *The Sphinx and the Commissar: The Rise and Fall of Soviet Influence in the Middle East*. New York: Harper and Row, 1978.

Israeli, Raphael (ed). *The Public Diary of President Sadat*. (In three volumes.) Leiden: E. J. Brill, 1978.

Kissinger, Henry. *White House Years*. Boston: Little, Brown, 1979.

Marcus, Yoel. *Camp David: The Key to Peace*. (In Hebrew) Tel Aviv: Schocken Press, 1979.

Perlmutter, Amos. *Politics and the Military in Israel 1967-1977*. London: Frank Cass, 1978.

Quandt, William. *Decade of Decisions*. Berkeley: University of California Press, 1977.

Rabin, Yitzhak. *Pinkas Sherut*. Tel Aviv: Maariv Library, 1979. (Hebrew edition). Abbreviated American edition, *The Rabin Memoirs*. Boston: Little, Brown, 1979.

Rubinstein, Alvin. *Red Star On the Nile*. Princeton: Princeton University Press, 1977.

el-Sadat, Anwar. *In Search of Identity*. New York: Harper Colophon Books, 1978.

_____. *Speeches by President Anwar el-Sadat: September 1970-March 1971*. Cairo: no date, no publisher.

Safran, Nadav. *Israel, the Embattled Ally*. Cambridge: Harvard University Press, 1978.

Segev, Shmuel. *Sadat's Road to Peace*. Tel Aviv: Massada, 1978. (Hebrew).

Sheehan, Edward F. *The Arabs, the Israelis and Kissinger*. New York: The Readers Digest Press, 1976.

Articles:

A., Lieutenant Colonel, (pseudonym): "Peace as Seen Through Egyptian Eyes," *Ma'arachot* (Hebrew), No. 269, June 1979, 8-12.

Aronson, Shlomo. "Israeli Views of the Brookings Report." *Middle East Review*, 10 (Fall 1977), 19-26.

Dellafar, William A. and Howard Pack. "Economic Benefits of Peace in the Middle East: Some Cautionary Notes—Some Potential Benefits." *Middle East Review*, 11 (Spring 1979), 10-17.

Goel, Yosef. "Anwar Sadat: Master of the Unexpected." *Jerusalem Post*, (November 20, 1977), 5.

Goldberg, Arthur J. "The Meaning of 242." *Jerusalem Post Weekend Supplement* (June 10, 1977), 2-3.

Heikal, Mohamed Hassanin. "Egyptian Foreign Policy." *Foreign Affairs*, 56 (July 1978), 714-726.

Israeli, Raphael. "President Sadat: The Image of a Leader." *Skira H' odsheet* (Hebrew), No. 6, June 1979, pp. 3-20.

Kimche, Jon. "The Riddle of Sadat." *Midstream*, (April 1974) 7-28.

_____."Sadat and the Russians: Why . . . and What Next?" *Midstream* (November 1972). 12-21.

Laqueur, Walter. "On the Soviet Departure From Egypt." *Commentary* (December 1972), 61-68.

Meir, Golda. "Israel in Search of Lasting Peace." *Foreign Affairs*, 51 (April 1973), 447-462.

Perlmutter, Amos. "A Race Against Time: The Egyptian-Israeli Negotiations Over the Future of Palestine." *Foreign Affairs*, Summer 1979, 987-1004.

_____. "Begin's Strategy and Dayan's Tactics: The Conduct of Israeli Foreign Policy." *Foreign Affairs*, 56 (January 1978), 357-372.

Ra'anan, Uri. "The Soviet-Egyptian 'Rift'." *Commentary*, 61 (June 1976), 29-35.

Raviv, Brigadier General Yehoshua. "Earlier Attempts at an Interim Settlement Between Israel and Egypt, (1971-1972)." *Ma'arachot* (Hebrew), April-May 1975, Nos. 243-244, 2-17.

el-Sadat, Anwar. "Where Egypt Stands." *Foreign Affairs*, 51 (October 1972), 114-123.

Safadi, Anan. "Sadat's Second Surprise." *Jerusalem Post Magazine*, (November 19, 1977), 4-5.

_____. "The Shock Therapist." *Jerusalem Post Magazine*, November 25, 1977, 5.

Safran, Nadav. "American-Israeli Relations: An Overview." *Middle East Review*, 10 (Winter 1977-1978), 30-42.

CONCLUSIONS

While surprise is considered to be the most effective and desirable means of accomplishing one's goals in military operations, in diplomacy, it is a tactic of last resort. Whenever possible, most leaders and bureaucracies participating in the formation of foreign policy prefer continuity to the risks inherent in radical, unexpected change. The frequent reorientation of foreign policy would undermine the credibility and alliance value of any state, thereby also impairing its ability to obtain political support within international organizations, procure the latest weapons, or conduct foreign trade. A major diplomatic surprise, unlike its military counterpart, always involves a trade-off in which future benefits are expected to outweigh potential problems such as a temporary reduction in alliance support or an increase in domestic opposition. Of course, not every surprise, even if initially successful, is guaranteed to achieve the intended long-term benefits.

Most radical foreign policy changes since the French Revolution have been the by-product of radical changes on the domestic scene. (This excludes major shifts in alliance patterns within a balance of power system where such shifts were the norm and did not involve a move across ideological barriers.) Since drastic foreign policy changes triggered by domestic upheaval or external pressures are not as unexpected, this book has focused on major surprises resulting from carefully planned diplomatic maneuvers.

This type of major diplomatic maneuver has been studied here from the vantage points of both the "victim" and the initiator. This approach stresses the problems and difficulties involved in trying to anticipate a surprise. The major findings confirm those arrived at in the studies of strategic surprise—namely, that despite an abundance of warning signals, the potential victim has found it virtually impossible to avoid being surprised.

From the initiator's point of view, a distinction is made between bilateral and unilateral surprises. In bilateral surprise, the surprise itself is rarely the goal, but is instead the unavoidable outcome of the secrecy required to facilitate a rapprochement between two formerly hostile states: the primary goal here is to build a new alliance or perhaps "neutralize" a former enemy. On the other hand, unilateral surprise is important in its own right (and thus more similar to strategic surprise in military affairs). When secretly prepared and initiated by one party, surprise can either paralyze an adversary into inaction, or conversely, shock the adversary into doing something he would not otherwise have done. Hitler's reoccupation of the Rhineland, for example, paralyzed the Western democracies as far as immediate action was concerned. Delayed action on their part could have seemed less justified and no longer relevant to the issues at hand. President Sadat provides us with excellent examples of surprise being used to shock an adversary into behaving in the desired manner: his ouster of the Soviet advisers in 1972 eventually "convinced" the Soviet Union to supply Egypt with additional sophisticated weapons; and his decision to come to Jerusalem in 1977 pressured Israel into making concessions that were previously thought impossible. The shock element of forcing an adversary into *action* or *inaction* as a result of a dramatic unexpected move can also be the intent of at least one party to a bilateral surprise. Hitler was convinced that the paralyzing impact of the German-Soviet agreement (August 1939) would enable him to occupy Poland without the intervention of the Western democracies.

Of course, the initial success of any type of surprise requires total secrecy in order to prevent an adversary from taking detrimental countermeasures. If the surprise involves more than one party, secrecy allows the participating sides to proceed with the delicate dialogue, but should the negotiations fail, the parties can still sever the contacts without damaging their existing alliances with, and commitments to, other nations. Naturally, it is easiest to maintain secrecy in the case of a unilateral surprise where the number of participants is minimal and the maneuver does not require any material preparations. Signals are apt to be more plentiful in bilateral surprises because more people are involved, negotiations are lengthy, and much of the dialogue—even if ambiguous to non-participants—must be carried out in public. Nevertheless, all of the case studies presented here, with the exception of Sadat's peace initiative, provided expert political observers with more than enough signals to warn of the ensuing events. It is therefore necessary to explain how and why surprise was effectively achieved.

One of the primary duties of an intelligence service is to collect, analyze, and present information sufficient to keep its government from being surprised by major new developments. None of the case studies dealt with here revealed direct evidence that intelligence organizations failed to obtain the information needed to perform this task. "Failures" in the collection of adequate raw data occurred only on those occasions in which one leader first reached a decision on his own, then revealed it to domestic politicians and military men at the same time that he announced it to the world. Authoritarian leaders such as President Sadat, who tend to make their decisions without consultation with anyone, pose very difficult problems for any intelligence organization. When faced with this type of adversary, the intelligence organization cannot be held responsible for failure, but it can nevertheless prepare a wide range of contingency plans and countermeasures, instead of relying on advance warning alone.

Most failures to anticipate major diplomatic changes in the international system therefore occur not in the collection of raw data, but in the analysis and consumption of intelligence. It must be emphasized that there are limits to what even the best intelligence organization can be expected to do. The work is plagued with uncertainties and paradoxes: wherever there is a signal, there is always noise; wherever there is accurate information, there is also the possibility of deception; and the larger the volume of information received, the less likely it is to be processed in time. Such failures can also result from a situation in which the victim-to-be receives a plethora of warning signals which are correct but premature. Frequent warnings tend to numb the senses, thereby reducing the attention paid to them. This was the principal cause of the Western democracies' failure to forecast the Rhineland crisis and the German-Soviet rapprochement. Though it cannot be proven, it is also reasonable to assume that Soviet leaders received more than one warning about possible changes in the Egyptian attitude toward the presence of Soviet advisers in Egypt, or about the likelihood of a Sino-American agreement.

A related problem is the existence of many contradictory signals that can be recognized as noise or deception only in retrospect. Before the German-Soviet non-aggression pact in 1939, England and France believed that the Russians were seriously interested in forming an alliance against Germany. While pursuing its secret negotiations with the People's Republic of China, the United States not only continued to maintain, but actually tried to improve, its relations with the Soviet Union. Kissinger and Nixon could thus honestly assure the Soviets of their friendly intentions. The Chinese, meanwhile, continued their media attacks on the United States and its involvement in Vietnam. Moreover, since most of the negotiations in a bilateral surprise are secret, top government officials who have not been apprised of the dialogue continue unintentionally to emit contradictory signals. For example, U.S. Secretary of State Rogers and Vice President Agnew made some negative statements concerning the possibility of an American-Chinese rapprochement while Nixon and Kissinger were making overtures to the

Chinese. These so-called contradictory signals can usually only be classified as such in retrospect because they were actually correct at the time they were emitted.

Of equal importance is the way in which the intelligence analysis is received or "consumed" by political and military decision-makers. Even if an intelligence organization correctly represents an opponent's intentions, the decision-maker may not believe that its observations are accurate or useful. Operating according to rigid perceptions which filter out contradictory information, top policymakers often regard ideological commitments as binding and immutable, whereas, in reality, other more powerful calculations can be decisive in the short run. History demonstrates that a swift dramatic move is often the only practical way to accomplish a radical change, for the incremental approach merely gives one's adversaries more of an opportunity to destroy the planned change in its incipient stages. Furthermore, the well-being of a state always takes precedence over its ideology or existing commitments. This is why, despite years of political, ideological, or even military conflict, German Nazis and Russian Communists, American capitalists and Chinese Maoists, or Egyptians and Israelis, could *at least temporarily* set aside their long-standing animosities.

Decision-makers can also misuse intelligence because of a tendency to plan in a vacuum or to rely on wishful thinking. Because the British were interested in developing friendly relations with the Germans prior to World War II, they assumed that the Germans desired their friendship to the same degree. Likewise, Stalin, who wanted to avoid war with Germany for as long as possible, projected this desire on Hitler between 1939 and 1941. In the Sino-American rapprochement, the Soviets may have hoped that as long as the United States was involved in the Vietnam War, such a rapprochement was impossible; and they may have also believed that "improvement" of Soviet-American relations precluded concurrent progress in Sino-American relations. Finally, in pursuing the policy of detente with the USSR, American leaders in the 1970s may have ignored information that contradicted their desire for detente. Even worse, they may have deliberately encouraged intelligence organizations to slant their reports to reflect this desire.

*   *   *   *   *

This book has been devoted to the study of surprise as an instrument of foreign policy, but this is only one dimension of the broader subject of intelligence and its influence on foreign policy. Intelligence organizations also contribute to foreign policy by studying the intentions and policies of other states, the character and influence of political leaders, the role of public opinion and the opposition, and of many other factors that determine the behavior of other states. This study suggests that despite the enormous investment in material, technological, and human resources for the improvement of intelligence work, such organizations seem to play a relatively limited role in the formation of foreign policy. Thus, there is still much to learn about the interaction between the intelligence community and its political clients. The neglect of this subject, which has yet to be the focus of a comprehensive theoretical and historical study, can perhaps be explained in the following way.

In the first place, intelligence work has always been considered more crucial and interesting in its application to national security and military affairs. A failure in military intelligence can lead to an immediate national disaster: an intelligence failure in diplomacy does not always entail equally dramatic or immediate results in the short run. In addition, most intelligence organizations were originally designed for the collection of military information, but also became involved—on a secondary level—in the collection and analysis of political and diplomatic information. Although the formation of national security and defense policy is closely related to the formation of foreign policy, the two are not identical and may even conflict with each other. There are many similarities between various types of intelligence work, but each type also has differences and unique problems that must be studied in their own right.

Secrecy is yet another explanation. Diplomatic historians often make passing references to the role of intelligence in this or that diplomatic episode, but they rarely elaborate on the subject because this is obviously the most difficult information for them to obtain. However, the fact that it is not readily available, or that it can only be obtained many years later, does not mean that the subject is unimportant.

The memoirs written by leaders soon after they leave office have not always been helpful in telling us how they interacted with their intelligence organizations; for reasons of state secrecy or political expediency, they prefer not to mention the contribution of intelligence services. For example, Churchill did not, in his memoirs, even hint at the existence and contribution of "Ultra," which means that his decisions must now be viewed in a different light. Another danger is that if secret information supplied by intelligence has led to successful decisions, the leader will be tempted to take the credit. If the leader has made a poor decision because he chose to ignore information provided by intelligence, he will obviously try not to publicize this error. The only occasion on which leaders would be inclined to refer to intelligence work is when it fails.

A study comparing how a number of leaders used, misused, or simply ignored intelligence work, would further aid us in understanding the relationship between the intelligence community and the political decision-making process. Did leaders such as Churchill and Roosevelt, for example, make better use of intelligence than Hitler or Stalin? What type of personality makes optimal use of such professional advice? Do early defeats or failures reinforce a leader's desire to consult intelligence on a more systematic and frequent basis? Conversely, do early victories (such as Hitler's) weaken the incentive to heed intelligence reports? Finally, how were intelligence reports adapted and presented to various types of leaders? Better knowledge of the collaboration and coordination required between intelligence work and foreign policy is crucial, because it will suggest not only how leaders can improve their decisions, but also how they can be made aware of both the limitations and the potential of intelligence in the political sphere.

It must be remembered that even perfect information cannot replace responsibility for action and creative diplomacy. Intelligence only complements and supports better decision-making—perfect information alone does not guarantee that correct decisions will in fact be taken. Although the tools and collection capabilities of intelligence organizations have increased many times over since the end of World War II, the quality of decisions made by political leaders has not improved correspondingly. Learning more about the relationship between the intelligence community and its political clients may contribute to a more intelligent use of intelligence in the future.

BOOKS WRITTEN UNDER CENTER AUSPICES

The Soviet Bloc, by Zbigniew K. Brzezinski (sponsored jointly with the Russian Research Center), 1960. Harvard University Press. Revised edition, 1967.

The Necessity for Choice, by Henry A. Kissinger, 1961. Harper & Bros.

Rift and Revolt in Hungary, by Ferenc A. Váli, 1961. Harvard University Press.

Strategy and Arms Control, by Thomas C. Schelling and Morton H. Halperin, 1961. Twentieth Century Fund.

United States Manufacturing Investment in Brazil, by Lincoln Gordon and Engelbert L. Grommers, 1962. Harvard Business School.

The Economy of Cyprus, by A.J. Meyer, with Simos Vassiliou (sponsored jointly with the Center for Middle Eastern Studies), 1962. Harvard University Press.

Entrepreneurs of Lebanon, by Yusif A. Sayigh (sponsored jointly with the Center for Middle Eastern Studies), 1962. Harvard University Press.

Communist China 1955-1959: Policy Documents with Analysis, with a foreword by Robert R. Bowie and John K. Fairbank (sponsored jointly with the East Asian Research Center), 1962. Harvard University Press.

Somali Nationalism, by Saadia Touval, 1963. Harvard University Press.

The Dilemma of Mexico's Development, by Raymond Vernon, 1963. Harvard University Press.

Limited War in the Nuclear Age, by Morton H. Halperin, 1963. John Wiley & Sons.

In Search of France, by Stanley Hoffmann *et al.*, 1963. Harvard University Press.

The Arms Debate, by Robert A. Levine, 1963. Harvard University Press.

Africans on the Land, by Montague Yudelman, 1964. Harvard University Press.

Counterinsurgency Warfare, by David Galula, 1964. Frederick A. Praeger, Inc.

People and Policy in the Middle East, by Max Weston Thornburg, 1964. W.W. Norton & Co.

Shaping the Future, by Robert R. Bowie, 1964. Columbia University Press.

Foreign Aid and Foreign Policy, by Edward S. Mason (sponsored jointly with the Council on Foreign Relations), 1964. Harper & Row.

How Nations Negotiate, by Fred Charles Iklé, 1964. Harper & Row.

Public Policy and Private Enterprise in Mexico, edited by Raymond Vernon, 1964. Harvard University Press.

China and the Bomb, by Morton H. Halperin (sponsored jointly with the East Asian Research Center), 1965. Frederick A. Praeger, Inc.

Democracy in Germany, by Fritz Erler (Jodidi Lectures), 1965. Harvard University Press.

The Troubled Partnership, by Henry A. Kissinger (sponsored jointly with the Council on Foreign Relations), 1965. McGraw-Hill Book Co.

The Rise of Nationalism in Central Africa, by Robert I. Rotberg, 1965. Harvard University Press.

Pan-Africanism and East African Integration, by Joseph S. Nye, Jr., 1965. Harvard University Press.

Communist China and Arms Control, by Morton H. Halperin and Dwight H. Perkins (sponsored jointly with the East Asian Research Center), 1965. Frederick A. Praeger, Inc.

Problems of National Strategy, ed. Henry Kissinger, 1965. Frederick A. Praeger, Inc.

Deterrence before Hiroshima: The Airpower Background of Modern Strategy, by George H. Quester, 1966. John Wiley & Sons.

Containing the Arms Race, by Jeremy J. Stone, 1966. M.I.T. Press.

Germany and the Atlantic Alliance: The Interaction of Strategy and Politics, by James L. Richardson, 1966. Harvard University Press.

Arms and Influence, by Thomas C. Schelling, 1966. Yale University Press.

Political Change in a West African State, by Martin Kilson, 1966. Harvard University Press.

Planning Without Facts: Lessons in Resource Allocation from Nigeria's Development, by Wolfgang F. Stolper, 1966. Harvard University Press.

Export Instability and Economic Development, by Alasdair I. MacBean, 1966. Harvard University Press.

Foreign Policy and Democratic Politics, by Kenneth N. Waltz (sponsored jointly with the Institute of War and Peace Studies, Columbia University), 1967. Little, Brown & Co.

Contemporary Military Strategy, by Morton H. Halperin, 1967. Little, Brown & Co.

Sino-Soviet Relations and Arms Control, ed. Morton H. Halperin (sponsored jointly with the East Asian Research Center), 1967. M.I.T. Press.

Africa and United States Policy, by Rupert Emerson, 1967. Prentice-Hall.

Elites in Latin America, edited by Seymour M. Lipset and Aldo Solari, 1967. Oxford University Press.

Europe's Postwar Growth, by Charles P. Kindleberger, 1967. Harvard University Press.

The Rise and Decline of the Cold War, by Paul Seabury, 1967. Basic Books.

Student Politics, ed. S.M. Lipset, 1967. Basic Books.

Pakistan's Development: Social Goals and Private Incentives, by Gustav F. Papanek, 1967. Harvard University Press.

Strike a Blow and Die: A Narrative of Race Relations in Colonial Africa, by George Simeon Mwase, ed. Robert I. Rotberg, 1967. Harvard University Press.

Party Systems and Voter Alignments, edited by Seymour M. Lipset and Stein Rokkan, 1967. Free Press.

Agrarian Socialism, by Seymour M. Lipset, revised edition, 1968. Doubleday Anchor.

Aid, Influence, and Foreign Policy, by Joan M. Nelson, 1968. The Macmillan Company.

Development Policy: Theory and Practice, edited by Gustav F. Papanek, 1968. Harvard University Press.

International Regionalism, by Joseph S. Nye, 1968. Little, Brown & Co.

Revolution and Counterrevolution, by Seymour M. Lipset, 1968. Basic Books.

Political Order in Chaning Societies, by Samuel P. Huntington, 1968. Yale University Press.

The TFX Decision: McNamara and the Military, by Robert J. Art, 1968. Little, Brown & Co.

Korea: The Politics of the Vortex, by Gregory Henderson, 1968. Harvard University Press.

Political Development in Latin America, by Martin Needler, 1968. Random House.

The Precarious Republic, by Michael Hudson, 1968. Random House.

The Brazilian Capital Goods Industry, 1929-1964 (sponsored jointly with the Center for Studies in Education and Development), by Nathaniel H. Leff, 1968. Harvard University Press.

Economic Policy-Making and Development in Brazil, 1947-1964, by Nathaniel H. Leff, 1968. John Wiley & Sons.

Turmoil and Transition: Higher Education and Student Politics in India, edited by Philip G. Altbach, 1968. Lalvani Publishing House (Bombay).

German Foreign Policy in Transition, by Karl Kaiser, 1968. Oxford University Press.

Protest and Power in Black Africa, edited by Robert I. Rotberg, 1969. Oxford University Press.

Peace in Europe, by Karl E. Birnbaum, 1969. Oxford University Press.

The Process of Modernization: An Annotated Bibliography on the Sociocultural Aspects of Development, by John Brode, 1969. Harvard University Press.

Students in Revolt, edited by Seymour M. Lipset and Philip G. Altbach, 1969. Houghton Mifflin.

Agricultural Development in India's Districts: The Intensive Agricultural Districts Programme, by Dorris D. Brown, 1970. Harvard University Press.

Authoritarian Politics in Modern Society: The Dynamics of Established One-Party Systems, edited by Samuel P. Huntington and Clement H. Moore, 1970. Basic Books.

Nuclear Diplomacy, by George H. Quester, 1970. Dunellen.

The Logic of Images in International Relations, by Robert Jervis, 1970. Princeton University Press.

Europe's Would-Be Polity, by Leon Lindberg and Stuart A. Scheingold, 1970. Prentice-Hall.

Taxation and Development: Lessons from Colombian Experience, by Richard M. Bird, 1970. Harvard University Press.

Lord and Peasant in Peru: A Paradigm of Political and Social Change, by F. LaMond Tullis, 1970. Harvard University Press.

The Kennedy Round in American Trade Policy: The Twilight of the GATT? by John W. Evans, 1971. Harvard University Press.

Korean Development: The Interplay of Politics and Economics, by David C. Cole and Princeton N. Lyman, 1971. Harvard University Press.

Development Policy II—The Pakistan Experience, edited by Walter P. Falcon and Gustav F. Papanek, 1971. Harvard University Press.

Higher Education in a Transitional Society, by Philip G. Altbach, 1971. Sindhu Publications (Bombay).

Studies in Development Planning, edited by Hollis B. Chenery, 1971. Harvard University Press.

Passion and Politics, by Seymour M. Lipset with Gerald Schaflander, 1971. Little, Brown & Co.

Political Mobilization of the Venezuelan Peasant, by John D. Powell, 1971. Harvard University Press.

Higher Education in India, edited by Amrik Singh and Philip Altbach, 1971. Oxford University Press (Delhi).

The Myth of the Guerrilla, by J. Bowyer Bell, 1971. Blond (London) and Knopf (New York).

International Norms and War between States: Three Studies in International Politics, by Kjell Goldmann, 1971. Published jointly by Läromedelsförlagen (Sweden) and the Swedish Institute of International Affairs.

Peace in Parts: Integration and Conflict in Regional Organization, by Joseph S. Nye, Jr., 1971. Little, Brown & Co.

Sovereignty at Bay: The Multinational Spread of U.S. Enterprise, by Raymond Vernon, 1971. Basic Books.

Defense Strategy for the Seventies (revision of *Contemporary Military Strategy*) by Morton H. Halperin, 1971. Little, Brown & Co.

Peasants Against Politics: Rural Organization in Brittany, 1911-1967, by Suzanne Berger, 1972. Harvard University Press.

Transnational Relations and World Politics, edited by Robert O. Keohane and Joseph S. Nye, Jr., 1972. Harvard University Press.

Latin American University Students: A Six-Nation Study, by Arthur Liebman, Kenneth N. Walker, and Myron Glazer, 1972. Harvard University Press.

The Politics of Land Reform in Chile, 1950-1970: Public Policy, Political Institutions and Social Change, by Robert R. Kaufman, 1972. Harvard University Press.

The Boundary Politics of Independent Africa, by Saadia Touval, 1972. Harvard University Press.

The Politics of Nonviolent Action, by Gene E. Sharp, 1973. Porter Sargent.

System 37 Viggen: Arms, Technology, and the Domestication of Glory, by Ingemar Dörfer, 1973. Universitetsforlaget (Oslo).

University Students and African Politics, by William John Hanna, 1974. Africana Publishing Company.

Organizing the Transnational: The Experience with Transnational Enterprise in Advanced Technology, by M.S. Hochmuth, 1974. Sijthoff (Leiden).

Becoming Modern, by Alex Inkeles and David H. Smith, 1974. Harvard University Press.

The United States and West Germany 1945-1973: A Study in Alliance Politics, by Roger Morgan (sponsored jointly with the Royal Institute of International Affairs), 1974. Oxford University Press.

Multinational Corporations and the Politics of Dependence: Copper in Chile, 1945-1973, by Theodore Moran, 1974. Princeton University Press.

The Andean Group: A Case Study in Economic Integration Among Developing Countries, by David Morawetz, 1974. M.I.T. Press.

Kenya: The Politics of Participation and Control, by Henry Bienen, 1974. Princeton University Press.

Land Reform and Politics: A Comparative Analysis, by Hung-chao Tai, 1974. University of California Press.

Big Business and the State: Changing Relations in Western Europe, edited by Raymond Vernon, 1974. Harvard University Press.

Economic Policymaking in a Conflict Society: The Argentine Case, by Richard D. Mallon and Juan V. Sourrouille, 1975. Harvard University Press.

New States in the Modern World, edited by Martin Kilson, 1975. Harvard University Press.

Revolutionary Civil War: The Elements of Victory and Defeat, by David Wilkinson, 1975. Page-Ficklin Publications.

Politics and the Migrant Poor in Mexico City, by Wayne A. Cornelius, 1975. Stanford University Press.

East Africa and the Orient: Cultural Syntheses in Pre-Colonial Times, ed. H. Neville Chittick and Robert I. Rotberg, 1975. Africana Publishing Company.

No Easy Choice—Political Participation in Developing Countries, by Samuel P. Huntington and Joan M. Nelson, 1976. Harvard University Press.

The Politics of International Monetary Reform—The Exchange Crisis, by Michael J. Brenner, 1976. Ballinger Publishing Co.

The International Politics of Natural Resources, by Zuhayr Mikdashi, 1976. Cornell University Press.

The Oil Crisis, edited by Raymond Vernon, 1976. W.W. Norton & Co.

Social Change and Political Participation in Turkey, by Ergun Ozbudun, 1976. Princeton University Press.

The Arabs, Israelis, and Kissinger: A Secret History of American Diplomacy in the Middle East, by Edward R.F. Sheehan, 1976. Reader's Digest Press.

Perception and Misperception in International Politics, by Robert Jervis, 1976. Princeton University Press.

Power and Interdependence, by Robert O. Keohane and Joseph S. Nye, Jr., 1977. Little, Brown.

Soldiers in Politics: Military Coups and Governments, by Eric Nordlinger, 1977. Prentice-Hall.

The Military and Politics in Modern Times: On Professionals, Praetorians, and Revolutionary Soldiers, by Amos Perlmutter, 1977. Yale University Press.

Bankers and Borders: The Case of the American Banks in Britain, by Janet Kelly, 1977, Ballinger Publishing Co.

Shattered Peace: The Origins of the Cold War and the National Security State, by Daniel Yergin, 1977. Houghton Mifflin.

Storm Over the Multinationals: The Real Issues, by Raymond Vernon, 1977. Harvard University Press.

Political Generations and Political Development, ed. Richard J. Samuels, 1977. Lexington Books.

Cuba: Order and Revolution, by Jorge I. Dominguez, 1978. Harvard University Press.

Raw Materials Investments and American Foreign Policy, by Stephen D. Krasner, 1978. Princeton University Press.

Commodity Conflict: The Political Economy of International Commodity Negotiations, by L.N. Rangarajan, 1978. Cornell University Press and Croom Helm (London).

Israel: Embattled Ally, by Nadav Safran, 1978. Harvard University Press.

Access to Power: Political Participation by the Urban Poor in Developing Nations, by Joan M. Nelson, 1979. Princeton University Press.

The Quest for Self-Determination, by Dov Ronen, 1979. Yale University Press.

The Rational Peasant: The Political Economy of Rural Society in Vietnam, by Samuel L. Popkin, 1979. University of California Press.

Legislative-Executive Relations and the Politics of United States Foreign Economics Policy 1929-1979, by Robert Pastor, 1980. University of California Press.

Insurrection or Loyalty: The Breakdown of the Spanish American Empire, by Jorge Dominguez, 1980. Harvard University Press.

Standing Guard: The Protection of Foreign Investment, by Charles Lipson, 1980. University of California Press.

The Collapse of Welfare Reform: Political Institutions, Policy and the Poor in Canada and the United States, by Christopher Leman, 1980. M.I.T. Press.

Palestinian Society and Politics, by Joel S. Migdal *et al.*, 1980. Princeton University Press.

Energy and Security, Joseph S. Nye, Jr. and David A. Deese, eds., 1980. Ballinger Publishing Co., Cambridge.

The Special Relationship Between West Germany and Israel, by Lily Gardner Feldman, 1981. George Allen & Unwin, London.

Weak States in the International System, by Michael Handel, 1981. Frank Cass, London.

On the Autonomy of the Democratic State, by Eric A. Nordlinger, 1981. Harvard University Press.

HARVARD STUDIES IN INTERNATIONAL AFFAIRS*

27. *The Law in Political Integration: The Evolution and Integrative Implications of Regional Legal Processes in the European Community*, by Stuart A. Scheingold, 1971. 63 pp. $2.95.

28. *Psychological Dimensions of U.S.-Japanese Relations*, by Hiroshi Kitamura, 1971. 46 pp. $2.50.

29. *Conflict Regulation in Divided Societies*, by Eric A. Nordlinger, 1972, 142 pp. $4.95.

31. *Italy, NATO and the European Community: The Interplay of Foreign Policy and Domestic Politics*, by Primo Vannicelli, 1974. 67 + *x* pp. $3.75.

33. *The International Role of the Communist Parties of Italy and France*, by Donald L.M. Blackmer and Annie Kriegel, 1975. 67 + *x* pp. $3.50.

34. *The Hazards of Peace: A European View of Detente*, by Juan Cassiers, 1976. 94 pp. $3.50.

35. *Oil and the Middle East War: Europe in the Energy Crisis*, by Robert J. Lieber, 1976. 75 + *x* pp. $3.45.

37. *Climatic Change and World Affairs*, by Crispin Tickell, 1977. 78 pp. $3.95.

38. *Conflict and Violence in Lebanon: Confrontation in the Middle East*, by Walid Khalidi, 1979. 217 pp. $13.95, cloth; $7.95, paper.

39. *Diplomatic Dispute: U.S. Conflict with Iran, Japan, and Mexico*, by Robert L. Paarlberg, ed. Eul Y. Park, and Donald L. Wyman, 1979. 168 pp. $11.95, cloth; $5.95, paper.

40. *Commandos and Politicians: Elite Military Units in Modern Democracies*, by Eliot A. Cohen, 1978. 136 pp. $8.95, cloth; $3.95, paper.

41. *Yellow Earth, Green Jade: Constants in Chinese Political Mores*, by Simon de Beaufort, 1979. 90 pp. $3.95, paper.

42. *The Future of North America: Canada, the United States, and Quebec Nationalism*, Elliot J. Feldman and Neil Nevitte, eds., 1979. 378 pp. $13.95 cloth; $6.95, paper.

43. *The Dependence Dilemma: Gasoline Consumption and America's Security*, Daniel Yergin, ed., 1980. 167 pp. $4.95, paper.

44. *The Diplomacy of Surprise: Hitler, Nixon, Sadat*, by Michael I. Handel, 1981. 369 + *xi* pp. $22.50, cloth; $11.95, paper.

* Available from Publishers Marketing Group, P.O. Box 350, Momence, Ill. 60954, (Tel.: 815-472-2661).